GLOBAL FEMINISMS SINCE 1945

Global Feminisms Since 1945 is an innovative historical introduction to the issues of contemporary feminism, with a truly global perspective. This book is a concise anthology considering the similarities and differences between feminisms in West and East, North and South, and highlighting class, racial, ethnic and imperial tensions, and claims in the twentieth century. The book analyzes the roots, development and, in some cases, the conclusions of feminisms and how they have interacted.

From the European and American feminist movements to those in the ex-Soviet Union and women's rights groups in Africa and East Asia, *Global Feminisms* examines the key economic, technological, sexual, reproductive, ecological and political debates.

Global Feminisms Since 1945 is essential reading for students of gender and women's history, world and comparative history, cultural and ethnic studies, and social movements.

Bonnie G. Smith is Professor of History at Rutgers University, and her many books include *Changing Lives* (Penguin, 1989), *The Gender of History* (Harvard, 1998) and *Imperialism* (Oxford, 2000).

Rewriting Histories focuses on historical themes where standard conclusions are facing a major challenge. Each book presents papers (edited and annotated where necessary) at the forefront of current research and interpretation offering students an accessible way to engage with contemporary debates.

Series editor **Jack R. Censer** is Professor of History at George Mason University.

D0188058

REWRITING HISTORIES
Series editor: Jack R. Censer

Already published

GLOBAL FEMINISMS SINCE 1945

Edited by
Bonnie G. Smith

London and New York

First published 2000
by Routledge
11 New Fetter Lane, London EC4P 4EE

Simultaneously published in the USA and Canada
by Routledge
29 West 35th Street, New York, NY 10001

Reprinted 2002

Routledge is an imprint of the Taylor & Francis Group

Typeset in Palatino by Keystroke, Jacaranda Lodge, Wolverhampton
Printed and bound in Great Britain by MPG Books Ltd, Bodmin

British Library Cataloguing in Publication Data
A catalogue record for this book is available from the British Library

Library of Congress Cataloging in Publication Data
A catalog record for this book has been requested

ISBN 0–415–18490–8 (hbk)
ISBN 0–415–18491–6 (pbk)

CONTENTS

v

CONTENTS

SERIES EDITOR'S PREFACE

Rewriting history, or revisionism, has always followed closely in the wake of history writing. In their efforts to re-evaluate the past, professional as well as amateur scholars have followed many approaches, most commonly as empiricists, uncovering new information to challenge earlier accounts. Historians have also revised previous versions by adopting new perspectives, usually fortified by new research, which overturn received views.

Even though rewriting is constantly taking place, historians' attitudes towards using new interpretations have been anything but settled. For most, the validity of revisionism lies in providing a stronger, more convincing account that better captures the objective truth of the matter. Although such historians might agree that we never finally arrive at the 'truth,' they believe it exists and over time may be better approximated. At the other extreme stand scholars who believe that each generation or even each cultural group or subgroup necessarily regards the past differently, each creating for itself a more usable history. Although these latter scholars do not reject the possibility of demonstrating empirically that some contentions are better than others, they focus upon generating new views based upon different life experiences. Different truths exist for different groups. Surely such an understanding, by emphasizing subjectivity, further encourages rewriting history. Between these two groups are those historians who wish to borrow from both sides. This third group, while accepting that every congeries of individuals sees matters differently, still wishes somewhat contradictorily to fashion a broader history that incorporates both of these particular visions. Revisionists who stress empiricism fall into the first of the three camps, while others spread out across the board.

Today the rewriting of history seems to have accelerated to a blinding speed as a consequence of the evolution of revisionism. A variety of approaches has emerged. A major factor in this process has been the enormous increase in the number of researchers. This explosion has reinforced and enabled the retesting of many assertions. Significant

ix

ideological shifts have also played a major part in the growth of revisionism. First, the crisis of Marxism, culminating in the events in Eastern Europe in 1989, has given rise to doubts about explicitly Marxist accounts. Such doubts have spilled over into the entire field of social history which has been a dominant subfield of the discipline for several decades. Focusing on society and its class divisions implied that these are the most important elements in historical analysis. Because Marxism was built on the same claim, the whole basis of social history has been questioned, despite the very many studies that directly had little to do with Marxism. Disillusionment with social history simultaneously opened the door to cultural and linguistic approaches largely developed in anthropology and literature. Multiculturalism and feminism further generated revisionism. By claiming that scholars had, wittingly or not, operated from a white European/American male point of view, newer researchers argued that other approaches had been neglected or misunderstood. Not surprisingly, these last historians are the most likely to envision each subgroup rewriting its own usable history, while other scholars incline towards revisionism as part of the search for some stable truth.

Rewriting Histories will make these new approaches available to the student population. Often new scholarly debates take place in the scattered issues of journals which are sometimes difficult to find. Furthermore, in these first interactions, historians tend to address one another, leaving out the evidence that would make their arguments more accessible to the uninitiated. This series of books will collect in one place a strong group of the major articles in selected fields, adding notes and introductions conducive to improved understanding. Editors will select articles containing substantial historical data, so that students – at least those who approach the subject as an objective phenomenon – can advance not only their comprehension of debated points but also their grasp of substantive aspects of the subject.

Although most other books in this series attempt to capture the current wave of scholarship, this one may be said to be a collection that represents the state of a field that is now taking shape. To be certain, for some nations, a number of histories of feminist movements have been written, but envisioning this subject from a global perspective is novel. Of course, not every practitioner in this book consciously makes cross-cultural comparisons, but these works do share a sympathy for women's rights and achievements from a global perspective. This allows for substantial diversity of approaches and subjects, with numerous contrasts, including those between East and West, as well as North and South. Yet it is this commitment to feminism, with an acceptance of variations, that characterizes the works included here and that constitutes these versions of a history only now being written.

ACKNOWLEDGEMENTS

The permission of the following publishers to reprint articles is gratefully acknowledged:

Chapter 1   'Competing agenda: feminists, Islam and the state' by Margot Badran. Reproduced from Deniz Kandiyoti (ed.), *Women, Islam and the State* (Macmillan, 1991).

Chapter 2   'Women and revolution in Vietnam' by Mary Ann Tétreault. Reproduced from Kathleen Barry (ed.), *Vietnam's Women in Transition*, (Macmillan, 1996).

Chapter 3   'Gender and nation-building in South Africa' by Zengie A. Mangaliso. Reproduced from Lois West (ed.), *Feminist Nationalism* (Routledge, 1997).

Chapter 4   'Female consciousness?' by Yvonne Corcoran-Nantes. Reproduced from Sarah A. Radcliffe & Sallie Westwood (eds), *Viva: Women and Popular Protest in Latin America* (Routledge, 1997).

Chapter 5   'The mother of warriors and her daughters: the women's movement in Kenya' by Wilhelmina Oduol and Wanjiku Mukabi Kabira. Reproduced from Amrita Basu (ed.), with assistance of C. Elizabeth McGrory, *The Challenge of Local Feminisms* (Westview, 1995).

Chapter 6   'Minjung feminism' by Miriam Ching Yoon Louie. Reproduced from *Women's Studies International Forum*, vol. 18, no. 4 (1995), pp. 417–30.

Chapter 7   Reproduced from Sara M. Evans, *Born for Liberty* (Simon & Schuster, 1989).

Chapter 8   Reproduced from Alkarim Jivani, *It's Not Unusual: A History of Lesbian and Gay Britain in the Twentieth Century* (Michael O'Mara Books, 1997).

Chapter 9   'Feminist critiques of modern Japanese politics' by Vera Mackie. Reproduced by kind permission of the author from

Monica Threfall (ed.), *Mapping the Women's Movement* (Verso, 1996).

Chapter 10   'Organising women before and after the fall' by Linda Racioppi & Katherine O'Sullivan. Reproduced from *Signs*, vol. 20, no. 4 (University of Chicago Press, 1995).

Chapter 11   'Eluding the feminist' by Zohreh T. Sullivan. Reproduced from Lila Abu-Lughod (ed.), *Remaking Women* (Princeton University Press, 1998).

Chapter 12   'Human rights are women's rights' by Saba Bahar. Reproduced from *Hypatia*, vol. 11, no. 1 (Winter, 1996).

Chapter 13   'The NGOization of feminism' by Sabine Lang. Reproduced from Joan Scott, Cora Kaplan & Debra Keates (eds), *Transitions, Environments, Translations* (Taylor & Francis/Routledge, 1997).

Chapter 14   'Some reflections on US women of color and the United Nations' Fourth World Conference on Women and NGO Forum in Bejing, China' by Mallika Dutt. Reproduced from *Feminist Studies*, vol. 22, no. 3 (Fall, 1996).

The editor would like to thank Tamara Matheson for her research assistance and Marlene Importico for helping preparing the manuscript.

INTRODUCTION

Bonnie G. Smith

This collection chronicles women's activism on behalf of equality, liberation, and more humane conditions for themselves and their families since World War II. Such activism took place in Asia, Africa, Europe, and North and South America, making it possible to claim that in the past fifty years there has been a global – though hardly unified or singular – women's movement. In fact the very diversity, complexity, and contested nature is what makes us think in terms not of feminism but of multiple 'feminisms.' Thus 'feminisms' refers to a variety of activism on behalf of social, political, economic, and personal justice. It also suggests the existence of global debates over what feminism is in the first place. Over the past half-century feminism has encompassed sometimes heated discussion over the meaning and acceptability of the term. It has comprised an incredible range of activity, from overthrowing the Western colonial powers to setting up local shelters for battered women to lobbying for major changes in constitutions and legal codes. The workplace, the environment, the household, the legislature, and the battlefield have all served as locations of feminism since 1945.

Of French and then English derivation, the word 'feminism' had its first sustained incarnation late in the nineteenth-century West. It increasingly replaced the term 'woman movement' that activists in Europe, the United States, Egypt, India, Austrialia, New Zealand, Canada, and some Latin American countries had developed in the course of that century. As the 'woman movement' focused its energy on obtaining the vote, it was also known as the 'suffrage' movement. When suffrage was obtained first in countries associated with European and US culture (between 1906 and 1945) as well as in decolonizing countries like India in 1947, the term 'suffrage' was dropped from the terms used to describe women's activism. In the 1960s and 1970s 'feminism,' 'women's movement,' and 'women's liberation' predominated in the West, with the term 'feminism' increasingly defined by media coverage. The media determined 'feminism' to mean a form of man-hating pursued by hateful, castrating women. As a result, some women who did not view their activism in those terms looked

1

for others. The US author Alice Walker devised the word 'womanist' and this had appeal. Others rejected any Western-sounding word as having imperialist connotations. Moreover, women in Africa and Asia in particular felt that even the range of causes covered by the non-media stereotype was still not inclusive enough for what they were doing. With all these disadvantages to the term, this book still uses it (as African and Asian authors also do), but adding the plural 's.' It invites readers to think about the term after digesting the chapters in order to test its usefulness.

This collection is historical, concentrating on the activism of women over time and often pushing to the margins today's debates over what feminism is or should be. The virtues of a historical approach include paying attention to specific activism in its various contexts whether these be the drive to free a region from the grip of imperialism, as in the case of Algerian women in the 1950s, or the fight for better working conditions in an emerging industrial economy, as in the case of Korean women in the 1980s. Women in Western Europe fought against the masculine privilege in so-called democratic society by struggling for a more equal place in the workforce and political life. Those in Eastern Europe, awarded equality by the Soviet government, struggled after the fall of that state in 1989 to keep their jobs, hold their families together, and prevent the increasing abuse of women. Such specificity allows for a more informed judgment of women's activist lives and of social movements. It helps produce a new understanding of global politics as comprising men's and women's aspirations – not just men's alone.

The historical context of the past half-century has been varied around the world: thus national histories (provided in the introductory material to the chapters) are important to understanding women's activism. This activism has also been shaped by other, more commonly experienced developments. The first of these was the legacy of World War II, which ended in 1945. Between 1939 and 1945 this war was the first with a truly global scope. All the great imperial powers – Japan, Great Britain, France, and the Soviet Union – as well as countries with global trade such as the United States and Germany had been involved. The continents of Asia, Africa, and Europe had been the recruiting ground for soldiers and had served the common battlefield, producing tens of millions of deaths and massive economic devastation. The war had gobbled up so many resources and taken so many people from farming that civilians at the war's end were often starving, whether in Europe or Africa. Amidst this chaos, the ties of empire had been loosened, with ideas of independence more widespread than ever before. In 1947 India became independent, while in 1949 the Chinese communists overthrew a government with strong, dependent ties to the US and Great Britain. For the next two decades, in the midst of recovery efforts and often persistent poverty, people in Africa and Asia successfully claimed their independence and set up new countries.

Women's movements in India and parts of the Middle East, North Africa, and Asia had grown up alongside the nationalist forces that led the postwar independence struggles. Nationalism, women's activism, and even feminism were thus closely intertwined, with the condition of women held up as emblematic in varying ways of rights and wrongs. Some women participated in national liberation struggles because for them, liberation from the grip of France, Great Britain, or the other imperialist powers would mean independence for everyone. Male leaders of national liberation movements promised women equality and opportunity for their help. Armed with these hopes, women from the 1940s on shouldered weapons, planted bombs, carried supplies, and cooked for rebel troops.

A second common theme of the second half of the twentieth century was the Cold War (1945–1989) between the Soviet Union and the United States, which divided the industrialized countries into strict systems of alliances. Cold War superpowers also intervened in the wars of liberation in many countries, complicating these armed struggles and at times intensifying resistance. The wars in Vietnam (1950s to 1970s) and Afghanistan (1979 to 1980s) were examples. Arms buildups of tanks, planes, and rocketry took place and the proliferation of nuclear weaponry was so great that the stockpile was said to be capable of annihilating life on the planet. As in 'hot' wartime, the governments provided an array of benefits like healthcare and subsidies for having children. Social security systems that gave pensions for the old or workman's compensation for the victims of accidents blanketed the male population and some of the women in the workforce. This array of programs was called the 'welfare state.'

During the 1950s and 1960s, women in both the East and the West started Ban the Bomb groups and lobbied for peace. They started counting the environmental cost of the Cold War, until in 1968 anti-war protesters joined with many other groups in a massive protest movement that spread across society. Foremost among these groups were civil rights activists who had taken seriously many promises made during the war and Cold War that the fight was for democracy, opportunity, and freedom against Nazis and communists. Women were at the forefront of the drive for people of color to obtain civil rights (such as the right to jobs, to have a good education, to eat at lunch counters, sit on buses, and to vote). They were arrested, beaten, insulted, and abused. But their breakthrough in terms of feminism was extraordinary, for during these struggles US and colonized women came to discuss how the sexist ways they were treated by men in their own movement were paralleled by the racist ways they were treated by whites, including feminists and reformers. The context of the Cold War helped shape Western feminist and civil rights movements and a complex body of reform-minded theory.

Another component of the Cold War was women's attraction to socialism. Millions of reformers aimed for more democracy and economic opportunity, but others found socialist values even better. Grounded in the nineteenth-century theories of Karl Marx, socialism was based first and foremost on the abolition of private property in industry, finance, and large amounts of land. Another way of putting it is that socialism was based on the abolition of the profit which capitalists made from owning the 'means of production.' Production of food and industrial goods would be done in large units under socialism but the direction of this production by the people themselves would permit the full value of their work to go to them. There was no need under socialism for a woman's movement, because women were held in subjection only as the result of private property. Passing down accumulated profits in the form of inherited wealth had confined them to the home where their sexuality could be monitored and the legitimate transfer of wealth thus ensured.

This was socialism in theory; the Soviet Union, its satellite states (East Germany, Hungary, Poland, the Baltic States, Czechoslovakia, Romania, Bulgaria, and others), and China were the main locations of socialist practice after 1945. By this time the name socialism had been changed to communism, with socialism being taken up by political parties that were more reform-minded, wanting to allow private property and simultaneously to make the lot of working people better. Where communism reigned, however, constitutions explicitly announced the equality of the sexes and women held a wide range of positions, not only in the economy but also in politics. Whether in medicine, government, the arts, the professions – all of these usually the prerogative of men – women were more visible than anywhere else in the world. Access to childcare and birth control added to communism's appeal.

The reality of women's lives under communism left much to be desired. Engaged in the Cold War, the government of the USSR diverted more resources to military production than to civilian needs. This decades-long strategy meant that women, most of whom worked full-time and did housework, spent long hours in line to get scarce consumer goods, even the most essential items. Because both China and the USSR were working to develop their economies, sacrifice was a fact of life, but women bore the brunt of it. In both societies, although women could do many more jobs and achieve in many more areas than in a 'free world,' the jobs that they held, such as physician, were the least well remunerated and less prestigious than those held by men. Finally, feminist protest was inconceivable and political conditions were harsh, even murderous. When late in the 1970s Moscow women produced a small underground newspaper, the secret police harassed them and their families and ultimately forced the editors into exile. In China, political life was even more brutal, with millions of women and men murdered in the Cultural Revolution of the 1960s. As in the rest of Asia, girls were held in such low esteem that they were regularly put into orphanages, killed at birth, or aborted as fetuses. All of these conditions

4

would come to be the subject for women's activism toward the close of the century, from the mid-1980s on.

Still another widespread development was the increasingly global economy that was said to produce a 'post-industrial' society. The decline of blue-collar manufacturing and the rise of a service economy characterized a 'post-industrial' way of life, especially in the West. Healthcare and information enterprises, financial institutions, the spread of universities and technical schools, and the increase in services like restaurants, cosmetics, beauty, and health salons also indicated that a society was post-industrial. Finally, the economy was said to be global in that 'multinational corporations' came to dominate economic life from the 1960s on. These corporations, unlike previous internationally focused enterprises, usually employed more people outside their national base than within it. Information and communications technology based on satellites and the Internet increased the possibilities for globalization of banking, manufacturing, and trade.

The development of 'post-industrial society' was uneven, however. The postwar years saw more women entering the paid workforce globally. Leaders in emerging economies like South Korea, Indonesia, Taiwan, and Singapore appealed to multinational corporations by promising them a docile female workforce in the blue-collar and unskilled sector that would cost far less than either male or female labor in the West. Grim workshops sprang up, where women worked a dozen hours a day and more at sweated jobs like garment-making that provided no benefits. On the positive side, many emerging economies improved their levels of education so that the workforce could be more attractive to high-tech companies. They also made contraception available so that women could be more available for factory labor. Countries like South Korea came to rank quite high in terms of conditions of life for women, and with improved education women's activism often heated up.

The large international structures like the World Bank, International Monetary Fund, and Common Market that sprang up with the global economy also had uneven consequences. So committed to large-scale global enterprises, they could severely handicap African women's traditional work in agriculture by funding men, but not women, to set up agribusinesses. The same forces also undermined women's traditional role as traders. Large foundations, mostly based in Western countries, sponsored 'non-governmental organizations' (NGOs) to advise, educate, finance, and organize women's activities. For some women, these NGOs were their entry-point into activism, as the NGO personnel trained them to be effective politicians or helped them to become candidates. NGOs sometimes financed women's institutes, battered women's shelters, birth control clinics, and wellness centers. At the same time, personnel of NGOs were sometimes totally ignorant of local conditions, and arrogantly saw women in emerging economies as somehow stupid or 'backward.'

The global economy was thus another context for activism. Where commercial agriculture spread, peasant women mobilized against the decline of their position as farmers and the large landowners' or agribusinesses' physical harassment. In the 1970s a group of women in India, angered at the extreme mistreatment that went unpunished by the law, charivaried a male landowner, rubbing manure on his faced and parading him before crowds of women in village after village. 'If men oppress us, we fight back,' they chanted. 'Women are not inferior.'[1] Women had traditionally exercised power in some dual-sex societies, for instance in Africa, where men and women shared well-defined segments of political authority. They often struggled to protect an already established position from threats posed by both old and newer forms of Western dominance, which aimed to place all power in the hands of men. Whereas the protests of women in India have been characterized as feminist because the women were fighting to attain an equal position, some scholars do not see as feminist struggles to *maintain* an equal position, and would like better distinctions and definitions.

Global technology based in information systems like computers, internetworking (the Internet), and other communication media also had real influence on women's lives. Computers had the first major impact when they changed the nature of women's work. Computers programmed to do the same task more rapidly could now do jobs that once took human skill. Although people gained skill when they learned to use a computer, other human skills were lost. Often computer operators mostly followed the commands of the machine. Much computer work became the area for further ghettoization of women. Communications systems allowed for instantaneous transmission of market and workforce information, in turn permitting the multinational corporation to move operations to where the cheapest women workers could be found. This established a pattern from the 1970s on of rapidly changing workforce conditions, in which jobs for women in highly industrialized countries moved to emerging economies. Finally, computers and the new information technology allowed for massive polling of women, for political targeting of women at elections, and for sophisticated ways of promoting candidates and causes. Because women possessed only a small percentage of the world's wealth, they had ever less possibility of influencing political processes because of this very costly technology. This lack of access and the threat this posed to women's well-being troubled activists around the world.

In spite of these common conditions, activists by the 1970s had become acutely aware of major differences in women's situations and started confronting one another about these differences. The most glaring one concerned wealth. Most of the world's women were desperately poor, but those in the 'South' were grossly disadvantaged by comparison with those in the 'North.' The term 'South' referred primarily to Africa, the Asian subcontinent, and Latin America, while 'North' indicated the industrialized countries of Europe, North America, Japan, and northern Asia. Some women of the South still worked in subsistence agriculture or were being starved by the transition to male-dominated agribusiness. They lacked access to modern medicine, were subject to famine and epidemic diseases like AIDS, and often paid the highest price for globalization in general. Civil war and political instability took a high toll on women and children in the 'South.' Thus, the issues which activists from these regions raised were different from those of interest to women in the North, who focused on greater economic opportunity, access to democratic politics, equitable treatment of lesbian and bisexual women, freedom from sexual harassment, and environmental safety. Finding common ground was a major undertaking for the international congresses of women that took place from the 1970s on.

Although the North–South distinction allowed differences to come to the fore along lines that focused on a common plight shaped by geography, other activists at international and national meetings discussed feminist differences in terms of class and especially in terms of Western middle-class domination. Non-Westerners were understandably distressed because many of the early feminists in India, Egypt, and elsewhere had been middle- and upper-class with ties to such Western ideologies as democracy, the free market, and individualism. They searched for a way to be 'authentic' in their feminism as opposed to mimicking the values of the imperialist powers. Others opposed the domination of prosperous women's issues whether these women were from the North or South, the 'West' or the non-West. Poor women's voices were underrepresented, whether from welfare mothers in the United States or from women facing AIDS in Thailand. In some cases the silencing of poor women was done by scholars and the media that interpreted feminism as a movement of (selfish) rich women and often did not take into account the centuries-old history of women's activism at all levels. None the less, the question of class has been paramount across this history, with common ground often proving elusive.

Another divisive condition was difference in color, race, and ethnicity. In the West, differences of skin color were starkly apparent to women of color because the legacy of slavery and imperialism gave 'whiteness' automatic privilege just as 'maleness' was automatically privileged. The privileges and punishments of race in the West were enormous, but at the beginning of postwar feminist activism, white women refused to acknowledge these issues and so focused on gender as to deny the legitimate claims of women of color. The insistence of women of color in the West that racism be acknowledged fragmented the women's movement late in the 1960s and early 1970s and produced such major statements by women of color as the Combahee River Collective Statement (1977). This fragmentation had the most important intellectual and political consequences, for it made the women's movement more complex, pushed it toward being more fair-minded, and helped people develop skills in coalition-building. Yet race and color in other parts of the world had different shapes, often making themselves felt in the class of different ethnic groups which could distinguish one another by religion, physical traits, and ways of behaving that allowed politicians increasingly to whip up political passions. As globalization took its toll economically, these political passions centered on race and ethnicity made women their victims. These differences became central to international feminist meetings too.

Sexuality was another divisive, complex issue, seen by women in many Southern countries as something that Western women could hardly comprehend. The pronouncements of Westerners on such practices as genital surgery, female seclusion, or infanticide were interpreted as highly bigoted and imperialist. Moreover, women in Southern cultures were themselves divided over practices and behaviors. In sub-Saharan Africa, Muslim women wrote novels showing the mental and social distress caused by male polygamy, but other women defended the practice. In the West lesbianism and heterosexuality initially divided the women's movement, but some practical ways of working together developed. However, for Southern women conflicts over sexuality of this kind were seen as utter luxuries compared to the real harms of sexual practice. Rape was common in ethnic and racial wars and often led to social ostracism if not death. Though rape was practiced against women globally, the rape increasingly inflicted on women in ethnic struggle became an urgent and unifying issue for many feminists around the world. It could simultaneously be divisive, if women saw the value or inevitability of rape in struggles to promote the liberation of their ethnicity, race, or nationality.

This book mainly covers feminisms as social and political movements based on material conditions and political and social aspiration. Because this subject alone is so vast, the collection gives virtually no space to the feminisms that were defined by great women theorists or expressed by artists, poets, novelists, and musicians. But we must remember that at no time in the past half-century did women in protest not lift their voices in songs of resistance or use their pens to give an aesthetic shape to their sense of womanhood, women's struggles, and women's accomplishments. Women artists have used visual irony to depict male privilege in a consumer society; they have also created visions of a feminist beauty, often involving mothering, women's love for one another, and women's spirituality. The development of feminist spirituality and religions (and challenges to male-dominated religious institutions), of feminist ethics, of feminist epistemology to challenge men's claims to being the sole possessors of reason, and of the field of women's studies, has been transformative. The challenges by theorists to everything from Buddhism to male domination of the art world can never be undone. Expressions of women's art, spirituality, and philosophy form part of the context of social movements. However, the uprising of women over the past half-century has also produced a vast quantity of new intellectual and aesthetic expression.

We have entered a global age in which women migrate across national borders to find work or to escape the political violence that has dominated politics in the past half-century. The world's peoples and cultures have become more hybrid as a result. Yet there is and has been no single global feminism, no single issue, nor single way of pursuing women's ends. Women have carried guns, written diatribes, used shaming and bodily gestures of ridicule against those who would oppress or exploit them. Women have acted heroically on their own, banded together informally, formed national and even transnational groups, and disagreed with one another, sometimes venomously, over politics and social goals. As a result there is a huge body of historical material charting their activism, and here the picture is clearer: women's activism is consistently rich, complex, and vast. That activism has operated over the past half-century in ways which still need analyzing for common themes, models of organization, tactics and strategies, useful paradigms, and long-term effects. When the first histories of feminism appeared in the 1960s, their tone emphasized that 'everyone was brave.' These histories stressed women's heroism, and although we admire our foremothers, the time is ripe for the hard, scholarly analysis of comparative work.

NOTES

1 Quoted in Amrita Basu, 'Indigenous Feminism, Tribal Radicalism, and Grassroots Mobilization in India,' in Josephine Diamond (ed.) *Women and Revolution: Global Expressions* (Dordrecht: Kluwer, 1998), p. 237.

BIBLIOGRAPHY

Basu, Amrita (ed.) (1995) *The Challenge of Local Feminisms: Women's Movements in Global Perspective*. Boulder, CO: Westview Press.

Butler, Judith and Scott, Joan (eds) (1992) *Feminists Theorize the Political*. London: Routledge.

Diamond, M. Josephine (1998) *Women and Revolution: Global Expressions*. Dordrecht: Kluwer.

Evans, Sarah M. (1997) *Born for Liberty. A History of Women in America*. New York: Free Press.

Jacquette, Jane (ed.) (1989) *The Women's Movement in Latin America: Participation and Democracy*. Boulder, CO: Westview Press.

Kandiyoti, Deniz (ed.) (1991) *Women, Islam and the State*. Philadelphia, PA: Temple University Press.

Nnaemeka, Obioma (ed.) (1998) *Sisterhood, Feminisms, and Power: From Africa to the African Diaspora*. Trenton, NJ: African World Press.

Radcliffe, Sarah A. and Westwood, Sallie (eds) (1993) *'Viva': Women and Popular Protest in Latin America*. London: Routledge.

Rives, Janet M. and Yousefi, Mahmood (eds) (1997) *Economic Dimensions of Gender Inequality: A Global Perspective*. Westport: Praeger.

Rueschemeyer, Marilyn (ed.) (1998) *Women in the Politics of Postcommunist Eastern Europe*. Armonk, NY: M. E. Sharpe.

Terborg-Penn, Rosalyn and Rushing, Andrea Benton (eds) (1996) *Women in Africa and the African Diaspora: A Reader*. Washington, DC: Howard University Press.

Tétreault, Mary Ann (ed.) (1994) *Women and Revolution in Africa, Asia and the New World*. Columbia: University of South Carolina Press.

Threlfall, Monica (1996) *Mapping the Women's Movement: Feminist Politics and Social Transformation in the North*. London: Verso.

Waylen, Georgina (1996) *Gender in Third World Politics*. Boulder, CO: Lynne Rienner.

White, Deborah (1999) *Too Heavy a Load: Black Women in Defense of Themselves, 1894–1994*. New York: W. W. Norton.

Part I

NATION-BUILDING

1

COMPETING AGENDA

Feminists, Islam, and the state in nineteenth- and twentieth-century Egypt

Margot Badran

As in Europe and the United States, an explicitly feminist movement had arisen in nineteenth-century Egypt among middle- and upper-class women. Alongside that movement a drive developed to liberate the country from British imperial domination, which siphoned off Egyptian resources and blocked independent rule. In the 1920s and thereafter, feminism and national liberation were intertwined causes in Egypt as they were in many other regions dominated by imperial powers such as France, Russia, Japan, Belgium, Portugal, and the Netherlands. To channel feminist activism into the anti-colonial cause, nationalists promised that independence would bring improvements in women's condition; but to their mind the national cause had to come first. Imperial domination affected everyone, it was argued, whereas the oppression of women only affected some of the people.

Debates over women played a surprisingly large part in anti-colonial theories used to argue for independence. In some of these debates it was said that imperialism made women too Western; independence would allow them to return to the safety and seclusion of the home. In India, women's spirituality in the privacy of the home was said to be akin to the spirituality of India before Western domination. Both needed to be restored. However, in other regions seeking independence, the Westernization of women was at the center of anti-colonial movements. The modernization of women in such areas as literacy would improve the general condition of the people and allow them a stronger position in the world of free nations.

Aided by women's activism and feminism, Egypt gained its full independence after World War II. The situation of women did not fulfill the promises made by nationalist leaders, however. This too was a common result of the anti-colonial struggles of the post-World War II period. None the less, the continuity in women's activism from the beginning of the twentieth century through the post-World War

II period was more visible in many decolonizing countries than in the United States and Europe over the same period. A strong women's presence shaped social and political movements for the entire century.

* * *

In Egypt the 'woman question' has been a contested domain involving feminists, Islamists, and the state. This chapter explores their competing discourses and agenda in nineteenth- and twentieth-century Egypt and how they have shifted over time.[1] Divergent discourses arose in the context of modern state and class formation, and economic and political confrontation with the West. These multiple discourses have been sustained in strikingly different political and economic cultures as state and society continually negotiate changing realities.

From the second quarter of the nineteenth century, the state in Egypt tried to draw women into the economic and technological transformations underway. As a consequence it began to wrest women away from the more exclusive control of the family, threatening the authority and domination of men over their women. Earlier in the century, after freeing Egypt from direct Ottoman rule, the new ruler, Muhammad 'Ali, while consolidating his power, had placed the Islamic establishment centred at Al Azhar under the control of the state. The former broad purview of the religious establishment was eroded piecemeal in the drive towards secularisation of education and law. The only exception to this was the sphere of personal status laws.[2] For women this created an awkward dichotomy between their role as citizens of the nation state (*watan*) and as members of the religious community (*umma*). In a division that was never precise, the state increasingly came to influence their public roles, leaving to religion the regulation of their private or family roles. The structural contradictions and tensions this created have to this day never been fully resolved.[3]

While promoting new social roles for women, the state could not afford unduly to alienate patriarchal interests and has therefore made various accommodations and alliances. Whatever their competing interests, the state and religious forces have retained patriarchal forms of control over women. It is this patriarchal dimension that feminists have identified and confronted and for which they have been variously attacked, contained, or suppressed by state authorities and Islamists alike. However, in Egypt there has been sufficient space – albeit more frequently taken than granted – within state and society for women to speak out as feminists and activists. Moreover, the authorities have at times deliberately encouraged women's initiatives for their own purposes.

The earliest articulation of women's feminist consciousness, first discernible in occasional published writings – poetry, essays, and tales – by the 1860s and 1870s, preceded colonial occupation and the rise of nationalism.[4] It was more widely expressed from the 1890s with the rise of women's journalism and salon debates. This new awareness (not yet called feminist; in fact the term 'feminism' was not used in Egypt until the early 1920s) was based on an increased sensitivity to the everyday constraints imposed upon women by a patriarchal society. Muslim, Christian, and Jew alike shared this sensitivity and they projected an

15

understanding, implicit or explicit, that these constraints were not solely religiously based as they had been made to believe. Furthermore, from the rise of feminism in Egypt to the present, its advocates across the spectrum from left to right have consistently used Islam, as well as nationalism, as legitimising discourses. In this chapter, feminism is broadly construed to include an understanding that women have suffered forms of subordination or oppression because of their sex, and an advocacy of ways to overcome them to achieve better lives for women, and for men, within the family and society. I am using a definition of feminism broad enough to be all-inclusive without intending to suggest a monolithic feminism. I indicate divergences within this larger framework while keeping the primary focus on the interplay among three major discourses, those of feminists, Islamists, and the state.[5]

Feminist, nationalist, and Islamist positions on the 'woman question' have seldom been considered together in the literature.[6] Moreover, although women's views come from the inside, their voices – whether as feminists or Islamists – have been subsumed within 'larger' (male) discourses. Here, I pay particular attention to the agenda of women who are feminists across the political spectrum and of women Islamists. Focusing on what women have to say makes it possible to discern their departures from their male counterparts as well as their own internal differences.

The exploration of the competing agenda and discourses on women is organised within the following historical framework: (1) the modem state-building and colonial periods; (2) the period of the liberal experiment; (3) the period of the revolution, Arabism, and socialism; and (4) the era of *infitah* capitalism and populist Islamist ascendancy.

The modern state-building and colonial periods: nineteenth century to 1922

During the nineteenth century, especially in the later decades, new contenders appeared in the shaping and control of discourse in general, and more particularly, discourses on women. With the broadening of opportunities for education and the rise of women's feminist consciousness, women who had previously been the objects of prescriptive pronouncements began to challenge patriarchal domination.

The expanding modem state promoted new educational and work opportunities for women, especially in health and teaching, but incurred resistance from families. In the early nineteenth century, for example, Egyptians did not initially allow their daughters to attend the new state midwifery school (Ethopian slaves were recruited as the first students).[7] In 1836, Muhammad 'Ali appointed a Council for Public Education to look into creating a state system of education for girls but it was found impossible to implement. Later, however, during the rule of Isma'il, one of his wives sponsored the first state school for girls which opened in 1873, serving the daughters of high officials and white slaves from elite households. Meanwhile, encouraged by the state, Shaikh Ahmad Rifa'i Al Tahtawi and 'Ali Pasha Mubarak published books in 1869 and 1875 advocating education for women, using Islamic justifications from the Quran and *Hadith*.[8] It was not easy, however, to draw women out of the realm controlled by the family.

Feminist discourse first emerged in the writings of women of privilege and education who lived in the secluded world of the urban harem.[9] Women gained new exposure through expanded education and widening contacts within the female world. They made comparisons between their own lives and those of women and men of other social and national backgrounds. Through their new education women also gained deeper knowledge of their religion. Some urban middle- and upper-class women began to contest the Islamic justification for their seclusion, *hijab* (meaning then the veiling of both face and body), and related controls over their lives.[10] In 1892, Zainab Al Fawwaz protested in *Al Nil* magazine, 'We have not seen any of the divinely ordered systems of law, or any law from among the corpus of (Islamic) religious law ruling that woman is to be prohibited from involvement in the occupations of men.'[11] When Hind Naufal founded the journal, *Al Fatah* (The Young Woman) in the same year, inaugurating a women's press in Egypt, women found a new forum for discussing and spreading their nascent feminism.[12]

This emergent feminism was grounded, and legitimised, in the framework of Islamic modernism expounded towards the end of the century by Shaikh Muhammad 'Abduh, a distinguished teacher and scholar from Al Azhar. 'Abduh turned a revolutionary corner when he proposed that believers, by which he meant the learned, could go straight to the sources of religion, principally the Quran and the *Hadith*, for guidance in the conduct of everyday life.[13] Through *ijtihad*, or independent inquiry into the sources of religion, 'Abduh demonstrated that one could be both Muslim and modern and that indeed not all traditional practice was in keeping with Islam. In dealing with gender issues, 'Abduh confronted the problem of patriarchal excesses committed in the name of Islam. He especially decried male abuses of the institutions of divorce and polygamy.[14]

The opening out encouraged by *ijtihad* had a number of consequences. While Muslim women's earliest feminist writing may not have been immediately inspired by Islamic modernism, it was not long before it developed within this framework. The progressive discourse of Muslim men was, however, situated within Islamic modernism from the start. It was generated by men of the upper educated strata, mainly new secular intellectuals, often men of law.[15] Later, towards the middle of the twentieth century, *ijtihad* would also be evoked by men and women of the lower-middle class to create a populist, conservative Islamist discourse (the method – that is *ijtihad* – rather than the content was inspired by Islamic modernism). Thus two marginalised groups; women and the lower-middle class, entered the debate.

After women had been producing their own feminist writing for some time, Murqus Fahmi, a young Coptic lawyer, published *Al Mar' a fi al sharq* (The Woman in the East) in 1894, criticising patriarchal tyranny over women in the home which he claimed no religion sanctioned. Five years later, a Muslim judge, Qasim Amin, published his famous book, *Tahrir al mar' a* (The Liberation of the Woman) in 1899, attacking the practice of female seclusion and the *hijab*, by which he meant face veiling (not modest covering of the head and body). He argued that women in Egypt were backward because they had been deprived of the legitimate rights accorded to them by Islam. He insisted that for the nation to advance and become modern, women must regain these rights. This pro-feminist discourse generated from within the establishment, by a Muslim lawyer and judge, drew wide criticism, especially from religious conservatives and members of the lower-middle class.[16] While it was perceived as more dangerous than women's feminist writing, less widely visible at the time, in the long run women's feminism would be more sustained and more threatening.[17]

Early in the twentieth century, women's feminist writing became more visible and reached a wider mainstream audience, when Malak Hifni Nasif, known by her pen-name, Bahithat Al Badiya (Searcher in the Desert), began publishing essays in *Al Jarida*, the paper of progressive nationalist party, *Al Umma*. These essays and her speeches were published by the party press in 1910 in a book called *Al Nisa'iyyat* (which can be translated as 'Feminine or Feminist Pieces', in the absence of a specific term for 'feminist' in Arabic). Women's feminism was becoming more explicit and was increasingly expressed within a nationalist idiom reflecting and fuelling the growing nationalist movement in Egypt.

Another principal producer of feminist ideas in this period was Nabawiyya Musa, who later published her essays in a book entitled *Al mar' a wa al 'amal* (The Woman and Work) 1920. These two women were both from the middle class: Bahithat Al Badiya from the upper and Nabawiyya Musa from the more modest strata. They were among the first graduates of the Saniyya Teachers School established in 1889, and both became teachers. In 1907, Musa was the first Egyptian woman to sit for the baccalaureate examination, and the last until after independence; the colonial authorities, with their policy of training men for practical administration, were not prepared to subsidise women's secondary education. Meanwhile, these two young women carried on consciousness-raising through their public lectures to strictly female audiences composed mainly of upper-class women and at special classes for women at the new Egyptian University (which were soon stopped and the money saved was used to send three men on study missions abroad).[18]

In 1911, Bahithat Al Badiya became a pioneer in feminist activism when she sent demands to the Egyptian National Congress for women's education and rights to employment and women's rights to participate in congregational worship in mosques.[19] While they were claiming women's rights to public space, feminists like Bahithat Al Badiya and Huda Sha'rawi early in the century actually opposed the unveiling of the face that male feminists advocated. As a tactical move, they wanted women to gain more education and to reclaim public space before they unveiled. While for progressive men unveiling had a key ideological and symbolic value, for women unveiling was a practical matter that they themselves would have to undertake, with the attendant risks of taunts and assaults on their reputations.[20]

The nationalists of the *Umma* Party led by Ahmad Lutfy Al Sayyid and other men of the upper class supported feminism, while those of the *Watani* Party, mainly men of more modest middle-class origins, headed by Mustafa Kamil, were antagonistic towards women's emancipation which they saw as an undermining Western influence. Unlike the *Umma* Party, which advocated a more secular society, the *Watani* Party favoured an Islamic society supporting the notion of a caliphate. It was within these respective frameworks that men as nationalists situated their views on women's place and roles and their own attitudes towards feminism.[21]

During the national revolution from 1919 to 1922, the first priority for Egyptian feminists and nationalists of both sexes was independence. To a large extent feminist and nationalist positions temporarily united in favour of the common cause. The extent and harshness of colonial oppression were underscored when upper-class women, mobilised by feminist and nationalist leaders among them, left the seclusion of their harems to demonstrate, and when poor women also filled the streets in more spontaneous protest. Members of the Wafdist Women's Central Committee (WWCC), created in 1920 as the women's section of the nationalist party, the *Wafd*, insisted on participating fully in decision-making, not just in auxiliary activities. In the midst of the revolution, these women at times took public feminist stands. In 1920 for example, when the male nationalist leadership did not consult the WWCC on the independence proposal they were circulating, the women publicly announced their objections.[22] Yet during colonial occupation a feminism that called for greater female participation in society was upheld by progressive male nationalists and generally tolerated by others. Moreover, during the ferment of revolution, male nationalists enthusiastically welcomed women's militancy.

While Islamic modernism, liberal nationalism, and the feminism of progressive men prevailed in the early modern state-building and colonial period, women's causes found a positive and supportive environment. The attacks of conservative *ulama* during this period focused on Qasim Amin's books, while the opposition to feminist ideas by nationalists like Mustafa

Kamil and Talat Harb did not create the broader conservative groundswell that expressions of anti-feminism would produce later in the century. During colonial occupation, women's feminism was not connected with a public, organised movement; it was the articulation of a broad new philosophy. Men's pro-feminism likewise expressed a philosophical position, and at the time was seemingly more radical than women's, for example, in calling for an end to face veiling. Men's feminist rhetoric, however, reached a climax during occupation. In the next stage, we find the more radical development of women's liberal feminism while men's earlier expression of liberal feminism faded for reasons that will become apparent later in our discussion.

In the late nineteenth and early twentieth centuries polemics were started that have plagued feminist and Islamist positions ever since and have had political reverberations in official discourse. These concern definitions of culture, authenticity, identity, and modernity – and their implications for women's roles around which a battle of legitimacy has raged. The debate has continued right up to the final decade of the twentieth century, as have the state's efforts to control competing discourses and to appropriate elements useful to itself.

The liberal experiment: 1923–1952

Early in this period, the feminist positions of progressive men and women which had drawn closest during colonial occupation and in the pre-independence nationalist movement started to diverge. Women had a rude awakening when it became clear that liberal men were not prepared to implement their promise to integrate women into public life after nominal political independence in 1922. Feminists became openly militant, while most men who had been pro-feminist nationalists, in the forefront of whom was Sa'd Zaghlul, grew silent as their attention turned towards their new political careers. A few others responded with concrete positive actions, such as Ahmad Lutfy Al Sayyid, whose championship of university education for women will be noted later.[23] There were moments, moreover, when feminists would be beleaguered, especially in the early 1930s during the government of Isma'il Sidki, a political and social reactionary. In the 1950s, the new more radical, socialist feminists would be harassed outright. During the same period, a rising activist, Zainab Al Ghazali, would move from feminism to Islamic fundamentalism, beginning a conservative women's religious and political movement.[24]

With formal independence (British troops remained on Egyptian soil until 1956), nationalist men become part of the new state. At first the official discourse articulated in the new Constitution of 1923 seemed to fulfil their promises to women when it declared: 'All Egyptians are equal before the law. They enjoy equally civil and political rights and equally have public responsibilities without distinction of race, language, or religion.' However, the principle of gender equality was soon cancelled when an electoral law restricted suffrage to males only. The following year women were barred from attending the opening of the new parliament, except as wives of ministers and other high state officials. The idealism of nationalist men gave way to political pragmatism in the new independent 'liberal' era.

At this point, women's feminist stance became explicit – the word 'feminist' began to be used – and their feminism became tied to an organised, political movement led by *Al Ittihad al nisa'i al misri* (the Egyptian Feminist Union, EFU) created in 1923 and headed by Huda Sha'rawi. The first unequivocal use of the term occurred in 1923 when the EFU feminists employed the term, *feministe*, in French, the everyday language of most of them. (To this day Arabic lacks a precise term for feminism.)[25] From 1923, feminism crystallised around a set of demands, a broad agenda of claims for political, social, economic, and legal rights. However, initial priority was given to women's education followed by new work opportunities and the reform of the personal status law. Some demands were granted relatively easily, such as equal secondary school education for girls and raising the minimum marriage age for both sexes (achieved in 1923 and 1924 respectively). The entry of women into the state university in 1929 as achieved, not without difficulty, by the Rector himself, Ahmad Lutfy Al Sayyid, one of the few nationalists who actively strove to implement his progressive ideas. Gains in the sphere of employment were mainly achieved in those areas which were most congruent with the immediate priorities of the state, such as in education and medicine. These were fields in which women professionals typically served the needs of other women and thus their new work also perpetuated gender segregation in public space. However, greater numbers of women were also drawn into employment in the expanding textile factories, where they worked more closely with men.

During the early 1930s, when the reactionary, Isma'il Sidqi was at the head of government, feminists encountered some setbacks, such as a conservative educational policy opposing higher education for women. With the change of government in 1933, however, the more characteristic liberal atmosphere was restored. Although feminists were able to conduct public activities, there were also to be disappointments. Most importantly, no headway was made in formal political rights for women, nor in the reform of personal status law. In addition, state-legalised prostitution was not abolished.[26]

During this period religious officials and feminists shared some common social concerns. When the feminists called for the prohibition of alcohol and the ending of state-licensed prostitution, the Shaikh of Al Azhar Muhammad Abu Al Fadl wrote to the president of the Egyptian Feminist Union (EFU) saying: 'We appreciate the value of your honourable association and its diligent efforts to spread virtue and combat vice. There are in Egypt now distinguished women whose impact on society is no less important than that of honourable men.'[27] However, when it came to demands for political rights for women, the same Islamic authorities pronounced them to be un-Islamic, both officially through *fetwas* (religious decrees) and through unofficial utterances.[28]

Official Islam was not the only Islamist platform during this period. A conservative popular Islamic movement emerged with the creation of the Muslim Brothers (*Ikhwan Muslimin*) by Hasan Al Banna in 1928. This movement drew on a wide base of support from the modest and lower strata of the middle class, strongly opposing the continued British military presence and economic imperialism. The Muslim Brothers, connecting Egypt's ills with a deviation from the practice of true Islam, went to the sources of their religion for fresh inspiration. They emphasised individual reform as the first step towards improving society, but their ultimate, more radical goal was the creation of an Islamic state. The ideology of the Muslim Brothers, laying stress on the moral foundations of society, articulated a conservative discourse privileging the patriarchal family, male authority over women, and clear-cut differentiation of gender roles.[29]

During the militancy of the 1919 revolution and its immediate aftermath, class differences between women as feminists and nationalists were of little importance in the face of larger common causes. However, in time, differences in class and culture produced cleavages between women and raised questions of cultural authenticity. The upper class had adopted elements of Western manners expressed in dress, in everyday life, and in the use of the French language. Indeed, the language of the EFU journal founded in 1925 was French. Because the EFU leadership was upper class and because its feminist ideas were mainly expressed in French, feminism came to be considered, especially by detractors, as foreign. The nationalism of Egyptian men who also spoke French and wore Western dress was not, however, denigrated in the same way.[30] The importance assigned to cultural symbols was different for the two sexes. Men could change and retain authenticity (the *tarbush* or fez, the Ottoman head-dress, was even forbidden to men by the state following the 1952 revolution) while the burdens of continuity were placed on women.

The tension between feminism and cultural authenticity is well illustrated in the case of Zainab Al Ghazali. The daughter of a prosperous cotton merchant with an Al Azhar education, she joined the EFU as a young woman in 1935. Around that time, Al Azhar initiated seminars for women at the *Kulliyya Shar'iyya* (the Islamic Law College) under the direction of Shaikh Ma'mun Shinawi (later, Shaikh of Al Azhar) which Al Ghazali joined. Within the year, Al Ghazali formed the Muslim Women's Society (MWS) – Shinawi was present at its inauguration – and left the EFU. In a recent interview Al Ghazali said, 'The Egyptian Feminist Union wanted to establish the civilisation of the Western woman in Egypt and the rest of the Arab and Islamic worlds.' She also remarked that when she left the feminist organisation, Huda Sha'rawi told her, 'You are separating yourself from me intellectually,' adding, 'I ask you not to fight the Egyptian Feminist Union.' And Al Ghazali confesses, 'I never fought it.'[31] In fact, there was occasional co-operation between the two organisations, mainly in nationalist activism, as Hawa Idris, the head of the EFU's youth group, the *Shaqiqat* (established in 1935) recalled recently.[32]

The division between feminist and fundamentalist women that originated in the late 1930s was to persist, and their divergent orientations, perceptions, beliefs, and agenda would be articulated in competing discourses. While the EFU women found their feminist ideology and programme compatible with Islam, and sought its legitimising force, their overall ideological framework was secular rather than religious. For Al Ghazali and the MWS, on the other hand, since the *Shari'ah* regulates all aspects of life, a separate ideology of feminism was at best redundant and at worst an undermining Western ideology. Al Ghazali, who extols the absolute equality (*musawa mutlaqa*) between women and men in Islam, finds women's liberation within the framework of religion.[33] Fundamentalist men and women typically speak of complementarity rather than equality and stress male authority over women. The EFU championed greater access for women to public roles while the MWS lauded women's family duties and obligations.

As a secular Egyptian organisation, the EFU included under its aegis Muslims and Christians alike, while the MWS as a strictly Muslim religious organisation did not cater to all Egyptians. The issue of 'secularism' (*'almaniyya*) has been contentious. Fundamentalist women called Egyptian feminism 'secular', thus implying that it was outside the bounds of Islam. However, Egyptian Muslim women distinguished their feminism which they based on Islamic principles from the 'secular' basis of Turkish feminism. An article in the EFU's journal *Al Misriyya* (The Egyptian Woman) in 1937 said, for example, that 'while the Turkish woman has attained her freedom by virtue of foreign laws [alluding to the 1926 Turkish Civil Code based not on the Islamic *Shari'ah* but on a Swiss model] the Egyptian woman will never ask for her rights except by basing her requests on the Islamic *Shari'ah*.'[34] The EFU and most other feminists later shied away from a secularism which severed all links with religion. This would be called *'almaniyya la dini'*, literally, secularism without religion, by some of today's fundamentalists. Women's fundamentalist leadership under Al Ghazali favoured an Islamic state with a theocratic ruler, while the EFU feminists accepted the notion of a secular state whose legitimacy was grounded in the basic principles of Islam.

Around the time of the creation of the MWS, Egyptian feminist activism broadened in response to the Arab Uprising in Palestine and to calls for support from Palestinian women to Egyptian feminists. Both Arab and religious – Muslim and Christian – identities were evoked in the drive to save Palestine. The EFU hosted the Conference for the Defence of Palestine in 1938, which religious and state authorities applauded equally. It was yet another instance when militant nationalism blurred gender lines. The feminists' collective nationalist action in 1938 led to the first pan-Arab Feminist Conference in 1944. Waving the banner of Arab unity, the pan-Arab feminist conference again won the praise of governments and the Islamic establishment for their nationalist actions.[35]

Towards the end of the 1930s and in the 1940s, feminism in Egypt broadened its outreach and new organisations proliferated. The EFU began its Arabic-language journal, *Al Misriyya*, in 1937, aiming to 'elevate the intellectual and moral level of the masses and to create lines of solidarity between the different classes of the nation.' The Arabic periodical aimed at a wider audience than *L'Egyptienne* and projected a self-consciously Islamic tone heralded in the journal's motto: 'Take half your religion from 'Aisha.' It was to be 'the *minbar* [pulpit] for feminist demands' as well as 'the tongue of the most noble nationalist hopes'. However, while EFU leaders Huda Sha'rawi and Saiza Nabarawi tried to serve the needs of a broader constituency, the rank and file of the EFU resisted opening up the organisation membership to women of humbler extraction. On two separate encounters with this author in the late 1960s and early 1970s, Duriyya Shafiq, from a middle-class family in Tanta in the Delta, contrasted Huda Sha'rawi's welcoming encouragement to her when she returned from France in 1939 with her doctorate with the grudging reception of the EFU membership.[36]

EFU resistance to broadening its constituency and the political and economic changes following World War II in Egypt encouraged a proliferation of more populist feminist organisations headed by middle-class women. Wishing to accelerate the struggle for political rights for women, former EFU members Fatma Ni'mat Rashid and Duriyya Shafiq founded respectively the *Hizb al nisa'i al-watani* (National Feminist Party, NFP) in 1944 and *Al Ittihad bint at nil* (The Daughter of the Nile Union, DNU) in 1948. Along with the advocacy of political rights for women, both the NFP and DNU mounted literacy and hygiene campaigns among the poor. They also sustained the concern with family law reform, education and work rights for women. Duriyya Shafiq, a protégée of Sha'rawi, was the more dynamic leader of the two, whose DNU was larger, longer-lived and more effective with branches throughout the country, whereas Rashid's NFP was a strictly Cairene organisation with limited outreach. Unlike their political goals, the social projects of these two feminist organisations could scarcely have antagonised the Muslim Brothers or the MWS.[37]

Despite the widening class base of the feminist movement through new organisations led by women who had come of age during the first phase of feminist activism, this new strand remained essentially within the liberal framework evolved by the EFU. It was the younger generation of women, university students and graduates of the mid-1940s, who moved in a new direction as socialists and communists. For them the liberation of women was tied to the liberation of the masses, and both necessitated the end of imperialism and class oppression in Egypt. A young leader of the new socialist feminists, Inji Aflatun, a landowner's daughter, discovered Marxism at the French Lycée in Cairo. After graduating from Fuad I University (later Cairo University) in 1945, she helped found the *Rabitat fatayat at jami'a wa al ma' ahid* (the League of University and Institutes' Young Women) which Latifa Zayyat, a student leader, soon joined. The League sent Aflatun and others to the first conference of the International Democratic Federation of Women, but it was closed down the following year in the drive to suppress communists. However, the socialist feminists went on to form other associations, such as the *Jamiyya al nisa'iyya at wataniyya al mu'aqata* (The Provisional National Feminist Association). Within the mainstream communist movement there was no room to address women's liberation, which was subordinated to the struggle against imperialist military occupation and class oppression. Aflatun linked class and gender oppression, connecting both to imperialist exploitation.[38]

The growing nationalist determination to expel British troops from Egypt led to coalitions among feminist and fundamentalist women. In 1950, the *Harakat ansar at salam* (the Movement of the Friends of Peace) brought together EFU feminist and then president, Saiza Nabarawi (Sha'rawi had died in 1947) and the young leftist, Inji Aflatun. The same year, Nabarawi created the *Lajnu al shabbal* (the Youth Committee), attracting women like Aflatun who went to poor quarters of Cairo to politicise women. In 1952 when violence broke out in the Canal Zone, the *Lajnu al nisa'iyyu lil muqawama al sha'biyya* (the Women's Committee for Popular Resistance) brought together women from the left and right including the socialist feminist, Aflatun, and the fundamentalist, Al Ghazali. Once again, women joined ranks with male nationalists in common cause and again men welcomed their support.

During this period, the religious establishment, as we have noted, at times supported women's demands and at other times opposed them. While fundamentalists did not support any of the feminists' demands, neither were they overtly anti-feminist. This changed, however, on the eve of the 1952 revolution when religious scholars held a conference to examine all aspects of women's status within the context of Islamic law. They now openly attacked the feminist movement, claiming it was influenced and supported by British imperialists, and saying that 'Colonialism had encouraged women to go out in order to destroy Islamic society.'[39] The conference condemned the Egyptian feminist movement for its disruptive effects on society and held Sha'rawi and Shafiq responsible. Evaluating the past, it attacked Murqus Fahmi and Qasim Amin and praised the (anti-feminist) stance of Mustafa Kamil.

The reactionary conclusions of the conference seemed to be in part a response to the growing numbers of women in the workforce. By the early 1950s, women were found in shops, factories, the professions and the social services in sufficient numbers to alarm the patriarchal sensibilities of male fundamentalists. The conference, wishing to turn the tide or at least to stem it, scorned women's forays into public life, lamenting that women 'wished to be degraded by going out to work and being seen by everyone.'[40] The conference reiterated the reactionary refrain 'a woman's natural place is her home', insisting that 'her entry into public life is unnatural.' The nub of the problem for these men was revealed in their declaration, 'The most serious threat facing our society is the oriental woman's refusal to obey men.' Although fundamentalist men raised the alarm in March 1952, it was not until 1978 that the conference proceedings would be published under the title, *Harakat nisa'iyya wa silatuha ma' al isti'mar* (Feminist Movements and Their Connections with Colonialism), edited by Muhammad 'Atiya Khamis. This occurred six years after Sadat had come to power, by which time religious fundamentalism in Egypt had won considerable public prominence. (Khamis in another book, *Mu'amarat didd al usra al muslima*, Conspiracies against the Muslim Family, n.d., charged that unveiling was a weapon of communism.) But during the period of Arab socialism under Nasser, these sentiments were not overtly expressed.

The period of the liberal experiment was a time in Egypt when a capitalist economy with ties of dependency to a dominant Europe still operated largely within a neo-imperialistic framework. The feminist or pro-feminist ideology that had served the nationalist cause during colonial occupation was no longer seen by most men to be useful or desirable during this new period of albeit incomplete independence. Thus feminists achieved limited gains. Their successes did not threaten the ruling class. In fact, these limited gains could be said to have helped construct a more viable, modern society by harnessing women to the development goals of the state. Feminist discourse was allowed public expression for the most part by the state, except in its most radical socialist form, but even this managed to survive more surreptitiously. When this period ended, women still lacked formal political rights, a symbol of their secondary status as citizens, while the stalemate on the reform of personal status laws affirmed their unequal positions within the family.

Revolution, Arabism and socialism: 1952 to the early 1970s

This was a time when independent feminist voices would be silenced. Radical Islamists were also suppressed, although the Islam of the establishment and the apolitical discourse of religious scholars would be tolerated. In short, it was a time when the state heavy-handedly silenced all political competitors, and did so publicly. The masses, whose liberation the state championed, included rank and file fundamentalists among those muzzled. Women, whose cause the state also claimed to support, and did so in certain ways such as granting them the vote, were likewise suppressed as independent political actors. However, the feminism of the leaders who had come of age in the previous period remained alive behind the scenes, while a rising generation of future feminists was nurtured as women took advantage of new state-sponsored opportunities in education and work. In this atmosphere of repression, feminists sharpened survival skills that would be useful in the battles they would encounter in the 1970s and 1980s.

The revolution of 1952, led by young military officers of the lower middle class supported in their struggle for power by members of the same class among the Muslim Brothers, promised to usher in a new era. Soon, however, the Muslim Brothers were suppressed as dangerous to the state, and the leader of the Muslim Sisters, Zainab Al Ghazali, was imprisoned. From the early 1960s Arab socialism, with its new economic measures such as land reform and industrialisation, challenged the old class system. It was an era of hope for the majority, including the leader of the next generation of feminists, Nawal Al Saadawi, a 1955 graduate of the Medical Faculty at Cairo University, who recently recalled the early enthusiasm and optimism of her generation.[41]

The Arab socialism of the state in the 1960s called for social equality and justice for all citizens and aimed at pan-Arab unity and wider Afro-Asian solidarity. While the tone of Arab socialism was secular, it accommodated religion. The 1962 Charter delineating the Arab socialist project declared: 'The essence of religious messages does not conflict with the facts of our life. . . . All religions contain a message of progress. . . . The essence of all religions is to assert man's right to life and to freedom.' The Constitution of 1964 stated in Article 1: 'The United Arab Republic is a democratic, socialist state based on the alliance of the working powers of the people. The Egyptian people are part of the Arab nation.' Article 5 declared Islam the religion of the state. The new state suppressed Islam as a political force but did not tamper with the Muslim identity of the society.

The stifling of competing discourses did not occur instantly. Feminist organisations continued their activism after the revolution of 1952. At this juncture, they made a final push for women's political rights in which Duriyya Shafiq of the DNU led the way. In 1953, when a proposed revision of the Electoral Law was under review, she published *Al Kitab al abiyad lil huquq al mar'a al misriyya* (The White Paper on the Rights of the Egyptian Woman), a compendium of pro-suffrage arguments by sympathetic secular liberals and politicians as well as pro and con views from within the Islamic

27

establishment. For example, a constitutional lawyer, Sayyid Sabri, argued that laws must change as the conditions and needs of society change. Since women were now part of the public opinion of society (*al ra'i al 'amm*) they should be able to participate in the formal political system. He noted that the Electoral Law contradicted the Constitution, which declared Egyptians equal in civil and political rights. However, the state and official Islam came down firmly against political rights for women. The Constitutional Affairs Committee of the Senate rejected women's suffrage and the *Fatwa* Committee of Al Azhar issued a decree saying that Islam did not condone it. The *Mufti* of Egypt, Shaikh Hasanayn Makhluf, contended that Islam opposed political rights for women. Shaikh Allam Nassar, who, it should be noted, was then a former *mufti* made the opposite claim, however. The day after the *Fatwa* Committee made its announcement, Islamic organisations held a conference in the office of the Muslim Brothers. Included in their lengthy statement was the demand that the government close once and for all 'the door to this *fitna*' (literally chaos, but here referring to political rights for women), claiming it had been proven that political rights for women were contrary to religion, the Constitution, and the public interest. Meanwhile Shafiq intensified her militancy in this heated battle through a sit-in at the parliament and a hunger strike. Finally, in 1956, thirty-three years after EFU feminists had first demanded suffrage, the revolutionary government in its fifth year granted women the right to vote.[42]

The intentions of the state, however, were made clearer in its actions than in its official discourse. Feminist leaders tried to continue their political struggle while the state put a final stop to their public activity. In 1956, the same year that the state granted women the right to vote, it paradoxically started to ban feminist organisations and to suppress public expression of feminist views, completing its task by 1959. The Egyptian Feminist Union, under pressure from the government, purged its membership of the alleged communist Saiza Nabarawi. The state dismantled the old EFU, but allowed a truncated version to continue as a social welfare society under the name of the Huda Sha'rawi Association. Meanwhile, after suffrage had been achieved, feminists formed *Al Lajna al nisa'iyya lil wa'i al intikhabi* (Women's Committee for Electoral Awareness) to make poor women aware of their rights, but the authorities closed down the committee within a year. Around the same time, a coalition of women of different political tendencies came together in *Al Ittihad al nisa'i al qawmi* (The National Feminist Union, the NFU). The authorities, however, blocked their project by withholding a permit for the NFU and finally shut it down in 1959. Aflatun was sent to prison in the same year. By then, Shafiq was under house arrest. Nabarawi and Rashid were also silenced. The clampdown on feminists occurred within the wider context of political repression. The state apparently perceived feminists as more dangerous than fundamentalists since the Muslim Sisters did not suffer the same fate until 1964, when they were banned; the following year their leader, Al Ghazali, was gaoled. The same year, new laws forbade the formation of women's political organisations.

The ideology of the new regime was set out in the 1962 Charter. The official discourse shifted from the more formal rhetoric of parliamentary democracy of the previous period to a fervent championing of the rights of the masses and socio-economic development. The grip of the old feudal class system was to be broken and the final vestiges of imperialist domination were to be eradicated. The Charter heralded Arabism expressed in language, culture, and pan-Arab political links. Now, also for the first time, the official state ideology confronted patriarchal supremacy. The Charter stated: 'Woman must be regarded as equal to man and must therefore shed the remaining shackles that impede her free movement so that she might take a constructive and profound part in shaping life.' This was situated in the context of the development needs of the country. The Constitution promulgated two years later declared in Article 8, 'The State guarantees equality of opportunity to all Egyptians.' This was translated into free university education and a guaranteed job for every graduate. State support for fuller participation of women in public life would before long, however, trigger conservative reactions.

Meanwhile, official educational and employment policies opened up new opportunities for women. Women's literacy rate increased and greater numbers of women graduated from university and entered the labour force. A corollary of this was a rise in the percentage of single women in the 1960s and 1970s and a decline in fertility. (Lower fertility rates, however, were also connected with birth control programmes which the state supported.) Because of the state's interest in increasing its scientific and technical capacities, it enforced policies to encourage greater enrolment in the applied sciences at university. Larger numbers of women were accordingly attracted to these subjects and subsequently into the professions. Nearly all women medical students graduating in the mid-1960s were reported to be practising their profession.[43] The marked increase of women with training in applied subjects and in the scientific and medical professions during this period should be noted for, as we shall discuss later, it was women university students specialising in these areas who were at the centre of the new wave of young fundamentalists in the 1970s and early 1980s.

As often happens historically, when objective conditions change there is a burst of idealist and prescriptive literature extolling the very roles that are being altered in the process. The decade following the proclamation of the National Charter of 1962 saw attempts to circumscribe the public roles of women through a reaffirmation of the doctrine of divinely sanctioned biological differences between men and women, and the renewed exaltation of wifely and maternal roles. There was also a call for different education for the two sexes corresponding to their different 'natures' and roles. Conservatives recognised that women's economic independence would reduce their need and desire to remain dependent upon men.[44]

This period also witnessed the rare entry of a woman into the domain of scholarly religious discourse. 'Aisha 'Abd Al Rahman, known as Bint Al Shati (a name purportedly taken as a pseudonym to hide her life of scholarship and writing from her *fallah*, relatives) became a professor of Islamic thought at Cairo University and a prolific writer of articles and books, including a series on the lives of the wives and female relatives of the Prophet Muhammad, held up as paragons for the modern woman. Neither feminists nor fundamentalists within their respective perspectives would consider her radical enough. But widely differing regimes through the years have considered her both safe and useful: she belongs to the *fuqaha al sultan* (the sultan's men of jurisprudence). Nasser, Sadat, and Mubarak have all decorated her.[45]

While Nasser gave Bint Al Shati space and awards, the fundamentalist, Zainab Al Ghazali was imprisoned in 1965 only to be released after Nasser's death. Her brand of Islamist discourse envisioning an Islamic state and insisting on the implementation of social justice for all, rather than just rhetoric, could not be tolerated during the Nasser period. She would only be allowed back on the scene from 1971 under the Sadat regime when competing discourses would once again surface.

We have already noted that under Nasser, Amina Sa'id was the exception to the suppression of feminists. Two years after the 1952 revolution she founded *Hawa* (Eve), a popular magazine for women, published by the large publishing complex, *Dar Al Hilal*. In 1956 she became a member of the Board of the Press Syndicate and three years later its vice-president. Sa'id wedded the message of liberal feminism to the socialist state's 'gender-neutral' agenda for the mobilisation of its citizens. She used her pen to promote women's causes within the framework of the Arab socialist revolution. Speaking to a Beirut audience in 1966 she said, '(Women) as a group form the greatest obstacle to national progress to be found in our country today', echoing the same notion differently phrased by male progressives at the end of the nineteenth century. While noting that recent declarations concerning sexual equality in Egypt and other progressive Arab states had provoked public hostility, she assured her Arab sisters that the Egyptian state had 'assumed responsibility for the emancipation of women.'[46]

Although her own brand of feminism coincided in large measure with the agenda of the state, Sa'id was not simply its spokesperson but a feminist who candidly criticised the failure of the state, then and later, to remedy inequities embedded in the personal status laws. She also decried women's new double burden, that accompanied their expanding economic roles, which the state did little to alleviate.[47] In fact, it was feminists with a social mission like Hawa Idris, who devoted her life to providing childcare for mothers working in the state system, and women belonging to social service societies who attempted to alleviate the double burden of poor working women.[48]

The education and work opportunities created after 1952 brought large numbers of women from middle- and lower-class families into the ranks of the educated and employed. However, while the new policies altered class and employment structures, gender inequalities persisted. The legacy of this partial change is apparent in the lives of two women born in the 1930s and educated at university in the 1950s, who in the 1960s and 1970s emerged as new feminist and Islamist activists.

Nawal Al Saadawi, after graduating as a medical doctor in 1955 found a mission as a practitioner among the rural poor. She was faced with physical and psychological health problems afflicting women relating to such matters as the practice of circumcision and the obsession with female virginity. The connections she made between patriarchy, class, and religion in structuring the oppression of women led her to publish *Al Mar'a wa al jins* (The Woman and Sex) in 1971, the first year of the Sadat regime. With Al Saadawi feminist discourse took a new turn: she introduced the issue of sexual oppression of women connected with everyday customs as well as the prevalence of deviant behaviours such as incest that victimised women inside the family. The feminist physician broke a cultural taboo by exposing the sexual oppression of women. The following year she lost her job. Silenced in Egypt, with her books and writings blacklisted and censored by the state, she went into self-imposed exile.[49]

Safinaz Kazim studied journalism at Cairo University, graduating in 1959. From 1960 to 1966 she studied in the United States where she received an MA from New York University while living and working Greenwich Village as a theatre critic. It was in the United States that Kazim began to move from the political left to right. The problem of identity nagged her. Around the same time she was inspired by the book, *Al 'Adala al ijtima'iyya fi al islam* (Social Justice in Islam), by the Muslim Brother, Sayyid Qutb who had himself become disenchanted with the West and looked to Islam as a force of revolutionary revival. The mentor whom she never met was killed not long after her return from the United States in 1966. Six years later, after a pilgrimage to Mecca, Kazim took up Islamic dress signalling her total commitment to Islam. In the 1970s she met Zainab Al Ghazali with whom she shared the view of Islam as '*din wa dawla*' (religion and state) and the desire to see an Islamic state in Egypt.[50]

Between 1952 and the early 1970s, feminist voices with the exception of Amina Sa'id whom the state found useful and safe, were muted. However, the state also created structures and conditions within which a new feminism incubated. The conservative pronouncements of Islamist scholars and thinkers were tolerated, even though they championed women's domestic roles at the very juncture when the state was encouraging women

31

to join the workforce. However, radical Islam which aimed at a more drastic overhaul of state and society was quashed. Yet, as we have seen, although these plural discourses were suppressed, they were by no means eradicated.

Infitah capitalism and populist Islamist ascendancy: the 1970s and 1980s

This period, which spans the rule of Sadat and the regime of Mubarak, witnessed a resurgence of competing discourses. Women's feminism became public once more while Islamic fundamentalists also found scope for new expression. In fact, the stated itself became an agent in the promotion of forms of feminist and Islamist discourse to further its own objectives. At the same time, controls were imposed on the more independent or radical expressions of these two positions.

Under Sadat there was a fundamental shift from socialism and anti-Western imperialist rhetoric to *infitah* (open door) capitalism and strong pro-Western rhetoric. This was accompanied by a shift from pan-Arabism to an inward focus on Egypt sealed when Sadat made a separate peace with Israel in 1979 and Egypt was expelled from the Arab League.

When Sadat came to power in 1970 the country was in a condition people wearily called 'no war, no peace' and still traumatised by the defeat of 1967 in the war with Israel. Sadat capitalised on the popular religious resurgence that followed the war and encouraged it, in part as a counterpoise to Nasser's Arab socialism with its more 'secular' cast.[51] After the war of 1973 and the acclaimed victory, there was a noticeable upsurge in the Islamic fundamentalist movement. It was popularly believed that victory had come because Muslims had returned to the correct practice of religion. The state encouraged the new emphasis on religion fuelling the spread of a fundamentalism which it subsequently needed to contain.[52]

Meanwhile, the advocacy of women's causes espoused by Jihan Sadat and inspired by the UN decade of women (1975–1985) was encouraged by the state. However, the more independent and radical feminism promoted by Nawal Al Saadawi and others was contained. This has been interpreted in part as a result of Jihan Sadat's drive, and her ability as the president's wife to style herself the supreme advocate of women's causes in Egypt and so to keep competing feminists out of the limelight.[53] However, on another front, the government could not tolerate independent feminist activism because of its need to appease conservative Islamist forces.

At the beginning of the Sadat period, for the first time since independence in 1922, the state promulgated a constitution spelling out a dichotomy between women as (public) citizens and as (private) family members governed by the *Shari'ah*. Thus women's right to the prerogatives of full citizenship became subject to male control. The new Constitution of 1971 stated in Article 40, 'Citizens are equal before the law; they are equal in public rights and duties, with no discrimination made on the basis of race, sex, language, ideology, or belief.' The unprecedented explicit declaration of no discrimination on the basis of sex would seem at first glance to represent a step forward. However, we must note the 1971 language: 'equal in public rights and duties' as opposed to the 1923 language: 'They enjoy equally civil and political rights and equally have public responsibilities.' Moreover, the 1971 Constitution declared:

> The state guarantees a balance and accord between a woman's duties towards her family on the one hand and towards her work in society and her equality with man in the political, social, and cultural spheres on the other without violating the laws of the Islamic *Shari'ah*.[54]

Meanwhile, Islamic fundamentalism continued to gain new adherents among women evidenced by the growing numbers of women wearing the *hijab*. Islamic groups became increasingly active on university campuses, spreading their word and actively recruiting. They were successful in appealing to large numbers of women, especially of the lower and more modest middle class. Many of the new recruits were among women studying medicine and the sciences who, moreover, tended to stay out of the workforce after graduation.[55] At the beginning of the movement to adopt Islamic dress, a young woman, Ni'mat Sidqi, published an account of her conversion to Islamic dress and an apology for the veil in a book entitled *Al Tabarraj* ((bodily) Display) published in 1971 which became a cult book among young women in the early 1970s. At the same time, Amina Sa'id mounted a counter-attack on veiling in the press, mainly in her magazine, *Hawa*.[56] However, the trend persisted and by the mid 1980s veiled women from the wealthier strata of society had appeared. Among these was Keriman Hamza, the first television announcer to wear Islamic dress, who has recounted her conversion in her book *Rihlati min al sufur ilal hijab* (My Journey from Unveiling to Veiling). Veteran feminist Sa'id had been the main opponent of veiling until recently when a young leftist, Sana Al Masri, attacked the practice and its wider implications in her book, *Khalf al Hijab* (Behind the Veil) (1989).

Released from gaol in 1971, the veteran fundamentalist leader, Zainab Al Ghazali, could return to discrete activism. Her prison memoirs, now in their tenth edition, have attracted new generations to her cause.[57] The year after Al Ghazali's release, Safinaz Kazim took up Islamic dress, becoming active as a 'committed Muslim' which she calls herself, rejecting the term 'fundamentalist'. The author of several books and drama critic for the weekly magazine, *Al Musawwar*, she has assumed the role of a crusading intellectual with a special concern for issues of culture, identity, and authenticity while Al Ghazali has been active as an organiser.

Both women wish to see an Islamic state in Egypt and both have experienced state surveillance and incarceration. Kazim was imprisoned three times under Sadat: in 1973, 1975, and 1981. Each time, interestingly, she was accused of being a communist.[58] This could be motivated by a wish to discredit a fundamentalist leader and demoralise the movement without being seen to challenge Islam.

The contradictory pressures on women under Sadat were enormous. The reversal of socialist policies became clear in the 1974 proclamation of the policy of *infitah* when the door was opened to foreign investment and the private sector was encouraged once again in Egypt. The state no longer promoted full employment but, on the contrary, propagated an ideology that curtailed women's public roles encouraging a retreat into the home. This was attempted in different ways, many of them illegal. Lawyers and other women prominent in public life exposed this in their booklet, *Al Huquq al qanuniyya lil mar'a al 'arabiyya bain al nadhariyyat wa al tatbiq* (The Legal Rights of the Egyptian Woman: Theory and Practice) (1988), writing,

> We have observed a retreat from the principle of equality regarding the woman at work. . . . This has become clear in certain practices that are contrary to the Constitution and Egyptian law such as in the newspapers for jobs specifying that applicants must be males.[59]

Meanwhile, rising inflation and the out-migration of men to neighbouring oil-rich countries, leaving women behind to cope, have pushed more women into the workforce.[60] In fact, the spread of the veil has been connected in part with women's need to work and their wish at the same time to protect themselves from exposure to male harassment. This security, however, is sought at the price of engaging in passive rather than active resistance to male intimidation.[61] On a different front, in yet another of its contradictory moves, in 1979 the government unexpectedly enacted a law guaranteeing women thirty seats in Parliament which led to an immediate increase of women in the legislature.[62]

However, the most dramatic and politically sensitive move was the presidential decree making fundamental changes in the personal status laws for the first time in fifty years. Excesses of patriarchal privilege were curtailed in an unprecedented manner with the expansion of women's ability to initiate divorce, added protection for women in divorce, and with controls placed on polygyny. The president's wife had pushed hard for the 1979 decree, issued when the parliament was in recess, which, indeed, became known as 'Jihan's law'. Many men, not only fundamentalists, were outraged, but for feminists the gains constituted an important, if still inadequate, step forward.[63]

The year 1979 was highly charged for Egypt abroad as well as at home. Egypt ratified the Camp David accord with Israel isolating itself from the

Arab world and antagonising both leftists and conservatives at home. The decrees favourable to women within the family and in parliament provoked Muslim conservatives. Meanwhile, the revolution in Iran brought Khomeini to power ushering in a new Islamic state which heartened fundamentalists in Egypt. As Islamist forces gathered momentum, the Egyptian state made an important placatory move in 1980 when it amended the Constitution to read: 'Islamic jurisprudence is *the* principal source of legislation', replacing the 1971 formulation that 'the *Shari'ah* is a principal source of law'.[64]

Egypt was in a period of new and dangerous tensions which the state could not control. In autumn 1981, massive arrests were made of women and men across the political spectrum including feminists and fundamentalists among whom were Nawal al Saadawi and Safinaz Kazim.[65] Not long after these arrests, Sadat was assassinated by a Muslim fundamentalist and the two women were released along with others by the new president, Mubarak.

The early 1980s witnessed the renewed visibility and organisation of independent feminism. Al Saadawi, who had by then gained both a local following and international repute, was active in feminist organising and politics. There was a significant number of highly educated women who espoused feminism practising law and medicine, teaching in university, working in business, and active as writers and journalists. A number of these women, under the leadership of Al Saadawi, struggled to establish the Arab Women's Solidarity Association (AWSA). In AWSA's own words: 'We knew that the liberation of the people as a whole could not take place without the liberation of women and this could not take place without the liberation of the land, economy, culture, and information.'[66] The process of institutionalisation was not easy. The Ministry of Social Affairs refused a permit to the feminist organisation in 1983. It relented, however, at the beginning of 1985 and AWSA registered the same year as a non-governmental organisation with the United Nations.

In 1985 in the face of growing opposition to the 1979 decree law revising the Personal Status Law, the government cancelled it.[67] This galvanised feminists into collective political action. Finally, within two months a new law was passed restoring most, but not all, of the benefits to women provided by the 1979 law. This occurred just before a large delegation of Egyptian feminists went to the United Nations Forum in Nairobi marking the end of the Decade for Women. It would have been impolitic for the Egyptian delegation to attend with such a major grievance.

There was marked concern among feminists at the growing conservatism in Egypt evidenced in efforts we have already mentioned to curtail women's public roles and push them back into the home. In 1986, AWSA held its first conference. Under the banner of 'unveiling the mind', its theme was Challenges Facing the Arab Woman at the End of the Twentieth Century.

The proceedings issued by the Associations's own publishing house declared: 'It has become clear that the traditional stance towards women and their rights undercuts progress in Arab societies. The present situation demands a deeper, more modern look at women's roles in society as well as in the family.'[68]

Meanwhile, the authors of *The Legal Rights of the Egyptian Woman* mentioned above, pooled their practical talents to advance the cause of women, reminding them of their constitutional and legal rights as well as their rights under international treaties and conventions ratified by the Egyptian state. They published an open letter warning against the retrograde trends threatening to curtail women's rights and calling for the establishment of a women's platform to counteract these trends articulated in mass publications.[69]

The proliferating popular conservative Islamist literature of the 1980s echoed writings from the 1960s. According to the Egyptian historian, Huda Lutfy, since the early 1980s an increasing number of Egyptian publishing houses have specialised in cheap editions of popular religious tracts. These tracts extol the domestic roles of women, held up as the cornerstones of a new virtuous society, and stress the need for male authority over women to guide them along the correct path.[70]

An important author of popular books with wide appeal is Shaikh Muhammad Mitwalli Al Sha'rawi, a former minister of *Awqaf* (Religious Endowments), who has spoken to Muslims since the 1970s through state television, which accords him prime time. In the quietist tradition he praises the virtues of obedience and patience for men and women alike while he preaches specifically to women about their family and domestic duties. In a reactionary vein, Sha'rawi has called the woman who works while she has a father, brother, or husband to support her, a sinful woman.[71] Shaikh Sha'rawi's tone supports the official line. In addition to enjoying continued television time, he received a state decoration in March 1988.

There is a different emphasis in the discourse of fundamentalist women leaders Al Ghazali and Kazim, who both play active public roles. Kazim finds no contradiction between women's public and private lives. Al Ghazali left a husband because he interfered with her Islamic activism. She told me, 'Woman companions (of the Prophet) have given as much to Islam as men, even more. The woman companion sacrificed herself, her husband, and her children while the male companion sacrificed (only) himself.' Yet, although Al Ghazali has carved out a public role for herself and has attracted working women to her cause, she continues to commend women's primary roles as wives and mothers.[72] In 1979, in an article in *Al Dawa*, Al Ghazali blamed feminists for encouraging women's public roles despite the dangers that await them in the public arena.[73] Fundamentalist intellectual and professor of English at Cairo University, Muhammad Yahia, in a recent interview said, 'The Islamic movement is seen as marginalising women but the Islamic movement, itself, sees attracting women to the movement (as public activists) to be its problem.[74] It seems that the mixed messages delivered by the movement contribute towards keeping women out of the public struggle.

Meanwhile, towards the end of the 1970s, there appeared what might be called a neo-Islamic modernism articulated by Al Ghazali Harb, a graduate of the languages section at Al Azhar and a former journalist, in his book, *Istiqlal al mara'a fi al Islam* (Independence of the Woman in Islam). Harb, like 'Abudh a century before him, called for a return to the sources of religion for a correct understanding of Islam.[75] Saying that women should consider themselves equal to men, he extolled women's work roles not only to meet economic needs but as a guarantee of their independence. In this he attacked patriarchal supremacy in the family and opposed the expulsion of women from public space. Harb took on the fundamentalists when he declared that there is no such thing as Islamic dress, saying that Islam does not require *hijab* whether veiling the face, or simply the head and body. He asserted that only a correct upbringing can protect women, not veiling. Harb was sternly criticised for these views by Muhammad Yahia, who saw the ideas of Harb (who he noted was far from the calibre and stature of 'Abduh) as useful to the state as a counterpoise to fundamentalism.[76] A few feminists have welcomed this position on women's liberation, argued in Islamic terms, because it suits them personally, while others simply acknowledged its wider political utility.

The state, trying to contain the spreading Islamic fundamentalist challenge, however, tries not to antagonise fundamentalist forces alternating between tough and conciliatory attitudes with the result that it generally displays a conservative stance regarding gender issues. It also favours more moderate conservative Islamicists such as Bint Al Shati who advocate an Islamic society, but not an Islamic state. The government bestowed a decoration on Bint Al Shati in 1988. However, women like Zainab Al Ghazali and Safinaz Kazim, who call for an Islamic state, and Nawal Al Saadawi, who advocates an end to patriarchal and class oppression, make the state very wary.

Conclusion

The 'woman question' around which competing discourses have flourished in Egypt has been, as we have seen, about more than women. It has been about gender relations and sexual hegemony, and broader issues of power. It has been a question through which the state, the religious establishment and Islamic movements have projected other designs. Women themselves helped to formulate the question on their own terms both as feminists and as actors in Islamist movements. While as feminists they generated their own terms of debate and as Islamists they mainly reproduced male discourses, as actors in everyday life both assumed new roles, and in so doing gave further definition to the question. While there has always been room in Egypt for alternative positions on the 'woman question' – with the state, Islamists, and feminists all keeping it alive – only feminists, for whom the 'woman question' is central, have meaningfully attacked patriarchal interests and opposed male supremacy.

The state has through different phases generated contradictory discourses and policies. It characteristically imposed its own agenda and in so doing attempted to define the 'woman question' to suit its own political ends. Thus we have seen that while the state has promoted new roles for women for pragmatic and ideological purposes, it has also upheld imbalanced gender relations and male authority out of political expediency. In the state-building, liberal, socialist, and *infitah* capitalist periods, there have been shifts in rhetoric and emphasis. But while the terms of discourse shift, a substratum of basic gender inequality is retained which does not ultimately challenge patriarchal relations nor the state's own power bases. Because of the state's own ambiguities, official discourses on the 'woman question' have often been discourses of deception.

Islam, in modern Egypt, has been controlled by the state. The Islamic establishment has had to negotiate with and accommodate the secular state. The last bastion of official Islam has been the regulation of family life. This is precisely the area where the state has allowed patriarchal control over women a free hand and where gender relations have been most unequal. Populist, fundamentalist Islam confronted the state but upheld conservative codes of gender relations and endorsed male supremacy. Uncompromisingly radical *vis-à-vis* the state, it has elicited a defensive reaction from the state taking the form of a show of 'Islamic toughness' in the area of gender relations, most notably demonstrated in conservative family laws. Women Islamists, normally excluded from the Islamic establishment, have joined the ranks of more radical, populist funda-mentalist movements. Their leaders have taken on daring social and political roles while acquiescing in an ideology that contradicts their own conduct as activists.

Secular feminists have created the only discourse that insists upon radical changes in gender relations. Feminists have held their own, despite repression by the state, and feminist ideology in Egypt has always managed to survive. In more liberal political climates, feminism can be absorbed into what appears to be a more supportive environment, as we have seen in the period of struggle for national independence. In more hostile contexts, when the agenda of the state and Islamists promote extreme conservatism, such as that of contemporary Egypt, feminism emerges as an oppositional discourse.

This chapter on competing agenda on the 'woman question' in Egypt has attempted to give a sense of the complex choreography of these discourses, how space is given and taken, and how for all but feminists the 'woman question' in the end is a matter of political expediency.

NOTES

For their comments and suggestions regarding this chapter I would like to thank Deniz Kandiyoti, Yesim Arat, John Esposito, Sarah Graham-Brown, Enid Hill, and Albert Hourani.

1 For general definitions of feminism (women's rights, women's emancipation, women's liberation) see Karen Offen, 'Defining Feminism: A Comparative Historical Approach', *Signs* (autumn 1988) no. 14, pp. 119–47 and Gerda Lerner, *The Creation of Patriarchy* (Oxford: Oxford University Press, 1986), appendix. For definitions of feminism in the Egyptian historical context see Margot Badran, 'The Origins of Feminism in Egypt', in Anna Angerman *et al.* (eds), *Current Issues in Women's History* (London: Routledge, 1989). In this chapter the various meanings of feminism should be gleaned from context and Margot Badran, 'Independent Women: Over a Century of Feminism in Egypt', in *Old Boundaries New Frontiers*, forthcoming; Margot Badran, 'Dual Liberation: Feminism and Nationalism in Egypt, 1970s–1985', *Feminist Issues* (spring 1988).

2 See Margot Badran, 'Huda Sha'rawi and the Liberation of the Egyptian Woman', Oxford D. Phil. thesis, 1977 and 'The Origins of Feminism in Egypt', and Judith Tucker, *Women in Nineteenth Century Egypt* (Cambridge: Cambridge University Press, 1985).

3 On this dichotomy see Nawal El Saadawi, 'The Political Challenges Facing Arab Women at the End of the 20th Century', pp. 8–26 and Fatima Memissi, 'Democracy as Moral Disintegration: The Contradiction Between Religious Belief and Citizenship as a Manifestation of the Ahistoricity of the Arab Identity', in Nahid Toubia (ed.), *Women of the Arab World* (London: Zed, 1988), pp. 36–43.

4 See Margot Badran and Miriam Cooke (eds), *Opening the Gates: A Century of Arab Feminist Writing* (London: Virago and Bloomington and Indianapolis: University of Indiana Press, 1990).

5 Badran, 'Over a Century of Feminism in Egypt', pp. 15–34.

6 See Deniz Kandiyoti, 'End of Empire: Islam, Nationalism and Women in Turkey', and Afsaneh Najmabadi, 'Hazards of Modernity and Morality: Women, State and Ideology in Contemporary Iran', in Deniz Kandiyoti (ed.) *Women, Islam and the State* (London: Macmillan, 1991), pp. 48–76 and Margot Badran and Eliz Sanasarian, 'Feminist Goals in Iran and Egypt in the 1920s and 1930s', paper presented at the Middle East Studies Association Meetings, San Francisco, 1984.

7 See Laverne Kuhnke, 'The "Doctoress" on a Donkey: Women Health Officers in Nineteenth Century Egypt', *Clio Medica* 9 (1974) no. 3, pp. 193–205.

8 The books are respectively: *Tariq al hija wa al tamrin 'ala qawa'id al lugha al 'arabiyya* (The Way to Spell and Practise the Rules of the Arabic Language) (1869), and *Al Murshid al amin lil banat wa al banin* (The Faithful Guide for Girls and Boys) (1875).

9 See, for example, selections by Warda al Yaziji, Aisha Taimuriyya, and Zainab Fawwaz in Badran and Cooke, *Opening the Gates*.

10 On the *hijab* in nineteenth-century Egypt see Qasim Amin, *Tahrir al mar'a* (The Liberation of the Woman) (Cairo, 1899). Bahithat Badiya has written on the changing modes of *hijab* in early twentieth-century Egypt. She generally favoured retaining the face veil for the time being for pragmatic reasons, but was aware this was not required by Islam. On the subject see, for example, her 'Mabadi Al Nis'ai', in Majd al Din Hifni Nasif (ed.), *Ta'thir Bahithat al Badiya Malak Hifni Nasif 1886–1918* (The Heritage of Bahithat al Badiya Malak Hifni Nasif) (Cairo, 1962), pp. 318–20. On the historical and contemporary context of *hijab*, see Valerie J. Hoffman-Ladd, 'Polemics on the Modesty and Segregation of Women in Contemporary Egypt', *International Journal of Middle East Studies* 19 (1978), p. 23–50. For various interpretations in general of *hijab* see Mostafa Hashem Sherif, 'What is Hijab?', *The Muslim World* (July–October 1978) nos. 3–4, pp. 151–63.

11 Zainab Al Fawwaz, 'Fair and Equal Treatment', *Al Nil* no. 151 (18, dhu al hujja, 1892) trans. Marilyn Booth, in Badran and Cooke, *Opening the Gates*.

12 The early years of the women's Arabic press in Egypt are the subject of a dissertation by Beth Baron presented to the University of California at Los Angeles in 1988.

13 See Albert Hourani, *Arabic Thought in the Liberal Age* (Cambridge: Cambridge University Press, 1983), pp. 130–63.

14 See 'Abd Al Razek, 'L'Influence de la femme dans la vie de Chiekh Mohamed Abdue', *L'Egyptienne* (August 1928), pp. 2–7. Abduh's writings include: 'Hajjat Al Insan lil Zawaj', 'Fatwa fi Ta'adud Al Zaujat', and 'Hukum Ta'adud Al Zaujat', in Muhammad 'Imara, *Al 'amal al kamila li Muhammad 'Abduh* (The Complete Works of Muhammad 'Abduh) (Cairo, c. 1971), pp. 49–54, 111–118, and 127–35.

15 See Juan Ricardo Cole, 'Feminism, Class, and Islam in Turn-of-the-Century Egypt', *International Journal of Middle East Studies* 13 (1981), pp. 397–407, and Thomas Philipp, 'Feminism and Nationalist Politics in Egypt', in L. Beck and N. Keddie (eds), *Women in the Muslim World* (Cambridge, MA: Harvard University Press, 1978).

16 On Qasim Amin see Hourani, *Arabic Thought*, pp. 164–70.

17 On women's feminist discourse from the 1860s to the present see Badran and Cooke, *Opening the Gates*.

18 On the public lectures see *Huda Shaarawi, Harem Years: The Memoirs of an Egyptian Feminist* (London: Virago, 1986), pp. 92–3. Writings and speeches of Bahithat Al Badiya and Nabawiyya Musa are found, among other places, in their respective books: *Al Nisa'iyyat* (trans. as either Women's or Feminist Pieces) (Cairo: Al Jarida Press, 1910) and *Al Mar'a wa al 'amal* (Woman and Work) (Cairo, 1920). Donald Reid communicated to me the information related here concerning the closing of the women's section and the new use of the funds saved.

19 See Majd Al Din Hifni Nasif, *Ta'thir*.

20 See Margot Badran, 'From Consciousness to Activism: Feminist Politics in Early 20th Century Egypt', unpublished paper.

21 See Philipp, 'Feminism and Nationalist Politics in Egypt', and Cole, 'Feminism, Class, and Islam in Turn-of-the-Century Egypt'.

22 Badran, 'Dual Liberation'.

23 Progressive men including Lutfy Al Sayyid, for example, acted as advisers to the Egyptian Feminist Union in their various professional capacities.

24 Fundamentalists, like feminist, is a term that needs to be understood in historical context but broadly it signifies the person who returns to the fundamentals of Islam, especially the Quran and *Hadith*, and is associated with a conservative

reading of Islam. Many persons generally referred to as fundamentalists reject the term, preferring to call themselves committed Muslims. In this chapter I use the term 'fundamentalists' in a broad way, aware of the inherent difficulties, hoping the contexts in which it appears add clarification.

25 In a paper published in Arabic, 'Nisa'iyya ka quwa fi al 'alam al 'arabi' (Feminism as a Force in the Arab World), in *Al Fikra al 'arabi al mu'asir wa al mar'a* (Contemporary Arab Thought and the Woman) (Cairo: Arab Women's Solidarity Press, 1989), pp. 75–90, I deliberately used *nisa'iyya* in the title to signify feminism, although this is not normal usage.

26 See Badran, 'Huda Sha'rawi and the Liberation of the Egyptian Woman', pp. 299–308.

27 *Mudhakirrat ra'ida al 'arabiyya al haditha Huda Sha'rawi* (Memoirs of the Modern Arab Pioneer Huda Sha'rawi) (Cairo: Dar Al Hilal, 1981).

28 See Duriyya Shafiq, *Al kitab al abiyad lil huquq almar'a al misriyya* (The White Paper on the Rights of the Egyptian Woman) (Cairo, 1953).

29 The most complete study of the Muslim Brothers remains Richard Mitchell, *The Society of the Muslim Brothers* (London: Oxford University Press, 1969).

30 On language, feminism, and cultural authenticity see Irene Fenoglio-Abd El Aal, *Défense et illustration de l'Egyptienne: aux débuts d'une expression feminine* (Cairo: CEDEJ, 1989).

31 Interview with Al Ghazali, Cairo, February 1989. On Zainab Al Ghazali see Valerie J. Hoffman, 'An Islamic Activist: Zaynab al-Ghazali', in E. Fernea (ed.), *Women and the Family in the Middle East: New Voices of Change* (Austin: University of Texas Press, 1985).

32 Interview with Hawa Idris, Cairo, April 1988.

33 Interview with Al Ghazali, Cairo, February 1989.

34 Fatma Ni'mat Rashid, 'Muqarana bain al mar'a al Misriyya wa al mar'a al Turkiyya', *Al Misriyya* (1 May 1937), pp. 10–13.

35 See Norma Salem, 'Islam and the Status of Women in Tunisia', in Freida Hussain (ed.), *Muslim Women* (London: Croom Helm, 1984), pp. 141–68, John Esposito, *Women in Muslim Family Law* (Syracuse, NY: Syracuse University Press, 1982), p. 92, and Maxine Molyneux, 'The Law, the State and Socialist Policies with Regard to Women: The Case of the People's Democratic Republic of Yemen', in Deniz Kandiyoti (ed.) *Women, Islam, and the State* (London: Macmillan, 1991), pp. 237–71).

36 Interviews with Duriyya Shafiq in Cairo in 1968 and 1974.

37 See Badran, 'Huda Sha'rawi and the Liberation of the Egyptian Woman', and 'Independent Women: A Century of Feminism in Egypt', and Akram Khater and Cynthia Nelson, 'Al-Harakah Al-Nissa'iyah: The Women's Movement and Political Participation in Modern Egypt', *Women's Studies International Forum* II (1988), no. 5, pp. 465–83.

38 Interviews with Saiza Nabarawi in 1968 and 1973 and with Inji Aflatun in 1975. On socialist feminism see Khater and Nelson, 'Al-Harakah Al-Nissa'iyya', pp. 473–7; Michelle Raccagni, 'Inji Efflatoun, Author, Artist and Militant: A Brief Analysis of Her Life and Works', unpublished paper, n.d.; Selma Botman, 'The Experience of Women in The Egyptian Communist Movement, 1939–1954', *Women's Studies International Forum* 2 (1988), pp. 117–26; Guiseppe Contu, 'Le donne communiste e il movimento democratico feminile in Egitto al 1965', *Oriente Moderno* (May–June 1975), pp. 236–48.

39 Muhammad 'Atiya Khamis (ed.), *Al harakat al nisa'iyya wa silatuha ma'al ist'mar* (Feminist Movements and Their Relations with Imperialism) (Cairo: Dar Al Ansar, 1978).

40 This and the following quotations in this paragraph from Khamis, ibid.
41 Interview with Nawal Al Saadawi, Cairo, February 1989.
42 Shafiq, *The White Paper*.
43 Kathleen Howard-Merriam, 'Woman, Education, and the Professions in Egypt', *Comparative Education Review* 23 (1979), no. 2, pp. 256–71.
44 Yvonne Haddad, 'The Case of the Feminist Movement', chap. 5 in *Contemporary Islam and the Challenge of History* (Albany: State University of New York Press, 1982), pp. 54–70 and 'Traditional Affirmations Concerning the Role of Women as Found in Contemporary Arab Islamic Literature', in Jane Smith (ed.), *Women in Contemporary Muslim Societies* (Lewisburgh, PA: 1980). For a broader look at Islamicist discourse see her 'Islam, Women and Revolution in Twentieth Century Arab Thought', *The Muslim World* 124 (July–October 1984), nos. 3–4, pp. 137-60.
45 Bint Al Shati' wrote two autobiographies: *Sirr al Shati* (Biography of Al Shati) (Cairo: 1952) and *'Ala jisr: ustur al zaman* (On a Bridge: A Myth of Time) (Cairo, 1967). See also C. Kooij, 'Bint Al-Shati': A Suitable Case for Biography?', in Ibrahim A. El-Sheikh, C. Aart van de Koppel and Rudolf Peters (eds), *The Challenge of the Middle East: Middle East Studies at the University of Amsterdam* (Amsterdam: Institute for Modern Near Eastern Studies, University of Amsterdam) (1982). Hasan Hanafi's epithet was taken from Valerie Hoffman Ladd, 'Polemics'.
46 'Amina Said', in E. Fernea and B. Bezirgan, *Middle East Muslim Women Speak* (Austin: University of Texas Press, 1978).
47 On the double burden see Mona Hammam, 'Women and Industrial Work in Egypt: The Chubra El-Kheima Case', *Arab Studies Quarterly* 2 (1980), pp. 50–69.
48 Interviews with Hawa Idris, 1968 and 1972.
49 Interview with Nawal Al Saadawi, Cairo, February 1989.
50 Interview with Safinaz Kazim, Cairo, February 1989.
51 Interview in Cairo, January 1989 with Sa'id Ashmawi, Judge in the High Court of Cairo, the High Court for State Security, and the High Court of Assize, and author of *Al Shariah al islamiyya* (Islamic Law) (Cairo, 1980) and *Islam al siyasi* (Political Islam) (Cairo, 1988) who spoke of Sadat's stress on Islam as a means to distance his regime from Nasser's.
52 General analyses of what is called the Islamic resurgence include: Hamied N. Ansari, 'The Islamic Militants in Egyptian Politics', *International Journal of Middle East Studies* 16 (1984), pp. 123-44; Said Arjomand (ed.), *From Nationalism to Revolutionary Islam* (Albany: State University of New York, 1984); Alexander Cudsi and Ali Dessouki (eds), *Islam and Power in the Contemporary Arab World* esp. Ali Dessouki, 'The Resurgence of Islamic Organizations in Egypt: An Interpretation,' pp. 107–19; R. H. Dekmejian, *Islam in Revolution, Fundamentalism in the Arab World* (Syracuse, NY: Syracuse University Press, 1985); Ali Dessouki (ed.). *Islamic Resurgence in the Arab World* (New York: Praeger, 1982), esp. Saad Eddin Ibrahim, 'Islamic Militancy as a Social Movement: The Case of Two Groups in Egypt'; John Esposito (ed.), *Voices of Resurgent Islam* (Oxford: Oxford University Press, 1983); Nazith Ayubi, 'The Political Revival of Islam: The Case of Egypt', *International Journal of Middle East Studies* (December 1981), pp. 81–99; Fadwa El Guindi, 'The Emerging Islamic Order: The Case of Egypt's Contemporary Movement', *Journal of Arab Affairs* (1981), pp. 245–61; Yvonne Haddad, *Contemporary Islam and the Challenge of History* (Albany: State University of New York Press, 1982); Hassan Hanafi, 'The Relevance of the Islamic Alternative in Egypt', *Arab Studies Quarterly* 4 (1982), pp. 54–74; Saad Eddin Ibrahim, 'Anatomy of Egypt's Militant Islamic Groups',

International Journal of Middle East Studies 12 (1980), pp. 481–99; Gabriel Warburg and Uri Kupferschmidt (eds), *Islam, Nationalism and Radicalism in Egypt and the Sudan* (New York: Praeger, 1983); and Fouad Zakaria, 'The Standpoint of Contemporary Muslim Fundamentalists', in Toubia, *Women of the Arab World*.

53 Nawal Al Saadawi mentioned this in her February 1989 interview. The need of Jihan Sadat to be the supreme woman – not just feminist – was mentioned by Safinaz Kazim in an interview in Cairo in February 1989.

54 On the 1971 Constitution and gender see Nawal Al Saadawi, 'The Political Challenges Facing Arab Women'.

55 The literature on women's turn to fundamentalism and veiling includes: Fadwa El Guindi, 'Veiling *Infitah* with Muslim Ethic: Egypt's Contemporary Islamic Movement', *Social Problems* 28(1981), no. 4, pp. 465–85; Fatima Mernissi, 'Women and Fundamentalism', *Middle East Reports* (July–August 1988), pp. 8–11; Zainab Radwan, *Bahth zahirath al hijab bain al jam'iyyat* (A Study of the Phenomenon of the Veil among University Women) (Cairo: National Centre for Sociological and Criminological Research, 1982); and John Alden Williams, 'A Return to the Veil in Egypt', *Middle East Review* 11 (1979), no. 3, pp. 49–54.

56 See Amina Sa'id, 'Hadhihi ithahira ma ma'naha' (This Phenomenon, What Does it Mean), *Hawa* (18 November 1972); ' 'Awda illi hadith at ziyy hadhihi al dajja al mufta'ana ma ma'naha?' (Back to the Issue of Dress, This Show of Fuss . . . What Does it Mean?), *Hawa* (2 December 1972); and ' 'Id at sufur 'id at nahada' (Feast of Unveiling, Feast of Renaissance), *Hawa* (24 March 1973). In the latter article, written to commemorate the fiftieth anniversary of the founding of the EFU and the public unveiling of Huda Sha'rawi and Saiza Nabarawi, she attacks the current return to the veil which is 'the greatest enemy of civilization'.

57 Zainab Al Ghazali, *Ayyam min hayati* (Days of My Life) (Cairo: Dar Al Shuruq, 8th printing 1986).

58 Interview with Safinaz Kazim, Cairo, February 1989.

59 A Group of Women Concerned with Affairs Relating to the Egyptian (Aziza Husain, Inji Rushdi, Saniyya Salih, Awatif Wali, Mervat Ittalawi, Muna Zulficar, Magda Al Mufti), *Al Huquq al qanuniyya lil mar'a al 'arabiyya bain al nadthariyya wa al tatbiq* (The Legal Rights of the Egyptian Woman: Theory and Practice) (Cairo, 1988).

60 On elite women in the workforce in the early 1980s see Earl Sullivan, *Women in Egyptian Public Life* (Syracuse, NY: Syracuse University Press, 1986), and for a general survey see Ann Mosely Lesch and Earl Sullivan, 'Women in Egypt: New Roles and Realities', *USFI Reports* 22, Africa (1986).

61 See El Guindi, 'Veiling *Infitah*', and Williams, 'A Return to the Veil'.

62 For an analysis of this see Kathleen Howard Merriam, ' "Affirmative Action" for Political Representation of Women: the Egyptian Example', *Women and Politics*, forthcoming. See also Sullivan, *Women in Egyptian Public Life*, on women in parliament.

63 See Aziza Hussein, 'Recent Amendments to Egypt's Personal Status Law', in E. Fernea (ed.), *Women and the Family in the Middle East* (Austin: University of Texas Press, 1985), pp. 231–2 and Kathleen Howard Merriam. 'Egyptian Islamic Fundamentalism and the Law: Connecting the "Private" and the "Public" ', *International Journal of Islamic and Arab Studies*, forthcoming.

64 For more on this see Enid Hill, *Al-Sanhuri and Islamic Law*, Cairo Papers in Social Science 10, monograph 1 (spring 1987), pp. 125–9.

65 For an account of her experience in prison see Nawal Al Saadawi, *Mudhakkirati fi sijn al nisa* (Cairo: Dar al mustaqbal al 'arabi, 1985), trans. Marilyn Booth, *Memoirs from the Women's Prison* (London: The Women's Press, 1986); and for her reflections inspired by prison see Safinaz Kazim, *'An al sijn wa al hurriyya* (On Prison and Freedom) (Cairo: Al Zahra' lil A'lam Al 'Arabi, 1986). On women's prison experience and writings see Marilyn Booth, 'Prison, Gender, Praxis: Women's Prison Memoirs in Egypt and Elsewhere', *MERIP* (November–December 1987), pp. 35–41.
66 'Challenges Facing the Arab Woman', in Badran and Cooke, *Opening the Gates.*
67 See Nadia Hijab, *Womanpower: The Arab Debate on Women at Work* (Cambridge: Cambridge University Press, 1988), pp. 29–35; Howard Merriam, 'Egyptian Islamic Fundamentalism and the Law', and Sarah Graham-Brown, 'After Jihan's Law: A New Battle Over Women's Rights', *The Middle East* (June 1985), pp. 17–20.
68 'Challenges Facing the Arab Woman', in Badran and Cooke, *Opening the Gates.*
69 *The Legal Rights of the Egyptian Woman*, pp. 5–6.
70 On this phenomenon see 'A Study of Muslim Popular Literature on the Role of Women in Contemporary Egyptian Society', presented at the Conference of the Middle East Studies Group, London, 1988 by Huda Lutfy, who has studied the recent literature, and Valerie Hoffman-Ladd, 'Polemics', for an analysis of the historical debate up to early 1980s on women in Islamicist literature, and the work by Yvonne Haddad cited in note 46.
71 See Mahmud Saif Al Nasr, 'Shaikh Sha'rawi wa imra'a al Khati'a' (Shaikh Sha'rawi and the Sinful Woman), *Al Ahali* (3 July 1985), p. 8. A popular book written by Sha'rawi is *Al Mar'a kama araduha allah* (The Woman as God Wanted Her to Be) (Cairo: Maktabat Al Quran, 1980). On Sha'rawi see Barbara Freyer Stowasser, *The Islamic Impulse* (London: Croom Helm, 1987).
72 Interview with Zainab Al Ghazali, Cairo, February 1989.
73 Zainab Al Ghazali, 'Al Jamiyyat al nisa'iyya' (Feminist Organisations . . .), *Al Dawa* (November 1979), no. 42.
74 Interview with Muhammad Yahia, Cairo, March 1989.
75 Al Ghazali Harb, *Istiqlal al mar'a fi al islam* (Cairo: Dar Al Mustaqbal Al 'Arab, n.d.). This book includes articles the author published in the Cairo daily, *Al Akhbar*, in the late 1970s.
76 Interview with Muhammad Yahia, Cairo, March 1989.

2

WOMEN AND REVOLUTION IN VIETNAM

Mary Ann Tétreault

Throughout their history Vietnamese people had fiercely resisted the incursions of Chinese, French, and Japanese, but the French had come to control the area in the last third of the nineteenth century. During World War II (1939–1945) the Japanese had taken over. Throughout the course of these successive foreign occupations the Vietnamese forged opposition movements, most notably a peasant and nationalist version of Soviet communism. Women were active in these struggles, and their activism was built on a centuries-old tradition of women's heroism in resisting foreign invaders.

As soon as World War II ended, a Cold War erupted between the Soviet Union and the United States – the new world superpowers. Many struggles for national liberation felt the effects of this Cold War and perhaps nowhere more destructively than in Vietnam. After the French occupiers were definitively driven out in 1954, peasants eagerly supported the Communist Party that had led the fight against French imperialism. Communism was often influential in shaping national liberation movements because it advocated and usually enacted land reform that broke up the massive estates of Europeans and local landlords. Distributing land to the landless, it was also successful in mobilizing women by theorizing that their condition would improve once socialism triumphed. The Vietnamese Communist Party, like the communists in the Russian Revolution of 1917, was scrupulous in including women in its leadership (though not always at the very highest levels).

As the war against the French ended in triumph for those who wanted liberation, the United States stepped in to keep Vietnam from going communist. The United States' allies in South Vietnam came in large measure from the wealthy landowning classes and the Catholic Church. Fighting these groups too, the peasant communists found the participation of women a crucial necessity. In a 'People's War' against a superpower with atomic and other massively destructive weapons, intense individual activity by women, men, and children pitted itself against technology. This chapter shows the complex ways in which women participated, often to guard their positions in government or improve their condition as peasants. Although holding leadership positions in government and agriculture according to the dictates of socialist theory, women's soldiering for national liberation resulted in fewer rights once liberation had been achieved, as US forces pulled out of the area in the mid-1970s. Vietnam is one country that officially commemorates women's wartime achievements through a separate museum to their efforts; it ranks higher in pay equity and human development potential for women than most Western nations. Yet women's wartime leadership has not translated into peacetime leadership. The question is 'why?'

* * *

Vietnam's Confucian tradition pictures revolution as a normal, cyclical process that restores an ideally imagined status quo ante. The state is believed to participate in the same ethical system of virtuous conduct as society as a whole and the families that comprise it; a ruler demonstrates his righteousness by presiding over domestic tranquillity.[1] Thus, domestic turmoil signifies a personal moral deficiency in the ruler. It shows that the 'mandate of Heaven', the correspondence between the ruler's rectitude and the cosmology of the universe, has been lost.[2] During such times, Vietnamese look for a new leader whose moral stature promises to restore harmony.

The 'occupation and "pacification" ' of Vietnam by the French undermined this Confucian order.[3] French dominance of Vietnamese rulers meant one of two things. Either the world was wrong and virtuous Vietnamese should withdraw from public life to set a moral example for their peers, or Vietnamese conceptions of 'the way', the proper ordering of society, had to be re-examined. Both strategies opened Vietnam to penetration by Western ideas: those who withdrew had no programme for change while those who looked for other answers ranged widely for them. As a result, Confucian ideas about social hierarchies were challenged.

In the early twentieth century proposals for women's formal education began to be made by Vietnamese intellectuals, and women were invited to attend public lectures at a short-lived but influential school in Hanoi. French support for women's formal education among the upper classes weakened, however, once women joined the anti-colonial movement. 'Women's' books – even cookbooks – often featured advertisements for overtly anti-colonial publications, and women's educational and social groups evolved into forum for public discussion of national issues. Vietnamese intellectuals also vacillated in their recognition of women's oppression and their support for women's rights. None advocated raising women's status by changing the law. Even Marxists 'failed to get the point entirely' by acquiescing in the conservative assumption that women belonged in the home, finding in their own analyses women's inborn 'feminine strengths such as virtue, patience, and loyalty'.[4]

In spite of their views about sexual equality. Vietnamese intellectuals used gender as a model for analysing conditions in Vietnam under colonialism. Censorship prevented an open political discourse that might criticize the regime directly. Thus 'debates on women became primary vehicles for arguing about topics that could not be addressed forthrightly'.[5] Both conservatives and radicals used women as symbols in their analyses. Conservatives argued that colonialism caused social change and corruption. Wanting to preserve the 'national essence', they took refuge in a neo-Confucianism that emphasized the family as the foundation of society and female subordination as the foundation of the family. Radicals adopted the image of Camille as the talisman of their revolution against both the colonial 'father' in France and 'the Vietnamese paterfamilias at home'.[6] They invited Vietnamese to see women as one of many oppressed groups in their society, and revolution as the way to liberate them all. 'This tendency to generalize grievances cannot be overemphasized. Without it, the Vietnamese would never have been able to mount a sophisticated mass attack on French rule.'[7]

Vietnamese revolutionaries did more than use gender as a code through which to discuss the penetration of their society by the French. They appealed directly to women to participate in the struggle to liberate their country, promising them in return equal political, social, and economic rights and status under a new regime. These appeals attracted women who felt oppressed by the old regime. Even though Vietnamese legends glorify female heroes like Trieu Au and the Trung sisters, the status of women in Vietnamese society from the Han invasions in the third century BC to the establishment of the Democratic Republic of Vietnam (DRVN) in 1954 was always formally and informally subordinate to men.[8] Vietnamese women seeking equality found revolutionaries to be the only group in their society willing to commit themselves to achieving it. It is not surprising that so many responded by joining the movement.

Women, the family, and revolution in Vietnam

The traditional Vietnamese family was patriarchal and authoritarian. Its relationship to the structure of society increased the value of women as a target group for political mobilization. The family was the economic unit of Vietnamese society. Polygamy remained legal throughout Vietnam during French rule, and was not even nominally abolished in the south until 1958.[9] As in other countries, polygamy in Vietnam underpinned a subsistence economy dependent on the labour of women – wives, daughters, concubines, and mostly female servants.[10] As forced labour, these workers worked because men made them, either through private coercion or by resorting to community sanctions against unco-operative behaviour.[11] In families where affection and consent motivated labour, women worked so that the family unit could survive.[12] For the revolution to succeed, women had to be motivated to work not only for themselves and their children, but also for the movement and its army. Many observers linked the mobilization of women by the revolution to improvements in the status of women in Vietnam, especially in the north.[13]

Women's political mobilization was mediated by the Women's Union, established under the auspices of the Indochinese Communist Party (ICP) in 1930. The focus of the Women's Union, like its name, has changed since its founding. What did not change was its role as the party organization responsible for the political mobilization, education, and representation of Vietnamese women. Organized at every level of society beginning with the village, the Women's Union can claim as a member virtually every woman who has held a position of authority in the Vietnamese government.[14]

The Women's Union was one of the 'functional organizations' established to build a social base for the ICP. From its inception, the ICP took a stronger line favouring women's liberation than any other group seeking to lead the revolution or Vietnamese society as a whole.[15] The statement of party principles made shortly after the ICP was founded listed the liberation of women as the party's tenth – and last – goal.[16] Women's liberation was part of the generalization of grievances that permitted a broad-based assault on the colonial regime. It was also an end in itself. In Ho Chi Minh's words, 'Women are half the people. If women are not free then the people are not free.'[17] The ICP recognized the importance of women to the revolution by sending a woman, Nguyen Thi Minh Khai, to represent the party at the Seventh International Congress in Moscow in 1935.[18] Female workers and peasants took part from the beginning in the upsurge of revolutionary activity following the foundation of the ICP and women carried the bulk of the supplies destined for the secret bases of the revolutionaries.[19] Some women became revolutionary martyrs: Nguyen Thi Minh Khai was captured and guillotined by the French in 1941.

The ICP was a key component of the Viet Minh, the united front coalition of Vietnamese formed by Ho Chi Minh in 1941 to combat the Japanese. The Japanese formally ended the French colonial administration in 1945. That August, during the confusion attending the end of World War II, Ho moved into Hanoi and proclaimed the establishment of the Democratic Republic of Vietnam. Women were policy-making members of the Viet Minh throughout the period, and a female Viet Minh leader, Nguyen Khoa Dieu Hong, took a public role during the August Revolution, making an 'appeal for national salvation' to an enthusiastic crowd at a large rally. The Viet Minh offered more than words to Vietnamese women. Women who previously had no rights to land were given a share in land in the areas taken over as the revolution proceeded in the countryside.[20] In 1946, the new constitution proclaimed the economic and political equality of women and men, defined the rights of women within the family, and provided for female suffrage. Vietnamese women voted for the first time in their history on 6 January 1946, sending ten women to the Chamber of Deputies, 2.5 per cent of the total.[21]

During the French war (1946–54), women assumed larger roles in local communities. Some engaged in combat, mostly as members of small bands of commandos. In the early 1950s about 840,000 female guerrillas operated in the north and some 140,000 in the south.[22] Women also engaged in local 'struggle' movements, community mobilization, intelligence gathering, and the transport of *matériel*. The latter was especially critical when main force units were engaged. The Dan Cong labour battalions ferried supplies to the front. Two-thirds of the Dan Cong were women.[23] During the battle of Dien Bien Phu, the Dan Cong transported virtually everything needed by the attackers on their backs or balanced on bicycles, moving through the monsoon rains that made using motor vehicles impossible.[24]

The quality of the revolution changed after 1954, and the role of women changed with it. Cochinchina, the most recently settled area of the country, was also the region that had been most deeply penetrated by the French and thus most affected, socially and economically, by colonialism. The greater wealth of the southern population and the looser structure of its rural life made villagers in the south harder to organize against the regime than villagers in the economically marginal northern and central sections of the country.[25] Prior to the expulsion of the French, the Communist Party in the south faced strong competition, primarily from the Catholic Church and the syncretic sects, for the leadership of the nationalist opposition.[26]

After partition, the new DRVN regime in the north was more interested in building its institutions and rebuilding its economy than in fighting a revolution in the south. The stability of the regime was threatened in 1957 as scattered local uprisings and a full-scale revolt in Nghe An province were mounted against its harsh land reform policy.[27] These uprisings and an internal struggle for control of the party contributed to the lack of involvement by the DRVN in the southern movement before 1960.[28]

Southern opponents of the US-backed, Roman Catholic, Ngo Dinh Diem regime were quiet, waiting for the elections promised in the 1954 Geneva Accords, which they expected would provide them with a bloodless victory. But in 1955 Diem announced that elections would not take place and he increased his efforts to liquidate his opponents. The southern insurgency resumed in 1957.[29] As the armed sects were decimated by Diem's army and police and the Catholic Church became more closely identified with the regime, the mostly communist Viet Minh, with its mostly Buddhist values and its emphasis on incorporating women into the struggle against Diem, assumed the dominant position in the continuation of the revolution in the south.[30]

Madame Nhu, Diem's sister-in-law, sought to counter the Viet Minh's appeal to women by forming her own women's groups, the Women's Solidarity Movement, which David Halberstam describes as 'an apparatus for family espionage', and the Paramilitary Girls, whom Madame Nhu called her 'little darlings'.[31] But like other 'popular' organizations created by the Diem government, they were ineffective. The regime was too Catholic and too brutal in its suppression of its domestic opponents to appeal to peasants in the countryside.[32] Even so, the size and reach of the Viet Minh contracted during this time. The Viet Minh got little assistance from the north, while the Diem regime was strengthened by economic and military assistance from the United States.

The material poverty of Diem's opposition dictated reliance on 'People's War' as a strategy. This required mobilizing the whole population against 'My-Diem' – the government of the south assisted throughout the period by US military and economic aid. People's War tactics included strikes, community action against local civilian and military officials, sabotage, and, most important of all, 'political struggle', intense and repeated attempts to persuade neutrals or partisans on the other side to join the revolution.[33] This emphasis on politics and ideology was intended to support partisans as much as to convert opponents.

The southern revolutionaries were 'remarkably committed, tough people, and their personal and political lives were largely inseparable'.[34] US troops, for most of whom ideology meant attachment to 'the big PX', could not understand why their enemies were such good fighters. Many attributed the bravery of the enemy to drugs.[35] Political motivation was the key to the success of the southern revolutionaries who had minimal resources and lived under constant fear of exposure and death. Northern party leaders were much more secure because they controlled the government and society in their half of the country.

> [W]hile the same men led the Party, its members in the north and south were becoming increasingly distinctive in terms of their local Party's internal life and styles of existence. Southern Revolutionaries were highly motivated and devoted, informal, and forced to make correct decisions quickly. . . . Party leaders in the south assumed ever-greater responsibilities . . . and were . . . in much closer contact with the masses. . . . To be a Party member in the North was a social asset and a . . . source of authority. . . . [I]ts huge size . . . offered ambitious people the possibility of abusing power.[36]

Differences in the nature and salience of the conflict from south to north shaped the conduct of the post-1954 war in each half of the country. In the south, the success of the revolution was literally a matter of life and death. In the north, the southern insurgency took second place to the desire to consolidate the regime, build the economy, and gain political power in the DRVN. Once US bombing of the north began, the interests of northern and southern party members converged, but their different situations affected the way they mobilized their resources, including women. US bombing threatened the infant economy of the north, already crippled by an economic boycott imposed by the United States. Women's activities during this phase of the war were critical to its eventual success and women, in turn, increased their autonomy in villages where patriarchal relationships had begun to be reasserted and reinforced as the new regime consolidated itself after the failure of its land reform programme.[37] As more men went into the armed forces after the mid-1960s, women became the majority of workers in many villages. In 1967 government regulations encouraging and even mandating women's participation in decision-making positions went into effect.[38] Industrialization in the north after 1954 had proceeded similarly to industrialization in other socialist developing countries, concentrating on heavy industry and collectivized agriculture. When the US bombing campaigns began in 1965, about half of the country's industrial infrastructure was still composed of small forges or a few machine tools located in huts or caves in the countryside.[39] US bombing encouraged further decentralization. Though it reduced overall efficiency, decentralization ensured the continued production of needed *matériel* despite the heavy bombing which reduced substantially production from the centralized factories owned by the state.

The feminization of agriculture partly reversed the post-1957 weakening of party commitment to collectivization because women were among the most likely villagers to eschew family-based work to join co-operatives.[40] This halted, for a time, the reversion to partiarchy – the 'family farm' – in many villages. The state's role in agriculture expanded as farmers became more dependent on chemical fertilizers and mechanical equipment such as pumps to flood and drain rice fields. Even so, local initiative remained strong. Production responsibility was vested in production brigades, hamlet-sized working groups, rather than in village leaders.[41] A free market in agricultural products existed throughout the war, despite vacillations in government policy toward it.[42] Food production remained stable from 1965, the first year of extensive bombing of the north, through 1972, when direct participation in the war by US troops officially ended. In agriculture as in industry, the basic organization of production remained highly decentralized and structurally resistant to disruption from the bombing.

The reliance of the DRVN on a premodern organization of its economy in order to decentralize sufficiently to preserve its productive capacity was echoed in the reliance of southern revolutionaries on the premodern structures of family and village to disperse and conceal personnel engaged in revolutionary activities. Vo Nguyen Giap, the leading general of the northern forces, said that 'until the war in the south [I] knew nothing about "people's war"', even though the earlier, anti-French phases of the revolution had depended heavily upon underground political actions and popular mobilization.[43] In the south after 1954, the distinction between friend and enemy was existentially as well as tactically unclear, and the war itself was not conventional in any sense.

Villages formed the main arena in which People's War was fought and peasants were the group that each side tried to win over. Many peasants, presumed by the Viet Minh to be the natural constituency of the revolution, were confused and frightened by the conflict. Unclear as to which side was 'right', given the pain inflicted by each[44] and the inability of either to take permanent control in most of the country, many preferred to sit the conflict out on the sidelines until one side or the other should capture the Mandate of Heaven.[45] Yet without peasant help, Viet Minh cadres would suffer massive casualties and the revolution would melt away, not only because of the lack of support from the north but, more crucially, because of the physical elimination of southerners committed to continuing the struggle against Diem.

The extent of domestic repression by Diem weakened the Viet Minh and threatened it with extinction.

> As early as January, 1954, police-state measures against *anyone* who disagreed with the prevailing edicts of the Diem regime forced all opposition into the agonizing choice of self-imposed exile (if rich), total silence (if less fortunate and thus forced to remain in Viet-Nam), or armed resistance.[46]

At the same time, the repression sparked massive resistance throughout the population. In January 1960, after Communist Party leaders finally authorized a resumption of armed struggle in the south, a series of demonstrations by thousands of peasant women began in Ben Tre province under the leadership of Nguyen Thi Dinh.[47] Reacting to large-scale indiscriminate killing and looting by government troops, the unarmed women had large numbers and the moral authority of passive resistance. Government forces were stymied in their efforts to drive the women away and the district chief was eventually forced to accede to their demands. Following these demonstrations, various local and regional groups joined individuals who had opposed Diem and formed the National Liberation Front.[48] The NLF membership was eclectic. At first even the Cao Dai and the Hoa Hao, the two largest religious sects, belonged to the organization, which embraced virtually all of the old Viet Minh coalition as well as three southern political parties, members of ethnic minority groups, students, farmers, and intellectuals.[49]

The NLF was a formidable force for two reasons. One was its land reform policy, which was far more appealing to Vietnamese peasants than the indifferently applied programme of the US-backed Diem regime.[50] The other was its policy of building on real and symbolic family relationships to sustain its cadres.[51] Frances Fitzgerald calls this the 'Children of the People' strategy. It meant that NLF cadres would depend upon village residents to protect them and, in return, would obey their wishes. Unlike representatives of the Diem government, the NLF reversed the normal hierarchy of family and nation. Villagers became the 'parents' and the cadres their 'children'. The NLF had to be accommodating because it depended upon villagers for sustenance and concealment. Unlike their opponents, NLF members could not exploit the population from the relative safety of national or provincial capitals, nor from behind a wall of native soldiers and foreign military and civilian advisers.[52] Even where the cadre had no blood relationship to local inhabitants, appealing to them as 'father' or 'mother' could evoke a protective response. Nguyen Thi Dinh writes about a time when she was arrested, beaten, and threatened with rape. She saw an old woman outside the hut where she was being held and shouted to her, 'Mother, I've been arrested. Please come in and ask them to release me so I can go back to my child.' The old woman came in and pretended that Madame Dinh was her daughter, enabling both women to escape when the soldiers were called away.[53]

NLF strategy relied on the fact that many of the original cadres sent to the villages were local residents and most of the families they appealed to were their own or had relatives in the revolution.[54] Where cadres were strangers, the NLF utilized other techniques to foster a family feeling between its members and local villagers. For example, the NLF retained the old Viet Minh practice of organizing older women in the villages into 'Foster Mothers' Associations' whose members were charged with serving as surrogate mothers to young guerrillas 'who were away from home for perhaps the first time in their lives'.[55]

Yet there were limits to this strategy. Not all villages could be supplied with local cadres, and strangers were looked at with suspicion, at least at first. This problem was aggravated by high levels of attrition in 1963–64 followed by the wholesale replacement of local cadres with strangers who frightened the villagers.[56] Despite their reputation not all cadres behaved like children of the village. Some showed favouritism, some were disrespectful of the elderly, and some committed crimes against the population.[57] Offenders were 'rejected' by villagers but, unlike villager rejection of government troops, this was the result of specific offences rather than general hostility.[58] After offenders were removed by their superiors, support for the NLF increased. But as attrition rates soared, some cadres were returned to villages where they had alienated members of the population.[59] The resulting disaffection of the villagers was aggravated by the bombing that a village 'liberated' by the NLF drew from US-GVN forces. The bombing showed that the Mandate of Heaven had not descended on the NLF, and weakened the faith of the villagers in the idea that it would eventually prevail.[60] Even so, the ability of the NLF to hold or reclaim villages in the south, and the tendency of villagers to protect individuals they knew against outsiders, enabled the Children of the People strategy to save the lives of many of the regime's opponents. When the NLF strategy was successful, cadres found refuge and built bases throughout the country-side from which they ambushed and harassed their enemies and recruited new adherents to their side. Throughout the war in the south, large areas of the countryside were unsafe for government troops, especially at night. The NLF also formed alternative village political systems throughout rural

South Vietnam, where local populations paid increasingly onerous taxes to the NLF.[61] This dual sovereignty period even supported underground societies located near US military bases.[62]

The Children of the People strategy rested on the cultural symbol of the nurturing mother. Another symbol underpinned the legitimacy of the 'Long-Haired Army', a term coined by the Diem regime to describe the women of the Ben Tre uprising. It gradually came to stand for all women fighting for the NLF. Madame Dinh's feats resonated with the legends of Vietnamese women in the past who had fought off occupying forces. This model for Vietnamese women was the antithesis of the nurturing mother who stayed in the background in a supporting role.

Madame Dinh was made a general of the People's Liberation Armed Forces (PLAF) based on her credentials as a co-founder of the NLF and the leader of the Ben Tre uprising. Her position also reflected the significance of women in the PLAF; Arlene Eisen reports that about 40 per cent of the PLAF regimental commanders were women.[63] As in the north, most southern women served in local and regional guards rather than in the national forces. Thus, the PLAF was only a small segment of the total number of female forces engaged in revolutionary activity.

> The regular forces were not very large but services, self-defence, and the guards were very large and mostly women. . . . [In the south] more women than men participated in the war. In enemy-occupied areas, the women were very important because if we wanted to send troops we needed places for them to stay, and to provide for them. After the women got ready, we could send troops in. All the supplies were carried by women. The forces that we sent in first to survey an area were women. Our struggle was carried with two principles: first, military and second, uprising. There women played a very important part.[64]

The extensive participation by women in the revolution in the south was reflected in high rates of female casualties. Le Tan Danh reports that from 1954 to 1965 female revolutionaries in the south suffered 250,000 deaths, 40,000 disabilities as the result of torture, and 36,000 imprisonments.[65] Nguyen Van Luong, president of the People's Committee of Binh Tri Thien province, tells of casualties from a broader perspective.

> The majority of the women in the workforce now are married. Most are not married who took part in the war. After thirty years of war, many could not marry. In many cases couples just married and went to the war. Afterward, they are too old to have children.[66]

Women also shared in the civilian leadership of the NLF and the People's Revolutionary Government (PRG). Memoirs of the period, such as Truong Nhu Trang's 1985 book, note instances when women took part in policy-making and planning, suffering the consequences of their activities when they were taken prisoner by the southern regime.[67] But despite their bravery and ubiquity in the movement in the south, women had difficulty gaining the respect of their male peers. They were not recruited to be cadres until the male pool was depleted by high casualties.[68] Eisen believes that women in the north occupied a higher status than their sisters in the south because the southern branch of the Women's Union was an illegal organization, retarding both the mobilization of women and the education of men.[69] Although some male party leaders from below the seventeenth parallel acknowledge the contributions of women to the success of the revolution in the south, Women's Union leaders from the south remain more cynical than their northern sisters about the extent of women' liberation in Vietnam.[70] This may be because women in the south exercised more authority during the war than northern women. They are more aware both of the extremity of the situation that was required to give them their opportunity, and the decline in their status today as compared to that time.

Symbols and status

The cultural symbols of the nurturing mother and the heroine who leads the people to expel the foreign invader are both interpreted as models of female autonomy in writings about the revolution by Vietnamese men and women. Unlike the analytical forms of discourse traditional in the West that emphasize abstract concepts, analytical discourse in Vietnam uses role models and personalization to convey values along with information. Such symbols carry multiple messages: the bravery of the Vietnamese people, the totality of national mobilization, and the extent of sacrifice demanded by the revolution.

Symbols featuring women were also used to mock or impeach the enemy. The most ubiquitous cartoon from the revolution shows a small Vietnamese peasant woman holding a rifle on a large US pilot, marching him off to POW camp. This is an ambiguous symbol from a feminist perspective because the weakness of the woman is the core of the message about the impotence of the enemy. Female revolutionaries also appear on postage stamps, such as the commemorative issued in 1969 to honour the women of Ben Tre and their leader, Nguyen Thi Dinh. Madame Dinh's face on the stamp memorializes a female leader at a crucial moment in the history of the revolution. The most famous of the many war memorials to be found throughout the country also features a woman. It is in downtown Hanoi and marks one of the sites of the 1972 Christmas bombing. The figures of a woman and a child are used to personalize the destruction of the bombing of civilians. Here also the use of a female symbol carries a mixed message, the sort of 'women and children' cliché common where the home front and the war front are depicted as gender-specific sites. Despite the ambiguity of some of the symbols, however, the depiction of women in art dealing with women's revolutionary roles tends to affirm their agency rather than their victimization or their status as 'helpers' of the 'real' revolutionaries.

The integration of these symbols into the cultural life of the nation is something else altogether, however. In the Museum of the Revolution in Hanoi, which boasts the most extensive collection of photographs and artefacts from the revolutionary period, little in the collection features or even includes women. Women have a separate museum but, as Americans know from their own experience, separate is not equal. Women's and men's pictures and artefacts are integrated most completely in the War Crimes Museum in Ho Chi Minh City, but this is an ambiguous situation in which to celebrate gender equality because it memorializes victims, not agents. The largest photograph from the American War is of the heaps of mostly female bodies left after the massacre at My Lai.

Although the symbolic representation of Vietnamese female revolutionaries shows agency and power, these symbols are not accorded equal status with those representing male revolutionary experiences. As a result, memories of women's contributions to the revolution are fading faster than memories of men's contributions. A similar mechanism can be seen in the Truong memoirs. Women in the photographs are seldom identified by name and only a few are discussed in the text, often in the context of victimization. The destruction of much of the NLF infrastructure during the Tet offensive, antagonism between the two halves of the ideologically and geographically divided party, and the experientially divided consciousnesses of the interpreters of the past obscure the NLF in the minds of the present generation. The status and contributions of the women in its ranks are the faintest of the shadows left behind.

Substance and status

La femme a une place importante, un grand rôle dans le mouvement, révolutionnaire, tout comme depuis plusieurs décennies, elle a participé activement au mouvement révolutionnaire dans son ensemble.[71]

This 1959 statement reflects the position of the leadership of the revolution with respect to the importance of women to the movement. The post-revolutionary regime did honour its promise to elevate the status of women in the new order. But despite great gains, the status and power of women in Vietnam today still compare unfavourably to the status and power of men.

Politics, the military, and the church tend to be the last bastions of male domination in most societies and Vietnam is no exception. Women have never held more than a few positions in the political leadership of the DRVN or the PRG. For example, women made up at most 17 per cent of the central committee of the PRG in 1965 despite their crucial role in the resumption of the southern insurgency and their large numbers among guerrillas and main forces fighting in the south.[72] This is unfortunate, as the revolutionary period was the high point of women's representation on central committees. Women headed five ministries in 1982, but only three in 1986, although gains were made during this period with respect to women's representation on provincial people's councils and committees. Women have been a minority in the National Assembly throughout the history of the DRVN. Their proportion rose from a low of 2.5 per cent in the first (1946) assembly to 32.3 per cent in the assembly elected in 1975. In the three subsequent elections, the proportion of victorious women dropped, falling to 17.5 per cent after the 1987 election.[73]

Nguyen Thi Binh explained the decline in the proportion of women elected to the assembly in 1976 and 1981 as the result of a heavier residue of feudal attitudes in the south.[74] The disappointing election result in 1987 was mitigated by the greater visibility of women in positions of leadership in the assembly. Women held no commission presidencies in the 1981 assembly but in the 1987 assembly led the legislative, social, and external affairs commissions. A woman was also chosen to head Vietnam's delegation to the United Nations.

The deterioration in Vietnamese women's electoral fortunes coincides with the gradual disappearance from public life of the 'grand old women of the revolution'. Both trends reduce women's political authority and the legitimacy of their claim to leadership positions in the national government. A counter-trend shows an increasing number of women holding office at the provincial level but, despite decentralization and increased local autonomy, the overall position of women in the political power structure of Vietnam is declining.

Conclusions

Vietnamese women responded in large numbers to appeals by revolutionary leaders to join in the struggle to free Vietnam from colonial rule and establish a socialist state committed to women's liberation. In return, from the earliest days of the August Revolution, the post-revolutionary government enshrined women's rights in its constitutions and laws. Ironically, given the greater level of integration of women and men in fighting forces in the south as compared to the north, reunification stalled women's progress in electoral politics. Still, the government has continued to reinforce and expand legal protection of women and families, and the rights of women to an education that enables them to compete successfully with men in the job market. State and party officials refer to the Women's Union as a powerful influence on policy, which itself raises the status of women and contributes to the legitimacy of their claims for social and political equality.

Legal intervention has characterized state policy to incorporate gains for women into social and political frameworks, providing remedies for women whose personal situations revert to 'feudal' forms. However, the decision of the regime to reinstate patriarchy in return for rural support also reinstated structural impediments to the realization of women's rights enshrined in Vietnam's constitutions and laws. These impediments are reinforced by gender inequality in the symbolic construction of the revolutionary past and memories of women's participation in the revolution, and are excused as persistent legacies of Confucian – or Confucianesque – social and cultural patterns. However, they undermine gains made by the revolution.

In his analysis of the French Revolution, Alexis de Tocqueville concluded that post-revolutionary France was not greatly dissimilar from the society of the *ancien régime*. Theda Skoçpol's analysis of the French, Russian, and Chinese revolutions comes to a similar conclusion.[75] Social revolutions make great changes in class relations and in the relative power of the state as opposed to society. Yet there are vast continuities between pre- and post-revolutionary societies and cultures. Over time, these can challenge novel social arrangements and keep old notions of legitimacy and old patterns of social relations alive, even when the identities of the groups occupying the various positions in the patterns change.[76] The Vietnam experience demonstrates how these continuities are constructed. Revolutionaries pay tremendous attention to who gets to run the state after the shooting is over. They compose a 'state class' of persons who have limited means for achieving high levels of status and power other than as their deserts from revolutionary success.[77] After 1954, the leadership in North Vietnam was concerned to maintain, consolidate, and gain power for itself. It was less concerned to maintain, consolidate, and gain power for the opponents of the southern regime, or for women and other marginal groups *in the north* who had supported the revolution but offered few resources to support men struggling for dominance in the new state. By ignoring the southern revolutionaries for so long, the DRVN contributed to the divergence in ideology, culture, experience, and identification that has made the reintegration of the country so difficult and so painful. By ignoring women, it ensured the continuation and strengthening of social groups and structures that undermine the legitimacy, power, and reach of the post-revolutionary state.

Conservatives and radicals believe that a harmony between personal life and larger social structures is necessary for long-term stability. English conservatives tried to restrict women's personal freedom as part of a strategy to stave off 'Jacobinism' and class conflict which they feared would break out in England in imitation of the revolution in France. They believed that preserving the patriarchal family would also protect the broader social and political status quo.[78] Some may doubt the logic or truth of this assumption yet its opposite is visible in post-revolutionary Vietnam. Failure to overthrow the patriarchal family along with the old regime validated the positions of conservatives who, from the beginning, wanted no more from the revolutionary process than the removal of the French. This validation keeps Vietnamese women and families in the private space, retarding the development of social policy that could make women's paper liberties realizable in practice. It also maintains a social structure that challenges the authority of the state to command resources and pursue its own interests.

The paucity of women in important positions in government and industry in Vietnam today demonstrates the failure of the regime to consolidate the cultural as opposed to the class and political gains made by the revolution. It is also indicative of a structural contradiction in the consideration of gender as an analogue to class. Women's interests as women may and often do conflict with their economic interests, group interests, and even their personal situations. Catholic and middle-class women under Diem's regime joined Madame Nhu's organizations even though Diem had abolished polygamy – reluctantly – only in 1958 and did not enforce the new law after it was passed. Women adjust to the desires of husbands and in-laws in socialist rural communes even when this means that they must work longer hours than men and neglect their infants in the process. The organization of women as a revolutionary class and expectations that they will be consistent in the pursuit of their class interests thus defined is borne out by events in only a minority of cases.

This helps to explain why gains made by women during periods of revolutionary upheaval tend to erode over time. Women themselves fail to maintain solidarity with one another; men, from their positions of structural superiority, place obstacles in the paths of even the ones who try. Though few women favour gender identity over other identities, most men do. The recurrence of patriarchy as a mode of social control in rural villages in Vietnam after 1957 and throughout the country after reintegration in 1975 provides strong evidence of the ease with which men can adjust their ideological prisms to block out inconsistencies arising from the pursuit of male gender interests. It also reflects the extent to which control over women is a measure of male 'success', both as a source of economic gain and as a counter in status competition. As in China, economic liberalization has intensified the rate of female exploitation. Recently the sale of female children into prostitution has become widespread once again in Vietnam.

This basic difference in the expression of gender in social organization, coupled to the political compromises that are routinely made in order for a new regime to entrench itself, keep social structures that oppress women alive and well despite the massive upheavals in political control and class structure that revolutionary transformation brings about. Even gains in legal protection made by women through participation in revolutionary movements may be more fragile than corresponding gains made by men. Women are uniquely vulnerable to the revival or resurgence of social patterns whose locus in society and connection to an idealized past make them seem innocuous or even irrelevant to male members of the state class. Yet the longevity of political changes brought about by revolutions is hostage to remnants of the past whose power rests in their ability to control people and other resources independently of the state. A revolution that fails to liberate women, leaving their fate to the whims of despots in the private sphere, also fails to protect the liberation of men from assault and erosion when these despots leave their houses to seize control in the public sphere as well.

NOTES

This chapter is taken from 'Women and Revolution in Vietnam', in *Women and Revolution in Africa, Asia, and the New World*, (ed.) Mary Ann Tétreault, Columbia: University of South Carolina Press, 1994.

1 David G. Marr, *Vietnamese Tradition on Trial, 1920–1945*, Berkeley: University of California Press, 1981, pp. 58–59.
2 Frances Fitzgerald, *Fire in the Lake: The Vietnamese and the Americans in Vietnam*, Boston, MA: Little Brown, 1972, p. 30.
3 Marr, p. 60.
4 Ibid., pp. 242–43.
5 Hue-Tam Ho Tai, *Radicalism and the Origins of the Vietnamese Revolution*, Cambridge, MA: Harvard University Press, 1992, p. 91.
6 Ibid., pp. 90, 92:
7 Marr, p. 235.
8 Ibid., pp. 191–99. Mai Thi Tu and Le Thi Nham Tuyet, *Women in Viet Nam*, Hanoi: Foreign Languages Publishing House, 1978, pp. 30–31.
9 Bernard B. Fall, *Street Without Joy*, New York: Schocken Books, 1972, p. 131.
10 V. Spike Peterson, 'An Archaeology of Domination: Historicizing Gender and Class in Early Western State Formation', Ph.D. diss., American University, 1988, pp. 173–75.
11 See, for example, Le Ly Hayslip, with Jay Wurts, *When Heaven and Earth Changed Places: A Vietnamese Woman's Journey from War to Peace*, New York: Doubleday, 1989, pp. 20–22.
12 Mai Thi Tu, 'The Vietnamese Woman, Yesterday and Today', *Vietnamese Studies* 10 (1978), p. 15.
13 See for example, Gerard Chaliand, *The Peasants of North Vietnam*, Baltimore, MD: Penguin Books, 1969.

14 Mai and Le, pp. 30–31; Arlene Eisen, *Women and Revolution in Viet Nam*, of London: Zed Books, 1984, pp. 119–34.
15 Marr, pp. 235–36; Douglas Pike, *Vietcong: The Organization and Techniques of the National Liberation Front of South Vietnam*, Cambridge, MA: MIT Press, 1966, p. 174.
16 Mai and Le, pp. 112–13; Nancy Wiegersma, *Vietnam: Peasant Land, Peasant Revolution: Patriarchy and Collectivity in the Rural Economy*, New York: St Martin's Press, 1988, p. 94.
17 The wording of this quote varies from source to source. This is the version told to me by Duong Thi Duyen, Secretary for Western Affairs of the Viet Nam Women's Union, on 4 January 1988 in Hanoi.
18 Eisen, p. 87.
19 Pike, p. 178; Mai and Le, pp. 118, 124.
20 Eisen, p. 97; Francois Houtart and Genevieve Lemercinier, *Hai Van: Life in a Vietnamese Commune*, London: Zed Books, 1984, p. 165.
21 Eisen, p. 244.
22 Mai and Le, pp. 101, 161.
23 Ibid., p. 163.
24 Douglas Pike uses this as evidence that women were exploited by male communist revolutionaries, for whom they were merely 'the water buffalo[es] of the Revolution'. Pike, p. 178.
25 Samuel L. Popkin, *The Rational Peasant: The Political Economy of Rural Society in South Vietnam*, Berkeley: University of California Press, 1979, p. 230.
26 Ibid., pp. 184–85; Fitzgerald, p. 155; Bernard B. Fall, *Viet-Nam Witness, 1953–1966*, New York: Praeger, 1976, p. 141–59.
27 Eric R. Wolf, *Peasant Wars of the Twentieth Century*, New York: Harper and Row, 1969, p. 191.
28 Wiegersma, p. 202; R. B. Smith, *An International History of the Vietnam War: Revolution Versus Containment. 1955–1961*, New York: St Martin's Press, 1983, pp. 93–99.
29 Fall, *Viet-nam Witness*, pp. 169–89.
30 Neil Sheehan, *A Bright Shining Lie: John Paul Vann and America in Vietnam*, New York: Random House, 1988, p. 122.
31 David Halberstam, *The Making of a Quagmire: America and Vietnam During the Kennedy Era*, rev. (ed.), New York: Knopf, 1988, pp. 24–28.
32 Sheehan, pp. 101–105.
33 Frank Denton, 'Volunteers for the Viet Cong', Rand Corporation Memorandum RM–5647–ISA/ARPA 1968, p. ix; Tam Vu, 'People's War Against Special War', *Vietnamese Studies* 11 (n.d.), pp. 50–55, 64–66.
34 Gabriel Kolko, *Anatomy of a War: Vietnam, the United States, and the Modern Historical Experience*, New York: Pantheon, 1985, p. 270; also W. P. Davison and J. J. Zasloff, 'Profile of Viet Cong Cadres', Rand Corporation Memorandum RM–4983–1–ISA/ARPA, 1968; Kondrad Kellen, 'A View of the VC: Elements of Cohesion in the Enemy Camp in 1966–1967', Rand Corporation Memorandum RM–5462–1–ISA/ARPA, 1969; Nguyen Thi Dinh, 'No Other Road to Take', recorded by Tran Huong Nam, trans. Mai Elliott, Data Paper 102, Southeast Asia Program, Cornell University, 1976.
35 Charles C. Moskos, Jr, *The American Enlisted Man: The Rank and File in Today's Military*, New York: Russell Sage Foundation, 1970, p. 152.
36 Kolko, p. 269.
37 Wiegersma, pp. 166–67.
38 Ibid., pp. 157–58.

39 Kolko, p. 266.
40 Wiegersma, pp. 159–60, 179.
41 Ibid., p. 161.
42 Kolko, pp. 265–66.
43 Quoted in Fitzgerald, p. 140.
44 For example, see Hayslip, pp. 94–97.
45 Fitzgerald, pp. 150–57; Rand Corporation, *Viet Cong Infrastructure in South Vietnamese Villages*, Rand Vietnam Interview Series PIE, Interim Reports 165–66, Santa Monica, 1972. This *attentisme* is clear in the Rand interviews. Questioners asked defectors and captives what percentage of their villages supported the NLF and what percentage did not. NLF supporters were generally reported as a positive number: 3 or 10 or 30 per cent of the villages the respondents came from. The remainder of the village populations were almost never judged to be GVN supporters, however. They were described as 'neutral'.
46 Fall, *Viet-Nam Witness*, p. 138, emphasis in the original.
47 Nguyen Thi Dinh, 'No Other Road to Take', pp. 62–74.
48 Wiegersma, p. 203.
49 Mai Elliott, 'Translator's Introduction', Nguyen Thi Dinh, 'No Other Road to Take', pp. 11–13; Pike, pp. 82–84.
50 Jeffrey Race, *War Comes to Long An*, Berkeley: University of California Press, 1972.
51 Rand Corporation, *Viet Cong Infrastructure*.
52 Fitzgerald. pp. 157–64.
53 Nguyen Thi Dinh, 'No Other Road to Take', p. 74.
54 Ibid. See also Rand Corporation, *Viet Cong Infrastructure*; Hayslip. *When Heaven and Earth Changed Places*.
55 William Andrews, *The Village War: Vietnamese Communist Revolutionary Activities in Dinh Tuong Province, 1960–1964*, Columbia: University of Missouri Press, 1973, p. 77.
56 Rand Corporation, *Viet Cong Infrastructure*.
57 Ibid. See also Hayslip, *When Heaven and Earth Changed Places*.
58 Konrad Kellen, 'A View of the VC: Elements of Cohesion in the Enemy Camp in 1966–1967', Rand Corporation Memorandum RM–5462–1–ISA / ARPA, 1969, pp. 9–10.
59 Rand Corporation, *Viet Cong Infrastructure*.
60 Ibid.
61 Ibid.
62 The term 'dual sovereignty' comes from Charles Tilly, 'Does Modernization Breed Revolution?', *Comparative Politics* 5 (1973). The juxtaposition of NLF and US bases is described in Tom Mangold and John Penycate, *The Tunnels of Cu Chi*. New York: Berkeley Books, 1986.
63 Eisen, p. 105.
64 Nguyen Van Luong, in an interview with the author, 6 January 1988, in Hue.
65 Le Han Danh, 'The Long-Haired Army', *Vietnamese Studies* 10 (1966), pp. 61–62.
66 Interview with the author, 6 January 1988, in Hue.
67 Truong Nhu Trang, *A Viet Cong Memoir*, New York: Vintage Books, 1985, pp. 110–11.
68 Rand Corporation, *Viet Cong Infrastructure*.
69 Eisen, p. 123.

70 Compare the views of southerner Nguyen Thi Dinh, reported in the *Christian Science Monitor*, 4 November 1987 (when she was president of the Women's Union), and those of northerner Duong Thi Duyen, vice-president of the Women's Union, revealed in an interview with me on 4 January 1988. Madame Duyen attributed the relative lack of women in top economic and political positions in Vietnam to the lack of formal education during the war (which should have affected men at least as much as women). She saw the drop in the number of women elected to the National Assembly in 1987 as due to a failure by the Women's Union to campaign effectively. Madame Dinh, in contrast, was reported as believing that the inferior position of women in post-revolutionary Vietnam was the result of men clinging to their outmoded Confucian values – and privileges.

71 Le Duan, then general-secretary of the Workers Party, cited in Nguyen Thi Dinh, 'La Loi Sur le Manage et la Famille et l'emancipation de la Femme', *Bulletin de Droit* 1 (1987), p. 4.

72 This figure was calculated from the list presented in Nguyen Huu Tho, 'Personalities of the Liberation Movement of South Vietnam', Commission of External Relations of the NLF, mimeo, n.d. It represents a high estimate. The list is incomplete; it omits the 'secret leaders' of the NLF discussed in Pike, pp. 216–17, also alluded to in Truong Nhu Trang, *A Viet Cong Memoir*. Trang identifies himself as one of these secret NLF leaders. It is unlikely that any secret member was female as the secrecy itself was necessitated by the high position in either the government of South Vietnam or a major private corporation that these NLF leaders held. None of these positions was occupied by a woman.

73 'Women's Participation in State Administration and Economic Management', *Women of Vietnam* 4 (1987), p. 27; Eisen, pp. 244, 246; interview with Doang Thi Duyen.

74 Quoted in Eisen, p. 246.

75 Alexis de Tocqueville, *The Old Régime and the French Revolution*, trans. Stuart Gilbert, Garden City, NY: Doubleday Anchor, 1955; Theda Skoçpol, *States and Social Revolutions*, Cambridge: Cambridge University Press, 1979.

76 Mary Ann Tétreault, 'Women and Revolution: What Have We Learned?, in *Women and Revolution in Africa, Asia, and the New World*, ed. Mary Ann Tétreault, Columbia: University of South Carolina Press, 1994.

77 Skoçpol, pp. 164–67.

78 Claudia L. Johnson, *Jane Austen: Women, Politics, and the Novel*, Chicago, IL: University of Chicago Press, 1988. For a discussion of revolutionaries and their efforts to harmonize politics and everyday life according to a new pattern, see Lynn Hunt, *Politics, Culture, and Class in the French Revolution*, Berkeley: University of California Press, 1984.

3

GENDER AND NATION-BUILDING IN SOUTH AFRICA

Zengie A. Mangaliso

South African women had participated in many battles against the system of segregation – known as apartheid – that had governed their society since the mid-twentieth century. Imposed by the white minority, apartheid legally restricted where people of color could live, limited their movements, prevented them from having a voice in government, and exploited them economically. By relegating people of color to certain areas, it allowed whites to claim land and resources. Deprived of land, men went to work in mines and performed other back-breaking labor. Women served as domestics for white families. Along with legal discrimination, Africans were harassed by police and suffered the other punishments of everyday life in a racist society.

Protest became a way of life for many black South Africans. In the 1950s and thereafter South African women boycotted bus and other transportation systems, protested the killing and imprisonment of activists, and demanded better wages and jobs. Informal networks sprang up with African-American women activists in the US civil rights movement, with each movement nourishing the other. But apartheid endured longer than the Jim Crow laws that kept Americans segregated by color. Over the decades women gained incredible experience, not only of hardship but also of activism. When apartheid was overthrown in the 1990s, South African women had hard-won political experience, diasporic connections with black activists on other continents, and the warning from the curtailed women's rights that followed on the heels of other national liberation movements' success. They were prepared to make demands and ensure their recognition as full citizens from the various parties that ran post-apartheid South Africa. The new constitution of South Africa reflects their insistent efforts.

* * *

On 26 April 1994, South Africa made a shift from a minority government led by the Nationalist Party (NP) to a new government elected by the majority of the people and led by the African Nationalist Congress (ANC) The electoral process, which for the first time included majority-age members of all racial groups, symbolized political fulfilment and first-class citizenship for all South Africans. In the new and transitional constitution the government stipulates categorically its commitment to equality for all South Africans. The preamble outlines their entitlement to a 'democratic constitutional state in which there is equality between men and women and people of all races so that all citizens shall be able to exercise their fundamental rights and freedoms.'[1] Chapter 3, the Bill of Rights in the interim constitution, lists equality as the primary and fundamental right, and protection before the law, clearly stipulating that no person shall be discriminated against directly or indirectly on various grounds including sex and gender.[2]

The constitutional reference to equality raises several fundamental questions. How does a society that is still rooted in old gender traditions transform itself into a modern democracy that recognizes equality between men and women? As an agent of socialization and of resources that different interest groups compete for, the government plays what role in facilitating or even obstructing the shift toward gender equality? This chapter attempts to address the questions.

We begin with a brief history of women's involvement in social movements. A discussion of the positions taken by the various political parties as they competed for representation in government follows. We end with a discussion of how the gap can be closed between what appears to be government rhetoric on gender equality, and women's reality.

Gender and nation-building

It is axiomatic that universally women have gained the right to participate in the electoral process, to cast their ballots as does the rest of the citizenry, and then have found their participation in public institutions to be limited, thus curtailing their efforts in nation-building. This is ironical in the sense that women will have joined the various political movements and will have participated in guerrilla movements aimed at deposing the enemy. At independence, women in most parts of the world have been excluded from the nation-building process and have been reminded that their rightful place and contribution are within the home. This trend, which is almost universal, raises questions about the South African situation. Again, for South Africa, the most pressing question is whether the intent and language of the constitution can become reality.

When one looks at the South African society, one sees its mosaic character. It is a society of several races and ethnicities that have been kept separate and unequal through apartheid. In reality, South Africa incorporates the Afrikaners, the English, and other smaller European groups who are considered part of the white group, a group that has been largely privileged under apartheid. South Africa also incorporates Coloreds, Indians, and Africans who are part of the black group that has been largely disadvantaged under apartheid. For simplicity, it can be asserted that apartheid in South Africa has produced two nations, a white South Africa and a black South Africa, each with its own historical and political experiences, its own sense of nationalism, and its own gender experiences.

As can be expected, what nationalism has meant for the white group, in particular the Afrikaner group that has been in power for more than forty years, is different from the nationalism articulated by disadvantaged black groups. Further, although similarities between the two groups could be drawn based on in-group hierarchical gender arrangements, gender experiences have also been different.

The origins of Afrikaner nationalism can be traced to the Afrikaners' defeat by the British in the Anglo-Boer War of 1899–1902.[3] The remnants of the scattered Boer communities had to forge a new identity in order to survive in the emergent British-driven, capitalist system. Originally, the Afrikaners had no monolithic identity and no single unifying language. They had to create a new community of the *volk*, with new and unifying traditions, highlighting their strong Calvinistic religion, and they also had to create a single written language.[4] In 1918 Afrikaans emerged as a legally recognized Boer language, reflecting the traces of the Dutch, French, and German origins of the Afrikaners. It can be argued that from the outset the Afrikaner identity had a clear class component. It was born primarily as a strategy of mobilization in order to overpower the British on the political and economic front, and to transform the South African system such that it would fit the Afrikaner ethos.[5]

Afrikaner nationalism has had a clear gender focus. A small elite group of Afrikaner men established in 1918 a secret society called the Afrikaner Broederbond (Afrikaner Brotherhood) whose strategy was to uplift the previously politically and economically downtrodden Afrikaner. The Broederbond became the custodian of Afrikaner nationalism, in that it strove to preserve Afrikaner values of cultural and racial superiority. It was synonymous with Afrikaner male economic and political interests. It is clear from its name that Afrikaner women were excluded from the society. Even though Afrikaner women had supported Afrikaner men during the war, as the men ascended to power, the women were assigned to motherhood, self-sacrifice, and stoicism.[6].

It was a position with contradictory outcomes. Denied formal political and economic power, Afrikaner women, however, shared the benefits of power accrued to Afrikaner men. In the process, they became complicitous in the operation of apartheid and the oppression of black people, including black women.[7]

It can be argued that African nationalism emerged as a response to the oppressive nature of apartheid. The African Nationalist Congress (ANC), founded in 1912 and ostensibly the first political organization established to challenge apartheid, in the preamble to its Freedom Charter called for national unity, asserting that 'South Africa belongs to all who live in it black and white', and highlighting that all South Africans deserve to be treated as equals. The initial position of the ANC was not to take over political and economic power but to extend that power to blacks. Drawn from the urban intelligentsia and mostly mission-educated, the early members of the ANC demanded full civic participation in the society rather than a radical alteration of the existing power structures. The ANC turned to guerrilla warfare when its demand went unheeded for decades and when it was instead met by violence from the apartheid government.

The language of the ANC was inclusive of people of color, and called for national unity, but its leadership was solidly male and hierarchical. This contradiction prompted the establishment of the Federation of South African Women (FSAW), a group within the ANC whose intent was to draw the attention of its members to the discrepancy between the language of the Freedom Charter and the experiences of women within the movement. It is important to note that even within African nationalism, the concept of motherhood was and still is prominent. Winnie Mandela has been hailed for her contributions to the struggle against apartheid as the 'Mother of the Nation', Miriam Makeba, the South African activist singer, has been addressed in most of Africa as 'Ma Africa'.[8]

The Pan Africanist Congress (PAC), an organization that broke off from the ANC because of the dispute over the inclusive language of the Freedom Charter, expressed stronger nationalist sentiments. The PAC vehemently opposed, and still opposes the language of the Freedom Charter. It argued that by proclaiming that South Africa belongs to all who live in it, the ANC is denying a historical fact and reality: South Africa belongs to the indigenous people, and their land was auctioned for sale to all who live in it. The PAC emphasized its commitment to the overthrow of the apartheid government and the restoration of the land to its rightful owners. The PAC's stance on African land ownership is expressed in its maxim: 'Izwe Lethu' (The land is ours).[9] To my knowledge, the PAC has been quiet on the issue of gender; however, it can be asserted that like most political movements, its hierarchy is gendered. It is axiomatic that most political movements whose primary goal is to take over ownership of government and land are dominated by males in all societies.

The primary question at this point is – considering that South Africa incorporates groups with divergent histories and gender experiences – what sort of national identity is needed in order to create a transformed and united nation? The process of creating a single nation has begun with the formation of the government of national unity, which is inclusive of most political parties, including parties whose numbers are former enemies. Different groups have their own notions of what a new South Africa should be like, and vociferously express their opinions. One group comprises some Afrikaners who prefer a homeland of their own where they can live separately and preserve their language, traditions, and identity. Another group is headed by Chief Mangosuthu Buthelezi, leader of the Inkatha Freedom Party (IFP), who is advocating the secession and self-determination of KwaZulu Natal, where a large proportion of the Zulus reside.

Gender equality within South Africa deserves special mention. In Western countries issues of gender equality are generally articulated by various women's groups and are largely informed by feminism. Western feminism within the South African context, and especially as it relates to the experiences of black women, has largely been viewed with skepticism. Black women assert that they have always dealt with issues of women's emancipation in their families, communities, and political movements without being aware of the existence of the term *feminism*. Also, the central tenet of feminist thought, which asserts that all women are oppressed, becomes contentious. The assertion implies that women share a common lot, that factors like race and social class do not create a diversity of experience that requires different strategies to challenge inequality in society. For black women in South Africa, issues of racial inequality are still primary and cannot be overlooked in the sense that they affect a larger collective. This sentiment has been succinctly expressed by women in the liberation movement in the following statement:

> In South Africa, the prime issue is apartheid and national liberation. So to argue that African women should concentrate on and form an isolated feminist movement, focusing on issues of women in their narrowest sense, implies African women must fight so that they can be equally oppressed with African men.[10]

This is not to argue that issues of gender inequality are an irrelevance. On 2 May 1990, the National Executive of the ANC, for instance, issued the historic Statement on the Emancipation of Women, in which it was acknowledged that women's emancipation is not a by-product of national liberation and needs to be addressed within the democratic movement. This reflects the conflictual situation that black women in South Africa are faced with: they have to figure out under what circumstances to advance the race issue, and under what circumstances to advance the gender issue. For white women in South Africa, their unequal position as women in society has been compensated for by their being members of a privileged racial group.

Historical considerations – women's struggles

Women in South Africa have been involved in every aspect of the struggle for freedom against apartheid. Some specific events that women have participated in can be highlighted. As early as 1913 (when African men were already mandated to carry passes), women successfully mobilized against the extension and implementation of pass laws, which were rescinded until 1950, when they were reinstated and forcefully implemented. It is worth noting that the effort drew support from women of various race groups.

Women have also been involved in various revolts and boycotts, including consumer boycotts. The revolts of rural women against the culling of cattle in Natal and their participation in the potato and bus boycotts to challenge certain unfair labor practices, which took place in the 1950s, are well documented.[11] Unfair labor laws eventuated in resistance movements, some of which were led by prominent women: Lillian Ngoyi is well known for her effective and brave leadership of the labor unions in the 1950s. Beginning in 1973, women increasingly participated in consumer and rent boycotts, many of which were sparked by real declines in standards of living. Because women have always had the responsibility of managing households, struggles against the escalating cost of living have had great appeal for them.[12] In the 1980s and 1990s women became active in the Congress of South African Trade Unions (COSATU) as it fought unfair practices in the workplace enabled by apartheid laws. Within the organization they addressed issues affecting them as women, such as night shifts, maternity leave and the implications of such leave, and sexual harassment in the workplace.

Aside from such involvement, the onslaught of the apartheid system on black families prompted women to join guerrilla forces such as the Umkhonto Wesizwe (Spear of the Nation) within the ANC. Interestingly, women have also actively advocated peace. A conference hosted by ZANU-PF Women's League, in Harare, Zimbabwe, in 1989, whose theme was 'Women in the Struggle for Peace,' drew women from all spheres of life and with a range of affiliations. These included women from the then-banned ANC, white South African women affiliated with the Black Sash, women engaged in community work, university lecturers, churchwomen, and many others interested in promoting peace in South Africa.

It needs to be noted that by and large, women's involvement in resistance movements initially derived from issues that directly impacted their lives as women and the lives of their families. Such issues were later perceived as 'soft issues.' Women's participation in broader national issues, those involving the well-being of everyone, began on a smaller scale, partly because the dominant ideology defined national political issues, 'hard issues,' as a male arena.[13] To illustrate, the *Who's Who in South African Politics* presents biographies of only seven women among its 122 entries.[14] In point of fact, white women, who have participated in the electoral process since the 1930s, in 1993 still had insignificant representation in government; for instance, they constituted only 3.5 percent of the Lower House, and 2.8 percent of the Upper House.[15] Overall, women's presence in most public institutions has been much smaller than men's, and increasingly smaller at higher levels of the hierarchies within the institutions.

In the rebuilding of South Africa, the gap between male and female representation in society's institutions needs to be addressed and redressed for several reasons. First, women have been negatively impacted by the apartheid order, like everyone else, and their situations and status in society need to be improved. Second, in various ways women have played a role in challenging apartheid laws, and have earned the right of full participation in a democratic society. Third, to build a democratic society, everyone's energy, effort, and input is critical, including women's. Said differently, involvement in the nation-building process should be open to everyone who is able and willing to be part of that process and not be subject to race or sex qualifications.

South African political parties on gender

Eleven political parties campaigned for representation in the current government of national unity. Four have been identified as major parties in that they drew more support than the others from the electorate: the reformed Nationalist Party (NP), the Inkatha Freedom Party (IFP), the Pan Africanist Congress (PAC), and the African Nationalist Congress (ANC). In their history and evolution, each has dealt with the issue of gender in its own way.

The Nationalist Party, which historically represented white interests, in particular Afrikaner interests, has taken a structural-functionalist perspective on gender. This perspective has had much to do with shaping the nature of gender relations in the society. According to this perspective, men and women are biologically different: men have superior physical strength; women bear and rear children. These differences suit men and women 'naturally' to different roles. Within the Afrikaner community, men are the family heads and, by extension, heads in the public sphere; women focus on the private and domestic sphere.

The pervasive gender arrangement supported by the Nationalist Party was neatly summed up in the now defunct males-only Broederbond. It worked for and symbolized Afrikaner male interests, aspirations, and politics. Participation in the national political scene by Afrikaner women was confined to voting and giving support to the political men in their lives. The women members of the Nationalist Party were part of what is known as the Women's Action group. At regional and national levels, they met as a constituency to discuss issues of importance to male political leaders or candidates and to raise funds. In short, their agenda was set by men. The meeting 'chairlady' was usually the wife of a prominent politician.[16] In the forty years that the Nationalist party was in power, leadership in public institutions has been overwhelmingly male; in a parliament with 103 National Party members, not one is female. Only one woman has been a member of Parliament: Helen Suzman, of British-Jewish heritage, representing the opposition Progressive Party. In sum, the Nationalist Party has supported a patriarchal society where ultimate control rests primarily with males.

The Inkatha Freedom Party has dealt with the gender issue in a manner that gives the appearance of being contradictory. Recognizing that African women in particular have suffered alongside men under apartheid and contributed toward challenging it, the party has publicly applauded women yet remains patriarchal and hierarchical in its treatment of gender. Chief Mangosuthu Buthelezi, its leader, in various speeches around Natal has clearly stated his view on the position of women in the party and society:

> My sisters, you are mothers in suffering inhumanity. Some of you are wives in an oppressed society and some of you are daughters in our oppressed society, and the full brunt of apartheid is borne by you more than by any other Blacks. . . . [W]hen others were quaking with fear, when others were intimidated . . . it was you who stood up to be counted.[17]

At the same time, Chief Buthelezi emphasizes that all party members should be under the direct authority of his leadership, just as a woman should be under a husband's authority at home. In one of the documents publicizing the party's position on gender, a high Inkatha official wrote:

> In the family the man is the head. The woman knows that she is not equal to her husband. She addresses the husband as 'father', and by so doing the children get a good example of how to behave. Women refrain from exchanging words with men and if they do, this reflects bad upbringing on their part.[18]

Women in the party by and large accept their secondary position and perceive their role as mother and defender of the home while men engage in public issues. They see their contribution in society to be fortitude, forbearance, and unfailing support to loved ones. In a sense, through the party, they have been trained to look upon themselves as the power behind the male throne.[19]

In the literature of the Pan Africanist Congress, the party appears silent on the question of women. Patricia De Lille, PAC secretary of foreign affairs, argues that historically the PAC has been anxious not to marginalize women by focusing on them separately from the overall population. The PAC premise is that national issues invariably incorporate both sexes and hence there is no need to address male and female equality. Curiously, after the lifting of the ban on all political movements in 1990, the PAC set up a women's wing that would have representation in its National Executive.[20] In other words, the PAC recognized the need to assist women's full participation in the public arena.

There is indication that within the ANC while it was a resistance movement, the issue of male and female equality was one of lively debate. As mentioned earlier, although racial equality was seen as primary, the gender issue lagged behind until it was brought to the front by the Federation of South African Women. Through women's insistence and persistence, the Women's Charter was written, highlighting the importance of gender equality. The Women's Charter begins by affirming the overriding commonality of interests women share with men:

> We women do not form a society separate from men. There is one society and it is made of both women and men. As women we share the problems and anxieties of our men and join hands with them to remove social evils and obstacles to progress.[21]

At the same time, the charter recognizes that women are discriminated against in society on the basis of sex, and commits women to working for the removal of discrimatory laws and practices. Throughout the charter, the dual nature of the women's struggle for equality is stressed:

> As members of the national liberation movements . . . we march forward with our men in the struggle for liberation. . . . As women there rests upon us also the burden of removing from our society all the social differences developed from past times between men and women which have the effect of keeping our sex in a position of inferiority and subordination.[22]

Needless to say, of the four major parties the ANC is the most progressive in regard to gender and could benefit all South African women regardless of racial background. The ANC policy guidelines unequivocally advocate women's equality in the public and private spheres, and encourage women's broad participation in post-apartheid socio-economic national development strategies.

> The emancipation of women must be an integral part of their lives, not just in legal statements, but in the reality of their lives . . . if women do not achieve equality with men, society will have failed. They have struggled within their homes, they have given their time, energy, and lives to the struggle for national liberation.[23]

The next, and most crucial, step for the ANC government is to move forward, to make certain that women are indeed part of the nation-building process.

Toward achieving gender equality in South Africa

A step already taken by the ANC government toward eliminating gender inequality was the introduction of affirmative action programs in all public institutions, ostensibly intended to encourage equal access to opportunities for all South Africans regardless of race and sex. Such programs elsewhere in the world, including the United States, do not translate into instant opportunities for the historically disadvantaged, and are also accompanied by a host of controversies.

Although the programs are welcome in that they indicate the willingness of the state to intervene to ensure equality, they are not by themselves sufficient. Women's representation in public institutions, particularly black women's, will not occur overnight. Some concrete steps are being taken to remove barriers created by apartheid, but cultural barriers remain largely untouched, and thus create circumstances unique to women.

Again, the South African culture clearly defines the positions of men and women in society: the public sphere is primarily the male sphere, and the private sphere is primarily the female sphere, and from birth everyone is socialized thereto. This pattern will not change soon because over time it has come to be perceived as 'natural,' the most convenient, and thus the most acceptable. Females may have access to quality public education, and, it is hoped, may have access to gainful work, but will run the risk of still having to fulfill customary domestic responsibilities.

The home, where gender inequality begins and is reinforced, can remain mostly untouched by outside institutional forces, including government policy. Also, the economies of rural communities function effectively on the basis of a distinct division of labor that is based on sex. Rural economies for the most part still rely on traditional farming arrangements, whereby it is the males who supervise animal-drawn ploughs or drive tractors, and it the females who do the planting and harvesting, as well as the managing of the household. Gender equality is easier to advocate and implement in urban areas, where farming is not the means of subsistence and resources are in relative abundance. Further, historically in societies where liberation has been achieved, national leaders, who predominantly were male, spoke unequivocally on race equality, ostensibly because it benefited more members of the societies, but were largely silent on gender issues. Thus far in South Africa, one has not heard any statement of serious concern about gender inequality from any leader. The prevailing sentiment is that issues of race still dominate and deserve top priority.

It is axiomatic that women who in various ways had participated in resistance against unpopular governments, at independence found themselves relegated to the margins, if not pushed back into the private, domestic sphere. Why is this so? A possible answer:

> The mobilization of women during the struggle that is necessary to gain national liberation is usually annulled after this has been achieved, and the number of women who continue to participate in political power, in theorization and decision-making is very small. One reason for this is the fact that although women participated in struggles in large numbers, they left the development of theory and of strategy to the male experts.[24]

In the press of daily activities, they overlook or neglect the need to prepare themselves, to be decision-makers – or are not given opportunities to do so. Accordingly, they are not equipped for advancement in the public-sphere.

It is imperative that more women acquire the skills required in the public sphere. Formal education provides women with specific skills and expertise; informal education can instill the motivation to move beyond the private sphere. Historically, women have played an important role in local community work, church work, and school committees. These are some of the areas that are deserving of acknowledgment and encouragement because they are 'natural' sites where women can learn and improve their leadership skills. Also, in most of Africa women have been dispropor-tionately active in the informal sector largely because participation in the formal sector was unavailable to them because of lack of education. South Africa is the exception; its informal sector is dominated by women, in particular black women. Government policies that promote the informal sector would benefit women by increasing their earning capacity. Women's improved incomes would in turn increase their bargaining power within the home. In other words, could be used to persuade men to share household duties, which would enable women's greater participation in public life.

Conclusion

In sum, the inclusion of women in the democratic process in South Africa is still a challenge. Black women in particular, who suffered the effects of apartheid and still face the daily pressures of a traditional culture, are doubly handicapped. Some expressed their condition pointedly on election day: they voted, and now have a government of their choice. The ritual of voting symbolized their political maturity and fulfillment. However, some still have to serve their white masters for a living, as well as manage their own homes.

Although the current ANC-led government speaks progressively on gender issues and has taken some steps toward gender equality in society, there is a long road ahead. Admittedly, the ravages of apartheid make racial equality more pressing than any other aspects of equality. Still, it cannot be assumed that women's meaningful participation in society will be a by-product of democracy for all. This has not happened even in socialist countries with clearly articulated principles of equality. Women's meaningful involvement in society has to be addressed within government, women's organizations, and the society at large.

NOTES

1 The Constitutional Assembly charged with writing the permanent South African Constitution (completion deadline May 1996), released a first draft and solicited comments and input from the general citizenry.
2 The use of the terms *sex* and *gender* highlights the prohibition of discrimination based on biological and cultural factors that prescribe men and women's positions in society.
3 The Anglo-Boer War arose out of the conflict between the British and the Afrikaners, the latter group then referred to as Boers, over the discovery of and access to diamond mines. The war also turned out to be a conflict between the two white groups for control over African land and labor. See Anne McClintock, 'Family Feuds: Gender, Nationalism, and the Family,' *Feminist Review*, no. 44 (summer 1993): 62–80.
4 Ibid.
5 James Leatt, Theo Kneifel, and Klaus Nurnburger, eds, *Contending Ideologies in South Africa* (Cape Town, 1986).
6 McClintock, 'Family Feuds.'
7 The benefits enjoyed by Afrikaner women were extended to white women in general. To my mind, this condition makes a coalition between white and black women in South Africa an uneasy one, if not problematic. Despite this problem, however, it needs to be acknowledged that there are white women who have used their privileged position and mobilized to challenge the oppressive laws of South Africa, including labor and pass laws that perpetuated the oppression of maids. One organization of such white women is the Black Sash.
8 McClintock, 'Family Feuds.'
9 PAC Manifesto, 1962 (abridged).
10 Frene Ginwala, 'ANC Women: Their Strength in the Struggle,' *Work in Progress*, no. 45 (1986): 10–11.
11 Cheryl Walker, *Women and Gender in Southern Africa to 1945* (Cape Town: David Phillip, 1990); Ivy Matsepe Casaburri, 'On the Question of Women in South Africa,' in *Whither South Africa*, ed. Bernard Magubane and Ibbo Mandaza (Trenton, NJ: Africa World Press, 1988); Julia Wells, *We Now Demand! The History of Women's Resistance to Pass Laws In South Africa* (Johannesburg: Witwatersrand University Press, 1993).
12 M. Sutcliffe, 'The Crisis in South Africa: Material Conditions and Reformist Response' (paper presented to he workshop Macroeconomic Policy and Poverty in South Africa, Cape Town, 29–30 August 1986; Jo Beall, Shireen

Hassim, and Alison Todes, 'A Bit on the Side? Gender Struggles in the Politics of Transformation in South Africa,' *Feminist Review*, no. 33 (autumn 1989): 32–56.

13 Casaburri, 'On the Question of Women in South Africa.'

14 Sheila Gastrow, ed., *Who's Who in South African Politics* (New York: Hans Zell, 1990).

15 Barbara Klugman, 'Women in Politics Under Apartheid: A Challenge to the New South Africa,' in *Women and Politics Worldwide*, ed. Barbara Nelson and Najma Chowhury (New Haven: Yale University Press, 1994).

16 Ibid.

17 Mangosuthu Buthelezi's speeches, various dates, quoted in Shireen Hassim, 'Family, Motherhood, and Zulu Nationalism: The Politics of the Inkatha Movement's Brigade,' *Feminist Review*, no. 43 (spring 1993): 1–77.

18 Praisley Mdluli, 'uBuntu-botho: Inkatha People's Education Tranformation,' *Public Address* no. 5, 1987.

19 Hassim, 'Family, Motherhood, and Zulu Nationalism.'

20 Klugman, 'Women in Politics Under Apartheid.'

21 Women's Charter; see Appendix, Cherryl Walker, *Women and Resistance in South Africa* (London: Onyx Press, 1982).

22 Ibid.

23 Zola S. T. Skweyiya, 'Constitutional Guidelines of the ANC: A Vital Contribution to the Struggle Against Apartheid,' *Sechaba* 23, no. 6 (1989): 5–10.

24 M. Mies, *Fighting on Two Fronts: Women's Struggles and Research* (The Hague: Institute of Social Studies, 1982).

Part II

SOURCES OF ACTIVISM

4

FEMALE CONSCIOUSNESS OR FEMINIST CONSCIOUSNESS?

Women's consciousness raising in community-based struggles in Brazil[1]

Yvonne Corcoran-Nantes

Where does feminist activism come from and what is feminist activism anyway? These two questions shape the analysis of Brazilian women since World War II. A dictatorship curtailed the opportunity for political participation as it was known in other parts of the world. Moreover, because politics is often defined as participating through activism around elections and through making organized demands of government for women's rights, women in the countries of Latin America have sometimes been interpreted as apolitical and without an ounce of feminist consciousness. There were socialist and guerrilla movements in Latin America, but the women involved were usually relegated to cleaning, cooking, and secretarial tasks and kept from roles thought of as 'political.' Yet it has become clear that Latin American women have been incredibly active, for example, taking to the streets in Argentina to protest the disappearance of their children. Believing that their children had been murdered because of the opposition to dictatorship, these women claimed the rights of motherhood, and occupied major city squares and spaces in front of government buildings. The demonstrations by the so-called 'Mothers of the Plaza de Mayo,' named after the square where Argentinian women kept their vigil, drew attention to a new source of women's politics.

In Brazil, as the economy grew more prosperous in the 1970s, the military dictatorship witnessed the growth of a variety of social movements – some for political liberalization and others for a revolution that would lead to socialism. During this period women became active socialists while some were influenced by the US and European feminism of the 1960s and 1970s. The Catholic Church also inspired women's activism, as did unions. In the early 1980s, elections took place with a spectrum of political parties shaping a public debate that acknowledged the legitimacy of women's issues. These showed the success of Brazilian feminism in highlighting claims ranging from the right to good jobs, to reproductive rights and sexual freedom.

But like the activism of the 'Mothers of the Plaza de Mayo,' a main source of reform energy was the urban poor of Brazil – among them thousands of poor women without access to government circles. Many women in the national liberation struggles described in earlier chapters were also poor, and men directed much of their activism. In the case of Latin American women the situation is different. The Brazilian women described in this chapter were poor, operating from the grassroots, and basing their claims to equal citizenship in the public sphere on their role as mothers in the private sphere. As they protested unemployment and bad living conditions in the 1970s and 1980s, their struggles challenge us to think both about the relationships among gender, class, and politics and about that between activism by women and feminism. Can or should poor women operating to benefit women, but doing so outside middle-class movements that claimed the name feminist, be considered as part of a women's movement?

* * *

Generally politics is thought of as a man's world, a place where women rarely appear. In Latin America in particular, it has been easy for political science to ignore women in institutional politics such as political parties and trade unions because their level of participation is low. In the 1970s, political research on the question of political participation focused on institutional politics in spite of the fact that democratic governments were not a prevalent feature of Latin American politics. Consequently, this focus produced a very superficial picture of the political participation of both women and men (Jaquette 1980). Blachman (1973), in a piece of political research on women, unique of its time, concluded that Brazilian women believed that politics was for men not women. What he failed to indicate was what kind of politics women were speaking about. In Brazil it was precisely in that period when the majority of the population were excluded from institutional politics that non-institutional politics, in the form of popular social movements, became the principal arena for political participation and opposition (Kucinski 1982).

My own research in Brazil, from which the empirical data in this chapter originates, was designed specifically to look at aspects of women's political participation in popular urban social movements in order to provide explanations for women's high profile in non-institutional politics. It was clear that by the 1980s women participated in and led popular protest around a wide variety of issues related to urbanization, employment and the provision of basic services, which suggests that this political arena represents something of fundamental importance to women (see Safa 1990; Corcoran-Nantes 1990; Moser 1987). Moreover, the issues that interest women represent the major social and economic problems in developing countries and are also becoming key issues in the advanced industrial nations.

Women of the working poor in Brazil have, over the past two decades, strengthened their presence in non-institutional politics by protesting about the lack of basic services, health provision, transport, housing and unemployment. The methods of organization and political practice of popular urban social movements demonstrate the influence of women in them and similar practices can be found in many developing countries both in grassroots protest politics and women's organizations (see, for example, Mies 1988; Mattelart 1980; Cutrufelli 1983). I have argued elsewhere that these movements were not specifically created *for* women. It is women who form the majority within a social group whose socio-economic experience in Brazilian society is neither reflected nor represented in other forms of political organization (see Corcoran-Nantes 1990). Consequently, women have played a major role in the formation and development of popular movements. Through their participation they have discovered a new public identity in a political sphere which, in many ways, they have made their own. Many women, through their political development in non-institutional politics, have gone on to extend their participation to political parties and trade unions as well as strategic gender protests along with women's organizations and feminist groups around issues such as birth control, rape and domestic violence.

What seems to have developed is a bifurcated political sphere: male/institutional politics and female/non-institutional politics, which are identifiable by the nature of political/gender organization and action. The political practice in either sphere bears little resemblance to the other as in one the majority of political actors are male and in the other female. What I wish to consider here is the gender specificity of political practices in non-institutional politics and their implications for the relationship between politically reproduced gender spheres.

This chapter will look at the development of political consciousness and solidarity among women of the popular urban movements in São Paulo. It is through these practices and women's influence on them that we can analyse the motivation behind their participation in this political sphere, how women view their role in society and what this represents for them. By looking at the various processes involved in conscientization and politicization such as forms of consciousness raising, self-help groups, oral history and the struggle for literacy, I will argue that the development of women's political consciousness is far more complex than present analyses demonstrate. In Brazil, as in many other Latin American countries, women have created a political role for themselves based on their social status as wives and mothers but through which they have struggled for recognition of their roles and rights as workers, residents and citizens.

Gender: the missing link in analyses of popular social movements

Despite evidence to show the predominance of women in non-institutional politics, those who have attempted to analyse popular social movements have tended to ignore the question of gender. Those who have acknowledged or tried to give some explanation for women's participation and political consciousness tend to fall into two different camps. First, there are those like Jaquette (1989) who subsume female participation under the auspices of feminism or women's movements, thereby removing the question of gender from their analysis of popular protest in Latin America. Second, there are those like Chaney (1979) who prefer to confine themselves to a matrifocal analysis where the traditional role of women as wives and mothers and their relation to the reproduction of the labour force becomes the universal explanation, the *sine qua non*, for women's political practice and participation. The role of women in Latin American society is far too multifaceted for us to be satisfied with unitary explanations of their participation in the political sphere.

Political division of labour exists in political parties and trade unions in Latin America and many other parts of the world. Within institutional politics women's groups and women's departments are formed to present programmes and drafts of new laws or to develop a strategy to place women's issues on the political agenda. What this actually does is to take strategic gender issues and other issues that are of importance to women out of the mainstream politics within these organizations. In short, it removes them from the political agenda. Tying women's political participation exclusively to the question of feminism and women's movements gives a wholly inaccurate picture of the extent of women's political participation and the motives and interests behind it. The majority of women who participate in the popular social movements are not motivated by a feminist consciousness; feminism for them has very little to do with the reality of their lives. In Latin American society the marked inequality in the distribution of wealth and resources has further reinforced the idea, among women of the urban poor, that feminism is a middle-class ideology for women who have all the social and economic advantages. Moreover, the institutionalization of domestic service on the continent has sustained the antagonism between classes whereby 'fortunate' women exploit 'less fortunate' women. The patron/client relationship which has evolved is a major barrier to any longstanding political association between them, and there have been occasions when this relationship has been politically exploited (Corcoran-Nantes 1988; Filet Abreu de Souza 1980; Chuchryk 1989). Consequently, there are considerable class differences in relation to how and in what forms of political organizations women participate.

Writers who do analyse women's participation in popular social movements tend to consider only one aspect (that of the sexual division of labour) as an explanation for their participation, either relating this exclusively to women's domestic role, or this, together with women's relationship to collective consumption (see Cardoso 1984; Safa 1990; Moser 1987; Evers et al. 1982). I have argued elsewhere that women's participation in social movements is also linked to their role in production and that most of the issues around which these movements are organized also affect men (Corcoran-Nantes 1990). Without doubt women do legitimate their entry into the political sphere as wives and mothers but there are tangible reasons why women do so. In Latin American society *marianismo*, or the cult of Mary, still exists whereby women's status comes from their reproductive role, and this has often been a source of power for women (Stevens 1973). By utilizing this image women can strengthen and legitimate their political involvement in the eyes of the state. Conversely the state has also exploited the cultural identity of women, *os supermadres*, to secure their political support (Chuchryk 1989). The *supermadre* approach to politics is legitimated by women, men and the state. Up to the present time no one has considered, for example, how far men take their role in the family into the political sphere.

Maxine Molyneux in her own work on women in post-revolutionary societies, has presented an excellent working hypothesis for considering the motivations and achievements of women's participation in political struggles. She divides gender interests into two broad categories. One is strategic gender interests which are directly related to women's subordination in a given society and the demands around which women's struggles are based on a strategy to overcome all forms of gender inequality. The other is practical gender interests which derive from women's ascribed role in the sexual division of labour, a response to their immediate practical needs and formulated by women themselves. These are shaped by class and ethnicity and are not necessarily part of a long-term strategy to achieve gender equality. She goes on to argue that in the formulation of strategic gender interests practical gender interests have to be taken into account and it is 'the politicisation of these practical interests and their transformation into strategic interests which constitutes a central aspect of feminist practice' (Molyneux 1985: 236–7).

It is practical gender interests which are the basis of women's political participation in popular social movements. The transformation of practical gender interests into strategic gender interests requires not only women's recognition of their power to represent their own interests but also that space exists within the prevailing political system to pressure the state into recognizing those interests. This is part of a complex political development process whereby women not only recognize gender interests but do so in relation to and in conjunction with other women, across class and ethnic boundaries.

Political practice - the development of political consciousness and solidarity

In Brazil the political *Abertura* (opening) of the 1970s stimulated the development of opposition forces outside institutional politics. By the 1980s the number and type of social movements multiplied as popular protest increased and state governments were constantly pressurized into taking action to ameliorate deteriorating socio-economic conditions amongst the majority of the population. In São Paulo, hardly a week went by without some form of political protest taking place and it was here that the sense of exclusion from the benefits of highly concentrated economic growth was most acute. São Paulo was the hub of Brazilian industrial growth, and with a migrant population growing by over 50,000 per month this exacerbated existing problems associated with economic development (Censo Demographico do Brasil 1990). In the urban periphery the *favelas* (shantytowns) expanded rapidly and this placed enormous pressure on the already limited capacity of public services such as water, electricity, sanitation, transport, housing and healthcare. The state of São Paulo was both unprepared and ill-equipped for such an influx of workers, having neither the infrastructure nor the resources to cater for the needs of its rapidly rising population. However, it is impossible to ignore the state government's neglect of public services during one of the most prosperous eras of Brazilian history, the period of the 'economic miracle', when it was undertaking some of the most ostentatious building projects in the capital of São Paulo. Nowhere were the socio-economic consequences of the government's political priorities more apparent than on the urban periphery, where the majority of workers lived and where most incoming migrants were forced to settle. The residential communities on the urban periphery of São Paulo were in turn, not surprisingly, the main political bases of the urban social movements (see Corcoran-Nantes 1990; Machado 1988).

It is on the urban periphery of São Paulo that the fieldwork on which this chapter is based was carried out and concentrated on three popular movements: O Movimento de Favela (The Favela Movement – founded in 1976 to secure land title and to improve services and infrastructure in the settlements), O Movimento de Saude (The Health Movement – formed originally in 1973 with the aim of improving medical services at both the local and regional level) and O Movimento dos Desempregados (The Unemployed Movement – formed in 1983 to solve the immediate problems of unemployment through demands for unemployment benefit, funding to set up worker cooperatives and so on).[2] These popular movements are representative of the wide range of movements which existed, and continue to exist, in the urban periphery of São Paulo. One common feature is that participants in these movements are either exclusively or predominantly women.

Health, housing and unemployment are typical of the kind of social questions that have attracted the interest of low-income women, and movements formed around these issues developed characteristics which reflect their involvement in them. The key factor to take into account here is that while the sexual division of labour tends in general terms to confine women for a large amount of their time to their homes and immediate neighbourhoods, low-income women are often involved in a wide range of activities which span the rather arbitrary divide between production and reproduction, with many having various modes of generating income (see Brydon and Chant 1989: 10–12). Women thus tend to be more responsive than men to issues that relate to socio-economic activities in both the public *and* private spheres. The political participation of women arises from the social bonds which are created via these activities in the community, through which they organize themselves and from which the political contexts of urban social movements are developed.

Moreover, the social, economic and even moral issues which have formed the basis of this type of political protest are directly associated with the nature of dependent capitalist development. They are issues which cannot be solved in the short term and are precisely those which have remained on the periphery of 'mainstream' politics or have been given little or no priority in the programmes of parties and successive governments. It is hardly surprising, therefore, that some social movements have been in existence for over two decades and have only gradually gained improvements in the conditions of life for the urban poor. Various forms of consciousness raising were used by the popular movements, and the ways in which they were implemented differed from one movement to another. First, there was instruction in socialist theories to explain the socio-economic conditions of the urban poor and the importance of the popular movements to the struggle for political change in Brazilian society. This almost always involved the help of supporters of the movements such as the Church or political parties who had political material designed for the conscientization of the urban poor. Second, there was a form of consciousness raising which was a means of self-education and collective counselling, and dealt with issues and problems arising from, and related to, their struggles. This was a method of consciousness raising which women preferred to use in which self-help and the dissemination of information was a part of the process of political participation. The question of self-help also led to the formation of cooperative schemes in low-income neighbourhoods to provide practical solutions to the immediate needs of the local community. Third was the use of oral history, which was probably the most important and effective way of creating political consciousness and solidarity. All the popular movements had some means of recording and registering their political history but it was only in those movements in which women had organizational control that a strong emphasis was placed on the use of oral history as a means of conscientization.

Class consciousness vis-à-vis female consciousness

Consciousness raising based on the propagation of socialist theory was undertaken in various ways. In many cases it was an integral part of the political meetings of the movement itself during which an individual or group, usually with experience in political parties or left-wing Church groups, discussed current political issues relating to the problems of the urban poor. Sometimes it was little more than speech making, but on other occasions simple visual aids such as diagrams or cartoon pictures were used to show the participants how and why they suffered in Brazilian society. Women were quick to point out that in much of this material they were underrepresented and *their* experience in Brazilian society was rarely discussed at all. More sophisticated material was sometimes used, such as films or slides borrowed from the Catholic Church which has produced entire courses for the politicization of the popular classes.

These forms of consciousness raising stimulated interest and discussion both inside and outside the meetings but this was difficult to sustain over a long period of time. Women, in particular, lost interest fairly quickly because their political concerns centred on practical difficulties rather than theorizing struggles. It was, however, a successful way of selecting potential political activists. Experienced activists from political parties or left-wing ecclesiastical groups who participated in the popular movements would often utilize this form of consciousness raising to 'recruit' new activists by inviting those people who demonstrated some 'political aptitude' to attend their meetings. A significant number of women entered local party politics in this way. The conflicting views of two women demonstrate the positive and negative aspects of this kind of consciousness raising:

'I liked the film best. It showed how we live and how we suffer. It made us think about why we are poor and always will be the way things are. But how are we going to change the world when it's all we can do to get a few changes in this one *and* after so many struggles . . . ? If we did change society would it be any different? I doubt it! It'd be alright for the men, it's always good for them. But what about us women? Nothing changes for us. It could be worse. . . . It's funny they didn't say much about our suffering in the film.'

(Reginalda, 32 years, São Matheus)

'Most people don't like to talk about politics, some of them leave the meeting but I think it's interesting. The pyramid was good, where they showed the different classes in different colours I think everyone liked that. . . . It was after that *favela* meeting that Manuel gave me a book to read about women and struggle and invited me to a meeting of the PT (Workers Party) group. I go to the meetings every week now. I think we women should participate in political parties, not just the popular movements, because we can learn a lot more but most of the women in the *favela* aren't interested in political parties. . . . I don't know why.'

(Valdiva, 23 years, Vila Sezamo)

This form of consciousness raising, although less successful at local meetings of the popular movements, tended to be used far more in the Encounters and Congresses held by the movements every year. Films and slides would be shown, speakers from the Catholic Church, political parties and the trade unions would be invited to discuss the role of the popular movements in class struggle in Brazil and debating groups would be set up to discuss the issues raised.

Female consciousness, women's groups and self-help

Consciousness-raising practices which dealt with issues and problems arising from the struggles of the popular movements were extremely popular amongst women participants. They invariably took place at separate small group meetings, often in people's homes. Meetings were extremely informal and were not necessarily held on a regular basis, depending on the role of the group within the movements and its aims. Irrespective of the form that this type of politicization took, it was fundamental to the continued participation of a large number of women in the popular movements. Support groups or self-education groups were quite common in the popular movements and arose from a basic need for women to discuss issues linked to their political participation or to the political demands of the movement. The Unemployed Movement and the Health Movement provide excellent examples of how these groups functioned.

In the Unemployed Movement the formation of women's groups spread swiftly from one region to another and the numbers of women committee members rose to 70 per cent. In some regions women's groups were formed as a result of initiatives by women themselves. In others, however, their formation was encouraged by men, who had organizational control of the Unemployed Movement, as a means of removing 'women's issues' out of the general political demands of the movement. Wherever they emerged, they became a forum for the discussion of a wide range of issues such as women's political participation, male domestic violence and women's role in society. Through the exchange of experiences, particularly those related to their own participation in the popular movements, many women were better able to face the problems arising from their political activities with the support of these groups which served to reinforce their commitment to the movement.[3]

Many women enjoyed the opportunity of talking about themselves and their lives, as well as finding out more about themselves and other women. These groups often developed into a mutual support collective wherein *companheiras* in the struggle became true friends who gave each other help in their personal, working and political lives. Some of these groups were little more than small women's meetings but others went on to join up with other women's groups and organize talks to which feminist speakers were invited to discuss topics such as 'The history of women's political participation in Brazil' and 'Female sexuality: my body, my choice'. Many of these groups joined with women's organizations and feminist groups on demonstrations and political protests about issues such as abortion, violence against women, and family planning. Consequently, these groups, although initially formed as a means of politicizing women within the popular movements through consciousness raising undertaken by women for women, sometimes became a vehicle for contacts with other women's groups or other women in a wide range of political organizations. Irrespective of how these groups developed, they gave women greater confidence in themselves, and many of the women who organized or participated in these groups went on to be elected local and regional coordinators of Committees of the Unemployed.

The Health Movement actually evolved from issues concerning women's health and that of their children. The use of self-education as a form of consciousness raising about these issues was a natural progression from the movement's initial aims and objectives. Their struggle to improve an inadequate and under-funded health service made women conscious of the need to take action themselves in the area of preventive medicine in an attempt to reduce the risk of health problems for themselves and their children. Women of the movement were principally interested in two main topics: first, ways in which they could prevent or reduce the risk of their children suffering from some of the more common childhood diseases in Brazil; second, access to information on contraception so that women could make an informed choice as to what methods were available and most suitable for them to use. In both cases, women turned to local doctors and nurses to help them produce booklets which they could use in their self-education groups.

The 'course' on family health was based on the prevention of common infectious childhood diseases such as dysentery, parasites and skin infections prevalent in poorer areas of the urban periphery. Inadequate and often polluted water supplies, the absence of proper sewerage and drainage systems and the questionable hygiene standards of local shops selling fresh foods were some of the causes of the high incidence of infectious diseases amongst children. Women discovered that it was possible to take preventive action against such illnesses and in the self-education groups they discussed ways in which they could help themselves and their families on the basis of the information in the pamphlets. Women learnt to sterilize their water supply, what to look for in fresh foods and how to identify certain diseases in their children to facilitate early diagnosis and treatment. The lack of emphasis within the Brazilian Health Service on preventive medicine meant that this form of self-education was extremely important.

The leaflets produced by the Health Movement on family planning were also an invaluable source of information for women. In Brazil there were no official family planning schemes or health advice services for women and the public health service offered little orientation for women who wished to use contraceptives, apart from advice on 'natural' methods of birth control supported by the Catholic Church. In practice, while there was no official line taken by the government on the question of family planning, women of the working poor were often pressured into using sterilization as a permanent solution to their 'problems' without being advised on alternative forms of contraception available to them.[4] The self-education groups and pamphlets were a means of informing women about the different methods of contraception available in Brazil, showing the advantages and disadvantages of each one to help women make an informed choice on what method was best for them. Women who did not participate in the Health Movement attended these informal groups on family planning and some of them went on to participate in the movement itself.

Meetings held by the Health Movement about the issues of family health and family planning were invariably held in people's houses, often as 'street meetings' to which women from the movement would invite their friends and neighbours. Working from the pamphlets, women would discuss the questions raised and any practical difficulties which arose. No professional people participated in the groups: they were run by ordinary women who sought practical solutions to health problems which were not resolved within the public health service. The existence of the groups demonstrated the importance of the Health Movement in the struggle for a better health service and they reinforced or developed women's commitment to the movement.

This type of consciousness raising developed for women by women raised female consciousness in relation to strategic gender interests. It stimulated and developed a complex matrix of inter- and intra-class alliances between women around gender-specific issues. As women acquired a greater sense of themselves and gender inequality through their political practices in popular struggles, women's organizations in the low-income neigbour-hoods emerged and grew in strength. By developing a political identity as women of the working poor, they were able to define their relationships clearly with other organizations, both inside and outside institutional politics. Consequently, when they entered political protests in association with political parties and trade unions on the one hand, or feminist groups and women's organizations on the other, in general or gender-specific political struggles, such as the Campaign for Direct Elections or Women against Violence Campaign, they were able to defend this identity and their practical gender interests from a position of greater political strength.

The demand for literacy and politicization

Adult literacy courses based on the methods of Paulo Freire, which use short literacy courses as a means of politicization, were also a popular and constructive form of conscientization.[5] Many of the urban poor who participate in the popular movements are illiterate. Women in particular have had few chances to educate themselves, and when they begin to undertake organizational roles in the movement there is tremendous pressure on them to obtain basic literacy skills. Dealing with members of the government, participating in negotiations and the need to take notes at meetings present difficulties to those who are unable to read or write.

Women often bypass these difficulties by using tape-recorders or by taking their children along to the regional or state meetings to take notes, so that they are able to recall the main points of discussion or proposals to report back to members of their group or the movement. However, the high rate of illiteracy amongst those who participate in the popular movements often gives a privileged position to people who can read or write. There are women with valuable political skills who have been elected as representatives or coordinators in the movements who hide the fact that they are illiterate. Whether it is from a feeling of inadequacy or as a result of internal or external pressure, it is invariably the leaders or representatives of the movements who instigate literacy courses as a means of educating both themselves and others in the popular movements.

Literacy courses are always undertaken with the help of activists from either the Church or the political parties who have experience in this field. These activists are invited by the movements initially to teach the literacy course, but eventually one or two members of the movement are shown how to deliver the course and this eliminates the need for outside help. The courses are nearly always over-subscribed and it is frequently women who are the most interested in becoming literate. This interest derives, primarily, from the desire to enhance and expand their new-found political skills; to be able to make notes, to vote in government elections, to read political material or even to write their own placards were all skills that these women wanted to acquire. Thus, it was these factors which made this type of literacy course based on politicization ideal for the popular movements.

Community action as political action

Cooperative work and mutualist schemes were two other activities which developed and strengthened the solidarity between those who participated in the popular movements. Amongst the urban poor they were a means of resolving immediate and socio-economic problems and could be of a short- or long-term nature. Cooperative work schemes usually entailed the sale of goods or commodities and only benefited those who participated in them. Mutualist schemes, on the other hand, involved the provision of services and frequently benefited those who did not participate in them as well as those who did. Irrespective of the schemes' beneficiaries they arose from the political practice of the popular movements. These schemes became an integral part of their political organization and extended the members' political commitment to the idea of collectivism into the local community.

It was the Unemployed Movement that used cooperative work schemes as an immediate solution to the subsistence problems of its members and in the period 1983–85 they became popular amongst the unemployed throughout Brazil. Some state governments financed projects submitted by the unemployed, but in São Paulo the majority of financing came from the Paulista Association of Solidarity in Unemployment (APSD) and was only given to groups registered with the Association.[6] Once again it was women who were most interested in the schemes which covered a wide range of petty commodity production such as bread making, confectionary, tailoring and craft production.[7] These schemes were 'tailor-made' for women: they were located near the home, they used flexible work rota systems and initially there were few expectations that the financial remuneration would do more than help to sustain the family unit during periods of unemployment. However, some of these cooperatives became extremely successful and the share of the profits was comparable to women's wages in the formal sector. Some cooperatives were more successful than others, in financial terms, but most of them managed to provide subsistence wages for the unemployed who participated in them. Furthermore, some of the cooperatives gave a small percentage of their profits to the funds of the Unemployed Movement to help finance political action.

The initiatives for the cooperative work schemes were encouraged by the Unemployed Movement as a whole, but individual projects were devised and organized by the local Committees of the Unemployed or Solidarity Groups of the Unemployed.[8] The cooperatives were organized along democratic lines and decisions were made by the collective about how it would be run. Those who wished to participate had to work a minimum number of hours per week in order to keep their place in the cooperative and receive a share of the profits. Anyone who did not comply with these regulations had to leave (there were usually plenty of people willing to take their place). In some cases people who did not participate in the movement were part of these cooperatives because the only qualification necessary to join was to be unemployed, and many people eventually began to participate in the Unemployed Movement through cooperative work schemes. Relationships built up amongst the unemployed within the movement were strengthened by these schemes, and the services they provided benefited not only the unemployed but also the local community.

Mutualist schemes were, at one time or another, used by all the popular movements to resolve problems within the local community on a short-term basis. The popular movements found that considerable onus was placed on the urban poor themselves to find solutions to many of their demands such as creches, house construction, refuse collection and other services. The *Favela* Movements, for example, set up many mutualist schemes due to the difficulty of getting general services installed in the *favelas* and the time it took for *favelados* (*favela* dwellers) to gain these services through their struggles.

Between 1983 and 1985, the *Favela* Movement in Vila Sezamo organized a mutualist scheme for rubbish collection as well as for the construction of the movement's headquarters. In both cases, volunteers came from within and outside of the movement and even *favelados* who did not participate in the scheme gave money, tools or supplied food for those who undertook the physical work. The rubbish collection scheme was probably the best example of how these schemes tended to work.

Despite several attempts by the *Favela* Movement in Vila Sezamo to get their rubbish collected, the local council had refused them an internal service. Rats, vermin and mosquitoes had created health problems and the movement proposed that the council send a truck to a point outside of the *favela* each week and the *favelados* themselves would deposit the rubbish. The council accepted their proposal and promised to provide placards to be posted around the *favela* to prevent dumping and to install large litter bins at various locations within the *favela*.[9] The mutualist scheme arose from this proposal. Part of the scheme was to educate people to take a pride in the *favela* and keep their environment clean. Members of the *Favela* Commission held consciousness-raising meetings about the importance of their scheme to people's health and its benefits to the community itself. They also made house-to-house visits telling people about the scheme and asked for volunteers or practical help to make it a success. The scheme was the first of its kind, and its success encouraged the *Favela* Commission to introduce other kinds of schemes, including cooperative work projects, to benefit the *favela* community.

Oral history: the story told and retold

The use of oral history as a form of politicization was fundamental to the creation of a political identity for the movements themselves and for those who participated in them. Many of the popular movements do write down the history of their organization and struggles and use this material for the conscientization of new members. But the use of oral history is a rich and personalized tribute to past events and the contribution of each of the participants to the movements' 'success'. An oral history is developed from individual and collective experiences of those who participate in the movements. It is a vivid, living testimony of their political defeats and victories which are recalled at any and every opportunity to demonstrate the courage, tenacity and commitment of those who participate in them. Women, without a doubt, are the most avid subscribers to this form of politicization. They take great pride in their ability to recall events and even conversations in the minutest detail, often dramatizing the conflicts and confrontations with government or the police during their struggles. It is the way in which they reaffirm the importance of their participation in this form of political organization and the viability of the popular movements as an instrument for political change and social change.

In the meetings held after a political protest has been carried out, those who participated recall their personal experiences of the struggle and how they felt about it. Not everyone who participates in the popular movements can or will participate in their protests and demonstrations. The practice of using individual accounts of events informs those who were not present, but it is also a means of encouraging far more people to participate. Everyone is given a chance to speak or ask questions; the emphasis is on the individual contribution to the collective; the relaxed, enthusiastic atmosphere of these meetings alleviates the inevitable anticlimax which follows the intense period of political activity leading up to collective action. For those who participate in the popular movement, *every* struggle is a success which is counted not only by the concrete victories obtained through the struggle in relation to the demands of the movement but also by its impact on both the government *and* the participants.

These meetings are an emotive and exciting vindication of the latest political protest organized and carried out by the popular movements. No one seems to tire of the inevitable repetition within individual recollections; each one is different because it discloses a personal interpretation and experience of the protest. Each moment of the protest is relived and retold in an atmosphere of excited interest and anticipation which conjures up an intricate web of mental pictures in the minds of those who listen attentively to these recollections of the latest act of political defiance. Individual acts of courage are recorded and acknowledged in these meetings; even those who suffered personal hardships through their participation in the protest are pointed out and applauded. It is here that the history of a movement is recorded and developed, not through the eyes of an observer but through the recollections of political actors themselves.

The oral history of the popular movements catalogues both the triumphs and tribulations of their political practice, and those who participate in the movements are the ones who make and develop this history. The past successes of a movement are often what sustains its organization and the political commitment of those who participate in the movements in some of the more difficult and less successful periods of its political action. Women in particular are eager to record their political experiences, to create for themselves and reaffirm a specific political identity, one in which women are not inconsequential but successful political actors. In this way, oral history is not merely an adjunct to the political action of the popular movements but one of the key elements of their political practice.

The transformation of gender interests

The many forms of political action employed by the popular urban social movements, as we can see here, have many different functions. The need for conscientization or the creation of solidarity within the movements themselves was not always the initial purpose of these practices but often became the reason for continuing or developing them. Some practices arose from a simple need or idea expressed by those who participate in the movements whilst others were a direct attempt to conscientize the popular classes. Irrespective of the impetus for or the development of such forms of political practice used by the popular movements, in most cases they reflected the desires and needs of the women who dominated this form of political organization. In doing so, it gave many women the chance to 'improve' themselves and develop both socially and politically by utilizing a wide range of skills to enhance and expand their new-found political ones.

The political mobilization of low-income women arose from their practical gender interests as well as structural class differences in Brazilian society. Their daily battles for economic survival prioritized political action around issues related to the access of the popular classes to the benefits of economic development. The provision of urban infrastructure, adequate healthcare and transport not only affect women's activities in the reproductive sphere but also have limiting effects on their access to employment and income-generating activities. Nevertheless, as opposed to gender-'neutral' analyses (Slater 1985), it would be wrong to describe urban social movements as women's social movements (Safa 1990); this would fail to acknowledge not only the participation of men in these movements but also the affects of gender relations within and between these movements and institutional politics.

In the popular movements men can account for up to 40 per cent of the participants. Gender relations in this context are different to those in institutional politics. Women acquire political experience in association with men, but in a sphere where they predominate it is frequently on their own terms. As we have seen here, the political practices of the movements are strongly influenced by women and as such their political development is directly related to their gender subordination in society. They are able to strengthen and legitimate their political role and become experienced political actors. Those who go on to enter institutional politics are able to do so from a much stronger position and with greater confidence in their political abilities (Corcoran-Nantes 1988; Moser 1987).

Through their struggles around practical gender interests, women who have a similar socio-economic experience in Brazilian society develop greater solidarity and awareness in relation to strategic gender interests. Opposition to women's political participation at a personal political level reinforces their experience of gender inequality in other spheres. Through their contact with political parties and trade unions they develop cross-class links with other women from feminist groups and women's organizations. These links have been strengthened by their association in struggles around strategic gender interests. By developing a political practice which emphasizes not only class inequality but also gender inequality, these women began to construct a gender identity around strategic interests based on their socio-economic experience. Consequently, low-income women were able to articulate their priorities and interests in relation to other class-based feminist groups and organizations and to pursue strategic gender interests through their political action.

Nevertheless, for low-income women practical gender interests take priority in their political struggles and it is here that they have built the necessary basis for unity and solidarity. Class oppression, to which their gender subordination is directly related, has forced women to organize around issues related to their very survival and that of their families. These issues comprise the major social and economic problems in developing countries, and in this context strategic gender issues take a secondary role or may not be considered at all. In Brazil, however, amongst women of the urban poor, female consciousness has developed around strategic gender interests, and whether they choose to describe these as feminist or not is irrelevant. What is important for women of the popular classes is that their concerns are firmly on the political agenda.

NOTES

I would like to thank Pepe Roberts, Lynne Brydon and the editors for comments on an earlier version of this chapter.

1 This chapter is dedicated to Elisabeth Souza-Lobo whose untimely death earlier this year represented a significant loss to Brazilian feminist research and to those, like myself, who had the privilege of knowing and working with her.
2 The material on which this chapter is based arises out of a wider research project conducted on the role of women in the organization and formation of popular urban social movements in Brazil during the period 1983–85. The research was funded by a postgraduate award from the Economic and Social Research Council. Fieldwork was carried out in nine low-income neighbourhoods from three different regions of the Greater São Paulo metropolitan area: Embu and Sta Emilia in the Southern Zone; Vila Rica, Vila Antonieta, Vila Sezamo and São Matheus in the Eastern Zone; and Diadema, São Caetano do Sul and Maua in the 'ABC' region to the far east of the metropolitan area. Interviews were held with over 200 women who were active participants in popular movements. All material and quotations used in this chapter are from the author's primary data, unless otherwise stated.
3 Many women faced strong opposition to their political involvement from their partners. In many regions women's self-help groups gave practical help and support to those who were victims of domestic violence or who wished to separate from their partners.
4 The Health Movement in conjunction with feminist groups and women's organizations had strongly opposed all family planning proposals by the government for being far too authoritarian. For example, in 1985 the Head of the Armed Forces insisted that the question of family planning should come under their jurisdiction because it was a matter of National Security!

5   Paulo Freire created a literacy course which utilized political material as subject matter to teach adults, in the space of forty lessons, the basic skills of reading and writing while at the same time developing a political consciousness in the student. In recent years the Brazilian Catholic Church has adapted this method for the conscientization of the popular classes and many political militants attend weekend courses, held by the Church, to learn how to deliver this course.

6   The APSD was one of the successful outcomes of political action by the Unemployed Movement. This Association was sponsored by various ecumenical bodies and Churches in São Paulo to give financial support to cooperatives and employment schemes initiated by the unemployed themselves.

7   In all the Brazilian states where help was offered by the government the majority of projects were either submitted by women or were to be carried out by them.

8   Not all the Committees of the Unemployed had cooperative work schemes as part of their organization. Some had allotment schemes which worked on a cooperative basis to grow fruit and vegetables to supplement the diets of the unemployed. These schemes were organized in the same way as other cooperatives, the only difference being that production was for use rather than for sale

9   People from adjacent neighbourhoods or towns often used *favelas* as dumping grounds for their rubbish. Part of the scheme was to prevent this happening by putting up official notices threatening the culprits with prosecution.

REFERENCES

Blachman, M (1973) *Eve in an Adamocracy*, Occasional Papers No. 5, New York University.

Brydon, L. and Chant, S. (1989) *Women in the Third World*, Aldershot: Edward Elgar.

Cardoso, R. C. L. (1984) 'Movimentos sociais urbanos: balanço critico', in B. Sorj and M. H. de Almeida (eds) *Sociedade e Politica no Brasil Pos 1964*, São Paulo: Editora Brasiliense: 226–39.

Censo Demographico do Brasil 1990.

Chaney, E. (1979) *Supermadre: Women in Politics in Latin America*, Austin: University of Texas Press.

Chuchryk, P. (1989) 'Subversive mothers: the opposition to the military regime in Chile', in S. M. Charlton, J. Everett and K. Staudt (eds) *Women, the State and Development*, Albany: State University of New York Press.

Corcoran-Nantes, V. (1988) 'Women in grass roots protest politics in São Paulo, Brazil', Unpublished Ph.D. Thesis, Department of Sociology, University of Liverpool.

—— (1990) 'Women and popular urban social movements in São Paulo, Brazil', *Bulletin of Latin American Research* 9(2): 249–64.

Cutrufelli, M. R. (1983) *Women of Africa: Roots of Oppression*, London: Zed Books.

Evers, T., Muller-Plantenberg; C. and Spessart, S. (1982) 'Movimentos de bairro e estado: lutas na esfera de reprodução na America Latina', in J. A. Moises (ed.) *Cidade, Povo e Poder*, Rio de Janeiro: Paz e Terra: 110–60.

Filet Abreu de Souza, J. (1980) 'Paid domestic service in Brazil', *Latin American Perspectives* 24(7).

Jaquette, J. (1980) 'Female 'political' participation' in Latin America', in J. Nash. and H. Safa (eds) *Sex and Class in Latin America*, New York: Bergin Publishers.

—— (ed.) (1989) *The Women's Movement in Latin America: Feminism and the Transition to Democracy*, London: Unwin Hyman.

Kucinski, B. (1982) *Abertura uma historia de uma crise*, São Paula: Brasil Debates.

Machado, L. (1988) 'The participation of women in the health movement of Jardim Nordeste, in the Eastern Zone of São Paulo, Brazil: 1976–1985', *Bulletin of Latin American Research* 7(1): 47–63.

Mattelart, M. (1980) 'The feminine version of the coup d'etat', in J. Nash and H. I. Safa (eds) *Sex and Class in Latin America*, New York: Bergin Publishers.

Mies, M. (1988) *Women: The Last Colony*, London: Zed Books.

Molyneux, M. (1985) 'Mobilization without emancipation? Women's interest, state and revolution in Nicaragua', in D. Slater (ed.) *New Social Movements and the State in Latin America*, Amsterdam: CEDLA, Latin American Studies 29: 233–60.

Moser, C.O.N. (1987) 'Mobilisation is women's work: the struggle for infrastructure in Guayaquil, Ecuador', in C.O.N. Moser and L. Peake (eds) *Women, Human Settlements and Housing*, London and New York: Tavistock Publications: 166-94.

Offe, K. (1985) 'New social movements: challenging the boundaries of institutional politics', *Social Research* 52: 817-68.

Safa, H.I. (1990) 'Women's social movements in Latin America', *Gender and Society* 4(3).

Slater, D. (ed.) (1985) *New Social Movements and the State in Latin America*, Amsterdam, CEDLA, Latin American Studies 29.

Stevens, E. (1973) 'Machismo and marianismo', *Society* 10(6).

Tabak, F. (l983) *Autoritarismo e Participação da Mulher*, Rio de Janeiro: Edições Graal Ltda.

Wanderley, L. E. (1980) 'Movimientos sociales populares: aspectos económicos e políticos', *Encontros com a Civilização Brasileira* 25: 107–31.

5

THE MOTHER OF WARRIORS AND HER DAUGHTERS

The women's movement in Kenya

Wilhelmina Oduol and Wanjiku Mukabi Kabira

As women's activism took on a 'womanist' or 'feminist' shape in the 1960s and 1970s, observers such as journalists began identifying it as a single movement. Indeed, in many Western countries, activists gave what they were doing the name 'women's movement,' 'women's liberation movement,' or 'feminist movement.' The African case does not fit any singular definition, argue the authors of this chapter on the Kenyan women's movement. Activism was plural, multiple, and thus barely resembled a unified entity. Moreover, in Africa as in other colonized regions, women's struggles targeted a constantly changing variety of forces, beginning with colonial oppressors late in the nineteenth century or the men in their ethnic groups who menaced their livelihoods. Welfare groups, choruses of women singing ballads critical of men with power, and even government-sponsored clubs, round out a portrait that is anything but simple.

Not only were the targets of women's activism multiple, but ways of agitating were multiple too. Support groups were common; so were the deeds of individual writers, researchers, judges, and volunteer workers. How do such individualistic and sometimes fragmented efforts constitute a social or political movement? What are the advantages and disadvantages of this pluralism for advancing women's causes? Are there lessons to be learned from the Kenyan experience?

* * *

When we were first approached about writing on the women's movement in Kenya, one question emerged in both of our minds: Is there a women's movement in Kenya? When we considered this, we simultaneously answered, 'No.' After more reflection, we began to ask, 'If there is no women's movement, what is this intense activity going on around us of women's group meetings, workshops, seminars, and even individual women agitating for women's rights in the courts, in the media, and on the streets?' We were thus faced with the dilemma of deciding whether a women's movement does exist in Kenya and, if so, what it implies in the Kenyan context.

Our conceptualization of a conventional definition of a movement, emphasizing a common objective, continuity, unity, and coordination, led to our initially negative reaction on the question of a women's movement in Kenya. It is true that the Kenyan context has always been characterized by women's active participation in activities aimed at improving the status of women in all spheres of development. These activities are manifested in individual efforts, self-help groups, occupational associations, non-governmental organizations, business enterprises, and social welfare activities, among others. In fact, women's group efforts are so vibrant that researcher and writer Patricia Stamp once described them 'as the source of the most radical consciousness to be found in the countryside providing women with a basis for resistance to exploitation.'[1] This vibrant activity is equally evident in urban settings, where women from all walks of life transcend individual, cultural, class, tribal, religious, and other barriers to identify issues of common concern and design strategies to address them.

However, these efforts are often uncoordinated and fragmented, with individual women or women's groups developing specific structures and agendas in response to local situations. This approach to the movement often beguiles both women themselves and the rest of the public into believing that the women's movement either does not exist or is insignificant. In a few instances the movement has manifested itself as being coordinated and cohesive. This occurred during the social and political upheavals of the 1950s, when the whole country was agitating for political independence from colonial domination. The same cohesiveness was apparent during the democratization process of the 1990s, when women organized two national conventions to map strategies for the future development of Kenyan women. However, these moments of cohesiveness have been so limited that few people recognize their significance for the movement as a whole.

Perhaps the diversity that characterizes the women's movement is a strength rather than a weakness. In a social context where tribal, class, educational, and geographical differences make the identification and pursuit of common issues of concern difficult, it seems realistic to highlight this heterogeneity and strategize accordingly rather than operate under an illusion of homogeneity, which in reality *does not* and *cannot* exist in the Kenyan context. Janet Burja underscores this point by asserting that 'we cannot belabor the fact that women cannot be thought of as a single category, even though there are important and occasionally unifying struggles in which they engage.'[2] For Diane Margolis, the major strength of the 1985 United Nations Third World Conference on Women held in Nairobi was 'recognizing and accepting that women have different perspectives, issues and priorities and strategizing to meet these needs.'[3] The diversity that characterizes the women's movement in Kenya does not in any way detract from the strength of the movement. On the contrary, it helps stimulate the movement's activism and creativity.

The women's movement is not a recent phenomenon in Kenya. Its origins lie in the precolonial period, when women formed self-help groups and work parties to assist one another during periods of economic and social stress. This tradition of forming women's groups to consolidate efforts for addressing problems has carried forward into the contemporary period. As a result of socio-economic and political changes occurring in Kenyan society, the women's movement now faces a number of major challenges. Kenyan society is still characterized by overarching patriarchal dominance and repressive sociocultural practices. Women are divided based on educational, economic, and geographic differences. Finally, the state and donor organizations have tended to be a cooptive and divisive influence.

In examining the evolution of the women's movement in Kenya from precolonial times to the present, we consider the women's movement to be synonymous with the emergence of women's groups. After providing a brief overview of Kenyan political and economic history and its impact on women, we examine these group activities at three levels: the women's group movement, largely rural and grassroots in nature; formal women's organizations; and the actions of individual women. We discuss the role played by the dominant patriarchal structures and existing sociocultural practices in shaping the women's movement. We analyze the extent to which the state has undermined these efforts by manipulating those in leadership positions and interfering with the autonomy of existing organizations. We examine the role of donor agencies and Western development approaches in shaping the movement. Finally, we assess women's efforts to empower themselves at the personal level.

Background: the social and political context

The country now known as Kenya encompasses diverse ethnic groups and geographical features. Along the coast its ports have supported an extensive and sophisticated trade economy for centuries. Its fertile highlands encouraged colonization and continue to support extensive cash crop production. However, it is estimated that only about 20 percent of Kenya's land is suitable for intensive agriculture. Much of the rest is semi-arid and can support only periodic grazing. Distinct societies developed in these diverse conditions; this diversity has at times led to bitter tribal competition and conflict, which remain a dominant feature of Kenyan political and social life.

As European influence in the region increased, these distinct and often conflicting groups were brought together as a British protectorate in 1895 and annexed as a colony in 1920. The temperate climate and fertile soil of the highlands drew large numbers of European settlers, who appropriated land for large plantations, which primarily produced coffee and tea. The colonial administration instituted a series of laws and policies to ensure adequate cheap African labor to support large-scale plantation production. Both men and women initiated organized protests against these policies and the appropriation of their land and independence. A number of smaller protests culminated in the guerrilla independence war of the 1950s that came to be known as the Mau Mau war.

After an experimental period of shared rule, Kenya gained independence in 1963. Jomo Kenyatta, a Kikuyu leader and head of the Kenya African National Union (KANU), became president. Sometimes bitter struggles for leadership occurred in the new nation, and loyalty to rival political parties closely followed tribal lines. Although there was official provision for multi-partyism, Kenyatta effectively silenced any opposition. His ability to quell the opposition and concentrate power within his own Kikuyu ethnic community led Kenyatta to become one of the most powerful leaders in Africa. In spite of his often repressive tactics and their lingering legacy for the country's political development, his reign, which lasted until his death in 1978, was marked by relative peace, political stability, and economic prosperity.

KANU continues to dominate Kenyan politics under Kenyatta's successor, Daniel arap Moi. Moi moved swiftly to consolidate his position by amending the constitution to legitimize a one-party state, silenced all dissident activity, and strengthened KANU's power. He effectively controls all three branches of government, his words and directives are law, and he brooks no opposition. The recent movement for democracy and the official emergence of multi-partyism in 1992 have done little to alter this situation.

For women, this increasingly repressive political climate has clearly not been conducive to challenging state policy or organizing protest. However, the women's movement has built on many of its strengths to overcome the legacy of patriarchy. Women have continued to build on their traditional modes of organizing to galvanize into an increasingly powerful economic and political force.

Collaborative effort: a strategy against cultural and patriarchal dominance

In traditional times women cooperated and mobilized themselves to assist one another through self-help groups; membership was based on friendship, kinship networks, and common need. Work parties were formed to perform crucial labor activities within the household and on the farms, especially during peak agricultural seasons and during illness and childbearing,[4] thus providing a form of maternity and sick leave. This tradition of community self-help was practiced by ethnic groups throughout much of Kenya,[5] providing a firm foundation for women's self-help activities and a strong women's movement.[6]

The formation of women's self-help groups evolved as a coping mechanism in male-dominated societies whose patriarchal structure ensured that most women did not have adequate access to and control of resources, including land, cattle, and other basic commodities. In an economy revolving around agriculture, women had only user rights to land passed through the husband's patrilineage; these traditional land tenure systems made few provisions for unmarried, divorced, or widowed women. In most societies all property was inherited through the male line. When women today ask for control of title deeds or access to credit, they are challenging these deep traditions.

These structures also denied women access to decision-making processes. Almost all societies now part of Kenya had political systems in which clan elders made decisions concerning the political and legal affairs of the community; these councils of elders were male dominated, and women rarely participated in them.[7] In some strongly male-dominated societies, such as pastoral communities, women were not even accorded adult status. This gender based ideology of oppression was institutionalized through a number of mechanisms, including the legal system, educational and religious institutions, and customary beliefs and practice.[8]

The gender-based division of labor also revealed the culturally determined and socially constructed power relationships evident in traditional societies. Despite this stereotyping of gender roles, in reality women performed all productive and reproductive functions in addition to off-farm community activities. They fetched water, cooked, collected firewood, and cared for both animals and family members; they also did most of the manual agricultural work, tilling the land, planting, weeding, harvesting, and processing food. In addition to ensuring that women and girls did most of the work, these norms accorded higher status to the male roles, a situation that continues in the present.

Women's realization that their marginalized position in society resulted in common problems not experienced by men motivated them to initiate ways of sharing and addressing these problems. Forming cooperative work parties was a positive strategy for coping with the work burden. Women also expressed their dissatisfaction through various cultural forms, such as song, poetry, and dance. In a Maasai prayer described by writer and researcher Wanjiku Kabira, a young woman describes her grief at the prospect of an arranged, polygamous marriage:[9]

> My father
> Why do you send me to
> Ole Kasero
> Why do you send me
> to such an old man
> Ole Kasero has eleven wives
> You say he can look after me
> but he is too old
> > Father why do you send me to
> > Ole Kasero

Such songs are not unusual in traditional Kenyan societies. Women challenged gender-based oppression in institutions such as marriage, polygamy, and political governance, which perpetuated their marginalized position, and found non-confrontational artistic methods of expressing their challenge.

The growth of the women's movement

During the colonial period the form and substance of women's resistance changed considerably. These changes were catalyzed by colonial policies and labor laws designed to meet the demand of a market-oriented economy, which disrupted traditional social structures and shifted responsibilities. The colonial period saw the strengthening of the women's movement. This was typified by two parallel movements that were formed almost simultaneously, and both drew their roots from the traditional support networks and self-help groups.

The first movement was composed of militant but informal associations of women who mobilized existing women's groups to rebel against those colonial policies that were destroying the local culture and economy and institutionalizing colonial structures and ideology. The colonial government imposed a series of laws and legislation that drew Kenya into the exploitative colonial global market economy. In 1902 an ordinance was enacted that 'empowered' traditional village headmen to enforce forced labor policies. Between 1912 and 1922 the Native Authority Ordinance reinforced this policy by legalizing forced labor on European farms with minimal pay. The 1926 Native Ordinance and the hut and poll tax further ensured the availability of labor in European farms by necessitating cash income to meet tax obligations.[10] This resulted in massive male out-migration in search of wage employment.[11] Traditional family and social networks were profoundly disrupted.

As a direct consequence of these policies, many women became heads of households,[12] and their labor time greatly expanded as they continued to shoulder all their traditional responsibilities while taking on those of men. Women relied on their traditional work groups to help meet these responsibilities. Furthermore, in areas where cash crops were predominant, women performed all the manual tasks, such as picking coffee and tea, while men dominated the mechanized agricultural work. The Swynnerton Plan of 1955 led to the privatization of land and the issuing of title deeds to men by the colonial government. The plan sanctioned large tracts of land for cash crop production while sharply reducing land available for subsistence production, a sector dominated by women. This resulted in the erosion of women's customary rights and further limited their access to land.

The situation was exacerbated by the exploitation of natural resources for cash crop production, which resulted in extensive overcultivation, overgrazing, and soil erosion. To rectify this situation, the colonialists forced women to undertake soil conservation measures such as terracing, planting trees, intercropping, and engaging in mixed farming. This compounded women's workloads and left them with limited time to attend to their numerous other responsibilities.

All of this led to intense debate among women, which culminated in open rebellion in the 1930s and 1950s. A few women mobilized existing women's groups in a series of riots. According to the colonial commissioner at that time, 'If left unchecked, [they] might have precipitated a landslide in government authority.'[13] Women in Muranga district mobilized their groups to resist soil conservation measures in 1948:

> 2,500 women from Muranga danced and sang and informed everyone that they would not take part in soil conservation mainly because they felt they had enough to do at home. [When the District Commissioner ordered their arrest,] they were quickly released by a large crowd of their own sex brandishing sticks and shouting Amazon war cries.[14]

Igembe women looted an Indian shop whose owner was not giving them a fair price for their produce.[15] In 1947 Kiambu women refused to pick coffee because they felt they were being underpaid.[16]

Numerous examples of women's mobilization also occurred during the Mau Mau war of 1952, which was fought to liberate Kenya from colonial domination and reclaim lost lands. Up to 5 percent of the forest fighters were women, and women also supported the war by organizing their work groups to prepare and carry food into the forest, hide firearms, and convey messages. As is discussed later, some women also rose to prominent leadership positions in the liberation struggle. In addition, women in central Kenya broke away from the most influential African political group of the time, the Agikuyu Central Association. Women characterized the group as chauvinistic in its approach toward issues and dominated by men, who assumed all the leadership positions and marginalized women. The women left to form their own group, the Mumbi Central Association, named for the mythical mother of the Agikuyu.

These examples of women's militant activities during the colonial era demonstrate that women were fighting oppression at two levels. They were fighting colonial domination, which denied them control of their lives in all spheres and totally disrupted the mechanisms that organized society. They were also fighting a patriarchal structure that provided all the opportunities to men while marginalizing women. Men engaged in cash crop production and reaped its benefits; they also reduced their workloads by using modern technologies, leaving the more menial tasks to women. As a result of disruptions in the traditional division of labor, women shouldered all responsibilities, while men worked away from home. The women resented this and fought against it.

Parallel to this more militant movement was the establishment in 1952 of a nationally based women's organization called Maendeleo Ya Wanawake (MYWO), which means 'Progress for Women' in Swahili. It was formed by a group of white settlers and administrators' wives who sought to advance the status of women according to Western values. They mobilized traditional women's work groups and trained them in childcare, hygiene, cooking, home sanitation, handicrafts, and other traditional activities.

The colonial government hoped that the interactions between white and black women within this organization would diffuse the tensions that were culminating in the liberation war. This is clearly evidenced in MYWO's close alliance with the colonial government during the Mau Mau uprising of the 1950s. In return for this support, the government awarded MYWO an annual grant for capital development and equipment, and its members were exempted from forced labor by the colonialists.[17] In fact, for many in Central Province in the 1950s and early 1960s, MYWO was synonymous with the colonial government and its homeguards. This created clear tensions between Mau Mau activists and those women's groups that supported them, on the one hand, and members of MYWO on the other. Ironically, after independence the new government sought to maintain this close association with MYWO. MYWO's close relationship with the ruling party, KANU, has created similar tensions with other women's organizations and activists in the contemporary period.

Scholarly opinion is divided on MYWO's success in promoting the cause of women. Some see MYWO as one of the few organizations that has successfully mobilized women's groups from all over Kenya and coordinated their activities in an effort to improve the status of women. Authors such as Ruth Nasimiyu and Shanyisa Khasiani, for example, quote escalating membership figures to support this assertion.[18] They argue that, while there were only 508 women's groups with a membership of 36,970 in 1954, today there are more than 3,000 registered groups coordinated by MYWO. They further assert that MYWO is the only women's organization that has provided a sense of continuity for the women's movement over the past three decades. It has weathered all sorts of obstacles since the colonial era, yet still retains its vitality.

Opposing views hold that MYWO has been vulnerable to political manipulation by the existing regime. Nzomo, for example, notes that in 1989 the organization was co-opted by the ruling party government.[19] Its elections were grossly interfered with by male KANU politicians who had picked their own candidates for the leading posts. Audrey Wipper also asserts that MYWO's acceptance of the status quo has limited its effectiveness as a membership organization since the leaders spend their time promoting the interests of the ruling party while ignoring the members' needs.[20] As already noted, KANU and the regime have used increasingly repressive measures to consolidate power. One tactic has been to try co-opting and controlling popular organizations, including MYWO. Because of MYWO's popularity and influence among women's groups all over the country, the government has a strong interest in co-opting it to win its members' support.

The women's movement in a postcolonial context

In addition to the efforts of Maendeleo Ya Wanawake, a number of other women's organizing and advocacy initiatives have emerged in the post colonial era. These efforts can be classified into three broad categories: the women's group movement, which is concentrated in rural areas; formalized women's organizations largely based in urban centers; and the efforts of individual women. The following sections highlight the objectives and activities of these categories of women's initiatives and assess the extent to which they have succeeded in improving the overall status of Kenyan women.

The women's group movement

The women's group movement refers to the informal voluntary women's groups that have proliferated all over the countryside and, to a lesser extent, in the urban centers. These groups are typically formed to engage in business enterprises, community projects, and revolving loan programs. The popularity of these groups is so marked that the 1988 *Women's Bureau*

Annual Report put the total number of groups at 27,000, with more than 1 million members.[21] Just as traditional self-help groups based their efforts on welfare-oriented and economic activities and utilized social, friendship, and kinship networks to draw their members, the women's group movement in the postcolonial era uses similar mechanisms as the basis for group formation. Membership is usually small (between five and twenty), with the majority coming from the same community and having little or no education. This reflects Kenya's low female literacy rates: of the 80 percent of women who live in rural areas, 62 percent are illiterate.[22] Leadership within the groups generally depends on popularity, although in some groups women with more education and higher socio-economic status tend to dominate leadership positions. They bring skills and exposure that facilitate managing their group's programs. For this reason, a few groups also have male members. Many of the groups are linked with national or international women's organizations, which act as channels for technical and financial assistance to the groups from donors or the government.

The groups' activities are wide-ranging and often defy generalization. Mazingira Institute describes the myriad activities in the following way:

> A group whose main goal is to own a business may also create an emergency welfare fund (through regular contributions) to help needy members, destitute children or homeless mothers in the community. Groups also incorporate educational activities in their meetings, welcome visits from health workers and agricultural advisors.[23]

Nevertheless, broad categorization is possible. Welfare groups generally concentrate on providing moral and material support to members during times of need, such a weddings, births, and funerals. Self-help groups organize to actively address community needs, such as constructing water cisterns, schools, bridges, dispensaries, and roads. Income-generating groups seem to have made the greatest strides toward the self-empowerment of women, particularly in the rural areas. Since traditionally women did not own resources or handle income, income earned and projects owned by women either individually or collectively to some extent help reduce their dependence. Illustrative examples of this include initiatives taken by women in Central Province to provide permanent roofing for their houses;[24] these efforts were so successful and prominent that the groups came to be known as *mabati* (iron roofing) women groups. Mazingira Institute also provides examples of women's groups that have transformed mutual welfare activities into revolving loan societies, investor groups, highly structured labor collectives, and so on.[25] Even more revolutionary, women's groups have bought land, business premises, and other properties. This signifies that women are moving away from merely coping with their traditional status to challenging and redressing it. The sense of empowerment derived from ownership of property is described by Rahab Wabici, a woman from Central Province, in referring to the land her group bought: 'I am a free woman. I bought this piece of land through my group. I can lie on it, work on it, keep goats or cows. What more do I want? My husband cannot sell it. It is mine:'[26]

However, while the women's group movement continues to make major strides in addressing issues of concern to women, it also faces major obstacles. The patriarchal administrative machinery blocks many of the women's attempts to challenge existing structures – land is not subdivided, title deeds are not released, and legal cases sometimes remain in court for decades. A formidable obstacle also emanates from the state and KANU, which realize that as a majority of voters are women, they have the potential to greatly influence the political direction of the country. Furthermore, if united, the women's group movement poses a major threat to male superiority and dominance in Kenyan society. To dilute this threat, the state has often manipulated and shaped the direction of the movement to suit its purposes. It does this by using divisive politics based on class, rural–urban, ethnic, and educational differences among women. Politicians often co-opt women's groups by appointing their own wives, relatives, or other partisan women as leaders, thereby ensuring votes during election periods.

Another threat to the women's group effort is the influence of donor agencies in shaping its structures, objectives, and activities. Donors' work with women's groups through national coordinating organizations such as MYWO, the National Council of Women of Kenya (NCWK), and the Young Women's Christian Association (YWCA). Because many of the donor agencies still adhere to a women-in-development (WID) approach, they focus largely on welfare-oriented projects. WID posits that women, as a disadvantaged category, need to be integrated into development projects. Carefully designed strategies and projects have been implemented in attempts to improve women's status, but without challenging fundamental gender relations. Typically, women engage in small projects in areas such as beehive keeping, poultry, goats, and kitchen gardens; often the benefits are minimal compared to the input. Other projects are based on outside ideas and technologies such as water pumps or grinding mills. When these break down, members tend to disassociate themselves from the project since the program idea was not internally generated. However, not all projects undertaken by women's groups are donor sponsored, nor do all those that are sponsored by donors fail. Nevertheless, groups that are affected negatively by donor influence find it difficult to achieve a sense of independence or empowerment.

Formalized women's organizations and associations

Apart from the women's group movement at the grassroots level, there are many formalized women's organizations and associations that have raised strong voices in the women's movement. These organizations are non-governmental, and most are formally registered under the statutes governing organizations in Kenya. Most of them are affiliated to international women's organizations whose objectives they largely adhere to. A few of them, such as the Kenya Finance Trust (KFT), the YWCA, and the NCWK, are umbrella organizations for grassroots women's groups.

The efforts of these organizations complement those of the small rural groups discussed above. They see women as agents of social change who should have their voices heard, and the activities and programs of these organizations are oriented toward empowering women at different levels. For many, empowerment implies the capacity of women to increase their self-reliance and internal strength through group effort and mobilization. Some also vocally challenge existing social structures and institutions and advocate the elimination of discriminatory practices against women at all levels.

These organizations use a variety of approaches. For example, while the YWCA primarily conducts welfare programs, it also worked aggressively for women's political empowerment during the democratization period of 1992, when it organized voter education for women throughout the country. The KFT focuses on economic empowerment of women by providing loans and business skills. This does not, however, prevent it from engaging in welfare activities such as childcare, family nutrition, and hygiene.

Perhaps the organization that best exemplifies these diverse activities is the NCWK. The NCWK was initiated as an affiliate of the International Council of Women in 1964 to coordinate women's organizations and groups in Kenya. While many of its programs, such as dressmaking, crafts, and home economics, reinforce women's traditional roles, it also works actively for women's empowerment. For example, during the multi-party era in the early 1990s, the NCWK launched the National Committee on the Status of Women to educate women on democracy and their political rights as Kenyan citizens. The organization also sponsors scholarships and training institutions for girls and women and initiated the well-known Greenbelt Movement to combat desertification in Kenya. It was instrumental in the First and Second Women's Conventions that took place in 1992 and 1993 and brought women together to strategize and demonstrate their solidarity in the struggle against gender-based oppression.

Several other organizations have been at the forefront of the women's movement and bear mention. The Kenya chapter of the International Federation of Women Lawyers has advocated for legal protection for children and women, especially widows; conducted outreach programs to educate grassroots women on their legal rights; provided legal counsel; and

112

challenged laws that discriminate against women. The League of Women Voters undertook a voter education program during the democratization process of 1992, published a booklet on women and democracy and advocates for women's rights in all spheres. The Antirape Organization conducts educational and policy programs against violence against women and provides support to women who have been physically assaulted by men.

Of special interest is the contribution of research organizations and writers to the liberation of Kenyan women. A major example of this is the Kenya chapter of the Association of African Women in Research and Development (AAWORD). AAWORD engages in action-oriented research on women's issues for policy implementation. Its publications, which include *Democratic Change in Africa*, *The Women's Movement in Kenya*, and *Women in Politics*, provide information to influence policy on a range of issues affecting women. AAWORD also conducts seminars in areas such as research methods, women and democratization, and violence against women. Its impact is largely felt in educated and professional circles.

Writers of fiction and poetry have continued the tradition of using cultural expression to articulate women's perspectives, concerns, and aspirations. In *Our Secret Lives*, by Wanjiku Kabira and Akinyi Nzioki,[27] women express their individual suffering. They reveal how the sanctioned status of women and girls continues to destroy the body, mind, and soul of women. In *They Have Destroyed the Temple*, women condemn their own alienation and the destruction of the temple within them and express the desire for full autonomy and a full life.[28] While these writers target both the public and academia, a major emphasis is on providing material to schools to reverse the socialization process in educational texts that portrays women as subordinate. While these writers have taken important and often courageous steps, given Kenya's strong patriarchal orientation, major changes in the perception of women require sweeping policy changes.

While formalized organizations work for women's rights, they face a number of problems. Just as the state developed mechanisms to weaken women's groups at the grassroots level, it also manipulates these formal organizations and employs divisive strategies that hamper unity. While the ruling party rewards and financially supports organizations such as MYWO that promote its interests, it harasses and heavily censures those organizations that challenge its oppressive patriarchal structure. For example, under the strong leadership of Professor Wangari Maathai, the NCWK was censored by KANU and the government for publicly challenging government policies that undermined women's progress and the promotion of human rights.

A major omission by the formalized organizations is that, while they concentrate on power relations in the public sphere, their members compromise their rights at the personal level. For many women, practicing at the personal level and within the home, what they advocate in public is impossible. Many women stay in unhappy marriages because divorce is culturally unacceptable. Many cannot make personal decisions on whether to stay single or whether to have children because they are going against societal expectations. Many activist women also continue to perform multiple roles at home and at work without expecting assistance from men because they risk being ostracized.

Without empowering themselves, women who advocate for female liberation cannot act as effective role models. It is therefore quite unfortunate that this vital element of women's liberation efforts has been largely ignored by existing organizations. Few groups have programs that deal with strengthening the personal lives of individual women through hotlines, counseling services, or centers for women who are victims of domestic and other forms of violence. Until these issues are effectively addressed, the impact of the women's movement will be limited in the real lives of Kenyan women.

Efforts of individual women

The importance of individual women's efforts toward individual and group liberation cannot be underestimated. While there is a paucity of literature on women's heroic actions during the precolonial era, colonial history abounds with examples of women who sacrificed their lives to fight for the cause of liberation and attain personal empowerment.

Scores of women joined men in the forests to fight colonial domination during the Mau Mau war of 1952. Of these women, a few rose to very senior ranks within the military. Likimani describes the case of Field Marshall Muthoni, a woman who attained this high military rank in a male-dominated army because of her courage and individual discipline.[29] She later defied all traditional constraints when she divorced her husband after the war by returning the dowry paid for her; he had told her that she needed to remember that she was just a woman.[30] At a time when divorce was a rare phenomenon and cultural inhibitions were at their height, this action was considered an extreme act of courage by female activists and total rebellion by the rest of society.

Wanjiru Nyamarata acted as a judge in the Mau Mau courts in Nakuru town in the center of Mau Mau activities. She passed sentences and was intensively involved in administering oaths and recruiting new guerrillas. As a result of these activities, she earned the name *Nyina-wa-Anake* (Mother of Senior Warriors).[31] This is particularly significant because during this period it was unheard of for women in any of the Kenyan ethnic communities to participate in judicial matters, let alone act as judges. The courageous feats of these individual women reversed societal perceptions of women from dependent and submissive to politically active, at least as long as the Mau Mau war lasted. Academic Tabitha Kanogo supports this assertion in noting that during this period 'leadership ceased to be a male preserve and there was no difference between male and female leaders.'[32]

In the post-independence period heroic women have persisted. Two cases that have had wide repercussions in Kenyan society are the famous 1987 Wambui Otieno case, where a woman fought to reverse patriarchal laws that prohibited her from burying her husband, and the case of Professor Wangari Maathai mentioned above.

S. M. Otieno, a legal practitioner from the western Luo tribe based in Nairobi, died in 1986. His wife, Wambui Otieno, a Kikuyu, and his relatives and clan members could not agree on a place of burial. She filed a suit in the high court claiming the right to bury her husband on their farm near Nairobi. Otieno's relatives claimed that no respected member of the Luo tribe could be buried away from his rural ancestral lands. This case generated heated debate and forced examination of a range of policies relevant to women. What are the rights of Kenyan women in relation to burial of their nearest kin and inheritance of property both in constitutional law and traditional customs? What is the relevance of constitutional law in a society in transition from a traditional to a modern economy? What are the tensions and conflicts resulting from ethnic intermarriages?

After four months of what the *Washington Post* described as 'the most sensational legal struggle in Kenya's history,' Wambui Otieno lost her case.[33] The judge declared that according to Luo custom, which is considered customary law, the deceased would be handed over to his brother, who would bury him in his rural home village. This case was illustrative of a society torn between adherence to familiar traditional norms and values and the need to adopt and respond to new values. More important, the case epitomized patriarchal gender-based oppression. The details revealed that in Luo customary law women were not only denied the right to bury their husbands and other close kin but were also not considered as their husbands' closest kin. After a man's death, his brother would be considered the next of kin and would look after the estate until the eldest son married; the wife would then be inherited by the husband's relatives. These customs also applied in many other Kenyan tribal communities.

The case also clearly revealed the openly discriminatory nature of Kenyan constitutional law. The court of appeal admitted that the constitution permits discriminatory laws on matters of personal law. The court did not even refer to the section of the constitution that specifically deals with the protection of fundamental rights and freedoms of the individual. In his concluding statement, the judge categorically stated that 'the plaintiff had no right to bury her husband under Luo customary law. She does not become the head of the family upon the death of her husband.'[34] Such blatant statements have led to a number of changes, such as the formation of a high-level commission dominated by women, to look into and change discriminatory laws and regulations.

Wangari Maathai has committed her life to the struggle against gender-based oppression and violation of human rights. A Ph.D., scientist, and internationally renowned environmentalist, Maathai headed the NCWK in the 1980s and initiated the Greenbelt Movement to mobilize women for environmental conservation efforts. During her participation in public life, she has spearheaded the women's movement by taking a position on national issues adversely affecting women's rights. In 1986 the NCWK challenged the validity of the queuing method, where votes are counted by persons publicly standing in line, rather than secret balloting. When Wambui Otieno was fighting for the right to bury her husband, only the NCWK under Maathai actively lobbied for the introduction of burial laws that protect the rights of women. She broadened the agenda of the women's movement by challenging the government on the environment and human rights. The most celebrated incident was her battle to stop the government erecting a skyscraper in the middle of the largest recreational park in Nairobi.[35] She was threatened, harassed, and thrown out of the offices she had occupied for over a decade. In March 1992 mothers of political prisoners being detained without trial went on strike; Maathai was the only elite woman who actively joined and fasted with the mothers. When these women were attacked and brutally beaten by the police, she was among the victims, beaten unconscious and admitted to the intensive care unit in Nairobi Hospital.[36] When she was endorsed as the presidential candidate by women delegates in June 1992, she turned the offer down, maintaining that she could best serve women in her capacity as an environmental conservationist and not as a politician.

Conclusion

At the beginning of this chapter, we emphasized that, while conventional notions of social movements do not fully explain the women's movement in Kenya, the movement does exist and is vibrant with activity. However, these efforts are often uncoordinated and fragmented, with individual women's groups developing specific strategies to suit local situations. We also noted that the movement has its roots in traditional forms of resistance to gender-based oppression. We argued that this resistance was expressed by developing strategies for coping with the burdens imposed by unequal gender division of labor and expressing silent resistance in artistic forms.

These less confrontational forms of resistance evolved in the colonial era to a more militant stand against colonialism and gender-based oppression, as embodied in protests and women joining in the guerrilla independence struggle. In the postcolonial context the movement has become more diversified. Women fight against male dominance as individuals and as members of groups. They strategize and formulate coping mechanisms ranging from welfare-oriented approaches to initiatives that aim at transforming the status of women in all areas of society. They are not satisfied with perpetuating the stereotyped roles of wife and mother that have been mapped out for them by society. They want equal pay for equal work, their own title deeds and other property, a share in reproductive work, and the freedom to shape not only their destiny but also the whole nation.

However, to attain their objectives, they must continue to fight the negative challenges posed by state, tribal, class, ideological, and cultural mechanisms that perpetuate their marginalized position. This requires more effective strategizing, the more vigorous pursuit of existent goals, and the ability to withstand opposition and harassment from a male-dominated society.

NOTES

1 P. Stamp, 'Kikuyu Women's Self-Help Groups: Towards an Understanding of the Relation Between Sex-Gender System and Mode of Production in Africa,' in C. Robertson and I. Berger, eds, *Women and Class in Africa* (New York: Holmes and Meier, 1986).

2 J. Burja, 'Urging Women to Redouble Their Efforts: Class, Gender, and Capitalist Transformation in Africa,' in C. Robertson and I. Berger, eds, *Women and Class in Africa* (New York: Holmes and Meier, 1986).

3 D. Margolis, 'Women's Movements Around the World: Cross-Cultural Comparisons,' *Gender and Society* 7, no. 3 (1993): 380.

4 R. Nasimiyu, 'The History of Maendeleo ya Wanawake Movement in Kenya,' in S. Khasiani and E. Njiro, eds, *The Women's Movement in Kenya* (Nairobi: Association of African Women for Research and Development, 1993).

5 B. Thomas, *Politics, Participation, and Poverty: Development Through Self-Help in Kenya* (Boulder: Westview Press, 1985), pp. 7–8.

6 Mazingira Institute, *Women and Development: A Kenya Guide* (Nairobi: Mazingira Institute, 1992).

7 W. M. Kabira and A. Nzioki, *Celebrating Women's Resistance* (Nairobi: Women Perspective Publications, 1993).

8 J. B. Ojwang and J. Mugambi, eds, *The S. M. Otieno Case: Death and Burial in Modern Kenya* (Nairobi: Nairobi University Press, 1989).

9 Kabira and Nzioki, *Celebrating Women's Resistance*, p. 27.

10 A. Pala, 'Daughters oft he Lakes and Rivers: Colonization and the Land Rights of Luo N Women,' in M. Eteinne and E. Leacock, eds, *Women and Colonization: Anthropological Perspectives* (New York: Praeger, 1980).

11 T. Kanogo, 'Kikuyu Women and Politics of Protest: Mau Mau,' in P. Halden MacDonald and A. Ardener, eds, *Images of Women in Peace and War: Cross-Cultural Perspectives* (London: Macmillan. 1987). Kanogo notes that in Central Province up to 50 percent of the men were short-term migrant laborers.

12 Republic of Kenya, *Agricultural Survey* (Nairobi: Government Printer, 1986). In Kitui district, male out-migration resulted in up to 36 percent of households being female headed.

117

13 Kenya National Archives, DC/FHI/ 27.1948, p. 1.
14 Kanogo, 'Kikuyu Women.'
15 H E. Lambert, *A Guide to Women's Organizations and Agencies Serving Women in Kenya* (Nairobi: Mazingira Institute, 1985), p. 100.
16 Kanogo, 'Kikuyu Women.'
17 J. Nzomo, 'The Kenya Women's Movement in a Changing Political Context' in S. Khasiani and E. Njiro, eds, *The Women's Movement in Kenya* (Nairobi: Association of African Women for Research and Development, 1993).
18 Nasimiyu, 'The History of Maendeleo ya Wanawake.'
19 Nzomo, 'The Kenya Women's Movement.'
20 A. Wipper, 'Equal Rights for Women in Kenya,' *Journal of Modern Studies* 9, no. 3 (1971): 427–42.
21 Republic of Kenya, *The Women's Bureau Annual Report* (Nairobi: Ministry of Culture and Social Services, Women's Bureau, 1988).
22 Republic of Kenya, *Kenya Literacy Survey* (Nairobi: Government Printer, 1988).
23 Mazingira Institute, *Women and Development*, p. 14.
24 M. Monsted, *Women's Groups in Rural Kenya and Their Role in Development* (Copenhagen: Center for Development Research, 1978).
25 Mazingira Institute, *Women and Development*, p. 8.
26 Kabira and Nzioki, *Celebrating Women's Resistance*, p. 75.
27 W. M. Kabira and A. Nzioki, *Our Secret Lives* (Nairobi: Phoenix 1992).
28 A. Nzioki and W. M. Kabira, eds, *They Have Destroyed the Temple* (Nairobi: Longman, 1993).
29 M. Likimani, *Women of Kenya: Twenty Years of Independence* (Nairobi: Giant Printers, 1983), p. 7.
30 Kabira and Nzioki, *Celebrating Women's Resistance*.
31 W. A. Oduol, 'Kenyan Women in Politics: An Analysis of Past and Present Trends:' in G. S. Were, ed., *TransAfrican Journal of History* Vol. 22: 166–80 (Nairobi: Gideon S. Were Press, 1993).
32 Kanogo, 'Kikuyu Women.'
33 *Washington Post*, 25 May 1987.
34 Okechi-Owiti, 'Some Socio-legal Issues,' in J.B.O. Ojwang and J.N.K. Mugambi, eds, *The S. M. Otieno Case: Death and Burial in Modern Kenya* (Nairobi: Nairobi University Press, 1989), p. 12.
35 Nzomo, 'The Kenya Women's Movement.'
36 *Standard*, 4 March 1992.

6

MINJUNG FEMINISM

Korean women's movement for gender and class liberation

Miriam Ching Yoon Louie

South Korea stands as a major example of a nation that has gained a modern industrial base because of globalization; its women appear a prime instance of those who have been victims first of colonialism and then of globalization of the economy. For the first half of the twentieth century, Japan subjected Korea to harsh and racist colonial rule. As Japanese militarism grew in the 1930s, thousands of Korean women were enslaved as prostitutes for the army and for a time continued as such for the US forces who defeated Japan in 1945. During the Cold War Korea was divided into a communist North Korea and a South Korea, which was allied with the United States. As a US ally, South Korea prospered from global investment of capital and from huge quantities of foreign aid, even though its government was a repressive dictatorship.

Oddly enough, the story of a postwar South Korean feminism begins here: in the labor movement, being crushed by squads of police in the 1970s. In fact, for almost two centuries women's common work experience has led to unionization and other organizations that build political unity. Women artisans in nineteenth-century Europe could be found agitating in front of city halls, parliaments, and factories for better working conditions. Many suffrage movements had large contingents of factory workers, and even after suffrage was obtained women workers lobbied for any number of causes to help their sex. Can meaningful movements for rights and social justice take shape when the trend of the past few decades has been the growth of global economic forces setting policies for small towns and entire nations alike? Since the postwar period, such globalization has brought large multinational corporations to set up plants in East Asia and other 'emerging' nations like South Korea. Governments in these countries have drawn the multinationals to install these factories by promising a docile female workforce that can be paid very low wages. As women flock to industries and sweatshops working for multinational firms, they suffer exploitation, putting in incredibly long hours for miniscule wages in addition to the tasks they have to perform as housewives and mothers. Sexual

119

harassment and political surveillance are also regular features of this work experience.

Studies show that women in emerging economies not only benefit from improved education and access to birth control, they find in factory work a source of solidarity and thus an avenue to political activism. This chapter hypothesizes that in the case of South Korea sexual harassment and the bad working conditions associated with the global economy shaped workers into feminists in the 1970s and 1980s. Workers, not the middle classes, built the road to South Korean feminism. This activism grew out of the mass movement of ordinary people seeking better work conditions and political democracy. However, women's agitation grew within an environment that was full of paradoxes.

* * *

Bad *koju chang* [pepper bean paste] is a grievance for 1 year; a bad wife is a grievance for 100 years

You can only get the real taste of dried fish and women if you beat them once every 3 days.

(Korean proverbs; Tieszen, 1977)

These two samples from the stockpile of misogynist folk sayings reveal centuries of socially sanctioned oppression of women. Yet from the rocky soil of sexism, a mass-based women's movement has sprouted. The feminist movement weds together the *minjung undong* (mass people's movement) with the struggle for *vo'song haebang* (women's liberation). The character of the Korean women's movement stems from two specific features: its intimate relation to the *minjung* movement, and the way the movement organizes around issues of gender and class.

First, the Korean women's movement developed in tandem with the broader *minjung* movement. *Minjung* movement origins are deeply rooted in the suffering of young women factory workers, whose super-exploited labor in export-oriented industries produced the precious start-up capital for South Korea's much touted 'economic miracle.' Their struggles riveted the attention and support of the budding democratic movement. As the movement grew, activists fleshed out feminist analysis and launched distinct women's organizations and coalitions.

Second, in terms of the intersection between gender and class, the movement brings its *minjung* orientation to organizing among women, focusing on the most oppressed women of the urban and rural poor. At the same time, within the broader masses, women are seen as 'the oppressed of the oppressed,' the core of the *minjung*. Subtle differences between socialist and Marxist feminists revolve around how to interpret the precise interpenetration of gender and class oppression.

Here a brief explanation of the concept of *minjung* is in order. The democratic movement reclaimed the term from the earlier anti-Japanese colonial movement, investing it with deep strategic, political, cultural, and spiritual meaning while fighting successive military dictatorships (1961–1992). *Minjung* ideology posits that the central thread running through Korean history is the oppression of the laboring masses and that the true national identity of Korea can be discovered in the lives, culture, and struggles of the *minjung* – the locked out, the exploited, the downtrodden, the have-nots. Populist in character, the *minjung* movement includes students, intellectuals, workers, peasants, church activists, writers, cultural workers, and other democratic forces (Koo, 1987).

This chapter will provide background on *minjung* feminism's origins and the tensions it is managing. Also included are specific examples of organizing work among workers and against sexual violence. The primary sources used are interviews with movement organizers and the materials they provided. Many movement leaders served time in prison and endured government repression. They bring years of experience, commitment, and sacrifice to their work. As a third-generation Korean Chinese working in support of Asian immigrant women workers and women of color in the United States, I thoroughly enjoyed listening to my Korean *ja mael* sisters share stories.

Women's movement roots

Minjung feminism's beginning includes two sub-stages. The first encompasses the struggles of women factory workers for democratic unions, battles which deeply influenced the beginning of the *minjung* movement. The second occurs when the women's movement takes distinct theoretical, practical, and organizational forms.

Yo'Kong Undong: *factory girls' movement*

Drawn from the countryside, *yo'kong*, or factory girls, toiled day and night in export-oriented industries, such as textiles, garments, electronics, plastics, wig and food processing (Koo, 1987, p. 105) under General Pak Chung Hee's regime (1961–1979). Their sweated labor financed South Korean economic development, providing seed capital for the later development of heavy industry, for example, chemicals, steel, autos, machinery, and shipbuilding. They endured the lowest wages, sexual harassment, exhaustion, and heartbreaking abuse to support parents and siblings and pay tuition for their brothers' education (Spencer, 1988). Some shop owners split single floors into two levels to house twice the production, stunting the women's physical and intellectual health by forcing them to crouch over their machines for long shifts. They often lived jammed together in company dormitory barracks, called 'chicken coops,' with mattresses rotated between shifts of workers. During this period South Korea gained international notoriety for the world's longest work week and highest rate of industrial accidents (Bello and Rosenfeld, 1990, p. 25).

These women spearheaded the democratic union movement throughout the 1970s when labor rights were completely suspended under martial law. They had to take on the interlocking repressive structures of foreign and domestic capital sponsored by the state, including the Korean CIA (KCIA), draconian national security and labor laws, *baekgo'ldan* (White Skull Squadron) police tactical squads, sell-out government-controlled unions, and ex-military male *kusadae* (Save the Company) thugs. For example, police beat striking women workers at the Dongil Textile Company in Inchon, dragging them by their hair, forcing human feces down their throats and across their breasts before throwing them into jail. Yet these workers went on to win their strike and elect a woman as union president in 1972, marking the first time in South Korean history for a woman to be elected to such a position (Committee for Asian Women [CAW], 1990, p. 38). The women managed to hold on to leadership and keep the union democratic for six years until they were finally overcome by the government and management.

The *Chunggye Pibok* Union (Garment Makers Union) headed by Lee So Sun, mother of martyred worker Chun Tae II, also managed to keep their democratic union alive until General Chun Doo Hwan's regime finally crushed it in the early 1980s. The union gave voice to the 20,000 young women who worked at Seoul's Peace Market in a one-block long, four-storey high maze of tiny cubicles for less than $30 a month (Ogle, 1990, pp. 72–75).

Liberation theologists such as Reverend Cho Wha Soon, religious organizations such as the Urban Industrial Mission, the Catholic Church's Young Christian Workers, and student-turned-worker organizers encouraged women workers using popular literacy, transformation, and conscientization methods. They urged workers to right injustices by examining their own lives and taking collective action for justice – to 'see, judge, act' (Ogle, 1990, p. 88). The *minjung* movement fused with women workers' struggles in a synthesis process which simultaneously politicized women workers' struggles while giving the cross-class *minjung* movement its working-class base and orientation.

Similar to many of the veteran activists in today's women's movement, Maria Chol Soon Rhie came to consciousness because of the struggles of women factory workers in the 1970s (Rhie, 1991). Now an organizer of the Committee for Asian Women, a pan-Asian workers' leadership development network, she explains the intersection of her feminist and class consciousness:

> I did not start out as a feminist. When I came into contact with the movement I was most concerned about my country and about workers' lives. The suicide of Chun Tae II really affected me and made me question what I was doing with my life. A Chonggye Garment Workers' Union organizer, Chun set himself on fire to protest the inhumane conditions of workers, shouting: 'We are not machines! Improve working conditions! Do not waste my death!' I felt compelled to understand the conditions that drove him to his death. College could not give me the answer. For 3 years I worked in a factory to learn about workers' lives. After 2 years I organized a small group of workers.
>
> (Rhie, 1991, p. 7)

> I began to learn more about women's lives. When you are born into a family and culture and grow up with inequality it is difficult to

be aware of it. In some ways it is easier for workers to recognize their condition after joining the workforce than it is for women who have grown up oppressed. Destroying old conceptions about women is difficult. Discussion of women's issues get [sic] squeezed because workers are busy fighting to change yellow [company] unions into democratic unions. . . . True democratic changes will come through the women's movement. Democracy must include women's democracy. Even now men ask why women need to struggle separately. Why not just fight for democracy? Have you heard of yo'song haebang [women's liberation]? Women have to come together autonomously to form their own voice so they can stand up.

(Maria Chol Soon Rhie, personal communication, 25 June 1991)

Throughout the 1970s women workers stood up for their rights, laying the foundation for the democratic union and *minjung* movements with pitched battles at companies like Dongil, Sygnetics, Bando, Songsa, Pangrim, Hankook Mobang, Dongsu, Yanghaing, Y. H. Trading and others. In fact, when women workers protested the Y. H. plant closure in Seoul, police bludgeoned them, killing one woman and provoking riots in the industrial zones of Masan and Pusan. As dictator Pak Chung Hee argued with his friend and head of the KCIA Kim Jae Kyu about how to handle the riots, Kim shot Pak to death in 1979 (Ogle, 1990, pp. 86–92).

Minjung *movement arises from ashes of Kwangju*

The dictator's death provided a potential democratic opening, and students and workers around the country demonstrated for change, taking over the city of Kwangju in the oppressed region of Cholla-do. But soon South Korean troops with the tacit consent of the US Military Command in Korea drowned the Kwangju rebellion in a sea of blood, leaving over 2,000 people dead (CAW and Korean Women Workers Association [KWWA], 1992, p. 6).

The Kwangju uprising catalyzed, radicalized, and cross-fertilized the student, labor, religious, and women's *minjung* movements. The massacre exposed the intractable dictatorial nature of the new regime and US complicity with its occupational army of 40,000 troops. Newly elected US President Reagan greeted General Chun Doo Hwan as the first foreign head of state received at the White House, further fanning the flames of anti-Americanism. Direct involvement in the Kwangju massacre hobbled Chun's regime (1980–1987) with a credibility crisis.

Spurred on by women's activism in the expanding student and labor movements, the women's movement assumed distinct theoretical, political, and organizational forms by the mid-1980s. Women students and organizers from the labor movement of the 1970s, together with a group of professors from Ewha University (the first institution to provide formal education for women and girls in Korea), organized study groups, put together the first women's studies courses, and developed the Institute of Women's Research. Discussion groups and seminars revolved around such topics as the history of Korean women's organizations since the end of the nineteenth century; work and family from a feminist viewpoint; women's literature; the relation between Korea's division, the denial of human rights, and women's oppression; and the connection between martial law and male domination (Cho Ailee and Nam Yunju, personal communication, 23 May 1992; Cho Haejoang, personal communication, 15 July 1991).

The pace of development of the women's movement escalated in tandem with the broader battle against the dictatorship. In 1985 organizers convened a giant women's rally with the theme 'Women's Movement in Unity with National Democratic *Minjung* Movement.' A cultural night co-sponsored by the Women for Equality and Peace and the government-controlled Federation of Korean Trade Unions drew 50,000 women workers and acted as the basis for a subsequent solidarity strike in Kuro, the main industrial area of Seoul. In 1986, women rallied in support of Kwon In Suk, a woman labor organizer who was raped and tortured by police at the Buchon police station. The fury unleashed by this incident and other sex torture cases sparked the formation of Korean Women's Associations United (KWAU), a national coalition of thirty-three worker, peasant, religious, research, environmental, housewife, and anti-violence organizations in 1987. KWAU was born amidst the explosion of tear gas canisters as protesters battled with riot police. The movement forced Chun to announce that he would step down at the end of his term, and led General Roh Tae Woo, Chun's hand-picked successor, to announce that direct presidential elections would be allowed (CAW and KWWA, 1992, p. 7).

Thus, the beginnings of the feminist and *minjung* movements are closely intertwined, from the struggles of young women factory workers to the full flowering of the women's movement during the pitched street battles to bring down the dictatorship during the late 1980s. The next sections on organizing among women workers and against sexual violence offer examples of how the women's movement tackles the intersection of gender and class.

Fighting for democracy in the union and the family

Women shoulder double burden

Gender discrimination intensifies the exploitation of women workers. Even the government-controlled Korean Federation of Trade Unions admits that women's wages are still only 53 percent of men's. Women must often work longer hours to compensate for low wages. Women work an average of 53.2 hours per week, not counting their unpaid work in the home.

Today's *yo'kong* (factory girls) are second and third generation urban dwellers. By 1987, women were 55 percent of the paid workforce, including 60 percent of service, 47 percent of commercial, 40 percent of manufacturing, and 38 percent of all office workers. Some one million women work in the service sector in restaurants, cabarets, room salons, saunas, public baths, tea houses, hotels, massage parlors, and barber shops. Women's movement activists say that almost 30 percent of these jobs are sex industry-related (Chung, 1991).

Women are punished for their marital status. The myth persists that a good wife and mother does not work outside the home. Meanwhile, growing numbers of women work and raise children without social or spousal support. Married women forced out of their jobs upon marriage do piecework at home to make ends meet. As their children grow older they return to work in factories at the worst jobs for the lowest pay, often as temporary workers. Some 45 percent of married women work, and married women now constitute 30 percent of all women workers. Due to the lack of childcare in Korea, many leave their children at home alone, resulting in stress for the mothers and tragic accidents among the children. Yet no matter how many hours women put in at work, most Korean men expect their wives to wait on them when they get home (CAW and KWWA, 1992, pp. 18–20).

According to Kim Eun Shil, a medical anthropology doctoral candidate at the University of California researching views of sexuality and reproduction among women workers, many working-class marriages are common law. She explains,

> Among the working class, consensual unions are common (i.e., living together without a marriage ceremony). With the increase in urbanization more young girls live separate from their family, often in factory dormitory, with little money. They feel lonely. Marriage is important to get parental recognition and exchange goods and gifts. But working class women's family networks are too poor to come up with the goods. A lot of working women have kids but have not gone through a marriage ceremony. Some get married after they have a couple of kids. They confided to me that they feel abnormal and ashamed, but that they could not afford to get married in a traditional way. ... Sex outside of marriage for men is supposed to be a customary practice, not morally correct, but allowable given men's supposedly 'lusty nature.' For women the standard is chastity.
>
> (Kim Eun Shil, personal communication, 12 July 1991)

History professor and editor of *Women & Society* magazine, Chung Hyun Back explains why women turned to the labor movement:

> Korean women workers used to have a little fantasy about marriage. In biographies written during the 1970s, women laborers voiced their dreams of marrying a 'man with a necktie,' that is a white collar worker who would help them escape from poverty. But they could never find this guy with the necktie. They began to realize that they would have to accept a manual laborer as their partner. When their fantasies of social mobility evaporated, they began to search for other solutions. That's when they turned to the labor movement as a means of improving their conditions.
>
> (Chung, 1991)

Organizing along the global assembly line

The Korean Women Workers Association (KWWA) organizes against gender discrimination at work and in the union movement, and presses for shared responsibility between women and men in the home. The formation of the KWWA in 1987 proved key in overcoming the fragmentation and break in the continuity of women workers' struggles caused by state repression and forced retirement upon marriage and childbirth.

The KWWA office sits in the middle of Kuro, the main industrial district of Seoul. Walls are plastered with leaflets. A doorway jammed with well-worn pairs of shoes leads into a room with a low table encircled by women workers sitting on the floor. Organizer Yoon Hae Ryun is gratified that KWWA allows blacklisted *son bae* (senior classmate) veterans such as herself to connect with their *hu bae* (junior classmate) workers to show them the ropes and bridge the gap between the generations of women workers fighting for their rights. Sitting in the tiny front room, she explains how she got involved in labor organizing:

> I started working in a factory when I was 14 when there were no democratic unions. I worked in a coat factory sewing from 8 a.m. to 2 a.m. every day. Our lives were really hard. We began to say that we should not have to work like this. I decided to get involved in the 1985 cooperative strike in Kuro launched by democratic unions. Chun Doo Hwan did his best to destroy the unions. When we started this strike, I told my family about it in order to prepare them for what might happen. They were shocked and cried and cried. I was the only wage earner in the family because the kids were in school and my father was too old to continue his job as a laborer lifting materials. I got arrested and spent 6 months in jail with workers and students. All of my friends from work were there. It

was so crowded that there was no place to sleep. You had to sleep like a knife. (She tautly presses her arms against her body to resemble a knife.) When I got out of jail I went back to the factory to work, but I kept getting dismissed from jobs. It got to the stage where I was blacklisted and could not get work. So together with other displaced women workers, I began to work with the KWWA to support women workers in their struggle.

(Yoon Hae Ryun, personal communication, 28 May 1992)

KWWA advocates higher wages and an eight-hour work day; ending sexual discrimination in the workplace; maternity protection, including menstruation leave, maternity leave, breast-feeding, and daycare facilities; halting sexual harassment and violence; solidarity among women inside and outside of the labor movement; and women's leadership training. Since 1989, KWWA has run a childcare center for workers as well as 'nolli bang / playroom,' an after school study program for older children. KWWA has chapters in the industrialized zones of Seoul, Pusan, Buchon, Inchon, Changwon-Masan, and Kwangju. KWWA discussion groups, educational materials, and comic books feature struggles to form women's sections within unions to build 'democratic unions' and 'democratic families' supportive of women workers (CAW and KWWA, 1992; KWWA, 1993).

Clerical and bank workers' unions are female dominated. Women office workers who have no hope of getting promoted and who, until recently, were forced to retire when they married, are more active in labor-organizing drives than men and often have a strong feminist consciousness. The Korean Women's Association for Democracy and Sisterhood was founded to support the struggle of the women office workers against discriminatory pay, petty errands, and having to deliver the 'three Cs' – coffee, copy, and cigarettes – to their male bosses. The membership of the highly progressive democratic teachers' union is also majority female.

Korean women workers' organizations also build links with other groups in Asia through participation in the Committee for Asian Women (CAW). Korea was one of the earliest outposts along the global assembly line. Now Korean women are fighting lay-offs and the replacement of permanent workers with contingency workers hired through a third agency and from other countries. Because these women are not protected by unions, they can be fired at will. Korean workers are also hard hit by factory flight to newer regions of transnational corporate penetration where workers are less organized and lower paid (CAW, 1993, p. 12). Korean women workers launched courageous campaigns against plant closures by Pico Products, Tandy Corporation, and Control Data Electronics of the United States and Sumida Corporation of Japan. Despite beatings and arrests, Pico Korea unionists who had produced cable TV parts chased the runaway company to corporate headquarters in Liverpool, New York with pickets, a hunger strike, a lawsuit, and national tour supported by the Korean American community and US labor unions (Liem and Kim, 1992).

CAW organizes exchanges between women workers' groups in Korea, the Philippines, Malaysia, Japan, Sri Lanka, Thailand, Indonesia, India, Taiwan, and Hong Kong so women workers can better confront class and gender abuse up and down the global assembly line (CAW, 1993).

Breaking the silence: organizing against sexual violence

Korea has a long history of subjugation and violence against women. But this legacy reached new lows under colonialism and imperialist domination when occupiers systematically raped the women of the raped nation. Division of the country into two antagonistic halves by foreign powers during the Cold War necessitated a huge military apparatus whose waste products were the sex industry and increased levels of male violence against women. South Korea has the world's third highest rate of sexual assault according to a 1989 study by the Korea Criminal Policy Institute (Korea Sexual Violence Relief Center (KSVRC), 1992, p. 11).

Confucianism, militarism, violence, and the sex industry

Jun Yeonny, a Korean Sexual Violence Relief Center volunteer, graduate of Ewha Women's Studies Department and now a Women's Studies professor at Kun San College in Seoul, explains how Confucian ideology subordinates and silences women:

> To understand why Korean women face such a high degree of sexual harassment and assault, you have to understand Korean social structure, especially the patriarchal system with its strong tradition of Confucianism. Under Confucianism women are subordinate to father, then husband, then son. Furthermore, Confucianism emphasizes the ideology of virginity and chastity for women as well as the supremacy of family. So if a woman is the victim of an attack she does not want to publicize it. In Korea, incest rape is a big problem. But under Confucian ideology, if there are problems in the family they should be settled in private or suffered in silence, not brought out into the open.
>
> (Jun Yeonny, personal communication, 24 April 1992)

Sexual violence also stems from foreign domination, military occupation, and represssion in Korean modern history, including Japan's forty-year colonization of Korea (1905–1945), the Korean War (1950–1953), the introduction of foreign troops including continued occupation by 37,000

US troops, military governments (1961–1987), the growth of the Korean military to 600,000 troops in the south and one million in the north, and compulsory military service and training in use of deadly force for all men in Korea. English literature professor Cho Ailee, member of the, Research Center for Women's Studies explains:

> You have to understand that Korea is a very violent society. We have lived directly under military governments for 30 years. Even though the sixth Republic of Roh Tae Woo [(1988–1992) was] ostensibly civilian, in reality the military still wields power. For Roh Tae Woo to reach the position of general, a lot of people had to die. The military and police have killed people demonstrating for democracy. *Kusadae* thugs beat up workers. In this violent military climate, men's violence against women is sanctioned.
> (Cho Alice, personal communication, 23 May 1992)

Militarism exacerbates the growth of prostitution and the sex industry as well as other forms of sexual violence against women. In addition to numerous Korean bases and posts, some forty US bases remain on Korean soil. An average of 2,000 altercations between local Koreans and US military personnel occur each year. In 1991, out of 1,373 reported cases of crimes committed by US soldiers, only eighteen were prosecuted (Lee Yeung Hee, personal communication, 27 May 1992). Many of these incidents are crimes against women, like the case of Kenneth Markel, a GI stationed at Tongduchon, who bashed the head of Yoon Geum Yi, a poor factory worker turned prostitute. He then stuck a Pepsi bottle into her vagina, an umbrella up her anus, a match between her teeth, and left her to die in a pool of blood (Lee, 1993a, pp. 16–17).

During the 1970s the Pak Chung Hee regime encouraged the development of the sex industry to entice foreign exchange out of Japanese businessmen. Korea also served as an 'R & R' (rest and recreation) center for US GIs during the Vietnam War. Thus, women factory and sex industry workers were called up to sacrifice themselves 'for the sake of the nation.' Sex tours included not only air travel, hotel, and transportation, but also the sexual services of Korean women (Haruhi, 1985; Lie, 1991; Louie, 1989). The women's movement educated the public about these problems, but the sex industry only went underground. The pornography industry, prostitution, massage parlors, hostess bars, and sex barber shops still abound in Korea. Although the sex industry's initial impetus was serving foreign soldiers and businessmen, these days its main customers are Korean men.

'Comfort women' caught in crossfire of militarism, colonialism, and sexism

Professor Jun Yeonny (1992) reflects, 'Perhaps the comfort women were the first victims of the sex industry' (Jon Yeonny, personal communication interview, 24 April 1992). Japan forced women to sexually service its Imperial Army and work its war industries during World War II, an act the Pak Chung Hee regime was to imitate three decades later. Euphemistically called *Chong Shin Dae* or 'Comfort Girl Corp,' this episode stands as one of the most humiliating reminders of the forty years Korea suffered as Japan's colony. Of the estimated 100,000 to 200,000 women drafted, more than 80 percent were Korean, with other women 'recruited' from China, Taiwan, the Philippines, Malaysia, Indonesia, and Thailand ('Presumed drafted,' 1992). Survivor Shim Mi Ja, of the Korean Council for Women Drafted under Japanese Rule, remembers her ordeal:

> When I was 16 years old [a] policeman tried to rape me so I punched him in the ear. Then they beat me so hard that I passed out. When I woke up I was in Fukuoka, Japan. They made me serve as a *Chong Shin Dae* prostitute for 6 years, between 1939 and 1945. . . . After I was kidnapped and sent to Japan I never saw my family again because my home town is in North Korea.
>
> (Shim Mi Ja, personal communication, 15 July 1992)

The hijacking and rape of Korean women embodied the ultimate subjugation of the colonized. Given its proximity to Japan, China, and the Soviet Union, Korea served as Japan's geostrategic bridgehead to take over the Asian continent and pilot Japan's plans for a 'Greater Asian Co-Prosperity Sphere' (Eckert *et al.*, 1990, p. 316). Korea acted as Japan's rice basket and source of raw materials and captive labor when the Japanese Imperial Army thrust into Asia and the Pacific after the declaration of war with China in 1937. Korean girls between the ages of 11 and 18 were gang raped almost every day after they arrived in the military camps. Japanese officers enjoyed the perk of sex with the teenage virgins, after which regular soldiers took their turn. The girls serviced between thirty and sixty men a day. They lived in dread of Saturday night when the numbers of men would increase (Chai, 1993a).

For these survivors of rape, bombings. murder, and suicide, deep scars remain. Dr Yun Chung-Ok, the first researcher to discover documents proving Japanese government complicity in 'recruiting' Korean schoolgirls, says that many women did not come home after the war because they were afraid of shaming their families. Others who did talk about what happened to them were shunned in a classic case of victim blaming (Neuberger, 1993).

131

Survivors break decades of silence with women's movement support

The *minjung* feminist movement provided shelter and support needed for comfort troop survivors to speak out after nearly half a century of silence and shame. Working together with the survivors in the Korean Council for Women Drafted under Japanese Rule are feminist professors, young women's movement activists, as well as the broader coalition of Korean women's groups, Japanese feminists, progressive lawyers, and Korean church and community groups in Japan. *Chong Shin Dae* became a hot issue in 1991 when survivors Kim Han Sun and Mun Ok Ju came forward and told their stories and Korean and Japanese journalists and lawyers began investigating. During June 1991 Korean reporters tracked down almost 200 survivors (Cho Nyeran, personal interview, 5 May 1992).

The Korean Council is also lobbying the Korean government to take a more active role in pressuring the Japanese government to pay reparations to survivors before they die. The Korean government had been silent, supposedly having settled the issue of reparations – not including *Chong Shin Dae* survivors' claims – with the Japanese government back in 1965. Apparently, the pay-off for government silence was a massive infusion of Japanese loan and investment capital.

The Korean Council, which is publishing a book of survivor interviews, has issued the following demands: Japanese government admission that Korean women were drafted as *Chong Shin Dae*, a government apology and full investigation, a monument dedicated to the victims, reparations for the survivors, full rights for Koreans in Japan, an independent position on the issue from the Korean government, a commitment that Japanese schoolchildren be taught the true history about this and other war crimes, and a commitment that Japanese people of conscience help Koreans reveal crimes committed during World War II.

Survivors' support groups

In addition to the comfort women's survivors group, activists have organized a number of support mechanisms for victims of sexual violence. The Women's Hot Line in Seoul was founded in the mid-1980s and belongs to the Korean Women's Associations United, the national *minjung* women's umbrella coalition. The group recently conducted a survey which revealed that one in ten married women are beaten by their husbands almost daily. Activists are now waging a campaign to save the life of Lee Sun Shim, recently charged with the murder of her husband who beat her constantly for twenty years ('One in ten,' 1994). Another women's center called 'My Sister's Place' assists Korean women involved with servicemen at the US base in Tongduchon (Moon and Yu, 1987). Ewha Women's Studies

Department graduates also founded the Korean Sexual Violence Relief Center to assist victims of rape and domestic violence and supported a Seoul National University teaching assistant who won a sexual harassment case against a professor, the first landmark decision of its kind.

Members of he Korean Council, Korean Sexual Violence Relief Center, and the Korean Women's Associations United, together with comfort troop survivors from other Asian countries, delivered their testimony and demands to the Human Rights Commission of the United Nations at its meeting in June 1993 in Vienna (Chai, 1993b; Lee, 1993b, pp. 16–19). Similar to mass rape victims of the war in Bosnia, Asian women demand an end to foreign domination, war, militarism, sexual slavery, and violence against women.

Minjung feminism in transition

Although radical *minjung* feminism exercises majority influence among feminist intellectuals and organizers, the movement is not monolithic. Differences exist over how to interpret the intersection between gender and class oppression. Another area of concern is how the collapse of socialism and the crisis of Marxism impact the South Korean movement. Still another challenge facing the movement is how to make the transition from organizing under a military dictatorship to organizing under a civilian government.

Transitioning from military to civilian rule

In order to survive blacklisting, imprisonment, torture, and decimation of leadership over decades of military dictatorship, the movement matured its political consciousness, ideological commitment, forms of organization, and breadth of alliances. Now Korean Women's Associations United, like the giant national worker and student federations, is shifting gear to the new political climate with a civilian president in the face of continued economic restructuring and recession. Although President Kim Young Sam's administration purged the military from key government positions and is waging a campaign against corruption, the basic structure of the army and police remains intact. The government has neither repealed the notorious National Security Law nor democratized labor laws, and has opened the rice market, threatening to further impoverish peasants. Kim has called on workers to make sacrifices 'for the sake of the nation' (KWWA, 1993).

At the same time the electoral process and expansion of civil society allows the citizenry to become more active, legitimizing Kim's government. Groups such as the Korean Women's Associations United have begun to register as legal organizations with the government, which both broadens the groups' appeal to women and also allows them to receive government and other sources of funding for their projects. Additionally, *minjung* women leaders from the labor and slum dwellers movements such as Choi Soon Young and Hong Mi Young ran for regional legislative positions and won. The Minister of Women's Affairs, Kwon Young Ja, journalist who lost her job because of her opposition to the former regime, is also working hard with a number of community women leaders to bring about reforms (Chung Hyung Back, personal communication, 13 May 1994).

Na Young Hee, who serves as KWAU's General Secretary and heads up daily operations surrounded by a staff of energetic young women out of the coalition's headquarters in Chung-dong, Seoul, describes the decision-making process:

> Debates and arguments arise about the political direction and focus of the movement. We have to organize a lot of open and participatory discussions before reaching a final conclusion. Because we target the mass of grassroots people we do not take extreme positions but try to act as a broad umbrella organization.
>
> (Na Young Hee, personal communication, 2 June 1992)

Forty-nine-year-old Han Myeong Suk, the current president of KWAU, works with the Christian Academy. A veteran of the democratic rights movement, she was incarcerated in the women's prison close to the army barracks during the Kwangju massacre in 1980, where she witnessed many violent acts committed against Kwangju citizens that she will never forget. Speaking to a group of Korean American women in Oakland, California about KWAU's work, Han Myeong Suk describes current challenges:

> Traditionally, the government tried to coopt our demands for reform while suppressing the leadership. But now is the time for our groups to dig in and work on the diverse issues that impact women. The people's movement is at another crossroads. In March there was a big conference summit of all the movements where it was decided that we would respond to government reform gestures in a positive manner. How many people were jailed and tortured, how many people died, how many people sacrificed so much to bring about the changes we have today?
>
> (Han, 1993)

Activists from the women's movement of the 1980s worry about the alienation of young women in the 1990s who are turning away from social movements and feminism. Yonsei University sociology professor Cho Haejoang, who comments on culture and the media, suggests that feminists critically re-examine 'compulsory motherhood' within the South Korean context and pay more attention to differences in experience, especially differences between generations:

> It seemed that the women's movement was going to pick up its tide on a large scale. However, in the 1990s, we find ourselves at a loss. Women of the younger generation who are eager to separate themselves from their mothers (the embodiment.s of colonial modernization) and who are free from the Utopian ideologies of the 1980s, find a way out in the 'Global postmodern culture.' . . . The roles and images of women were transformed without accompanying change in the deep structure of sexism. Women exist for men's everyday living and to cater to the male ego. Modernity, understood as the birth of the individual, is only for the male gender.
>
> (Cho, 1995, p. 29)

KWAU details how women are 'the primary victims of the "development dictatorship"' (KWAU, 1995, p. 16) in a report analyzing the impact of structural adjustment policies on women for the UN World Summit on Social Development in Copenhagen in March 1995. KWAU chronicles how women remain vulnerable to exploitation as cheap labor and contingency workers, lay-offs during periods of structural adjustment, poverty as the heads of households, as well as state reinforced patriarchy, sexual discrimination, and violence, both within and outside of the family.

Going to the source: learning from *minjung* women

Women are the *minjung* of the *minjung*. They were the bottom of a Confucian hierarchy that exploited and spurned the peasant, the laborer, the female. Under Japanese colonial domination they embodied the analogy of Korea as the raped nation, force to submit to the lust of the occupier's war machine. After the war their slave-like labor in export-oriented factories and the sex industry yielded the capital accumulation necessary to skyrocket South Korea into coveted Four Little Dragons status. They continue to enrich foreign and domestic capitalists and act as modern-day comfort women soothing soldiers and businessmen.

When Korean women stood up for even the most basic rights, they immediately confronted the interlocking structures of male privilege, foreign domination, state-supported capitalism, and a repressive military apparatus, which, though supposedly erected to protect them against the communist enemy from without, increasingly turned inward to slaughter the *minjung* within. If the goal of the *minjung* movement is to empower the oppressed masses to realize democracy, human rights, workers liberation, national independence, and peaceful reunification, then women are the movement's primary constituency core, the oppressed of the oppressed.

In fact, the *minjung* movement has developed hand-in-hand with the struggles of poor women for class and gender liberation. The international women's movement can learn much from the advanced experiences of our Korean sisters. First, we can learn from the movement's *minjung* orientation of focusing analytical and practical organizing energies on the struggles of grassroots women, utilizing the methodologies of popular literacy, transforming and giving witness to enable poor women to release their voices, and then flanking them in their struggles for justice. Second, we can learn from their combination of theoretical and practical organizing work; from their careful process of building unity through constant discussion, debate, compromise, and evaluation; and from their experiences in organization and coalition building to break isolation and fragmentation between regions, sectors, and generations. The Korean women's movement has begun to share its experiences within international forums and networks of women workers and survivors of sexual violence.

Today the movement faces new challenges, including the global economic restructuring process which continues to abuse and discard workers similar to worn-out shoes, the diversification of Korea's class and occupational structure, the collapse of alternative left ideologies and solutions, and a government whose rhetoric about change does not match its conservative actions. But, whatever the future brings, Korean women have begun their search for liberation. Whereas desperate women once turned to shamans to exorcise evil spirits and change their luck, today's vibrant *minjung* feminists use shamanistic rituals (*kut*) to purge foreign domination, militarism, capitalism, and sexism; to release the *han*, the accumulated suffering and grief of tortured political prisoners, *Chong Shin Dae* comfort women, and rape victims so their souls can find peace. The past suffering, sacrifice, dedication, experience, and leadership of Korean women gives the movement every basis to chart a new course where feminism will be at the core of *minjung* liberation.

ACKNOWLEDGMENTS

Special thanks to Korean women's movement activists who took time from hectic organizing schedules to swap stories. Many thanks also to Linda Burnham and Elizabeth Martinez of the Women of Color Resource Center and Max Elbaum of *Crossroads* Magazine for their helpful editorial comments.

REFERENCES

Bello, Walden, and Rosenfeld, Stephanie (1990) *Dragons in distress: Asia's miracle economies in crisis*, San Francisco: Institute for Food and Development Policy.

Chai, Alice Yun (1993a) Presentation about comfort women at Asian Resource Center, Oakland Chinatown, California, 3 June.

Chai, Alice Yun (1993b) Violated women: why, everywhere, a 'wall of silence?' *Honolulu Advertiser*, p. B3, 25 July.

Cho Haejoang (1986) *Male dominance and mother power: The two sides of Confucian patriarchy in Korea*, Paper presented at workshop of the International Cultural Society of Korea, Seoul, Korea.

Chao Haejoang (1995) *Living with conflicting femininity of mother, motherly wife and sexy woman – a transition from colonial-modern to postmodern*. Paper presented at the Workshop on 'Gender and Social Change in Late Twentieth Century Korea,' Columbia University, New York, 10–11 March.

Chung Hyung Back (1991) *Women in Korea*. Paper presented at meeting of Korea Reunification Symposium Committee and the Department of Asian American Studies, University of California, Berkeley, C.A., 14 March.

Committee for Asian Women (CAW) (1990) *Moving on: Education in organizing.* Hong Kong: Author.

Committee for Asian Women (CAW) (1993) *Asian Women Workers Newsletter*, 12(3).

Committee for Asian Women (CAW) and Korean Women Workers Association (KWWA) (1992) *When the hen crows ... Korean women workers educational programs*. Hong Kong: CAW.

Eckert, Carter, J., Lee, Ki-baik, Lew, Young Ick, Robinson, Michael and Wagner, Edward (1990) *Korea old and new: a history*. Seoul, Korea: Ilchokak Publishers for the Korea Institute of Harvard University.

Han Mycong Suk (1993) Presentation on Korean women at Asian Resource Center, Oakland, California, 18 April.

Haruhi, Tono (1985) Military occupation and prostitution tourism. In *Female sexual slavery and economic exploitation: making local and global connection.* UN Non-Governmental Liaison Service Consolidation held in San Francisco. 25 October 1984.

Koo, Hagen (1987) Women factory workers in Korea. In Eui-Young Yu and Earl Philips (eds), *Korean women in transition: at home and abroad* (pp. 103, 112). Los Angeles: California State University.

Korea Sexual Violence Relief Center (KSVRC) (1991) *Korea sexual violence relief center pamphlet*. Seoul: KSVRC.

Korean Women's Associations United (1995) The effects on women of the Korean economic development model. In *Effects of economic development in South Korean society* (pp. 16–22). Seoul: Korea NGO Forum for Social Development.

Korean Women Workers Association (KWWA) (1993) Working women. *KWWA Journal*, 1.

Lee, Jin Sook (1993a) The murder of Yoon Geum Yi. *Korea Report*, 16: 16–17.

Lee, Jin Sook (1993b) Korean NGOs raise human rights issue at the UN world conference on human rights in Vienna, *Korea Report*, 18, 16–19.

Lie, John (1991) *From kisaeng to maech'un: the transformation of sexual work in twentieth-century Korea*. Unpublished manuscript.

Liem, Ramsey, and Kim, Jinsoo (1992) The Pico Korea workers' struggle., Korean Americans, and the lessons of solidarity, *Amerasia Journal*, 18(1): 49–68.

Louie, Miriam Ching (1989) Third world prostitutes. *Off our Backs*, 6(10): 14–15.

Moon, Fay II., and Yu, Bok Nim (1987) My sister's place reports. Eijungboo, Korea, Home of 8th US Army: My Sister's Place.

Neuberger, Mary Jo (1993) Violence is global. *Village Voice*, 20 April, p. 20.

Ogle, George 1: (1990) *South Korea: dissent within the economic miracle*, London: Zed Books.

One in Ten Korean Wives Beaten Every Day (1994) *San Francisco Examiner*, 10 April, p. A17.

200,000 Presumed Drafted as 'Comfort Girls' (1992) *Korea Times* 17 January, p. 1.

Rhie, Maria Chol Soon (1991) Korea: starting small, growing strong. In Committee for Asian Women (eds). *Many paths, one goal: organising women workers in Asia* (pp. 6–19). Hong Kong: CAW.

Spencer, Robert F. (1988) *Yokong: factory girl*. Seoul: Royal Asiatic Society.

Tieszen, Helen Rose (1977) Korean proverbs about women. In Sandra Mattielli (ed.), *Virtues in conflict: tradition and the Korean woman today* (pp. 49–66). Seoul: Royal Asiatic Society.

Part III

WOMEN'S LIBERATION

7

DECADE OF DISCOVERY
'The personal is political'

Sara Evans

The United States has a history of feminist activism dating from the mid-nineteenth century. Many issues engaged the early feminist reformers, leading to heated discussion, schism, and an eventual compromise late in the century that reunited many factions to focus on achieving the vote for women. Thus the 'woman movement,' as it was then called, came also to be known as the suffrage movement. Gaining the vote in 1920, mostly white women entered mainstream politics in some numbers. Some became medical, educational, and legal professionals, while still others entered government bureaucracy. By 1945 most found their lives changed by hard times during the Depression, by momentous political events like World War II, and by more subtle social forces like the birth control revolution.

Despite the vote, a belief that women and girls were less important than men continued to be dominant in the West. In response, in the 1960s new and very vocal feminist movements arose in the United States and Europe, and the press associated these movements with the outspoken, rich, and middle class. Postwar feminism, by this view, was elitist, high falutin', and out of touch. Two names came to the fore in the publicity: the journalist Betty Friedan and the French philosopher Simone de Beauvoir. In 1949 de Beauvoir had published a pathbreaking book, The Second Sex, *that evaluated women's lives as never attaining the status of freedom. For de Beauvoir, freedom entailed making decisions and taking considered actions. Women, she maintained, lived in a world of unfreedom where they merely did the work of nature and tried to live up to men's expectations. Men were autonomous, authentic, and the measure of true value; women were an inferior 'other.' In the US Friedan popularized these ideas in a blockbuster book,* The Feminine Mystique, *and helped found the National Organization of Women (NOW) that lobbied for equal political and economic rights for women.*

Yet historians have shown that this was only a small portion of the feminist movement, although the media liked to focus on a few 'stars' because they were easier to caricature. Instead, in the climate of Cold War where dissent of any kind was cast as working for the enemy, a far-flung women's activism that challenged the status quo took shape. From the 1950s on, a wide variety of US women had formed activist groups to 'Ban the Bomb,' to achieve civil rights, and to protect the environment, which in the US was deteriorating rapidly. In European countries women worked variously for the right to contraception, for an end to laws against homosexuals, and for the right to divorce. This chapter captures the diversity in the US movement in the 1960s alone and outlines the profound disagreements that reflected how complex women's liberation movements were and remained. It sets this activism in the tumult of the 1960s, with their assassinations, wars, civil protest, and social turmoil.

* * *

The chair of the House Un-American Activities Committee (HUAC) subcommittee was beside himself. For three days in mid-December 1962 his hearing room had been packed with hundreds of women who hissed, booed, applauded, and shushed their wailing babies. He was trying to prove that Women Strike for Peace (WSP) was infiltrated by communists, and he was accustomed in such cases to interviewing terrified witnesses. But these witnesses baffled him. They claimed their organization had no members, that they were all leaders. Retired schoolteacher Blanche Posner took the Fifth Amendment time after time, even when the committee counsel asked whether she wore a paper daisy to identify herself as a member of WSP. The audience cheered. Over the sputtering objections of the chair, Posner lectured the committee:

> You don't quite understand the nature of this movement. This movement was inspired and motivated by mothers' love for children. . . . When they were putting their breakfasts on the table, they saw not only the Wheaties and milk, but they also saw Strontium 90 and Iodine 131.[1]

By the time Women Strike for Peace founder Dagmar Wilson appeared, Chairman Clyde Doyle was near the end of his tether. He had outlawed standing when the audience stood in silent solidarity with the first witness. Next they applauded and he outlawed that. Then they ran to the front of the room to kiss the witnesses. Journalists described Doyle's defeat with delight: 'By the third day the crowd was giving standing ovations to the heroines with impunity.'

As Dagmar Wilson headed for the stand, a woman with a baby on her hip pushed through the crowd to hand her a large bouquet of flowers. Trim, serene, and impeccably dressed in red wool, Wilson calmly answered questions that in the 1950s had made other witnesses cower. Was it her idea to send a delegation to a peace conference in Moscow? 'No, I wish I had thought of that.' Well then, whose was it? 'This is something I find very difficult to explain to the masculine mind.' Finally, the committee counsel asked if she 'would knowingly permit or encourage a Communist Party member to occupy a leadership position in Women Strike for Peace.' 'Well, my dear sir,' she said, 'I have absolutely no way of controlling, do not desire to control, who wishes to join the demonstrations and the efforts that women strikers have made for peace. In fact, I would also like to go even further. I would like to say that unless everybody in the whole world joins us in the fight, then God help us.'[2]

HUAC's defeat came at the hands of an organization of middle-class housewives who proclaimed their concern for peace in the name of mother love. Their actions were harbingers of women's re-entry into political action in the name of womanhood and the initiation of a decade of activism that would shatter Cold War assumptions. By the end of the decade, growing numbers of women possessed a new sense of rights, sisterhood, and language with which to describe personal experiences in group and political terms. This re-emerging feminism issued a broad challenge to American culture – a challenge that would reverberate for the rest of the century. The politicized femininity of Women Strike for Peace was not the source of the new feminism, but it helped create an environment in which the passivity and apolitical nature of the feminine mystique could be challenged.

Signs of change

Movements for women's rights generally emerge in the ferment of widespread social change when women discover and create spaces in which they can develop a collective identity and a shared sense of rights and possibilities. In 1960 there were signs of change on many levels, though no one at the time could have put the pieces together to find a pattern. In February four black college students in Greensboro, North Carolina, sat at the lunch counter of Woolworth's and refused to leave despite violent threats and finally arrest. Their action inspired young blacks across the south who began to sit-in, kneel-in, stand-in, wade-in, and otherwise challenge racial segregation wherever they could. The civil rights movement that grew from these activities provided a new model for social change and a language about equality, rights, and community that transformed public discourse in a decade. 'Freedom now,' the movement proclaimed. Movement-sponsored citizenship schools taught the basic skills of public participation and reinvigorated the ideals of civic duties and rights. All such ferment changed the idiom of politics, re-emphasizing themes of community and civic participation that had long been eclipsed. The election of youthful and energetic John Fitzgerald Kennedy in 1960 further encouraged the new civic idealism as he challenged Americans to 'ask not what your country can do for you. Ask what you can do for your country.' A renewed public life for middle-class women in the 1960s was a far cry from the politics of domesticity a hundred years before; this public life carried with it the burdens, as well as the freedoms, of the modern age.

The changes of the 1950s had left women in a new and unsettled position, experiencing new dimensions of work, education, and community action but trapped in a language of domesticity that suppressed the broader implications of these new realities. The mass media in 1960, including the *New York Times, Newsweek, Redbook, Time, Harper's Bazaar*, and CBS Television, suddenly discovered the 'trapped housewife.' Twice as many women attended college as a decade before, leading *Newsweek* to worry about 'Young Wives with Brains: Babies, Yes – But What Else?'[3] Obviously the 'what else' in most cases included labor force participation, but the concentration of women in low-paid clerical and service jobs had reduced women's wages from 63.9 percent of men's in 1955 to only 60 percent in 1960. A few universities began experiments to help women cope with their 'dual role' as housewives who would also work outside the home at some stage in their lives. The continuing education movement opened higher education to older women who wanted to complete degrees or plan for returning to the labor force in meaningful jobs.[4]

The re-emergence of the single young woman represented another alternative obscured by the popular obsession with domesticity. After 1957 marriage ages had begun to creep up and birthrates to fall. Slowly, invisibly, the headlong rush into domesticity had begun to reverse, revealing itself as an aberration in the longterm trends. At the same time, in 1960 the Food and Drug Administration approved a new form of contraception, the birth control pill. For the first time contraception was thoroughly separated from the act of sexual intercourse. And the effectiveness of the pill broadened the possibilities of recreational sex, enjoyed for its own sake in contexts not linked to procreation or even domesticity.

The convergence of these ongoing changes and vaguely sensed possibilities took place in a context in which Cold War verities were rapidly dissolving. From the late 1950s, world events signaled the end of self-congratulation and a re-emergence of social criticism. New countries in Asia, Latin America, and Africa met in 1955 to declare themselves uncommitted either to the Russian-led communist world or the United States-led capitalist world. The Cold War bifurcation into 'free' and 'communist' countries no longer sufficed. In 1957 Ghana won independence from British colonialism, to be followed by a flood of newly liberated nations in the late 1950s and early 1960s; each new nation joined the non-aligned movement. Also in 1957 Russia launched the first artificial satellite and sent shock waves through a complacent American educational establishment. Then in 1959, Cuban guerrillas led by Fidel Castro overthrew an American-supported dictatorship and proclaimed a socialist state only ninety miles from the Florida coast.

Americans were suddenly on the defensive and they began a new self-examination. Intellectuals and 'experts' of all kinds began to ask new questions and challenge bland orthodoxies. The passivity of the child-mother image no longer fitted the times. Several studies of working women and a National Manpower Council report indicated both that working women with children required substantially increased social support for the double burdens they carried and that educated women remained significantly underemployed.[5] At a time when leaders worried that the United States was losing the Cold War, underemployed women suddenly looked like a wasted resource.

On the fringes of college campuses, young people gathered to listen to folk music, to talk about the terrors of nuclear war, and to criticize the materialism and hypocrisy of American culture.[6] Beatniks like Jack Kerouac challenged American mass culture but hardly its sex roles. Their praise of sex, drugs, and Zen tended to portray women as simply the mechanism for achieving the cosmic orgasm. There were few liberating possibilities for women in this subculture, though it prepared the way for more egalitarian sexual experimentation. By contrast, when pacifists in the Committee for Non-Violent Action and the Fellowship of Reconciliation discovered a new audience concerned about the morality of warfare and the dangers of the nuclear arms race, groups like Women Strike for Peace found their voice. And when Michael Harrington, former associate of Dorothy Day, shocked optimistic liberals with descriptions in *The Other America* of millions of Americans who remained hungry and impoverished in the midst of affluence, he shocked young women and men alike into idealistic activism.[7]

For all kinds of women changes in the 1960s paradoxically generated greater stresses, new possibilities, and new consciousness. Housewives, still the majority of adult women, perhaps faced the most difficult dilemmas. Sociologist Helena Lopata spent most of the 1960s interviewing women in the Chicago area to produce a profile of urban and suburban, black and white, and middle- and working-class women. She found tremendous variation, but most of all a continuing conflict between the very restrictive cultural definition of women's proper domestic roles, reflected in the self-denigrating response, 'I'm just a housewife,' and women's own descriptions of varied, creative, and active lives.[8]

Suburban housewives, in particular, had arrived in their new suburban environment during the 1950s leaving behind the old neighborhoods and the extended family networks that defined much of their mothers' daily lives. Relying largely on one another and on 'experts,' they began to construct a lifestyle with few concepts to describe or validate what they did. The more educated women had evolved an activist lifestyle in which they extended mothering roles into the community and through voluntary associations brought community into the home. Such organized domesticity began to change the texture of public life in local communities. Suburbs vibrated with the activities of PTAs, girl scouts, churches, charitable fund-raisers, and volunteer-supported neighborhood recreation programs. Yet most women understood their activities simply as 'an attempt to fill empty time.' American culture offered them no way to explain and justify their increasing competence and experimentation.[9] At the same time, few recognized the social and economic vulnerability of their position as housewives as divorce rates, which had dropped during the 1950s, began to rise again in the 1960s.[10] The multifaceted life of a middle-class suburban housewife could become, overnight, a single mother's struggle for economic survival.

The growing community activities of middle-class women briefly generated a new form of politicized domesticity, a political claim on society in the name of family loyalty. Five women who had been active in the

Committee for a SANE Nuclear Policy started Women Strike for Peace. They were disgruntled with the way Cold War witch-hunts had turned peace activists against each other and wanted a way to act quickly in response to international events such as the atmospheric testing of nuclear weapons. Updating a tradition that began with the WCTU, they wanted an organization that could raise 'mother's issues,' such as radioactive contamination of milk, to their rightful place on the public agenda.

They issued a call for women to go on a one-day 'strike' for peace on 1 November 1961, as a radioactive cloud from a Russian nuclear test floated across the United States. Word of the strike spread through female networks in PTAs, the League of Women Voters, peace organizations, and personal contacts. By 1 November an estimated 50,000 women left their jobs and kitchens to lobby government officials to 'End the Arms Race — Not the Human Race.' Within the next year they organized local groups in sixty communities. Most activists in WSP were educated, middle-class mothers. Sixty-one percent did not work outside the home. Intellectual and civic minded, these middle-aged women had been liberal or radical in the 1940s and then had withdrawn into domesticity in the 1950s. They found themselves impelled, by growing fears for their children's futures as well as by the courageous examples of civil rights activists in the south, back into politics, this time in positions of leadership. Women's rights were on their agenda only so far as they emphasized the right of housewives to be heard as citizens. Conscious that 'the housewife was a downgraded person,' Dagmar Wilson set out to show 'that this was an important role and that it was time we were heard.'[11]

Although WSP enjoyed a momentary triumph, domesticity could not provide the political base it had for Victorian women. For too many the home was conceptualized as a 'closed off cloister unconcerned with what goes on outside,' and while the actual boundaries between public and private were fuzzy, political life that involves citizens, as opposed to politicians, had lost a distinctive, vibrant dynamic of its own.[12] Working-class and lower-class housewives had a far more restrictive definition of domesticity than their middle-class counterparts, along with far less self-confidence about their own achievements. Less neighboring and less involvement in the community reinforced women's isolation inside a constantly precarious family economy and gave them little sense of control over their lives or their children. When such women did not work outside the home, they frequently explained that their husbands would not let them. Researcher Lillian Rubin described a painful discussion with a mother of four who, like her house, appeared 'unkempt and uncared for.' The woman explained, 'No, I don't work.' 'My husband doesn't like me to work. He thinks a wife ought to be home taking care of the children and her husband.' In a wistful voice she remembered how much she had enjoyed her work at a bank, where 'I was the best girl in the office, too. You know, it's funny, but

I'm very organized when I work. . . . I even used to be more organized around the house when I was working.'[13]

Economic dependence on men whose own opportunities were severely restricted led many such women, both white and black, to express considerable anger at men for failing to fulfill their roles as breadwinners. One woman complained that she never got enough money from her husband 'to feed and clothe my family,' not recognizing that with a total income of less than US$5,000 he did not have 'enough' to give. Others complained about unemployed men: 'They don't care to work' and 'Men just think women are work horses.'[14]

Among poor black women, especially in northern urban ghettos, decades of severe unemployment among black men left growing numbers with sole responsibility for the support of their children. As the numbers of female-headed households rose, so did illegitimacy rates, from 17 to 29 percent of all black births between 1940 and 1967. The proportion of black women in the labor force reached 58 percent in 1960.[15] A government report by Daniel Patrick Moynihan issued in 1965, *The Negro Family: The Case for National Action*, appeared to place the blame for black poverty on the 'pathology' of this 'matriarchal' black family.[16]

Yet the survival strategies of poor black women drew on the traditional elasticity of the black family that had never conformed to middle-class images. Kin and fictive kin (that is, friends referred to with the labels of kinship: 'sister, 'aunt') formed networks within which resources could be shared and children cared for. Women were central to such networks while men floated in and out of them, depending largely on their level of employment. When one member of the network had a job or a welfare check, resources flowed out to the network as a whole. When members were jobless, homeless, or ill, resources in the form of gifts and services flowed to them. Such gift-giving and swapping exchanges contrasted sharply with middle-class competitive and individualistic values. As one woman said, 'You ain't really giving nothing away because everything that goes round comes round in my book.'[17]

Struggles for minority rights: black women and Chicanas

For middle-class black women domesticity as organized through church and community groups had always been politicized. From the earliest black women's clubs, through settlements like the Atlanta Neighborhood Union, or work in the colored YWCA, black women had worked for the welfare of the black community. By the 1960s, however, the black community was becoming increasingly diverse – ranging from north to south, from city to countryside, and from extreme poverty to educated middle class.

In contrast to the white middle class, black community activists for the most part worked outside the home as well. Indeed, working black women's intensely active lifestyle involved them in religious and community groups more than any other group of women.[18] The activist tradition of black women, primarily through their churches, placed them in central leadership positions in the civil rights movement that spread across the southern states after 1960. As young blacks throughout the south confronted segregation, they drew on the courage and experience of earlier actions such as the Montgomery bus boycott. When the movement shifted its focus to voter registration, it became essential to mobilize entire communities; organizers quickly learned that, as in Montgomery, churches were the key institutions within the black community. On one level this emphasized the public leadership of black male ministers. On another, it required the active support of community women. Young volunteers in southern communities quickly learned to know the 'mamas,' powerful women whose courage and strength provided the backbone of the local movement as they had within their churches.

Born in 1917, Fannie Lou Hamer was the twelfth of twenty children; her parents were Mississippi sharecroppers. Until she went to her first mass meeting in 1962, she

> didn't know that a Negro could register and vote. . . . When they asked for those to raise their hands who'd go down to the court-house the next day, I raised mine. Had it up as high as I could get it. I guess I'd had any sense I'd a-been a little scared, but what was the point of being scared. The only thing they could do to me was kill me and it seemed like they'd been trying to do that a little bit at a time ever since I could remember.[19]

When her employer in Sunflower County, Mississippi, instructed her not to register to vote, she replied, 'But you don't understand, I'm not registerin' for *you*, I'm registerin' for *me*!'[20] As a result, she and her husband lost their jobs and were evicted from their home. But for Hamer the movement had become a way of life. She organized citizenship schools and voter registration projects, endured brutal beatings in jail, and founded the Mississippi Freedom Democratic party to challenge the all-white political structure in that state. Young black and white volunteers recalled the transforming power of women like Fannie Lou Hamer singing gospel hymns, organizing their communities, risking and suffering for freedom with indomitable pride and dignity.[21]

The opportunities for female leadership in the civil rights movement were most open at the grassroots. Within Martin Luther King, Jr.'s Southern Christian Leadership Conference women such as Ella Baker, Septima Clark, and Dorothy Cotton conceived and led the Citizenship Education program that laid the groundwork for many local civil rights demonstrations. Women were also key leaders in the youthful radical wing of the civil rights movement, the Student Nonviolent Coordinating Committee (SNCC). SNCC was founded because Ella Baker had persuaded SCLC to sponsor a meeting in April 1960 for participants in the sit-in movement. SNCC set out to embody the goals of the movement, 'the beloved community,' as people called it. Blacks would claim their dignity and citizenship rights regardless of intimidation or violence. Blacks and whites would live and work together equally, showing to the world the meaning of the equality for which they were fighting.

The intensely personal nature of participation in SNCC and the openness to youthful initiative made it possible for many women to join and lead demonstrations against segregation and to organize communities for voter registration. Refusing bail, they experienced jail again and again, gaining the respect and admiration of their colleagues. Rubye Doris Smith Robinson, a central staff member of SNCC, according to one of her co-workers was

> The nearest thing I ever met to a free person. I mean really free, free in the sense that be you Black or white, you could not commit a great indignity or injustice about Rubye and have it go undealt with. . . . Rubye just stood up to *anybody*. . . . That's just not the way Blacks acted in the south. As a result, she made you stand taller.[22]

The civil rights movement transformed many parts of the south between 1960 and 1967 by eliminating the humiliations of public segregation, integrating school systems, and empowering black voters. On other levels its achievements seemed excruciatingly minimal. Black Americans remained disproportionately poor while discrimination assumed increasingly subtle forms. For black women, however, there were some dramatic consequences. Public opinion shifted decisively toward a belief that racial discrimination was wrong, and the Civil Rights Act in 1964 made it illegal. In 1960 black women remained confined to domestic and other segregated, menial jobs or professional jobs within the black community. After 1964, however, their economic opportunities broadened to include jobs previously open only to white women. The proportion of black women in clerical and sales jobs increased between 1960 and 1970 from 17 to 33 percent in northern states and from 3 to 11 percent in the south. The proportion of black women in domestic service dropped from 36 percent in 1960 to 15 percent in 1970. And in the north, black women earned 95 percent of the wages of white women compared to less than 80 percent in 1960.[23] Of course, white women's wages remained about 60 percent of white men's.

Black women were left with a dilemma. The poorest faced deteriorating conditions as single parents in inner-city ghettos. Swirling around them in the late 1960s was not only the rage expressed in ghetto riots but also the arguments, sometimes echoed by black men, that their very strength and survival undermined the black community. On the other hand, working- and middle-class black women found new opportunities in the late 1960s in spite of continuing racial prejudice. By the 1970s they also found a new voice.

The infectious nature of the black struggle, with its stirring stories of courage and reclaimed dignity, spurred numerous other groups to action as well. Chicana farm workers like Jesse Lopez de la Cruz had labored for decades in the grape, apricot, beet, and cotton fields of the southwest, moving from farm to farm, setting up house in shacks and fields. When Cesar Chavez visited the home of 43-year-old de la Cruz in 1962 and talked about building a union of farm workers she immediately joined as a volunteer organizer.

Chavez's background in community organization led him to emphasize community issues and communal solidarity, matters of deep concern to women. The farm workers' union combined the spirit of labor organizing with that of a civil rights movement rooted in the culture of Mexican Americans. In the beginning it focused not on workplace issues, where a series of union efforts had failed in recent decades, but rather on strength- ening the Mexican-American community. Union members built a credit union and a consumer co-op. They offered counseling for welfare recipients and immigrants seeking citizenship, and waged battles against racism in the schools and rent-gouging landlords. When workers in the Delano, California, grape fields struck in 1966, the United Farm Workers drew on the deep cultural symbolism of the religious pilgrimage as workers marched 230 miles to Sacramento, staying in farm workers' homes each night, drawing new marchers every day, and becoming a presence on the national nightly news for twenty-five consecutive days.[24]

Though Chicanas experienced continuing resistance to activism even within their own communities, many joined and a few emerged as leaders in la causa. De la Cruz, who joined the staff of the United Farm Workers in 1967, saw her principal task as bringing women into the union. 'Women can no longer be taken for granted – that we're just going to stay home and do the cooking and cleaning,' she would tell them. 'It's way past the time when our husbands could say, "You stay home! You have to take care of the children! You have to do as I say!"'[25] A new generation of Chicana leaders emerged from this struggle. The farm workers' movement, in turn, inspired student activists who joined a massive grape boycott in the late 1960s. And in the 1970s it served as a model for new forms of organizing among urban working women.

Re-emergence of feminism

The civil rights movement in the black community also inspired a renewed struggle for women's rights. From the beginning a number of black women were involved: Dorothy Height, president of the National Council of Negro Women, lawyer Pauli Murray, union leaders Aileen Hernandez and Addie Wyatt, Representative Shirley Chisholm, and Fannie Lou Hamer herself. The dual oppression of women in racial minorities and the difficulties of fighting sexism while maintaining racial solidarity, however, took black and other minority women, for the most part, on a different trajectory toward feminism in the 1970s.

The initiation of a new feminist sensibility came from two groups of middle-class women, both inspired by the civil rights movement. The first group consisted primarily of professional women. The second, in many ways parallel to feminists in the 1910s, drew on younger radical activists and posed a broader cultural challenge to accepted definitions of femininity and sexuality but without the seasoned political expertise of the older, more moderate group.

Through the 1950s a small network around the Women's Bureau of the Department of Labor and the tiny remnant of the National Woman's Party had sustained mutually antagonistic voices on behalf of women's rights. But when President Kennedy appointed Esther Peterson to head the Women's Bureau, he brought back into the center of the federal government a female reform sensibility shaped by the labor movement. Peterson had served as recreation director of the Bryn Mawr Summer School for Women Workers in the early 1930s and had worked as a labor lobbyist in Washington for several years.

Peterson persuaded Kennedy to appoint a Presidential Commission on the Status of Women. Chaired by Eleanor Roosevelt and strongly directed by Peterson, the commission set about reassessing women's place in the economy, the family, and the legal system. Membership on the commission, its staff, and seven technical committees was drawn from labor unions, women's organizations, and government agencies.

Not surprisingly, a strong majority of the commission opposed the Equal Rights Amendment that had been kept alive by the National Woman's Party, gaining some new support from business and professional women in the postwar years. Striving for a position less divisive than in the past, their report declared that 'equality of rights under the law for all persons, male or female is so basic to democracy . . . that it must be reflected in the fundamental law of the land.' They argued that this was already achieved under the Fifth and Fourteenth amendments to the Constitution. Therefore, they could conclude that a constitutional amendment was not needed 'now.' The only member of the commission who supported the ERA, feminist lawyer Marguerite Rawalt, insisted on the insertion of the word 'now' to leave the door open for change if the Supreme Court failed to accept their interpretation.[26]

The commission's final report, issued in 1963, together with numerous subcommittee reports documented in great detail problems of discrimination in employment, unequal pay, lack of social services such as child care, and continuing legal inequality. Though the committee paid careful obeisance to the centrality of women's traditional roles, it also spelled out the realities of inequality. One immediate consequence was a presidential order requiring the civil service to hire for career positions 'solely on the basis of ability to meet the requirements of the position, and without regard to sex.'[27] A second was passage of the Equal Pay Act in 1963 that made it illegal to have different rates of pay for women and men who did equal (i.e., the same) work.[28] For the first time the federal government restricted discrimination against women by private employers.

The commission itself activated a network of professional women whose growing concerns during the past decade had found no outlet. Its various subcommittees drew on a large number of women who had been active both in their professions and in their communities. Within a year of their report, most states had also formed commissions. These environments fostered concern about women's status and creative thinking about solutions. No longer bifurcated by their positions on the ERA, union women, lawyers, academics, and organizational leaders were stunned by what they learned. The depth and pervasiveness of discrimination and the hardships accompanying women's 'double burden' in the home and the labor force gave quantified validation to problems they themselves had experienced or observed in more individual ways.[29]

The same year the commission issued its report, Betty Friedan published her book *The Feminine Mystique*. Blaming educators, advertisers, Freudian psychologists, and functionalist sociologists for forcing women out of public life and into a passive and infantilizing domesticity, Friedan advocated meaningful work outside the home as the solution to 'the problem that has no name.' She was unprepared for the deluge of mail that her book inspired. From all over the country, women by the thousand wrote to thank her for naming their unhappiness and to tell her their own painful stories. 'My undiluted wrath,' wrote one, 'is expanded on those of us who were educated and therefore privileged, who put on our black organza nightgowns and went willingly, joyfully, without so much as a backward look at the hard-won freedoms handed down to us by the feminists (men and women).' Another upper-middle-class housewife and mother of five explained, 'In seeking that something "more" out of life, I have tried large doses of everything from alcohol to religion, from a frenzy of sports activities to PTA . . . to every phase of church work. . . . Each served its purpose at the time, but I suddenly realized that none had any real future.' While she saw herself as about to make some different choices, other writers conveyed notes of despair. A suburban housewife claimed that she and her female neighbors were depressed and self-destructive. Describing herself as brilliant with 'an I.Q. in the 145–150 range,' a compulsive eater, and occasionally suicidal, she summarized her life: 'I "caught" a husband at 19, married him on my twentieth birthday, quit school pregnant, and now have six children! I am the typical stay-athome, domineering mother and wife. I love my children yet I hate them, have actually wished them dead.'[30]

All of this set the stage for debate on the 1964 Civil Rights Act. Howard Smith, an elderly congressman from Virginia, encouraged by constituents in the National Woman's Party, suggested that the prohibition in Title VII against discrimination in employment on the basis of race, creed, and national origin should also include 'sex.' As a long-time supporter of the ERA he offered the amendment seriously, but as an ardent segregationist he probably also hoped it would help to kill the bill.[31] While their colleagues chuckled at the very idea of including sex in a civil rights bill, Congresswoman Martha Griffiths and Senator Margaret Chase Smith set to work to pass the amendment which made Title VII the strongest legal tool yet available to women.

Once the Civil Rights Act was passed, the newly created Equal Employment Opportunity Commission (EEOC) found itself flooded with women's grievances. Most people, including the EEOC, still considered the inclusion of sex a bit of a joke. The *New York Times* referred to it as the 'bunny law.' What, the editors worried, would happen if a man applied to a Playboy Club for a position as a bunny? Could he charge discrimination if the owners refused to hire him?[32]

Friedan and others within the networks surrounding the presidential and state commissions became increasingly alarmed. Women, they realized, had no organized advocates in Washington or the states. The EEOC had even approved the continued use of separate want ads for male and female employment. Organizations such as the League of Women Voters and the American Association of University Women were decidedly uninterested in working specifically for women's rights or being labeled 'feminist.' Clearly women lacked the political clout to demand that laws similar to Title VII be enforced.

Several delegates to the third National Conference of State Commissions on the Status of Women, including women from the United Auto Workers and leaders of several state commissions, arrived with this concern. They held an informal meeting in Betty Friedan's hotel room and decided first to submit a resolution to the conference. When they learned that the conference would not allow resolutions or action of any kind, even the reluctant members of the group decided a new organization was required. Friedan recalled that they 'cornered a large table at the luncheon, so that we could start organizing before we had to rush for planes. We all chipped in $5.00, began to discuss names. I dreamed up N.O.W. on the spur of the moment.'[33] Thus the National Organization for Women, NOW, was born with a clear statement of purpose: 'To take action to bring women into full participation in the mainstream of American society now, assuming all the privileges and responsibilities thereof in truly equal partnership with men.'[34]

NOW articulated the clear dilemmas of professional women for whom continuing discrimination violated deeply held convictions about their rights to equal treatment and for whom traditional attitudes about family roles were obsolete. 'It is no longer either necessary or possible,' they argued in their founding statement, 'for women to devote the greater part of their lives to child-rearing.'[35] NOW represented in some ways a modernized version of the Seneca Falls Declaration by reclaiming for women the republican ideals of equal participation and individual rights. But its organizers were skilled at lobbying, not movement building.[36] For the first year, organizational mailings went out from the offices of the United Auto Workers' Women's Bureau, and local chapters were slow to develop. Activities targeted the enforcement of federal anti-discrimination laws. This included pickets and demonstrations against the continued existence of sex-segregated want ads; pressure for the inclusion of 'sex' on the list of discriminations prohibited for federal contractors and for enforcement of Executive Order 11375 once it was amended on 13 October 1967; and continuous pressure on the EEOC to enforce Title VII. As the cases piled up, it became clear that Title VII could eliminate the use of protective legislation to discriminate against women as well as such blatant discrimination as the airlines' policy of firing stewardesses who married or turned 32.

With some successes, several lawsuits pending, no organized local base, and an increasingly diverse membership, the NOW national conference in 1968 encountered serious disagreements. Endorsement of the Equal Rights Amendment forced United Auto Workers women to withdraw. Within their union they were working for change, but until their union changed its position – which it did two years later – they could not remain within NOW. The issue of abortion precipitated another split as lawyers who wanted to focus on legal and economic issues left to found the Women's Equity Action League (WEAL).

NOW did not immediately grow into a national movement in part because its founders did not have the required organizing skills. In addition, its focus on rights and individuals, abstracted from communal relations, did not speak to large numbers of women. The founders of NOW understood that women were seriously disadvantaged in the American political and legal system, but they presumed a model of political activity which was essentially individualist, recalling the late suffragist focus on the direct relationship between citizen and state. In the beginning, the bonds of sisterhood remained unarticulated and depoliticized. Indeed, NOW was very careful to insist that it was an organization 'for' women but not necessarily 'of' women, a sharp contrast to the centrality of female solidarity (without the feminism) in Women Strike for Peace.

The fact is that most women still could not identify with the clear-cut dilemmas of the professional woman. Trapped in the mystifying complexities of a popular culture that simultaneously endorsed individual opportunity and the feminine mystique, a gender-segregated economy that drew women into low-paid, low-status jobs, and a child-centered family premised on the full-time services of a wife / mother, they could not abstract issues of rights from the underlying questions of identity.

Even younger women preparing for professional vocations found themselves caught in a web that was both internal and external. Sara Ruddick finished four years of graduate work at Harvard and followed her husband to his first academic job planning to write her dissertation. She found herself paralyzed, unable to work because she had no models, no image of herself as a worker. 'In my generation, women's work histories were so buried in our life histories as to be barely visible.'[37] Similarly, Marilyn Young with a Ph.D. in Chinese history found herself caring for young children and playing the role of the faculty wife in the mid-1960s. She wrote in her journal in 1967 at the age of 30: 'How ineffective. I shall live out the rest of my life as if it weren't really happening and then die surprised. . . . I have no proper work, and for me that is hard. And I grow lazier, mentally, by the hour.'[38] Both Ruddick and Young found new direction in the intense relationships and personal support of another, younger branch of the emerging women's movement. They were not so much interested in changing the EEOC's enforcement policies as in transforming their own sense of self. Ruddick recalled that the women's movement 'enabled me to achieve a new self-respect at home, made me confident and clear about my need for the friendship of women.' It also transformed her sense of women's aspirations. 'I had carried an invisible, almost amorphous weight, the weight of guilt and apology for interests and ambitions that should have been a source of pride. When that weight was lifted, I felt almost literally lighter, certainly more energetic, more concentrated.'[39]

The groups in which Young could speak of 'the bitterness of those years' and Ruddick could find a new definition of selfhood were part of another, younger branch of feminism that emerged about a year after the formation of NOW.[40] What was called the 'women's liberation movement' grew from the angry critique of a small group of radical young women who challenged the very definitions of public and private, of politics and personal life, and who asserted women's needs for personal support and group solidarity as well as for political action.

The young women who proclaimed, in the late 1960s, that 'sisterhood is powerful' were children of the postwar middle class. Their parents had achieved unprecedented material success in a culture characterized increasingly by rootlessness. The student movements of the 1960s represented a backlash on the part of such youth against the materialism of American society, the absence of authentic community, and the failure of America to live up to its moral claims. In the process young people not only demanded changes but also began to experiment with new and visionary forms of democratic relationships.

These movements provided young women with a social space within which they could question received definitions of domesticity and female nature. They shared their generation's intense search for community and discovered there the power of sisterhood. As a result, they challenged the definitions of politics more fundamentally than women had done since the days of the WCTU, and definitions of gender more radically than anyone had since the Greenwich Village radicals in Heterodoxy. With their declaration that 'the personal is political' they repoliticized the bonds among women and rediscovered the ground for collective action.

Within the black civil rights movement, middle-class white women experienced a politicizing transformation analogous to that of their abolitionist and settlement house foremothers. In the beginning there were very few whites, but in the summers of 1964 and 1965 hundreds of college students flooded the south at the invitation of civil rights organizations, particularly SNCC. Many women found that they had to stand up to the opposition of parents frightened by the continuing violence in the south. 'It is very hard to answer to your attitude that if I loved you I wouldn't do this,' wrote one woman to her parents. 'I can only hope you have the sensitivity to understand that I can both love you very much and desire to go to Mississippi. . . . There comes a time when you have to do things which your parents do not agree with.'[41]

Bolstered by a radical commitment to equal rights, often with religious roots, they broke the mold of passive domesticity by organizing voter registration drives and freedom schools, risking arrest, enduring jail, and witnessing firsthand the dignity and self-respect of impoverished rural black communities. They also learned from black women on whose strength much of the movement rested. These 'mamas' offered a vision of womanhood that further reinforced an emerging sense of self-assertion.

When Students for a Democratic Society (SDS) initiated a series of community organizing projects in imitation of SNCC's southern projects, it unwittingly created an environment in which women could develop new skills and self-confidence. Even more than in the civil rights movement, women's experiences in SDS were filled with irony and mystification. Men were the public leaders of every project, but women were frequently the most skilled organizers. While men tried to organize street gangs and winos, young women effectively organized a large, stable, female constituency, many of them welfare recipients, around community issues. Yet everyone worried about the 'problem' of having so many women leaders, and community issues never received the respect and attention of strategies focused on male employment.

Nevertheless, community organizing projects offered women opportunities to develop leadership skills and political analysis talents, as well as supplying role models – all of which they later used to begin a new women's movement. Within SDS projects, women developed communal bonds among themselves and a deep identification with the female leadership of poor communities both in the north and in the south.

The new left student political movement as a whole became a less hospitable environment for women after the mid-1960s. In the south, racial anger and the need of the black community for self-definition made it impossible for whites to participate in an increasingly nationalist black movement. 'Black power,' often defined as a movement to reclaim black 'manhood,' also rendered black women increasingly invisible. President Lyndon Johnson began, in the spring of 1965, an escalation of the war in Vietnam that quickly provided the central focus for student activists in the north. In the traditions of the Women's International League for Peace and Freedom and Women Strike for Peace, many women devoted themselves to the cause of peace. Nonetheless, the anti-Vietnam War movement, with its emphasis on draft resistance, was far more male dominated than community organizing had been.

The emergence in the late 1960s of a youthful counterculture celebrating love and community – feminine values – might have reversed this trend, but its focus on drugs and sex was often extremely exploitative of women. The counterculture represented a complex continuation of the sexual revolution that had been working its way through American culture since the beginning of the twentieth century. By the 1960s the association between pleasure, consumption, and heterosexuality thoroughly permeated popular culture. With the availability of the birth control pill in 1960, for the first time contraception could be separated from any specific sexual interaction and could be almost 100 percent effective. Heralded as 'the perfect contraceptive,' the pill made it possible for women to separate sexuality and procreation with a confidence never before known. Yet, as young people experimented with new frontiers of sexual freedom, they did so with no critique or re-evaluation of female sexuality. Instead, the promiscuity, emotional detachment, and consumption orientation associated with cultural definitions of male sexuality became defined as sexual 'freedom.' Women raised with needs for security and affection found themselves accused of being 'uptight' and 'out of it.' In the midst of these new pressures some did indeed explore new dimensions of themselves, others withdrew in distrust, and still others experienced what they would later name as abuse.

As early as 1964, women in the student movement had begun to explore the possible consequences of applying democratic principles to their relationships with men. Just at the moment when women had begun to apply the egalitarian ideology of the new left to themselves and their condition in American society, they discovered the realities of sexual inequality. The very settings that had taught them the value of egalitarian community also harbored the prejudices of the broader society.

When women raised the question of their equality within the student movement, they met a combination of indifference, ridicule, and anger. In 1964 SNCC leader Stokeley Carmichael joked that 'the only position for women in SNCC is prone.' At a conference in 1967 Shulamith Firestone stood at the microphone demanding to present a set of women's rights resolutions. After effectively preventing the resolutions from reaching the floor, the chair patted Firestone on the head and said, 'Move on little girl; we have more important issues to talk about here than women's liberation.' Like the founders of NOW in a similar situation, sponsors of the resolutions met immediately to begin organizing a separate movement for women. Using their organizing skills and the networks of activist women across the country, they began to set up small discussion groups and to create a process they called 'consciousness-raising.'

The early meetings were intense and exhilarating. In a style they had learned in the civil rights movement and the new left, women explored the political meaning of their personal experiences. Again and again, individuals were shocked to discover that their lives were not unique but part of a larger pattern. The warm support and understanding of other women empowered them as they reclaimed the lost legacy of sisterhood.

Convinced that they would and could change history, radical young women initiated a variety of forms of outreach. While theoretical papers circulated – What is the root cause of women's oppression? Who is the enemy? – guerrilla theater attracted the mass media. At the 1968 Miss America pageant they crowned a live sheep, tossed objects of female torture – girdles, bras, curlers, issues of the *Ladies Home Journal* – into a 'freedom trashcan,' and auctioned off an effigy: 'Gentlemen, I offer you the 1969 model. She's better every year. She walks. She talks. She smiles on cue. *And* she does housework.' Other groups leafleted bridal fairs and 'hexed' Wall Street.

The lack of structure in this new movement contributed to its growth because it had such a large, ready-made base of activist women in every city. The small consciousness-raising groups proved a brilliant organizing tool. Anyone could start one, in an office, a school, a neighborhood. Soon it had spread well beyond the boundaries of the new left.

In Washington, DC, Arvonne Fraser, a longtime activist in the Democratic Party who worked in her husband's congressional office and managed his campaigns, invited about twenty women to her home in 1969 to talk about the new women's movement. She had tried to join NOW but her letter had been returned – probably a casualty of NOW's disorganization after the

UAW withdrew support. Like many of her friends she found women's liberation groups too young and too radical, but she easily adopted their organizing strategy by organizing her own group. At the first meeting women decided not to introduce themselves through relationships with men (though many were related to or on the staff of prominent men). They said they would be a discussion group, not a consciousness-raising group. 'Many of us realized later,' according to Fraser, 'that the main difference between the two was in name only.'[42] Out of that group came key insider networks that in the 1970s carried out major legislative advances for women.[43] Fraser herself went on to become not only a national officer in the Women's Equity Action League (WEAL) but also increasingly active in international women's networks.

Del Martin, one of the founders of the Daughters of Bilitis, became an early activist in NOW. DOB had made some slight and controversial shifts in the mid-1960s toward a more militant stance, but remained a tiny organization, still distant from the growing lesbian culture that flourished in urban bars. Feminism added a dynamic and stressful dimension. Activists debated whether their primary loyalties lay with the homophile movement, where many experienced sexist treatment from gay male activists, or the new feminist movement where they painfully discovered the homophobic prejudices of other feminists. With feminism, however, they had a powerful analytic tool for examining their own social realities as well as an experience of solidarity and community – sisterhood – which provided a 'psychic space' that allowed many women to claim their identity as lesbians.[44] The explosive emergence of gay liberation in 1969 further fueled this process and set the stage for more dramatic changes in the 1970s.

By the late 1960s, feminist challenges were in the headlines and opposition to the war in Vietnam had toppled a president. Inflation aroused anxiety that the boom might be ending. Race riots and a divisive war abroad destroyed the optimism of the early 1960s. Both Cold War verities and their cousin, domestic ideology, were under serious stress. Indeed, Women Strike for Peace, so effective at the beginning of the decade, found itself accused of being reactionary. Younger radical women pointed out that WSP still played on traditional roles of wife and mother, roles in which women's identities remained derivative and dependent.

In January 1968 women in the peace movement mobilized thousands to march in Washington in opposition to the war in Vietnam. They called their march the Jeanette Rankia Brigade to honor the first woman in Congress and the only congressperson to vote against American entry into both world wars. A small contingent at the march called a separate meeting of women interested in struggling for their own liberation. Among themselves there was immediate division over ideological issues: Were men the enemy or was it 'the system'? Should women continue participation in the male-dominated left or should they break away and work only with other women?

For the moment these angry young women seemed a rude and irritating interruption of the mass movement of women in the mold of Women Strike for Peace. In fact, they were the core of the burgeoning new women's liberation movement that by 1970 had eclipsed and apparently rendered obsolete agitation based on women's traditional roles. Declaring that 'the personal is political,' they introduced a radical challenge to the cultural definitions of male and female. Yet with youthful ingratitude, they failed to recognize the debt they owed previous generations as well as the complex power of women's traditional identities and associations. That failure also prevented them from understanding the long-run import of the movement they had begun.

NOTES

1 Amy Swerdlow, 'Ladies Day at the Capitol: Women Strike for Peace versus HUAC,' *Feminist Studies* 8 (fall 1982): 493–520. See also Amy Swerdlow, *Women Strike for Peace: Traditional Motherhood and Radical Politics in the 1960s* (Chicago: University of Chicago Press, 1993), and Susan Lynn, *Progressive Women in Conservative Times: Racial Justice, Peace and Feminism, 1945 to the 1960s* (New Brunswick, NJ: Rutgers University Press, 1992), chap. 4.

2 This description draws on the account by Mary McGrory quoted in Swerdlow, 'Ladies Day at the Capitol,' p. 508.

3 *Newsweek* 55 (7 March 1960): 57–60.

4 Sara Evans, *Personal Politics: The Roots of Women's Liberation in the Civil Rights Movement and the New Left* (New York: Alfred A. Knopf, 1979), pp. 15–16.

5 See Alva Myrdal and Viola Klein, *Women's Two Roles: Home and Work* (London: Routledge & Kegan Paul, 1956); Robert W. Smuts, *Women and Work in America* (1959; reprint, New York: Schocken Books, 1971); National Manpower Council Reports, *Womanpower: A Statement with Chapters by the Council Staff* (New York: Columbia University Press, 1957–58); National Manpower Council Reports; *Work in the Lives of Married Women: Proceedings of a Conference on Womanpower Held October 20–25, 1957* (New York: Columbia University Press, 1957–58).

6 See James Putnam O'Brien, 'The Development of a New Left in the United States, 1960–65' (Ph.D. diss., University of Wisconsin, 1971), pp. 83–84, 214–22.

7 Michael Harrington, *The Other America: Poverty in the US* (New York: Macmillan, 1962).

8 Helena Z. Lopata, *Occupation: Housewife* (New York: Oxford University Press, 1971), pp. 362–76.

9 Ibid., pp. 31–41.

10 Divorce had soared in the immediate postwar years and declined during the 1950s. Divorce rates increased steadily through the 1960s, presaging a more dramatic acceleration in the 1970s. US Bureau of the Census, *Historical Statistics of the United States: Colonial Times to 1970*, pt. 1 (Washington, DC: US Government Printing Office, 1975), p. 64; Fig. 1, 'Marital Status and Living Arrangements: March 1984,' US Bureau of the Census, *Current Population Reports: Population Characteristics*, series p–20, no. 299, p. 3.

11 Swerdlow, 'Ladies Day at the Capitol,' pp. 493–520, quote on p. 510.

12 Quote from Lopata, *Occupation: Housewife*, p. 376.

13 Lopata, *Occupation: Housewife*, Lillian Breslow Rubin, *Worlds of Pain: Life in the Working-Class Family* (New York: Basic Books, 1976), quotes on pp. 181–82.

14 Lopata, *Occupation: Housewife*, quotes on pp. 122, 128.

15 See Reynolds Farley, *Growth of the Black Population: A Study of Demographic Trends* (Chicago: Markham Publishing, 1970), pp. 145–47.

16 Daniel Patrick Moynihan, *The Negro Family: The Case for National Action* (Washington, DC: US Government Printing Office, 1965).

17 Carol Stack, *All Our Kin: Strategies for Survival in a Black Community* (New York: Harper & Row, 1974), p. 42.

18 Lopata, *Occupation: Housewife*, pp. 291–94, 340.

19 Fannie Lou Hamer, *To Praise Our Bridges: An Autobiography of Mrs. Fannie Lou Hamer* (Jackson, MI.: KIPCO, 1967), excerpted in *Eyes on the Prize: America's Civil Rights Years: A Reader and Guide*, ed. Clayborne Carson *et al.* (New York: Penguin Books, 1987), pp. 133–34.

20 Quoted in Tracy Sugarman, *Stranger at the Gates: A Summer in Mississippi* (New York: Hill & Wang, 1966), p. 115.

21 See Evans, *Personal Politics*, chaps. 2–4. See also Kay Mills, *This Little Light of Mine: The Life of Fannie Lou Hamer* (New York: Dutton, 1993).

22 Stanley Wise quoted in Bernice Johnson Reagon, 'Rubye Doris Smith Robinson,' in *Notable American Women: The Modern Period* (Cambridge, MA.: Belknap Press, 1980), p. 586. See also Cynthia Griggs Fleming, '"More Than a Lady": Ruby Doris Smith Robinson and Black Women's Leadership in the Student Nonviolent Coordinating Committee', in *Hidden Histories of Women in the New South*, pp. 204–23; Cynthia Griggs Fleming, 'Black Women Activists and the SNCC: The Case of Ruby Doris Smith Robinson,' *Journal of Women's History* 4, no. 3 (winter 1993): 64–82; *Women in the Civil Rights Movement: Trailblazers and Torchbearers, 1941–1965*, ed. Vicki L. Crawford, Jacqueline Anne Rouse, and Barbara Woods (Brooklyn: Carlson Publishing 1990); Belinda Robnett, 'African-American Women in the Civil Rights Movement, 1954–1965: Gender, Leadership, and Micromobilization,' *American Journal of Sociology* 101, no. 6. (May 1996): 1661–94, and 'The Voices of African American Women in the Civil Rights Movement,' special issue of *Journal of Black Studies* 26, no. 5 (May 1996).

23 Jacqueline Jones, *Labor of Love, Labor of Sorrow: Black Women, Work and the Family from Slavery to the Present* (New York: Basic Books, 1985), p. 302; Bureau of the Census, *Black Population: Historical View*, p. 74.

24 See J. Craig Jenkins, 'The Transformation of a Constituency into a Movement: Farmworker Organizing in California,' in *Social Movements of the Sixties and Seventies*, ed. Jo Freeman (New York: Longman, 1983), pp. 52–70; Ronald B. Taylor, *Chavez and the Farm Workers* (Boston, MA: Beacon Press, 1975); Dick Meister and Anne Loftis, *A Long Time Coming: The Struggle to Unionize America's Farm Workers* (New York: Macmillan, 1977).

25 Ellen Cantarow with Susan Gushee O'Malley and Sharon Hartman Strom, *Moving the Mountain: Women Working for Social Change* (Old Westbury, NY.: Feminist Press, 1980), pp. 94–151, quote on p. 134. See also Margaret Rose, '"Woman Power Will Stop Those Grapes": Chicana Organizers and Middle Class Female Supporters in the Farm Workers' Grape Boycott in Philadelphia, 1969–1970,' *Journal of Women's History* 7, no. 4 (winter 1995): 6–36.

26 Cynthia E. Harrison, 'A "New Frontier" for Women: The Public Policy of the Kennedy Administration,' *Journal of American History* 67 (December 1980), 630–46; quote on p. 640.

27 Ibid., pp. 641–42.
28 Ibid., p. 642.
29 Jo Freeman, *The Politics of Women's Liberation: A Case Study of an Emerging Social Movement and Its Relation to the Policy Process* (New York: David McKay, 1975), pp. 52–53.
30 Quotes from Friedan Manuscript Collection, Schlesinger Library Manuscript Collections, Radcliffe College, Cambridge, MA., quoted in Elaine Tyler May, *Homeward Bound: American Families in the Cold War Era* (New York: Basic Books, 1988), pp. 209, 210, 212.
31 Leila Rupp and Verta Taylor, *Survival in the Doldrums* (New York: Oxford University Press, 1987), chap. 8, esp. pp. 176–79. See also Cynthia Deitsch, 'Gender, Race and Class Politics and the Inclusion of Women in Title VII of the 1964 Civil Rights Act,' *Gender and Society* 7, no. 2 (June 1993): 162–82.
32 *New York Times*, 'Editorial,' 21 August 1965.
33 Judith Hole and Ellen Levine, *Rebirth of Feminism* (New York: Quadrangle Books, 1971), p. 84.
34 Ibid.
35 Freeman, *Politics of Women's Liberation*, p. 74.
36 Ibid., p. 73.
37 'A Work of One's Own,' in *Working It Out: 23 Women Writers, Artists, Scientists, and Scholars Talk about Their Lives and Work*, ed. Sara Ruddick and Pamela Daniels (New York: Pantheon Books, 1977), pp. 128–46, quote on p. 129.
38 'Contradictions,' in Ruddick and Daniels, *Working It Out*, pp. 213–27, quote on p. 223.
39 'A Work of One's Own,' in Ruddick and Daniels, *Working It Out*, p. 145.
40 Ibid., p. 223. This section draws primarily on Sara Evans, *Personal Politics*. See also Alice Echols, *Daring to Be Bad: Radical Feminism in America, 1967–75* (Minneapolis: University of Minnesota Press, 1989).
41 Elizabeth Sutherland, ed., *Letters from Mississippi* (New York: McGraw-Hill, 1965), pp. 22–23. On the experiences of summer volunteers see also Mary Aiken Rothschild, *A Case of Black and White: Northern Volunteers and the Southern 'Freedom Summers'* (Westport, Conn.: Greenwood Press, 1982), and Doug McAdam, *Freedom Summer* (New York: Oxford University Press, 1988).
42 Arvonne S. Fraser, 'Insiders and Outsiders: Women in the Political Arena,' in *Women in Washington: Advocates for Public Policy*, ed. Irene Tinker (Beverley Hills, CA.: Sage Publications, 1983), p. 122.
43 Ibid.
44 John D'Emilio, *Sexual Politics*, p. 236.

8

IT'S NOT UNUSUAL

Gay and lesbian history in Britain

Alkarim Jivani

As preceding chapters have shown, feminism is part of an intersection of interests, identities, and causes. While activists in the West protested the Cold War and lack of economic and political rights for women and minorities, activists in national liberation movements could want rights for women as well as political independence from the imperialist powers. Women activists in particular felt themselves dislocated and sometimes pulled apart by these intersections, especially when competing groups demanded full loyalty. Civil rights activists could not see that women of color had legitimate grievances as women, while feminists could not see that women of color had grievances other than as women. In the 1960s neither group initially could see that lesbians and gays suffered discrimination except as a result of sex or race.

Gays and lesbians in the West had been active on behalf of many of these other political causes but some had also been struggling to overturn discriminatory laws since World War II ended. They were acutely aware of the long history of persecution, including famous trials of homosexuals and even executions for those judged to have engaged in sodomy. In England the drive to end discrimination had resulted in the setting up of commissions to study legislation against homosexuals, and one commission in turn had resulted in curtailing some of the worst police abuses. This chapter in Britain immediately opens after the 1967 reform of a nineteenth-century law criminalizing homosexuality. In the face of continuing discrimination, the radicalization of the homosexual rights movement burst upon society, dramatically and permanently changing culture. This radicalization occurred not only because of the police, but also because straight people in the women's and civil rights movements turned out to be as prejudiced as anyone else. It took a while for the women's movement in the West not only to see its racism but also to acknowledge and deal with its homophobia.

This chapter also reminds us that history comes not only from professional scholars but also from activists and witnesses to the events of the day. Accounts by participants have a special urgency, and sometimes their bias is more evident than that of professionals who are better at hiding or sometimes overcoming it. The story of gay rights also raises questions of male/female co-operation and of whether anyone can have a singular identity or set of causes when one is an activist, or an 'ordinary' person for that matter. It ends in the 1970s before there was a rapprochement *during the AIDS crisis of the 1980s, when lesbians and gays banded together to fight the epidemic and to help its victims.*

* * *

The distinct lack of euphoria that greeted law reform was not misplaced. Parliament had provided too little too late. When gay men sat down and analysed what had actually happened, they wire bitterly disappointed. The Homosexual Law Reform Society – whose contribution was rejected when it came to drafting the Leo Abse bill – pointed out that the new law applied only to England and Wales. Even worse, in many ways it was more restrictive than what had gone before. For example, the definition of private was such that a locked hotel room was deemed to be a public place and therefore two men in such a situation could still be prosecuted. Worst of all, the people who had pushed through reform made it clear that gay men (and by implication lesbians) should be grateful for what they'd got and should now shut up.

Lord Arran's final statement in Parliament made his feelings plain. 'Homosexuals must continue to remember that, while there may be nothing bad in being a homosexual, there is certainly nothing good,' he argued. He added that legislation or not, homosexuals would continue to be objects of 'dislike, derision and, at best, self-pity'. He had misread the writing on the wall, even though it had been daubed on in five-foot psychedelic letters. The mood of the times was not one of self-pity but of self-celebration.

Peter Burton was running a club called Le Duce in 1967 which was one of the trendiest places to be seen in London. It was filled with young people who were defining what society should be like, regardless of what the law said. 'My generation was not going to be tied down by their laws and their constraints,' he explains. 'So, whether the law changed in 1967 or whether it had to wait till 1977, we would have been like we were at that point in history.' Peter's clientèle at Le Duce included David Hockney and Andy Warhol, as well as straight stars like Rod Stewart (who later employed Peter as his tour manager) and Paul Simon, who used to strum away on his guitar on the club's folk nights. Dislike and derision were not what Peter experienced, and self-pity about being gay was as alien to him as a gas mask.

The emphasis was on fun, and the first gay magazines which began to be published, soon after the law was changed, had one thing in common – they concentrated on the lighter side of life. There was *Spartacus* and *Jeremy* – of which the latter was the more frivolous. Its glossy pages were filled with pictures of good-looking men, chic clothes that could be bought in Carnaby Street, just a stroll away from the magazine's offices, and the latest movies, carrying stills from Fellini's *Satyricon* and the Hollywood adaptation of Gore Vidal's *Myra Breckinridge*. It even carried stories about the latest in underwear for men, with special offers for those of its readers who wanted to buy some. It was clearly aimed at a young, metropolitan group.

The 1960s, as well as being a time of hedonism, were also noted for their head-expanding movements, with a proliferation of single-issue campaigns and the beginnings of grassroots politics. Many people, emboldened by the change in public attitudes towards gay men and lesbians, formed self-help groups of the sort that had never existed before. The Minorities Rights Group was one such organization which had been set up as early as 1963 by Esme Langley and Diana Chapman. It was notable for being the first explicit and dedicated lesbian social and political organization. By the mid-1960s it had reached its high point, and subsidiary groups were being set up all over the country.

That was how Barbara Bell came across it. She was living on the south coast at the time, saw an ad for a meeting in London and decided to attend. '[I went] into this seedy pub up a seedy staircase . . . dusty wooden floor and tables that looked awful, but to see all these women who were lesbian . . . was quite a revelation.' The Minorities Rights Group was in a confident, expansionist phase and wanted regional representatives, and Barbara found herself putting her hand up to volunteer to be the representative on the south coast.'

> 'We used to meet in our little house, we'd have parties which was wonderful. It was a cul-de-sac so we weren't disturbing anybody. We told the gay boy on the corner he could come and join us, of course he never did. We didn't really want him but we didn't want anybody to be upset.'

Far from being disliked or derided, as Lord Arran had predicted, Barbara found her straight neighbours eager to help:

> 'The woman was in amateur dramatics and the husband commuted to London every day and they had two little girls. But . . . she saw at once that Joan and I were in a partnership and how much in love we were. So, when we had the parties, she used to say, "Come into my house and I'll make all the puddings." It was lovely having neighbours like that.'

Many gay men and lesbians had always been politically active in other single-issue campaign groups, notably the peace movement, and many of them carried on with this. One of the most prominent activists for the Campaign for Nuclear Disarmament was Pat Arrowsmith, who had been one of the original members, having been one of the prime movers in the Aldermaston March. According to Pat, the peace movement appeared to harbour no prejudices against homosexuality:

> 'The question of being open about my lesbianism barely arose. Wendy and I were living together and there was no particular reason for stating we were lesbians. We just took for granted that everybody knew we were and I think it's true that anybody who knew us at all did know.'

In her career as a peace campaigner, Pat has been sent to prison eleven times. During the course of it, she noticed the changes in lesbian culture inside Holloway, from a rigid division between butch and femme to a more relaxed attitude.

> 'On the first of my long sentences in the mid-Sixties . . . the butch-type lesbians would strap back their busts and pad themselves out with mock cocks using sanitary towels for that purpose . . . I can remember looking up to one of the galleries, thinking am I in Wandsworth or Holloway? . . . [It] wasn't always easy to tell what sex a woman was until she spoke, not even necessarily then. . . . But when I was in prison for my second six month sentence a couple of years later in the late Sixties, it wasn't that stratified any more – you could see lesbian couples both of whom were dressed as women.'

This shift in emphasis was caused initially by the hippie movement, where jeans and caftans were interchangeable garments to be worn by either sex. This was reinforced by the rise of the Women's Liberation Movement, which told lesbians that they didn't need to dress like men to have power. In any case, being butch all the time was too much of an effort, as Luchia discovered.

> 'Dressing up in men's clothes, I can assure you, had its advantages because you could leap over a wall, you could run like the blazes. . . . But in another context you didn't like it . . . you felt as if you were actually performing to people. . . . At the end of the day, when everybody's gone home and there's nobody there, only you, you look in the mirror and what's looking at you is a sort of male version of yourself.'

One day, while she was in the Union bar, Luchia had her conversion from a world where a drink always meant a pint and clothes always meant a suit and tie. Two women walked in who didn't fit either the butch or the femme mould. They had long hair and they had smudges of blue make-up on their eyelids, and blouses with small pieces of mirrored glass embroidered on to them, and they smelled of patchouli oil. What's more, instead of seeing the Union as a refuge from a hostile world, they were criticizing it for exploiting a captive clientèle. Luchia was intrigued by their conversation, particularly by the word 'exploited', and asked if she could sit at their table. 'And I said, "Well, I was thinking about what you were saying about landlords and, you know, what's the word – exploitation? What's exploitation?" So they told me and I said, "You're right, they are exploiting."' It turned out that what Luchia had encountered were two lesbians from the local university who were to pull her into a new milieu.

First, however, they had to effect a transformation on Luchia's dress sense. 'I started to buy myself a nice pair of slip-on sandals, I got myself a nice little pair of bell bottoms. I asked the girls to come and help me to buy one of them little blouses with glasses on and I got right into Janis Joplin.' Luchia also started attending meetings at the local university and familiarizing herself with the vocabulary of agitprop groups which extended far beyond the word 'exploitation'.

For some lesbians, the Women's Liberation Movement, in its early days, was less welcoming. Angela Mason recalls a particularly hostile response. 'We tried to join Women's Liberation. We sent a letter to the secretary, who was this Maoist, with a postal order for seven shillings and sixpence, and she wrote me back a letter saying that lesbians shouldn't be part of the Women's Liberation Movement and returned my postal order.' Sharley McLean recalls a similarly disagreeable attitude. 'I left several groups of liberation-type women because on the whole they could not hack lesbianism. I think they felt threatened . . . in awareness-raising around women's issues you could always tell who were lesbians because they had a far clearer idea . . . on women's rights.'

The hippie movement was not much better when it came to gay men and lesbians. Despite its credo of free love and peace towards all, the attitudes of many hippie men were inevitably unreconstructed and gay men got taunted while lesbians were expected to make exceptions when it came to sex. This combination made the time ripe for gay men and lesbians to set up their own organization. The new grouping was to combine the Women's Movement's philosophy, that the personal is political, with the hippie movement's tactics of 'zapping' hostile organizations in a spirit of jovial insolence which gave the press the photo opportunities they wanted. The result was the Gay Liberation Front (GLF).

There were plenty of things that distinguished GLF from all the other campaigning organizations – not least some of its members who went everywhere dressed in radical drag – but the most obvious one was the use of the word 'gay'. Just as the use of the word 'homosexual', at the beginning of the century, had marked a shift in the way gay men and lesbians were perceived, the use of the word 'gay' signified another major change – not only in the way that gay men and lesbians were regarded by society as a whole but, more importantly, how they viewed themselves.

All the words used to describe gay men and lesbians until that point – sodomite, invert, homosexual – either had religious, scientific or legal origins, and then there were all the pejorative slang terms. What was needed was a word which was neither abusive nor clinical. Many attempts had been made to coin such a word. In the nineteenth century a German lawyer, Karl Heinrich Ulrichs, who campaigned for law reform in the German states, came up with the singularly unmellifluous 'urning'. It didn't catch on. At the beginning of this century, Edward Carpenter, the writer and thinker, came up with another neologism. He suggested 'Uranian' – taken from Plato's *Symposium*, in which the Greek philosopher had used the word to describe his theory of an idealized love between men. Although the word acquired a brief currency among Carpenter and his associates it too fell by the wayside, but when GLF fell upon the word 'gay' it was the obvious choice, not least because it was the term that gay people had already been using to describe themselves.

The origins of the word, as applied to homosexuals, are unclear, but it had certainly been in existence since the nineteenth century. It could have been borrowed from the French, where the word *gaie* meant homosexual – interestingly the feminine form of the word was used to describe males. By the 1930s, 'gay' had become a codeword to describe homosexuality but its use was fairly restricted, although it did make a mainstream appearance from time to time as an in-joke. So, for example, in 1936, a Broadway musical called *Bittersweet*, which was a satire on Oscar Wilde and Lord Alfred Douglas, had a line-up of chorus boys singing a song whose refrain was: 'We are the reason for the Nineties being gay.' Similarly, in the 1938 film *Bringing Up Baby*, the character played by Cary Grant – about whom there were many rumours at the time – loses all his clothes and has to wear a borrowed frilly négligée. Exasperated by persistent questions about why he is in that unusual ensemble, he retorts: 'Because I just went gay all of a sudden.'

Certainly by the 1950s, gay had become a common word of self-description by homosexual men and women, most particularly in America where it served the same purpose as Polari did in Britain – a way of communicating without being generally understood. So friends could talk about being gay or advertise for 'gay' roommates where only the right person would understand the real meaning. Donald Webster Cory in his 1951 survey of homosexuality in America wrote: 'Needed for years was an ordinary, everyday, matter-of-fact word that could express the concept of homosexuality without glorification or condemnation. It must have no odium of the effeminate stereotype about it. Such a word has long been in existence and, in recent years, has grown in popularity. The word is "gay".'

The fact that the word was more prevalent in America than in Britain was no impediment to the pioneering gay liberationists on this side of the Atlantic who took all their early inspiration from America. Indeed, gay rights activists in Western Europe all date the beginning of the struggle back to the Stonewall riots in New York when a group of gay men and lesbians fought a pitched battle with the police after years of harassment. To this day, Gay Pride parades across the Western world are timed to coincide with the anniversary of that event.

The Stonewall riots take their name from the bar in Greenwich Village where, on 28 June 1969, a group of gay men and lesbians fought back for the first time in modern history. Police raids were a regular occurrence at the Stonewall – so much so that there was a secret signal to warn customers. The Stonewall, which was run by the Mafia, would often get tipoffs from its contacts in the New York Police Department that a raid was imminent. When this happened or when a plain-clothes officer was suspected of having gained entry, the tinted lights on the dance floor would be switched off and the white lights switched on. These had to be deployed at frequent intervals and any members of the same sex who were dancing together would stop instantly. However this in itself was no protection. The police would still harass anybody who was wearing more than three articles of clothing that could be construed to be garments intended for the opposite sex – this apparently contravened a state law – and most people would be turned out of the bar regardless.

On that night in 1969, the Stonewall was raided as usual, but, as each person was questioned and turned out of the bar, instead of dispersing, they hung around. As the paddy wagons arrived the mood became angry, and missiles rained down on the police who retreated into the bar. Parking meters were uprooted and hurled into the bar, lighter fluid was squirted in followed by burning matches. Howard Smith, reporter from the New York paper, *Village Voice*, who found himself inside the bar with the police, reported: 'The sound filtering in [didn't suggest] dancing faggots any more, it sounded like a powerful rage bent on vendetta.'

The drag queens had discovered that a stiletto could be as powerful a weapon in the hand as it was decorative on the foot. Thus empowered, they fought back, tooth and varnished claw. Martin Duberman, in his account of the events, recalls how, when the police turned up the next night, they were confronted by more angry drag queens – all dressed to kill. They had their arms round each other's waists and proceeded to high-kick their way towards the police lines, chanting: 'We are the Stonewall girls, we wear our hair in curls, we wear no underwear, we show our pubic hair.' What had happened was that gay men and lesbians suddenly discovered that they didn't have to put up with the harassment. Even during the course of the Stonewall riots, this lesson was not as obvious as it seems. Duberman describes how 'some hundred people were being chased . . . by two cops, someone in the crowd suddenly realized the unequal odds and started yelling: 'There are only two of 'em! Catch 'em!' . . . As the crowd took up the cry, the two officers fled.'

Symbolically, the riots began on the night of Judy Garland's funeral. Garland had been the archetypal gay icon because she represented bravery through adversity, but that bravery was characterized by a passive stoicism. With the death of Judy Garland, that image of the gay man died too. The beat poet, Allen Ginsberg, expressed it thus: 'You know those guys were so beautiful – they've lost that wounded look that all fags had ten years ago.'

What the clientèle of the Stonewall had done was express their anger; there was no planning or political agenda behind it, but interested onlookers saw how it could be used to spark off the last of the 1960s revolutions and people like Ginsberg hurried down to Greenwich Village. The decade had been marked by grassroots agitation, starting with the civil rights movement, followed by the student revolution and the Women's Liberation Movement. Many gay men and lesbians who had been active in one or more of these other movements saw their chance. Within twenty-four hours, political slogans were appearing on the boarded-up windows of the Stonewall which read, among other things, 'Support Gay Power'. The following day another notice appeared on the Stonewall windows. It read: 'We homosexuals plead with our people to please help maintain peaceful and quiet conduct on the streets of the Village. Mattachine.'

The Mattachine Society had been going for a number of years and represented professional gay men and lesbians who wanted to lobby for equal rights by proving that they were no different from heterosexuals except in their sexual preferences. The Mattachine Society advice to its members when going out on pickets and demonstrations was that men should don white shirts, suits and ties and women should appear in skirts and dresses. Both sexes should wear glasses, if they had them, to give an added air of authority. While the Mattachine Society had done some good work in the past, its tactics were rooted in an era when respectability was what gay men and lesbians craved. What was beginning to emerge was a conflict between older, staider gay men and lesbians and their younger, angrier counterparts. Exactly the same conflict was to show itself when the Gay Liberation Front unfurled its banners in Britain.

The Stonewall riots were described by one American observer as 'the hairpin drop heard around the world', and young gay men and lesbians in Britain heard the reverberations loud and clear. In the years after law reform, police harassment was on the rise again and the gay voice was largely ineffectual. The Homosexual Law Reform Society was running out of steam. Plans to set up a series of social clubs around the country came to nothing and there seemed to be a lack of direction. The northwest branch of the Homosexual Law Reform Society, which had always been more adventurous, renamed itself the Committee for Homosexual Equality (CHE, later renamed the Campaign for Homosexual Equality), which, like the Mattachine Society in America, believed in doing things properly and, also like the Mattachine Society, it found itself in conflict with Britain's emergent Gay Liberation Front.

The first and most obvious difference between the Committee for Homosexual Equality and the Gay Liberation Front was one of semantics. The gay liberationists felt that to accept the word 'homosexual' as a self-definition meant also accepting all the baggage that went with it. The word 'homosexual' was clinical in a literal sense – it was a word that had emerged

172

from and belonged in psychiatrists' clinics. More importantly, it was a word that defined a sexual category, whereas the word 'gay' defined a lifestyle. It might seem a trivial distinction but it mattered enormously, not only to gay men and lesbians but to heterosexuals too.

Soon after GLF began to make waves, British newspapers began to get upset about their use of the word 'gay'. The *People* ran a story about gay men and lesbians with the headline: 'They Call This Gay – But We Have Another Word For It – Ugh.' There was a stream of readers' letters about the hijacking of the word gay. In the early 1970s, the *Daily Telegraph*, the *Sunday Telegraph* and the *Observer* all ran letters in their correspondence columns on the issue. The general complaint was that a perfectly good English word had been misappropriated. The newly revolutionized gay men and lesbians responded by saying that plenty of other good English words – like fairy and pansy – had also been misappropriated, but nobody seemed to be complaining about them. The correspondence in the *Observer* finally came to a halt when a certain Nick Rogers wrote the following:

> It is not up to her [the previous correspondent] as a heterosexual to decide how we should describe ourselves. It is up to us to produce a description and she can like it or lump it. Why should we accept what she deems . . . to be 'dignified' . . . or are we also allowed to define her identity and lay down that from now on all heterosexuals should call themselves 'giraffes'?

This jokey impertinence was typical of GLF's tactics which were transported to Britain in 1970 – by students and staff at the London School of Economics, one of the most radical campuses in Britain. During the summer of 1970, Aubrey Walter, who had just finished his sociology degree, took himself off to the States, having read about the Gay Liberation Front in *The Times*. While demonstrating in New York, he came across Bob Mellors, who was at the London School of Economics. Back in Britain, at the end of the summer, Bob Mellors and Aubrey Walter decided to hold a meeting to test out the water. Accordingly, on 13 October 1970, the first meeting of the British branch of GLF took place in a basement seminar room at the London School of Economics. That first meeting was attended by fewer than twenty people most of whom were students or staff at the London School of Economics, but over the next few months, as the core group went round London handing out leaflets, the attendance at meetings burgeoned.

For many gay men, like Michael James, GLF articulated what they had been feeling, but couldn't quite express. Michael, who had been living in London and frequenting the commercial gay scene, felt that 'they actually gave words to our feelings and experiences . . . it was almost as if somebody had cracked open our heads and allowed other parts of our consciousness to blossom out and start asking questions.' GLF's approach to rigid gender distinctions was radical drag. This differed from conventional drag in that it wasn't female impersonation – men with moustaches would varnish their nails and flounce around in dresses with handbags hanging from the crooks of their elbows. They knew that this would be shocking at first but that was the idea. The hope was that, after the initial indignation wore off, it would make people think about sex roles and why a piece of fabric should carry so much significance. Radical drag was something that Michael took to with alacrity. 'It was instant transformation. I stepped out of a three-piece suit and into a frock and that was it.'

GLF was just as much of an eye-opener for the lesbians who joined it. Juno Jones, who had earlier in her life joined the Carmelite nuns as a postulant, came across an article about GLF in a discarded copy of the *Daily Mirror* and decided to go along to one of the meetings which were held in a cavernous venue in Covent Garden called Middle Earth. 'I made about four or five attempts and eventually I went inside . . . and there were guys with sequins in their beards and lots of patchouli oil in the air and flowing robes . . . it was just astonishing. It really was like dipping your toe in magic,' she recalls.

Like Michael James, Juno found that GLF shifted perspectives so that her world view was now proud rather than apologetic. More importantly, she recognized that anything was possible. 'It was like somebody had taken my brain out of my head, washed out all the crap and put it back in,' she says. 'It's like trying to describe what an orgasm is. You can't describe what an orgasm is and I can't really . . . put into words what it was like for me. It was just mind-blowing. It was like the top of your head zips open and powwww!'

Most of GLF's founding members had come from other political groupings which were informed by Marxist politics, and it was one of GLF's central tenets that, by transforming the individual, society would be transformed. All mainstream *modi vivendi* came under scrutiny, from the nuclear family to private property and personal incomes. For those who were committed to GLF, the logical next step was to move into a commune with other GLF people.

There were numerous demonstrations, the most notable being the one mounted against the Festival of Light. In May 1971, two ex-missionaries set up the Festival of Light to counter what they regarded as the moral pollution that had confronted them on their return to Britain. The organization quickly gained an enormous influence. Within a few months, the Festival of Light had become a national organization and announced plans for a huge rally in London which would compel the government to act against the 'forces of evil' as they described it. The manifestations of this evil, as cited by the Festival of Light, were Ken Russell films, sex outside marriage and the growth of open homosexuality.

This was the kind of challenge GLF was waiting for. One of the leading lights in GLF, John Chesterman, organized the event with impeccable élan. The first task was to infiltrate the organization, and one of the GLF women volunteered to work in the Festival of Light's main office, from where she filched mailing lists. These were used to send out fake mailings and misleading parking plans for coaches that were bringing Festival of Light members to their rally in Central Hall in Westminster. The most important acquisition, however, was tickets for the rally, which GLF then forged in such large numbers that were were enough to hand around to anyone who wanted to go. An early form of networking was employed and other sympathetic groups like members of the Women's Liberation Movement were brought in to join in the disruption.

Chesterman co-ordinated it so that everyone was split up into small groups and asked to come up with an inventive form of disruption. No one was aware of the complete battle plan, they only knew what the group before them was going to do. When the previous group had finished, it was the cue for the next group to do their stuff, and so on, in a chain of events that was to burst like so many water bombs over the heads of the people in the hall. In her history of GLF, Lisa Power quotes from a note handed out by Chesterman to each group. It reads:

> Enter the hall in small groups. Ones or twos. Act unobtrusively. Dress conservatively. Act cool. Make no sign of protest until it is your turn. Do not speak to each other. Sit as close to the centre of the row as possible. Let the previous demonstration finish completely before you start yours. Let everyone settle down and the speeches start again. Part of the purpose is to slow down and delay proceedings. . . . Offer passive resistance only. Do not fight back. A general brawl will only confuse the media image. If there is any aggression, let them look like the villain in the press reports. Do not carry anything that could be construed as an offensive weapon . . . You may be arrested so make any arrangements . . . beforehand. Make no statements to the police until you have legal assistance. They cannot force you to do so. Do not speak to the press or TV.

A number of participants went one better when advised to dress conservatively – they came dressed as clerics and nuns. 'Men really sacrificed their long hair, they got their long hair cut off and had short backs and sides,' recalls Juno Jones. 'They wore suits and ties which had us on the floor laughing because we'd never seen them looking so straight.'

Michael James decided to wear a beige lace dress with pearl buttons and a voluminous lacy skirt – but under suitable disguise: 'We all met at the Embankment . . . and I had my evening dress stuffed underneath my suit, with a little bag of make-up and heels and a wig, and we got to Westminster Hall and dotted ourselves all the way around and the proceedings started.'

The first event was the release of white mice which scurried down the aisle almost as if they were clockwork toys, but the two women who released the rodents didn't escape lightly – one of them was repeatedly hit over the head with a handbag by a woman who kept shouting, 'Jesus loves you.' Then two old ladies sitting in the balcony unfurled a banner saying, 'Cliff for Queen.' Then the 'nuns' started. They consisted of a group of men and women who until then had stayed quietly in their seats, but when their cue arrived they rose as one, walked to the front and started doing the cancan.

Michael's cue was Bette Bourne – a trained actor who later started up the theatre troupe Bloolips – who was sitting on the other side of the aisle dressed like a Blimpish colonel.

> 'Bette has got this absolutely fabulous voice and people were being really manhandled very badly by the stewards – you know beaten and kicked, that's Christians for you – and Bette said, 'This is not right,' and this wonderful voice resonated throughout the hall . . . 'People are being injured here, this is not right. We're supposed to be Christians. I see a steward there hitting somebody.' Course they twigged that Bette was part of the demo and shoved her out.'

Finally it was Michael's turn.

> 'By this time they'd wheeled Malcolm Muggeridge up to the microphone and he was wittering away about this, that and the other. So I gave him two or three minutes to get into his stride and then I thought now or never. I just stood up in the back in this lovely coffee-coloured frock and screamed, "Hallelujah! I've been saved," and went into the whole southern belle trip – "I've seen the light, I've seen the Lord," and of course they couldn't get to me. They had to empty the row either side and I was just standing there proclaiming the Word. Eventually they got to us and I just sort of drifted this frock over everybody as I was going down the stairs proclaiming my love for Jesus.'

Finally, it was time for the *pièce de résistance* which involved GLF people, dressed as members of Ku Klux Klan, standing up to demand 'perverts' be burnt at the stake. Afterwards, the protesters stood outside to hand out leaflets and discuss the issues with any Festival of Light members who cared to. The event was given wide coverage in the national press, which found GLF enlivened what would otherwise have been very dull stories. There were dozens of other such demonstrations but the disruption of the Festival of Light rally exemplified GLF's approach to campaigning.

Branches of GLF were being set up outside London, and Luchia Fitzgerald was introduced to the Manchester offshoot of it by the women she had met in the Union. Although she didn't understand all the political rhetoric, she knew she had found a way of living that would make her happy. But she had to deal with all the baffling jargon in some way.

> 'I went out and bought a dictionary and every night when I heard a new word at these meetings I would go home and I would open the dictionary and have a look for the word and so a whole new vocabulary was opening up to me.'

It wasn't all talk and no action. Like their London counterparts, the Manchester group were activists first and foremost. Luchia remembers going out with a pot of yellow paint one night and daubing 'Lesbians Are Everywhere' on the most prominent surfaces she could find in the city. 'It went up on every bridge in and out of the city – north, south, east and west – and you should have seen it the next morning, the traffic all jammed up against one another, sitting there staring at "Lesbians Are Everywhere".'

This wasn't to last long. GLF was a rainbow coalition and after a while the differences began to show. There had always been small rifts – between the women and the men – between those who espoused radical drag and those who didn't – but after a few years, those rifts widened into chasms. The gaps loomed as women felt that the men were not even interested in listening to them, let alone joining them in their fight.

'The lads from GLF were very contradictory,' Luchia explains.

> 'They were very loud in the meetings, they always wanted to chair the meetings. They were very butch, if you will, and we felt that they didn't have an understanding of our sexuality. They were very reluctant to share jobs and to share power and so we were fighting a battle within a battle.'

Juno Jones recalls that even though there had been divisions, the split took her aback. 'It came as quite a surprise to me when it actually happened but in retrospect I had to agree with what happened,' she explains.

> 'It was really the attitude of the men, just because they were gay men didn't mean that they weren't men and they basically treated us like shit. . . . The women were getting more involved in Women's Liberation by that stage and our consciousness was changing more into wanting to separate from the men because we

had completely different issues. We had a different agenda by
that stage like equal pay for women, wages for housework, why
should women look after the children, why should women do the
clearing up.'

The women involved in the London branches of GLF – still the largest and
most influential in the country – were feeling much the same and now they
had an alternative. The early hostility of the Women's Liberation Movement
had dissipated after a group of GLF activists went to the Women's
Liberation National Co-ordinating Conference. Initially, they were told that
they were a 'bourgeois deviation', but GLF women were not going to be put
off so easily. They seized the microphone and led a grassroots revolt which
changed the tenor of the conference and put lesbianism firmly on the
feminist agenda. That was in October 1971, and by the following February,
women had walked out of GLF announcing that they wanted to work
separately.

On 1 July 1972, when Britain's first Gay Pride parade took place, the
women returned, wearing wonderful face paint, and marched under a
banner reading 'Gay Women's Liberation'. The radical drag queens got
decked out in fabulous frocks and the single-issue activists came as they
were. The trouble was, the groups barely spoke to each other or, worse,
they argued. 'The divisions were so deep that it could never have been
reconciled although it did paddle along for a couple of months after that,
but once the women split and the drag queens split that was it – you know,
the final thing,' Michael James explains.

The demise of GLF has as much to do with a change in society as with
the inherent tensions within it. GLF was an essentially 1960s organization
with its emphasis on the counterculture, its suspicion of hierarchies, its
opposition to capitalism and its emphasis on the individual. By the early
1970s that approach was beginning to die off, along with the rest of the
1960s' counterculture. In all, GLF had lasted for less than four years, but its
influence extended far beyond its short life. During the heady days, when
nobody saw beyond the next demonstration and the biggest dilemma was
what you were going to wear to it, GLF members could hardly have
foreseen how far-reaching their actions would be. With hindsight it has
become clear.

Not only did GLF start off Britain's Gay Pride parades – which have taken
place in an unbroken chain for the lest twenty-four years – but it was
also the catalyst for Britain's first national gay newspaper – *Gay News* was
started up as a joint initiative between GLF members and CHE. Finally,
GLF was also responsible for establishing a help and information line – Gay
Switchboard. Indeed, when the GLF office in King's Cross closed down, it
was handed on as a present to Gay Switchboard which has gone from
strength to strength since then. *Gay News* soon cut itself off from its radical

roots and established itself as a non-partisan, middle-of-the-road newspaper. Even though major distributors like WH Smith refused to carry the paper in the early stages, within four years it had established a circulation of 20,000 which made it the largest circulation newspaper for homosexuals in the world. In 1977 it gained even greater fame when Mary Whitehouse brought a private prosecution against the paper under blasphemy laws which had remained dormant for so long everybody thought they were defunct. Gay men and lesbians – even those who disagreed with the editorial stance that *Gay News* had adopted – rallied around staging fundraising events and benefits to help pay the enormous costs of the court action so that the paper's future could be secured. Peter Burton, who was working for *Gay News* at this time, believes it might have even done *Gay News* some good:

> 'Dear Mrs Whitehouse found this [a poem published by *Gay News*] offensive and . . . took a private prosecution for blasphemous libel against *Gay News*, thereby doing the publication a great kindness, because she made us international news. Really, it was a big worldwide story, thereby raising our visibility, raising the readership, letting lots of lonely people, who didn't know we existed, know [that we were there]. We couldn't buy publicity like she gave *Gay News* and gays generally.'

GLF's highly visible campaigning of the early 1970s had another effect which is far more difficult to quantify – it taught gay men and lesbians not to be fearful and to ask for what they wanted. It seems that what they wanted was hedonism. What characterized gay culture throughout the rest of the 1970s was the pursuit of pleasure. The number of gay clubs, pubs and restaurants grew with such speed that it was difficult to keep pace. Gay men no longer wanted to demonstrate – they wanted to dance, and disco was the beat that they wanted to dance to.

9

FEMINIST CRITIQUES OF MODERN JAPANESE POLITICS

Vera Mackie

Since the late nineteenth century Japan has been an industrial power and one that commanded an important Asian empire until 1945, when it was defeated as a result of World War II. As in India, Egypt, and the West, the women's movement in Japan had begun long before 1945. Japanese movements on women's behalf had been liberal, socialist, and even anarchist, putting forth a variety of proposals in the first half of the twentieth century. The diverse approaches to improving women's lives stemmed from the variety of Japanese experiences: women staffed the industries that created its economic wealth, and these workers fed into working-class movements. A widespread 'good wives' ethos made others favor educational and moral reform above economic change. A few were conscious of their relationship with the subjects of Japanese colonialism.

Feminist fervor declined in the 1930s, as Japan's government became involved in conflicts in Asia and the Pacific between 1937 and 1945. The dropping of the atomic bomb on Hiroshima and Nagasaki in August 1945 ended that war. This experience and the threat of more atomic warfare because of superpower rivalry encouraged Japanese women to lead the way in global pacifism in the 1950s. Yet Japan became powerful once again because of the Cold War, supplying the US military with jeeps and other manufactured goods for its wars in Korea and Vietnam. From the 1960s US soldiers also snapped up electronic goods like cameras, hi-fis, and televisions while on breaks from combat. It was in the context of a booming capitalist economy that Japanese feminism revived, targeting the university, the household, work life, and the parliament for reform. Describing a movement half a world away from feminism in the West yet one with many similarities, the following chapter raises issues of capitalist prosperity as a precondition for a certain kind of activism that seems to cross cultural and geographic lines. An East–West comparison also allows us to consider that despite women's activism in lobbying and electoral politics, their actual success in national representative politics remains incredibly low. What lies behind the persistent practices in these societies, even in the face of constant critique, that it is masculine values which should inform political and social life? The goals of Japanese feminism invite questions about regions as the basis for either investigation or politics.

* * *

Feminist activists in modern Japan have addressed a number of questions that will seem at once familiar and highly distinctive to an international readership. Discussion of women in other Asian countries often focuses on issues of development and underdevelopment, but the problems faced by contemporary Japanese women are the problems of advanced capitalism. What is the role of women's labour, and how have capital and the state attempted to regulate women's labour? How have women themselves theorized this relationship? What is the ideological importance of motherhood? How has the state attempted to use or to regulate women's reproductive capacity? Since the late nineteenth century, feminist activists and critics in Japan have analysed how government policies affect women, and have outlined strategies for transforming such policies. Whether under the Imperial system before 1945, or under the more liberal postwar system, women have aspired to the full rights of citizenship. Before 1945, women petitioned for the removal of legal and institutional barriers to political participation. Since 1945, with the removal of these formal restrictions, women have addressed the operations of gender ideologies in the family, education and the workplace which determine the possibilities for women's political participation.[1] In this chapter I will take a broad view of feminist politics in Japan, and not seek to push all of women's political activities into a falsely coherent 'women's movement'. Women have also been active in, for example, consumerist, pacifist, and anti-pollution groups, often contributing through these to a critique of modern Japanese society.

From subject to citizen

After World War II, Japan was occupied by the Allied forces under General MacArthur until 1952. In these years the legal system was completely overhauled. In effect, women were transformed from subjects (subject to the Emperor and subject to the patriarch) into citizens, with rights explicitly spelt out in the Constitution and Civil Code. The changes in the legal position of women were dramatic, although it is debatable how much real change was effected in women's lives. According to documents of the Occupation forces, the rationale for granting female suffrage was that women would be more 'peace loving' and challenge the militarist traditions of the pre-war state.[2] These legal changes were backed up with a programme of civic education for women.[3] MacArthur is often given credit for the granting of female suffrage from above, but this view ignores the existence of the pre-war suffrage movement which demanded all of the legislative changes eventually granted. In fact, several women had petitioned on this and other issues immediately after the surrender.[4]

The Constitution of 1947 is one of the most liberal in the world. Article 14, paragraph 1 stipulates: 'All of the people are equal under the law and there shall be no discrimination in political, economic or social relations because of race, creed, sex, social status or family origin.' This is extended to cover marriage, divorce and inheritance, and the Civil Code was revised after 1947 to meet the conditions outlined in the Constitution:

> Marriage shall be based only on the mutual consent of both sexes and it shall be maintained through mutual co-operation with the equal rights of the husband and wife as its basis. With regard to choice of spouse, property rights, choice of domicile, divorce and other matters pertaining to marriage and family, laws shall be enacted from the standpoint of individual dignity and the essential equality of the sexes.[5]

Divorce is granted almost automatically by mutual consent of both parties, and the grounds for judicial divorce are the same for husband and wife.

However, remnants of the patriarchal family system remained in the Nationality Law and family registration (*Koseki*) system. The Household Registration Law gave the famly an official legal status and implicitly recognized the father's headship. According to the postwar Nationality Law, only men had the right to pass on Japanese nationality to their children, reflecting a patriarchal view that the father had the major power to determine the domicile and nationality of family members. The welfare system, although expanded in the postwar period, continued to be based on the assumption that the family would be the major provider of welfare services, with the remainder of services being shared between the state and private companies.[6] The Eugenic Protection Law of 1947 and so-called 'protective' provisions of the Labour Standards Law encoded a view that women's primary role concerned motherhood – in both cases it was the abstract concept of 'motherhood' which was to be protected (*bosei hogo*), rather than the welfare of individual women.

The Labour Standards Law of 1947 prohibited differential treatment in wages and on the basis of sex. It provided women with menstruation leave, maternity leave and nursing leave, and women were prevented from working late at night or in dangerous occupations.[7] Thanks to Article 14 of the Constitution, and articles of the Labour Standards Law concerning equal pay, it has been possible to sue employers guilty of discriminatory practices throughout the postwar period. However, as we shall see, this was no easy matter.

In the first postwar election on 10 April 1946, an estimated 67 per cent of the 20 million eligible women cast their votes, and in more recent years, women's voting rates have even exceeded that of men.[8] As early as 1946 several women were elected to the Diet. Although there have been prominent individuals, women have generally been less than 3 per cent of the total membership of both houses until very recently, and only a few women have been appointed to cabinet in the postwar period.[9] Despite their marginalization from mainstream politics and union activities, women have been active in various kinds of grassroots political activity.

In the immediate postwar period, women's political activities focused on questions that were bound up with a perception of their role as wives and mothers. Some of the most active of citizens' movements concerned consumer affairs and pollution – women united to protest against food shortages and high prices. After the 1946 election the new female members of the Diet united in pressuring MacArthur to take action on the shortages.[10] The Chifuren (League of Regional Women's Organizations) and Shufuren (Housewives' Association), two of the largest national organizations, were formed at this time. Both groups are concerned with consumer issues, and the Shufuren has large laboratories in Tokyo for testing products. It also handles consumers' complaints about defective products and has been involved in campaigns to boycott overpriced goods.[11] It has often been women who have brought pollution problems to the attention of the nation; for example, they were particularly important in the campaign against mercury poisoning by the Chisso Corporation in Minamata. Because most men in the Minamata area were on the Chisso payroll, they could not challenge the company without endangering their livelihood.[12]

Women have been involved in peace movements throughout the postwar period. In 1952, the first and second meetings of Nihon Fujin Kai took place – women workers, housewives and students called for peace, and the abolition of nuclear weapons. Chifuren took up the peace issue in 1954, and Hahaoya Taikai (The Mothers' Convention) grew out of this into a national pacifist movement. The names of these groups are revealing of the identification of these women with an expanded domestic sphere. Shufuren even used a rice serving spoon as its symbol.[13]

In the 1960s the preconditions for more radical political participation by women appeared. From the 1960s, the Japanese economy showed spectacular economic growth, largely based on steel processing and manufacturing. The influence of the United States was crucial, for Japan provided bases for American military activity in Korea and Vietnam, which acted as a stimulus to the Japanese economy. In 1960 Japan was due to renew a security pact ('Ampo') with the United States. Protest against the pact provided impetus to left-wing groups, unions, students and over forty women's groups. The Ampo struggle was linked with opposition to American military bases on Japanese soil. In Kitafuji, at the foot of Mount Fuji, struggles against the appropriation of 'common land' by American forces supported by the Japanese self-defence forces have carried on for several decades. Years before the massive women-led protests against the US base at Greenham Common in the UK, the women of Kitafuji occupied huts on the military practice grounds and employed various forms of active and passive resistance. The women of Kitafuji continue to provide inspiration for peace activists.[14]

Although women's involvement in such movements may initially have been seen as an extension of their role in the home, the contradictory effect was to make many of them more receptive to a radical critique of gender relations in their society. In the 1960s there was increased student militancy, culminating in the occupation of several universities.[15] Many women, however, experienced similar contradictions to those of their sisters in America and France, quickly becoming disillusioned with the malestream Left's lack of awareness of gender issues. This provided impetus for a feminist critique of politics. Saitô Chiyo,[16] the founder of Agora, a women's resource centre in Tokyo, had watched with concern the demonstrations against the security pact with the US in 1960. She abhorred anything which might lead to a revival of militarism.[17] When one of the demonstrators died in confrontation with the police, Saitô was moved to join the demonstrations, despite problems in finding childcare for her young child. This experience radicalized her and revealed to her that it was impossible for women to take an active role in the world – through labour or political activity – while inadequate childcare facilities tied them to the home.[18] She embarked on a three-year campaign to establish a childcare centre in her area, in the course of which she met many housewives, and helped to establish a 'talent bank' so that women could employ their skills in the public sphere.

Eventually, Agora was created as a resource centre where women could engage in consciousness-raising and assertiveness training, and gather information as a resource for feminist activity such as the talent bank, which served as a kind of labour exchange. Agora has survived longer than many other feminist groups, and the story of its founding is instructive. It grew out of the experiences of women themselves, and now has centres all over Japan – each centre having evolved to meet the needs of local women. This pattern recurs in feminist politics in Japan. A group of women meet to try to solve some problem close to their own lives – pollution, childcare, consumer issues, the usurpation of community land by military bases. Although they may not initially describe themselves as 'feminist', they are led inevitably to a critique of the politics of gender in Japanese society.

Fighting women

By the 1970s Japan's economy was firmly established on the basis of spectacular growth, largely in steel processing and manufacturing. By 1978, 65 per cent of all working women were married – many of whom had returned to temporary or part-time labour in their late thirties or early forties, after childrearing responsibilities had been eased.[19] Women's political activity in this period became more explicitly feminist, growing directly from their experiences of oppression as women, and challenging the identification of women with motherhood and the family.

185

In the early 1970s the Tatakau Onnatachi (Fighting Women) group was formed to combat conservative moves to amend those clauses in the abortion law which allowed pregnancies to be terminated on the grounds that the mother's welfare would be affected for 'economic reasons'. Members experimented with communal living and communal childcare, and set up the Shinjuku Women's Liberation Centre.[20] The journal *Onna Eros* (Woman – Eros) provided a forum for discussion of marriage, sexuality, prostitution, labour and politics from a literary and theoretical perspective.[21] Countless small groups were formed in the 1970s, and their newsletters formed the basis of *'mini-komi'* (mini-communications), providing an alternative to the *'masu-komi'* (mass-communications) which had no place for discussion of women's issues – except in a sensational or patronizing manner.[22] The term *uuman ribu* ('women's lib') became a focus of attention in the mass media, but was often the butt of ridicule.

Radical lesbian groups and a lesbian feminist 'L.F.' centre, which ran consciousness-raising and self-defence classes, were also formed at this time, while publications such as *Subarashii Onnatachi* (Wonderful Women) and *The Dyke* attempted to retrieve a history of lesbians in Japan,[23] a significant gap in accounts of Japanese feminism until recently.[24] Veterans of these groups later founded the first Rape Crisis Centre in Tokyo. Lesbian feminist groups have often been on the periphery of Japanese feminist activity, but have always had strong international links. Recently an Asian Lesbian Network was set up, and has held two conferences so far, one in Thailand and one in Japan. An annual gay and lesbian film festival has also been established.

It is no accident that the 1970s' flowering of feminist activity roughly coincided with similar activities in Europe, the United States and Australia. In all of the advanced capitalist nations women were experiencing the contradictions of an education which seemed to promise self-fulfilment, and a labour market based on inequalities of class and gender.[25] In Japan, too, many women had become disillusioned with left-wing politics which ignored or dismissed feminist demands. If Japanese women turned to the US and Europe for theoretical tools to explain their situation, this was because they were experiencing similar contradictions. Several feminist classics were translated into Japanese in the 1970s, and their influence was marked.

While many women pursued 'liberation' at an individual level, by engaging in consciousness-raising around themes of sexuality, the body and ideology, there was also a strong strand of reformism. Women were demanding institutional changes such as an equal opportunity act and reform of the education system, in the hope that the guarantees of equality encoded in the Constitution could be translated into reality. Women's underrepresentation in the elite national universities which feed graduates into public administration and the management sectors of large corporations is one of the factors contributing to the relative lack of women in decision-making positions in government, the civil service and private industry.

International Women's Year in 1975 and the ensuing International Decade for Women had an incalculable effect on Japanese feminist politics. Such groups as the International Women's Year Action Group were able to combine domestic political activity with international pressure through such forums as the International Women's Decade conferences at Copenhagen, Mexico and Nairobi. A large number of the group's members were educated working women such as teachers or public servants, and their activities were closely related to these sectors' concerns, with publications on non-sexist education, family law, problems of working women and divorce. The group also showed considerable skill in attracting media attention through demonstrations and sit-ins, and led a campaign to have a sexist TV commercial for instant noodles removed.[26]

In 1977, feminist poet and academic Atsumi Ikuko founded the journal *Feminist*, subtitled 'The New *Seitô*' to acknowledge its heritage in the pre-World War I feminist paper, which was much more ambitious than many of the '*mini-komi*'. It was interested in the development of a women's culture, and had an academic rather than an activist orientation. It carried work on labour conditions, the media, the family, education and motherhood, and introduced such writers as Adrienne Rich and Sylvia Plath to the Japanese audience. It also published two English-language editions in an attempt to integrate the journal into an international network of feminist communication.

Equal opportunity and Labour policy

By 1978 the International Women's Year Action Group had framed a clear set of demands for legislative change: an equal opportunity act and the removal of sexist provisions from the Nationality Law. Even in 1978 it was possible to sue a company for sexual discrimination on the grounds that it contravened Article 14 of the Constitution, but such legal action was expensive and time-consuming, and each case had to be argued on an individual basis. Though several judgments upholding equal pay for equal work referred to the Constitution, they could be circumvented by means of reclassification of job titles.[27] Furthermore, equality provisions of the Labour Standards Law only covered wages, and not promotion or retirement, and also prohibited women from excessive overtime or night-work. This was to be the most controversial aspect of demands for legislative change, for women demanded an equal opportunity act as well as the retention of 'protective' provisions for women.

The International Women's Year Action Group was able to mobilize sufficient international pressure to embarrass the government into signing the Convention on Ending All Forms of Discrimination Against Women (CEDAW) in Copenhagen in 1980 with a commitment to ratify the Convention by 1985. Over the next five years, women campaigned ceaselessly in the hope that Japan would introduce an act which had some potential for changing the situation of working women in Japan.[28] All opposition political parties produced draft legislation, and the most progressive was presented to the Diet by Socialist member Tanaka Sumiko.

Although the union federations paid lip-service to the principle of equality, unions provided little support in anti-discrimination cases. One reason is that most labour contracts only cover individual companies, and national union federations have little jurisdiction over contracts at the company level. Furthermore the union hierarchy is male-dominated – even in industries with large numbers of female workers. Responsibility for childcare often makes union activity practically impossible for women. Mainstream unions have shown little interest in providing representation for temporary or part-time workers.[29]

The Equal Employment Opportunity Law (EEOL) was promulgated in May 1985, effective from 1 April 1986. The law, based on a philosophy of 'equality of opportunity' rather than 'equality of result', was not backed up by affirmative action programmes and is virtually free of punitive provisions. Companies are encouraged to 'make efforts' to abolish discrimination in recruitment, hiring, transfer and promotion and are prohibited from discrimination on retraining, welfare, retirement and retrenchment, but no penalties are specified. Where a dispute arises, there are three stages of conciliation – within the company, through the local Women and Minors' Bureau of the Department of Labour, or through the local 'Equal Opportunity Board'.[30]

Immediately after the implementation of the EEOL, judgments were handed down in some long-running cases. In the case against the Japan Association of Steel Manufacturers, the Tokyo District Court in its 1986 verdict recognized that having separate career tracks for men and women was in violation of Article 14 of the Constitution, but that the company had discretion in the matter of deployment of staff within the company. In another case, in the Tottori District Court, female teachers were awarded compensation and costs on the grounds that they had been discriminated against in retirement provisions.[31]

During International Women's Decade, public money was poured into conferences, resource centres and a National Education Centre for Women, and as a result nearly every prefecture and major city boasts some kind of women's centre, which provides an important focus for information-sharing.

There has been some change in attitudes in the last few years. There are women who pursue careers and an independent lifestyle without undue pressure, and it is possible to see some men sharing childcare and taking children to and from crèches. For the majority of men, however, working conditions preclude any participation in domestic labour, and their long working hours are the major stumbling-block to any change in the sexual division of labour. Indeed, such commitment to their companies would be impossible without the support of women's domestic labour.

Masculinity, femininity and the media

The mass media, however, continue to present a stereotypical view of men and women. Women are seen as mothers, sexual objects or non-threatening child-figures. In the pages of the comics read by male students and workers on rush-hour trains, women are subjected to violence, rape and mutilation. Similar fantasies are enacted in pornographic movies. Media stories are also instrumental in instilling a sense of guilt in working mothers. When, for example, a death occurred in a private childcare centre some years ago, media rage was directed against the mother rather than the inadequacy of public childcare facilities.[32]

In the media's portrayal of women from other Asian countries, sexism overlaps with racism.[33] Weekly pulp magazines provide guides to brothels in Manila and Seoul; articles on Philippine women link them with the spread of HIV/AIDS in Japan – with no discussion of the responsibility of their male customers. The issue of 'sex tours' to South-east Asia by Japanese men forced Japanese women to think of the economic, political and ideological links between their own situation and that of other Asian women, instead of always looking to Europe or the US for inspiration.

Japan and Asia

One reason for Japan's spectacular economic growth in the postwar period was the stimulus provided by its support facilities for the United States' military operations in Asia. In the 1970s it was Japan's economic activities in Asia which came under scrutiny. Japanese industry went through a process of restructuring, as manufacturing industry moved offshore in search of cheaper labour and fewer controls over environmental pollution. Philippine, Korean or Indonesian workers – often women – provided labour for these enterprises. Japanese workers were affected by this restructuring as jobs were lost in manufacturing and created in service industries. South-east Asian women were affected as their local economies were integrated into the international division of labour. Women often had to make a dubious choice between sweated labour in electronics or textile plants, or providing sexual services for the tourist industry.[34]

The Asian Women's Association and Christian groups were most active in raising these issues. Matsui Yayori – one of the Association's founders and one of the few women to reach an editorial position in a major Japanese newspaper – used the pages of the *Asahi Shinbun*, often meeting opposition from senior editorial staff.[35]

The Asian Women's Association conducted research into Japan's economic activities in Asia, the structure of the tourist industry, the Nationality Law, the sexual division of labour in Japan and South-east Asian countries, and attitudes to the issue of prostitution in Japan. Their findings were published in the journal *Ajia to Josei Kaihô* (Asian Women's Liberation). The Association pointed out that the food, clothes, electrical goods and cosmetics the Japanese use every day were often produced by Asian women under shocking working conditions and curtailment of political rights. The Asian Women's Association also reacted to political repression and liberation struggles in Korea, the Philippines and other countries. These concerns arose out of an awareness of Japanese history, with Japan's military activities in the 1930s and 1940s being associated with present economic imperialism. The link was made between current prostitution tourism and the history of Japan's exploitation of women's sexuality during its process of modernization.

One of the most successful campaigns by the Asian Women's Association concerned the Nationality Law, during which Socialist Diet member Doi Takako called for the removal of its sexist provisions. It was revised in January 1985. Japanese women may now pass on Japanese nationality to their children, and their non-Japanese husbands may be naturalized under the same conditions as non-Japanese wives.

More generally, members of the Association have seen it as their responsibility to act in solidarity with Asian women, rather than pitying them as 'victims'. The Association has particularly strong links with Philippine and Korean groups, and often staged joint demonstrations with Korean or Philippine women on the issue of prostitution tourism during the 1980s. The most recent manifestation of the interaction of different systems of inequality based on gender, class and ethnicity in the relations between Japan and South-east Asia concerns immigrant women who come to Japan to work, and are often tricked into prostitution.[36] Japan's Women's Christian Temperance Union has set up a shelter for such women and has produced a slide presentation called *Sachiko's Story* to encourage Japanese women to think of the plight of Asian women in Japan's bars and massage parlours as well as in their own countries.[37]

The shelter, established by a grant from the Ichikawa Fusae Foundation[38] and widely supported by feminist groups, originally set out to rescue exploited immigrant women but is also used by Japanese women who are victims of domestic violence, thus creating a further link between the oppression of women in Japanese society and the oppression perpetrated by Japan in South-east Asia. Such activities provided one more strand of the coherent critique of structures of domination and subordination developed by Japanese feminists in the 1980s.

The 'Japanese-style welfare state'?

In the 1980s it seemed that the conservative Liberal Democratic Party (LDP) had firmly consolidated its hold on power, under the ultra-rightist Nakasone Yasuhiro. Military matters were the focus of attention, with a new note of nationalism apparent. In 1987, for the first time, military spending passed the notional boundary of 1 per cent of GDP, with growth in welfare spending curtailed.[39] Privatization of national industries put a strain on the labour market, and weakened Sôhyô, the left-wing Japan Council of Trade Unions, a major source of support for the Japan Socialist Party.[40] At the same time, the high value of the yen weakened export industry and intensified the trend for large companies to protect their profit margins by moving offshore,[41] while exploring possibilities for the development of high-tech and knowledge-intensive industries in Japan. Between 1970 and 1982 most new jobs were created in technical, clerical and service industries, and 40 per cent of new jobs were temporary positions.[42] Women in casual and temporary jobs constituted the most vulnerable sector of the labour market.[43]

Between 1975 and 1985 the number of female workers increased by 35 per cent, with women representing 36 per cent of all salaried workers. By 1984 the number of female salaried workers exceeded the number of full-time housewives. The most dramatic increase in female employment was in information services and advertising (160 per cent increase); commodity leasing (156 percent); food and beverage marketing (106 per cent); department stores (65 per cent), and healthcare (62 per cent). By 1985, 22 per cent of female employees worked part-time, over 3 million women. Statistics, however, probably give little indication of the number of women involved in the *mizushôbai*: bars, massage parlours and entertainment industries. At the same time, it has proved hard for women to climb the corporate ladder.[44]

The vulnerability of women workers is increased by the trend towards seconded labour and outworking. Many workers formerly employed as regular employees are now employed on a casual basis through agencies[45] and much word-processing is now carried out at home on a piecework basis. Though *ME Kakumei* – micro-electronic revolution – and *OA* – office automation – were the buzz-words of the 1980s, these trends have done nothing to improve the situation of working women.[46] Furthermore, the Equal Opportunity Act is of little use to women in vulnerable positions in small companies,[47] and most new jobs are being created in the least-organized sectors. In addition, the government had granted the EEOL at the price of weakening restrictions on working hours in the Labour Standards Law.[48] The situation of women workers, casual workers in the computer industry, and other part-time workers and outworkers has been seriously weakened, and 'part-timers' unions' have developed as a response to the failure of the mainstream unions to address these issues.[49]

Some recent social policy decisions recognize the situation of women workers. The Childcare Leave Law (Ikuji Kyûgyô Hô), which took effect in April 1992, provides for either the father or mother to take up to one year of childcare leave. Payment of all or part of the employee's salary during such leave is a matter for negotiation between employer and employee, or in a unionized workplace may be the subject of a union agreement.[50] As it need not be paid, it is likely that a father will have no incentive to take childcare leave if he is the more highly paid parent.

The Law Concerning the Improvement of Working Conditions for Part-time Workers came into effect on 1 December 1993. It allows for the setting up of part-time workers' centres which provide advice, guidance and assistance. Nevertheless, women are encouraged to 'choose' part-time labour because tax exemptions and welfare benefits are provided for wives who earn less than the threshold of 1 million yen.[51]

Another factor which affects gender relations at work and at home is the ageing of Japanese society. The percentage of the population over the age of 65 has more than doubled, from 5.7 per cent in 1960 to 12.6 per cent in 1991, yet the proportion of people aged between 15 and 64 has hardly risen (from 64 per cent in 1960 to 70 per cent in 1991). At the same time, the decrease in those aged under 15 has been dramatic. While 30.2 per cent of the population in 1960 were under 15, in 1991 the figure had fallen to 17.7 per cent. Such figures reflect greater life expectancy (76 years for men and 82 for women) as well as declining birthrates since the immediate postwar baby boom of 1947 (33.8 births per 1,000 population). Between 1955 and 1975, the birthrate fluctuated between 17.1 and 18.8, but had fallen to 11.9 per 1,000 in 1985.[52] At the moment there are five working people for every elderly person, but this ratio is expected to decrease to under 4:1 by the year 2000, and to 2.5:1 by 2020.[53]

Despite this increase in the numbers of the elderly requiring welfare support, growth in the state contribution to medical and other expenses has been curtailed. Following the dominant ideology, the elderly have traditionally been cared for in an extended family where three generations share the same residence. But this is unrealistic in the latter decades of the twentieth century, when most families live in houses or apartments barely large enough to house a basic nuclear family, and many 'salarymen' are transferred out of the cities (with or without their families) for part of their careers, thus putting further strain on the extended family.

Although the nuclear family may still be the norm, the number of households headed by females is rising, and such families are severely disadvantaged. The mean annual income of a female-headed household was 39 per cent of the national average; 36 per cent of such families had no savings compared to a national average of 12 per cent. Furthermore, as few as 27 per cent of female-headed households owned their own home compared to the national average of 63 per cent. Yet only 13 per cent of these families received welfare benefits. Almost 80 per cent of divorced wives received no support from their former husbands.[54]

In this context the emphasis placed on the 'unique' Japanese family system and the Liberal Democrat Party's calls for a specifically 'Japanese-style welfare state'[55] are no more than a desire to make ordinary families shoulder the major burden of care for the elderly or handicapped. As long as women are mainly engaged in part-time labour, they will be able to look after such relatives – a burden not easily shared by men if they continue to work some of the longest hours of any developed country. In the future the 'Japanese-style welfare state' is likely to be propped up by promotion at the local level of volunteer work by women.[56]

Feminists are attempting to expose the links between increased military spending and reduced welfare spending, and to show how women's vulnerable position in the labour market 'frees' them to take over the major burden of welfare, and supports the over-extensive commitment demanded of male workers in the primary labour market.

Beyond 'women's issues'

After International Women's Decade, with the ratification of CEDAW in 1985, the modification of the Nationality Law, and the implementation of equal opportunity legislation in 1986, many feminist groups went through a period of 'stock-taking'. Women celebrated the fortieth anniversary of female suffrage and witnessed the celebration of Doi Takako's elevation to the position of leader of the Japan Socialist Party: the first woman to lead a major political party, she provided further inspiration for women activists.[57]

The Asian Women's Association celebrated its tenth anniversary in March 1987; it continued to monitor the activities of Japanese companies and aid agencies in South-east Asia and to denounce the misuse of development aid.[58] By the time of its fifteenth anniversary in 1992, it had turned its attention to advocacy for illegal immigrant workers.

The International Women's Year Action Group, reborn as the Women's Action Group in 1986,[59] campaigned on education issues such as the removal of sexist educational practices, compulsory home economics courses for girls only and the segregation of sporting activities in schools. Other members of the group focused on pornography as an expression of derogatory attitudes towards women in Japanese society, and the economic structure of the porn industry.[60] Sexual harassment is an issue which has achieved national press coverage, with the first legislative decision on sexual harassment being handed down in the early 1990s.[61]

Agora, the women's research centre whose publications have often provided the necessary information for a range of feminist campaigns, celebrated its twentieth anniversary in 1992, and marked the occasion with a publication which charts feminist interventions over the past twenty years.

One organizational trend of the 1980s which has intensified in recent years is the cooperation of single-issue groups. Women's groups, consumer groups, and citizens' groups work at a grassroots level on matters which affect them directly, but unite in national coalitions on questions that require coordinated national activity. It had often been suggested that citizens' movements in Japan are fragmented, divided and ineffective,[62] yet in recent years there has been a trend towards linking seemingly disparate campaigns in a coherent critique of the masculinist nature of modern Japanese political institutions and policy decisions. This occurred over proposed changes to the Eugenic Protection Law in 1982, and campaigns on the Equal Opportunity Act and labour legislation.

As noted above, the Eugenic Protection Law carries a clause which allows a woman to have an abortion if her welfare would be affected on 'economic grounds', a clause whose removal is regularly demanded by conservative groups. In 1982, Murakami Maskuni, Diet member and leader of the right-wing religious and political group Seichô no Ie led renewed pressure for the removal of the 'economic reasons' clause.[63] This was resisted by Soshiren, a broad coalition of over seventy groups, including anti-war, anti-pollution, anti-nuclear organizations and groups supporting the rights of the disabled. They argued that moves to restrict the abortion law were part of a coherent conservative philosophy which relegates women to the private sphere of domestic labour and denies them reproductive freedom. The proposed restrictive amendment was defeated. In addition, women have continued to demand the removal of the crime of aborticide from the Criminal Code, to question the eugenic philosophy behind the law, and to monitor the use of new reproductive technology, while the conservatives panic about the declining birthrate (now down to 1.53 children per couple).

Feminist research and feminist activism

Activism has been supported by a revival of interest in Japanese women's history. The research of the Asian Women's Association in the 1980s linked Japan's former military activities with present-day economic imperialism, and also raised the issue of military prostitution, which is now the subject of international concern. The Association also raised the question of *women's* share in the responsibility for the oppression of other Asian peoples – were Japanese women victims or supporters?[64] Feminist historians have reconsidered Japanese history in the light of this dilemma, examining the role of women in the national mobilization of the 1940s.[65] If women are to be seen as active participants, then the next task of feminist historians is to expose the ideological pressures which persuaded women that supporting national mobilization was a suitable sphere for women's public participation. This whole issue also sheds light on recent theoretical debates on the connections between gender and fascism in Italy and in Germany.

There has also been great interest in rediscovering the history of feminist activism in Japan. The reissue of feminist classics and journals, and facsimile editions of documents – even those of the 1970s – has made the history of feminist activism more accessible.[66] A reappraisal of family history may challenge the aforementioned myth of the 'unique Japanese family system' which has so often been used to justify women's relegation to the domestic sphere. Such research is supported by women's studies associations[67] and feminist bookstores in the major cities.

Discourses of motherhood and maternalism have attracted attention from Japanese feminist theorists, who have questioned the equation of *josei* (femaleness) with *bosei* (maternity).[68] Recent debates on motherhood often refer to French theories of the body, sexuality and language, or apply deconstructive methodology to a consideration of Japanese ideologies of motherhood and the body.[69] Others have been interested in tracing the transformations of concepts of motherhood through Japanese history.[70]

An area where research has had a close relationship with feminist activism is the issue of enforced military prostitution during World War II, now the subject of petitions for compensation from the Japanese government.[71] The stories of the women who had been enforced labourers in military brothels came to light in the early 1970s, as Japanese and Korean historians found that not only had hundreds of thousands of Koreans been subject to conscripted labour, but that many women had been forced to engage in sexual labour. When Japanese feminists became aware of the history of the military prostitutes, their careful involvement demonstrated an increasing sensitivity to the international context in which they must operate. The issue of enforced military prostitution also highlighted the inconclusiveness of Japan's attempts to come to terms with the legacy of World War II, and the ways in which gender relations can be intimately connected with foreign policy issues.[72]

A consciousness of the history of Japanese women is thus linked with an emphasis on international solidarity. Japanese women use theoretical tools from other countries, where appropriate, in an attempt to understand their own situation. They seek links with other Asian women, but realize that Japanese women, too, may be 'oppressors'. In turn, feminists from other countries may learn from the international consciousness of Japanese feminism.

From the margins to the political mainstream

Japanese women's experience in the postwar period demonstrates the limits of liberal feminist strategies for political change. The most liberal consti-tution in the world is ineffective without affirmative action programmes and support for women workers in the form of adequate childcare and welfare services. The barriers to women's political participation under this system lie not in political structures and the legal system, but in the familial structures, educational institutions and employment practices which shape women's and men's activities in the public sphere.

There is a long tradition of socialist activism in Japan, and socialist women attempted to bring a gendered perspective to the socialist movement in the early years of the twentieth century. In the postwar period, the socialists and communists have had a much better record than the conservatives in raising women's issues in the national assemblies, and in standing women candidates and having them elected. In 1986, Doi Takako became the first female leader of a political party in Japan, with her election to the leadership of the Japan Socialist Party. While socialism and feminism can provide a conceptual critique of the limits of liberalism in postwar Japan, it is unlikely that we will see a viable government from the ranks of the socialist and communist parties.

The landscape of Japanese politics has changed since 1989, when the LDP lost its Upper House majority for the first time in the postwar period.[73] Between 1989 and 1993 the LDP suffered a crisis of legitimacy, racked by factional disputes and splintering into smaller parties. Since 1993 Japan has been governed by a series of coalitions including the Socialists, now called the Social Democratic Party of Japan, but their presence is unlikely to have the influence to transform the inadequate welfare and employment policies for women described above. Conservatives still form the majority of participants in the recent coalition governments.

Feminist activists in Japan have hitherto joined pressure groups which have attempted to influence government policy on welfare issues, labour policy, environmental policy, and local community issues. They have often stated a preference for independence from government institutions. Given the importance of the bureaucracy in Japan, interesting comparisons can be made with the Australian situation, where feminists have taken a strategy of entering the bureaucracy and attempting to change policy from within, while retaining links with an autonomous feminist movement.[74]

Since 1989 there has been a moderate improvement in the numbers of women elected to the Japanese parliament. For most of the postwar period, women have been around 3 per cent of the total membership of both Houses, excepting the unusually high number of women elected in 1946. In July 1992 women were 2.4 per cent of Lower House members and 14.7 per cent of Upper House members, making an overall percentage of 6.5 per cent.[75] Until 1989, only five women had held cabinet positions, but women have been members of the recent coalition cabinets, and former Socialist Party leader Doi Takako is now speaker of the House. The recent modest increase in the numbers of women standing for the Japanese Diet (and being elected) suggests a shift of strategy in some women's political activities.

Rather than remaining in pressure groups which try to influence national and regional government policies from outside, these women are attempting to gain access to the centres of political power.

At present, the lack of women in decision-making positions in large corporations makes it unlikely that the conventions of these workplaces will be transformed to make them more congenial to women with families; while the continued absence of women from decision-making positions in the public sector results in the persistence of gender-blind policy-making procedures. Furthermore, women's marginalization from decision-making positions in the mass media makes it difficult to create a forum for the discussion of alternative visions of gender relations. The following years will demonstrate whether women can bring a feminist critique to the most powerful institutions of Japanese society: the mainstream political parties, business, the bureaucracy and the mass media.

ACKNOWLEDGMENT

This is a revised and updated version of 'Feminist Politics in Japan', originally published in New Left Review, no. 167, January–February 1988. I would like to reiterate my thanks to Saitô Chiyo, Aoki Yayoi and the women of the Asian Women's Association who gave time to be interviewed in January 1987, and all of those other friends who have generously provided books, articles, resources and time for informal discussion of the issues addressed in this chapter. Subsequent research trips to Japan have been supported by the Japan Foundation, the Arts Faculty at the University of Melbourne, and the Australian Research Council Small Grants Scheme.

NOTES

1 Discussed in more detail in Vera Mackie, 'Gender Citizenship and the Limits of Liberalism in Postwar Japanese Politics', in Susan Blackburn, ed., *Gender in Asian Politics*, Sydney, forthcoming.
2 Susan Pharr, *Political Women in Japan*, Stanford, CA 1981, p. 20.
3 Dorothy Robins-Mowry, *The Hidden Sun: Women of Modern Japan*, Boulder, CO 1983, pp. 89–95.
4 Aoki Yayoi, 'Yakeato no Jeanne d'Arc tachi', *Ushio* [Tokyo], May 1975, pp. 175–97.
5 Lois Naftulin, 'Women's Status under Japanese Laws', *Feminist International*, no. 2, 1980, p. 13.
6 Christopher Rudd, 'Japan's Welfare Mix', *Japan Foundation Newsletter*, October 1994, p. 15
7 Naftulin, pp. 13–14.
8 Robins-Mowry, p. 247.
9 There has been a moderate rise in the number of women elected to the Diet

in the early 1990s. On 1992 figures, women were 6.5 per cent of the total membership of both houses, 2.4 per cent of members in the Lower House, and 14.7 per cent of members in the Upper House. Nihon Fujin Dantai Rengôkai, eds, *Fujin Hakusho*, Tokyo 1992, p. 281.

10 Aoki, 'Yakeato no Jeanne d'Arc tachi', p. 189.

11 Robins-Mowry, pp. 190–202.

12 Matsui Yayori, 'Asian Women in Struggle', paper presented at the Second Women in Asia Workshop, Monash University, Melbourne, 1983, pp. 8–9.

13 Robins-Mowry, p. 200.

14 Andô Toshiko, *Kitafugi no Onna Tachi*, Tokyo 1982; Leonie Caldicott, 'At the Foot of the Mountain: the Shibokusa Women of Mount Fuji', in Lynne Jones, ed., *Keeping the Peace*, London 1983.

15 For discussion of the student Left, see Muto Ichiyô and Inoue Reiko, 'The New Left, Part 2', *Ampo*, vol. 17, no. 3, 1985.

16 Author's interview with Saitô Chiyo, January 1987.

17 Saitô's thoughts on pacifism and feminism, and her experiences during World War II, are related in her 'Feminism to Sensô', *Agora*, no. 24, May 1981.

18 Cf. Sylvia Lawson's discussion of the difficulties of women with children exercising the rights of citizenship: Sylvia Lawson, 'La Citoyenne, 1967', in Drusilla Modjeska, ed., *Inner Cities: Australian Women's Memory of Place*, Melbourne 1989, pp. 99–108. I am indebted to Susan Sheridan for this reference.

19 Ôhashi Terue, 'The Reality of Female Labour in Japan', *Feminist International*, no. 2, 1980, pp. 17–22; Kaji Etsuko, 'The Invisible Proletariat: Working Women in Japan', *Social Praxis*, 1973, pp. 375–87.

20 Aoki Yayoi, *Josei: sono sei no shinwa*, Tokyo 1982, p. 55.

21 *Onna Eros* survived until 1982, and the final issue focused on discussion of pacifism and women's liberation. *Onna Eros*, no. 17, *Josei Kaihô nakushite, hansen nashi*.

22 Sandra Buckley and Vera Mackie, 'Women in the New Japanese State', in Gavan McCormack and Yoshio Sugimoto, eds, *Democracy in Contemporary Japan*, Sydney 1986, p. 181; Vera Mackie, 'Feminism and the Media in Japan', *Japanese Studies*, August 1992, *passim*.

23 *The Dyke*, no. 2, June 1978, pp. 3–9.

24 I am indebted to Sharon Chalmers for discussion of these issues. See Jennifer Robertson, 'Doing and Undoing "Female" and "Male" in Japan: The Takarazuka Revue', in Takie Sugiyama Lebra, ed., *Japanese Social Organization*, Honolulu 1992; Jennifer Robertson, 'Gender-Bending in Paradise: Doing "Female" and "Male" in Japan', *Genders*, no. 5, summer 1989; Jennifer Robertson, 'The Politics of Androgyny in Japan: Sexuality and Subversion in the Theater and Beyond', *American Ethnologist*, vol. 19, no. 3, August 1992; Sharon Chalmers, 'Inside/Outside Circles of Silence: Creating Lesbian Space in Japanese Society', in Vera Mackie, ed., *Feminism and the State in Modern Japan*, Melbourne, Japanese Studies Centre 1995.

25 Most young people go as far as senior high school: 95 per cent of girls and 93 per cent of boys advance to senior high school from middle school (Iwao Sumiko, *The Japanese Woman: Traditional Image and Changing Reality*, Cambridge, MA. 1993, p. 37). Although the numbers of males and females advancing to higher education are roughly equal, women are disproportionately represented in two-year colleges. In 1980, women made up 91 per cent of the student population in junior colleges, but only 31 per cent of students at four-year universities. At four-year universities, female students are concentrated in the non-technical

subjects in humanities (35.9 per cent), social sciences (16.4 per cent), education (16.1 per cent) and social welfare (9.3 per cent) which affects their likelihood of gaining a prestigious occupation. Mary C. Brinton, *Women and the Economic Miracle: Gender and Work in Postwar Japan*, Berkeley, CA. 1993, pp. 202–3.

26 English Discussion Society, *Japanese Women Now*, Kyoto 1992, pp. 86–94.
27 Miyo Nakamoto first sued the Nissan Motor Company over discriminatory retirement provisions in 1969, but it was not until 1982 (after several appeals) that the Supreme Court decided in her favour. Alice Cook and Hiroko Hayashi, *Working Women in Japan: Discrimination, Resistance and Reform*, Ithaca, NY 1980, pp. 38–63.
28 *Agora – Tokushû: Kintôhô, Hakenhô, soshite . . .*, no. 100, August 1985, p. 13.
29 Cook and Hayashi, pp. 83–5.
30 Vera Mackie, 'Equal Opportunity in an Unequal Labour Market: The Japanese Situation', *Australian Feminist Studies*, no. 9, autumn 1989; Julieanne Long, 'The Ministry of Labour and the Implementation of Equal Opportunity Policies in Japan', in Vera Mackie, ed., *Gender, Power and Public Policy in Contemporary Japan*, forthcoming.
31 Nakajima Michiko, 'Hataraku Josei no Sabetsu: Teppai e Zenshin', *Fujin Tenbô*, January 1987, p. 8.
32 Fujieda Mioko *et al.*, *Japanese Women Speak Out*, White Paper on Sexism in Japan Task Force, Tokyo 1975, pp. 17–25.
33 Matsui Yayori, 'Contempt for Women and Asians in the Japanese Press', *Feminist International*, no. 1, 1978, pp. 12–14.
34 Vera Mackie, 'Division of Labour: Multinational Sex in Asia', in Yoshio Gavan McCormack and Yoshio Sugimoto, eds, *The Japanese Trajectory: Modernization and Beyond*, Cambridge 1988; Vera Mackie, 'Japan and Southeast Asia: The International Division of Labour and Leisure', in David Harrison, ed., *Tourism and the Less Developed Countries*, London 1992.
35 Matsui Yayori, *Women's Asia*, London 1989.
36 The popular label for these women is *Japa-yuki-san* ('women who come to Japan'), a pun on *karayuki-san*, the women who travelled to Asia in the late nineteenth century. Today activists prefer to reject the sexual connotations of *Japa-yuki-san* and emphasize that these women are exploited as workers in the sex industry, and as such have much in common with other groups of illegal immigrants to Japan.
37 Presented at a meeting of the International Feminists of Japan, February 1987.
38 Ichikawa died in 1981, and left money for the establishment of a fund for feminist activities.
39 The share of the national budget devoted to welfare spending rose rapidly in the 1970s, but LDP policy in the 1980s re-emphasized of the family as the source of welfare provision, and sought to curtail increases in welfare spending. Rudd, p. 16.
40 Peter Hartcher, 'Why Japan's Industrial Muscle Has Atrophied', *Sydney Morning Herald*, 15 April 1987. Sôhyô has since amalgamated with the more conservative Dômei union federation, which mainly organized private sector enterprise unions. The new Rengô federation thus forms an umbrella organization for most organized workers in Japan, but left-wing voices have been marginalized in the new federation, and unionization rates have dropped, particularly among women, who are more likely to be in casual or temporary positions, in less stable enterprises, in the least well-organized sectors of the labour market. This had further implications for party politics, as Sôhyô has been the major power base for the Japan Socialist Party.

41 R. Richardson, 'The End of Jobs for Life', *Far Eastern Economic Review*, 29 January 1987, pp. 44–5.

42 Tessa Morris-Suzuki, 'Sources of Conflict in the "Information Society"', in McCormack and Sugimoto, *Democracy in Contemporary Japan*.

43 Rôdô shô fujin kyoku, *Fujin Rôdô no Jitsujô*, Tokyo 1986, quoted in *Fujin Tenbô*, November–December 1986, pp. 14–15.

44 See Patricia G. Steinhoff and Kazuko Tanaka, 'Women Managers in Japan', in Nancy J. Adler and Dafna N. Israeli, eds, *Competitive Frontiers: Women Managers in a Global Economy*, Cambridge, MA. 1994.

45 The situation of these workers is discussed in Isobe Akiko *et al.*, 'Tadayou Rôdô Yabukareru Onna Tachi', *Shin Nihon Bungaku*, no. 469, January 1987, pp. 60–1. This trend was given official recognition in the Labour Dispatch Law (*Haken Rôdô Hô*) of 1985.

46 Committee for the Protection of Women in the Computer World, 'Computerization and Women in Japan', *Ampo*, vol. 15, no. 2, 1983, p. 18. Konpyūtá to Josei Rôdô o Kangaeru Kai, *ME Kakumei to Josei Rôdô*, Tokyo 1983.

47 Glenda Roberts, *Staying on the Line: Blue Collar Women in Contemporary Japan*, Honolulu 1994, pp. 171–5.

48 In 1991, 28.5 per cent of male workers were unionized, but only 17.7 per cent of female workers. Of the 12,322,884, unionized workers in 1991, only 3,455,932 (28 per cent) were women, while women were 12.8 per cent of the membership of union committees. *Japanese Women Now*, p. 52; *Fujin Hakusho*, 1992, p. 271. On debates about equal opportunity and so-called 'protective' provisions, where feminists argued for a retention of provisions which addressed the needs of the more vulnerable women workers, see Mackie, 'Equal Opportunity in an Unequal Labour Market'; and Vera Mackie, 'Equal Opportunity and Gender Identity', in Johann Arnasson and Yoshio Sugimoto, eds, *Japanese Encounters with Postmodernity*, London 1995, pp. 95–113.

49 See Isobe *et al.*, 'Tadayou Rôdô', p. 49; Community Union Kenkyûkai, *Community Union Sengen*, Tokyo 1988.

50 Sugeno Kazuo, *Japanese Labour Law*, Seattle 1992, pp. 304–6.

51 Shiota Sakiko, 'Gendai Feminism in Nihon no Shakai Seisaku: 1970–1990', *Joseigaku Kenkyû*, no. 2, Tokyo 1992, pp. 29–52.

52 *Fujin Hakusho*, 1992.

53 Kôrei ka shakai o yoku suru josei no kai, *Dai yon kai josei ni yoru rôjin mondai symposium*, 1986, p. 74.

54 *Japan Foundation Newsletter*, June 1985; *Japanese Women Now*, pp. 20–1.

55 McCormack and Sugimoto, *Democracy in Contemporary Japan*, p. 53; Rudd, p. 16.

56 Kôrei ka shakai o yoku suru josei no kai, p. 73.

57 After a stint as a Speaker, Doi was reinstated as leader of the JSDP.

58 Matsui Yayori, 'Josei no tachiba kara mita "kaihatsu" to wa nani ka', *Ajia to Josei Kaihô*, no. 18, 1987, p. 1.

59 Ueno Chizuko, 'Feminism – Nihon no undô no kore kara', *Kôdôsuru Onna*, no. 9, December 1986.

60 Kôdôsuru Kai, 'Rasshu Awaa wa Poruno Awaa?' Meeting held at Kinrô Fukushi Kaikan, Tokyo, 1 February 1987.

61 Tsunoda Yukiko, 'Recent Legal Decisions on Sexual Harrassment in Japan', *US – Japan Women's Journal*, no. 5, 1993.

62 Iida Momo, 'Aka to midori no dai gôryû: ishitsu no kyôwa no tameni', *Crisis*, 30 November 1985.

63 This campaign and the feminist response are discussed in detail in Buckley

and Mackie, 'Women in the New Japanese State', pp. 179–85. The Eugenic Protection Law was modified and renamed in 1996.

64 *Ajia to Josei Kaihô*, no. 12, 1984.

65 The *Jûgo Shi Nôto* collective has documented women's experiences of militarism in the period from 1931 to 1945, both as victims of war and as supporters of Japanese militarism. See also Suzuki Yûko, *Feminizumu to sensô*, Tokyo 1986.

66 Witness the two-volume set published by the Shôkadô Women's Bookstore in Kyôto.

67 Junko Kuninobu, 'Women's Studies in Japan', *Women's Studies International Forum*, vol. 7, no. 4, 1984, pp. 301–5.

68 A pioneering book divided the concept of motherhood into three areas – reproduction, childcare and other nurturing activities – pointing out, in terms reminiscent of Juliet Mitchell, that only reproduction is essentially carried out by women. Aoki Yayoi, *Bosei to wa nani ka*, Tokyo Kaneko Shobô 1986.

69 See, for example, Tanazawa Naoko, Horiba Kiyoko and Takayoshi Rumiko, 'Josei, Gengo, Sôzô', *Shin Nihon Bungaku*, no. 469, January 1987.

70 Kanô Mikiyo, *Jiga no Kanata e: Kindai o Koeru Feminizumu*, Tokyo 1990; Kôuchi Nobuko, ed., *Bosei Hogo Ronsô*, Tokyo 1984; Suzuki Yûko, Joseishi o hiraku 1: Haha to Onna, Tokyo 1989; Wakita Haruko, ed., *Bosei o Tou: Rekishiteki Henkô*, 2 vols, Kyôto 1985; Ôhinata Masami, *Bosei no Kenkyû*, Tokyo 1988.

71 I prefer to avoid the phrase 'comfort women', the translation of the Japanese euphemism for these women. Some translators prefer the phrase 'sex slaves', as they feel that to describe the women as prostitutes implies some degree of volition. I prefer to refer to 'enforced military prostitution' in order to focus on the *institutionalized* use of sexual violence by the military.

72 Cf. Cynthia Enloe, *Bananas, Beaches and Bases: Making Feminist Sense of International Politics*, London 1989; Rebecca Grant and Kathleen Newland, eds, *Gender and International Relations*, Bloomington, IN 1991; J. Ann Tickner, *Gender in International Relations: Feminist Perspectives on Achieving Global Security*, New York 1992; V. Spike Peterson and Anne Sisson Runyan, *Global Gender Issues*, Boulder, CO 1993; Cynthia Enloe, *The Morning After: Sexual Politics at the End of the Cold War*, Berkeley, CA. 1993.

73 Yuriko Ling and Azusa Matsuno, 'Women's Struggle for Empowerment in Japan', in Jill M. Bystydzienski, ed., *Women Transforming Politics: Worldwide Strategies for Empowerment*, Bloomington, IN 1992, p. 58; Iwao Sumiko, *The Japanese Woman: Traditional Image and Changing Reality*, Cambridge, MA. 1993, pp. 225–8; Iwai Tomoaki, '"The Madonna Boom": Women in the Japanese Diet', *Journal of Japanese Studies*, vol. 19, no. 1, 1993, p. 105; Nuita Yôko *et al.*, 'The U.N. Convention on Eliminating Discrimination against Women and the Status of Women in Japan', in Barbara J. Nelson and Najma Chowdhury, eds, *Women and Politics Worldwide*, New Haven, CT 1994, pp. 408–9.

74 This has given rise to the coining of the label 'femocrat', resulting in debates on problems of cooperation and cooptation. See Suzanne Franzway *et al.*, *Staking a Claim: Feminism, Bureaucracy and the State*, Sydney 1989, pp. 133–55; Marian Sawer, *Sisters in Suits: Women and Public Policy in Australia*, Sydney 1992; Sophie Watson, ed., *Playing the State: Australian Feminist Interventions*, Sydney 1990; Anna Yeatman, *Bureaucrats, Technocrats, Femocrats: Essays on the Contemporary Australian State*, Sydney 1992; Anna Yeatman, 'Women and the State', in Kate Pritchard Hughes, ed., *Contemporary Australian Feminism*, Melbourne 1994.

75 *Fujin Hakusho*, 1992, p. 281.

Part IV

NEW WAVES IN THE 1980s AND 1990s

10

ORGANIZING WOMEN BEFORE AND AFTER THE FALL

Women's politics in the Soviet Union and post-Soviet Russia

Linda Racioppi and Katherine O'Sullivan See

In 1917 Russian communists installed a revolutionary government that called for an end to private property and the beginning of collective ownership of industry, agriculture, and commercial ventures. Their system – called communism – was based on the ideas of Karl Marx, who maintained that human oppression developed principally from inequalities in systems of producing goods (including food) necessary to sustain life. Collective ownership, communists believed, would eliminate those equalities. Between 1917 and the collapse of the Soviet Union (as Russia became known) in 1989, official communist decrees had also declared women equal and had set quotas to ensure women jobs and government offices.

Late in the 1920s, Joseph Stalin came to full power intending to modernize the economy through massive industrialization. His crash program brought women into the workforce at perhaps the highest rate in the world. After 1945 the Soviet Union forced countries of Eastern Europe to become communist too. As part of a Soviet empire, Poland, Czechoslovakia, Hungary, Bulgaria, Romania and other states instituted similar policies to bring women into the industrial workforce and into politics.

The collapse of the Soviet Empire in 1989 opened a debate about the place of women in post-Soviet societies in Russia, Hungary, Poland, the Czech Republic, and other states in East and East-central Europe and in Asia such as Kazakhstan. The fall of this system and the turn to the free market brought drastic unemployment to women, their departure from government, and the curtailment of services such as daycare centers that had allowed women to work in the first place. Equality of women – which they had never actually enjoyed – was seen as part of evil Soviet oppression; inequality was equated with being modern and Western, as the West had visible inequities in wages and in women holding public office. Thus, feminism was a taboo subject, because it was discredited with the communist past even though communists had hated feminists because so many were middle class.

This meant that defending women's position, bad though it had been under communism, was difficult, if not impossible, in the new political and social order. Those who watched the situation of women become worse found few models for activism. US and Western European feminism was interpreted as 'man-hating,' whereas under the Soviet system women saw their men being oppressed and kept out of politics too. Women accepted and men expected the reinstallation of patriarchy, whether in government or in jobs. Moreover, under Soviet censorship the household and private life had become a refuge, and public debate and experience in conducting civil society had become virtually non-existent.

How, then, could women turn back the tide that was ending their rights to contraception and abortion, to daycare and medical treatment, and even to jobs? What would their relationship be to the state that had simultaneously declared them equal and kept them unequal? As one government after another ended the right to abortion or put women out of work (they usually constituted two-thirds to three-quarters of the unemployed), would-be activists searched for answers. This chapter gives an account of what happened in the largest post-Soviet state, Russia, where old Soviet agencies for women and new leaders struggled to address women's position under the new political conditions. Despite horrendous living conditions and growing violence in everyday life, they built a variety of organizations.

* * *

We want to cross the border of isolation; we want to act and be together but we still have not understood ourselves and sometimes move in very different directions.

(Ol'ga Besolova)

For women here, it is very important to have their own voice, to speak independently. To speak not from a position of class, or one half of the population which has been rescued by somebody else, but to set up their own agenda. . . . This accent on independence is very crucial for understanding Russian feminism. . . . Our women have to understand after years of forced solidarity, not real solidarity, that only realy solidarity of women could help them, could change their position in society.

(Anastasia Posadskaya)[1]

Two conclusions emerge from the most recent scholarship on women in the former Soviet Union and Eastern Europe: that the transition from communism has had numerous negative political and economic impacts on women, and that this transition has also opened up opportunities for independent women's organizations to challenge the centralized, state-sponsored women's organizations and to forge a new feminist politics (see e.g. Konstantinova 1992; Lipovskaia 1992; Rimashevskaia 1992). In this chapter, we build on these insights and seek to show how women have organized in response to these dilemmas. We argue that although appreciation of the historical development of the state's policies toward women and of the severe socio-economic gender consequences of the transition from communism is essential to understanding contemporary women's politics in Russia, any analysis that assumes persistent dichotomies between independent and formerly state-sponsored women's organizations or that emphasizes only resource constraints for women's mobilization misses the purposive and dynamic character of women's politics in Russia.

Our analysis is based on bibliographic research and information collected during four research trips to the Soviet Union and to post-Soviet Russia in which we interviewed leading activists in traditional and emerging women's groups. These groups focus on women's issues, broadly defined, at the national and Moscow regional levels.[2] Before we move to the interview material itself, we will briefly survey the historical legacy of the Soviet period for women's rights and women's activism. We will then examine the present political and economic context, discuss some of the women's organizations we have been following, and analyze the main factors influencing the development of a unified women's movement in Russia.

The historical context and legacy

The Bolshevik Revolution of 1917 brought with it the great promise of women's equality in Russia: Marxism-Leninism held that as socialism was established, women would achieve equality with men. Important Bolshevik feminist activists like Inessa Armand and Alexandra Kollontai challenged the new regime to hold fast to that egalitarian goal. As a result, the state examined a range of issues important to women and implemented policies designed to improve the position of women in Russian society.[3] Consideration of those issues, however, was always undertaken within parameters defined by the Communist Party. In part because the party faced acute difficulties in consolidating its rule and establishing socialism, women's interests were sacrificed to what was defined as the greater good. In fact, from the Revolution forward, women's equality was never an end in and of itself, women's political participation never a primary goal.[4] As the Soviet state became increasingly centralized and repressive under Stalin, it placed sharper limitations on women (and on men), cut off the relatively wide-ranging discussion about women's rights and equality that characterized the early 1920s, and designed and implemented policies to ensure that women served the causes of national political consolidation, economic construction, and, later, the war effort. Even with the post-Stalinist thaw in Soviet society and policies in important areas affecting women, no one in the government fundamentally questioned the state's right to establish priorities and to define women's role in them. Despite the opening up of the political system under Gorbachev and in the post-Soviet period, the legacy of the state's manipulation of women for its own purposes continued to shape the discussion about women's rights and position in Russian society and state policies affecting women, especially in labor, family, and reproduction.

Debates

The leaders of the 1917 Revolution may have taken their philosophical bearings from Marx and Engels, and Lenin may have expressed interest in the plight of women's domestic work, but concerns about women and the family were not central issues to most Bolsheviks. The challenge of liberalism to Russian patriarchal institutions and attitudes, however, forced revolutionaries to pay closer attention to the incorporation of women into the state (Lapidus 1978). The well-known and lively debate about the ways in which to increase women's political participation, improve their status *vis-à-vis* traditional institutions, and achieve sexual equality came to be known as the 'woman question'. With the establishment of the *zhenotdel'* (women's department) in the Communist Party, Bolshevik activists hoped that women's interests would be represented and other women inspired to take up the cause of the new communist state (see Stites (1991) for a discussion of the *zhenotdel'*). As a consequence, a series of laws on marriage, abortion, and property lifted restrictions on women's rights.

With the accession to power of Josef Stalin, the discussion shifted dramatically and feminist views were silenced entirely. Stalin eliminated the *zhenotdel'* in 1930, declaring the woman question 'solved'.[5] As a replacement for the *zhenotdel'*, *zhensektory* (women's sections) were established in the agitation and propaganda departments of the Communist Party. The mission of these short-lived organizations was simply to rededicate women to Stalin's economic program (Clements 1991: 268–70).

Women's position in Soviet society was re-examined, in limited fashion, in the Khrushchev era, prompted by the recognition that women had not assumed positions of political and economic leadership at a level comparable to men. In response, the Khrushchev regime created the *zhensovety* (women's councils); the goals of these councils were not generated by their members, however, but by the party or government organization with which they were associated.[6] Furthermore, there was no attempt to overturn the Stalinist assertion that the woman question had been solved. Indeed, it was not until the Brezhnev era that the woman question was officially reopened, allowing the state to more candidly attack the problems of a faltering economy that demanded women's participation in the labor force and the demographic predicament of decreasing Russian birth rates (see Buckley 1989). Although reopened, the woman question was again being addressed in terms dictated by the policy needs of the state.

Policies

In the early years of the Revolution, Bolshevik policy-makers had operated under the assumption that socialist economic and political transformation would produce women's emancipation, not that such transformations would reinforce women's secondary status. The Bolshevik regime passed important laws striking at some traditional patriarchal institutions and increasing women's rights both in the public and private spheres. Divorces could be attained without the consent of both parties, for example; marriage was made a civil rather than a religious institution, and legislation was passed to require that marriage be freely entered into by both parties. Furthermore, women were no longer required to follow their spouses to a new residence or to take their surnames. It became illegal to restrict one's spouse's property rights, and daughters were given inheritance rights equal to sons. Finally, in response to the problem of back-alley abortions, an abortion bill was passed in 1920, making free abortions available at Soviet hospitals. There were some suggestions even in the 1920s, however, that women's rights would be sacrificed to the needs of the state. As Elizabeth Waters puts it:

> For all that women's rights were part of the Bolshevik program,
> they were seen as a secondary matter, subordinate to the political
> and economic struggles of the (male) working class. Bolshevik
> Marxism viewed change first and foremost in terms of production:
> the worker and the factory took the center of the revolutionary
> stage. By the same token domestic life was on the periphery: if
> home and family were transformed as a by-product of revolution,
> well and good; if not, there was no point in a special allocation of
> time and energy to their reform, as other issues took priority.
>
> (Waters 1991: 232)

The Leninist state's image of woman as worker, was soon modified by the Stalinist regime to create a new 'superwoman' image that combined woman as worker with woman as mother. Because Stalin needed women to support the building of the centralized economy, heavy industrialization, and collectivization and to minimize the social disruption that Stalin's policies wrought, the regime decided to cultivate pre-revolutionary family values and the traditional nuclear family. 'Dead-beat' fathers were forced to provide support for their children through tough new child support legislation. Couples were encouraged to stay together by state regulations that made divorces more difficult to acquire, and abortion was once again made illegal in an effort to ensure a rising birth rate. The regime declared that in the Soviet Union women were equal to men, and assumed that women in the socialist state would provide the state with ever-increasing productivity at work and reproductivity at home.[7]

In the post-Stalinist thaw, there was reinstatement of some rights rescinded under Stalin: for example, abortion was once again legalized and divorces made easier to obtain. In addition, the state made available a wider range of social support services to assist women in balancing their arduous work and home lives. The system of daycare centers and summer camps was expanded, and subsidies were made available to mothers for support of their families.[8] The prevailing image continued to be that of the superwoman, and the myth of women's equality was faithfully promoted by the state.

The production/reproduction dilemma

From Stalin's time, the critical issue for the state was how to sustain and, if possible, to increase women's reproductive capacities while maintaining their presence in the workforce. Some early Bolsheviks, like Armand and Kollontai, were committed to improving women's position in the labor force as a means of attaining sexual equality, but there were no Armands or Kollontais under Stalin; economic productivity and the construction of the centrally planned economy became the state's primary consideration.

It was not until the Brezhnev era that the production/reproduction dilemma was addressed outright in the face of increasing economic deterioration. As economic and demographic pressures mounted in the late 1970s and early 1980s, the image of woman as worker-mother (superwoman) became more apparent. Birth rates in the Russian and European parts of the Soviet Union dipped to among the lowest in all Europe; Russia was facing a labor shortage and was having difficulty attracting workers from high-birth-rate areas (i.e. Soviet Central Asia). At the same time, policy-makers were faced with a stagnating economy in which women made up over half of the workforce. As the centrally planned economy disintegrated in the late 1980s and early 1990s and transition from state socialism, however limited, caused redundancies and displacement in the labor market, the production/reproduction dilemma still generated a new response from the regime. To quote Mikhail Gorbachev:

> Over the years . . . we failed to pay attention to women's specific rights and needs arising from their role as mother and home-maker, and their indispensable educational function as regards children. Engaged in scientific research, working on construction sites, in production and in the services, and involved in creative activities, women no longer have enough time to perform their everyday duties at home – housework, the upbringing of children and the creation of a good family atmosphere. We have discovered that many of our problems – in children's and young people's behavior, in our morals, culture and in production – are partially caused by the weakening of family ties and slack attitude to family responsibilities. This is a paradoxical result of our sincere and politically justified desire to make women equal with men in everything. Now, in the course of perestroika, we have begun to overcome this shortcoming. That is why we are now holding heated debates in the press, in public organizations, at work and at home, about the question of what we should do to make it possible for women to return to their purely womanly mission.
>
> (Gorbachev 1987: 103)

In the Gorbachev era and in post-Soviet Russia, therefore, the image of woman as worker-mother has been steadily replaced by an image of woman as wife, mother, and homemaker. That is, as the state no longer requires her labor in the economy, the Russian woman is being asked to return to the home to her 'traditional' duties and position in the family.

211

The contemporary social, economic, and political context for women

I started working at the factory in 1975 and I've given it, or to be more precise, I've given the foundry shop, my whole life and my health. I fell in love there and got married. My husband went to school and worked. No matter how we tried, we couldn't get our own place to live. We had a tough time and he left. He found an easier life. We were left alone. We've been living in a dormitory since 1984. There are ten families on our floor, and each of them has two kids. Imagine the hell we have in the kitchen, in the bathroom, in the laundry room? Lord, how tired I am of living! I earn 250 rubles and the child support payments are paltry. My older son is fourteen years old already. . . . Believe me, I don't want to live anymore. But I feel sorry for my children – who needs them?! Our life is humiliating, poor and hungry.[9]

The arduous life of women in the former Soviet Union has been well documented: in a society with an almost 90 percent female labor participation rate, women also do almost all the housework, childcare, and family work (such as shopping) without much labor-saving technology. Since the 1980s, although women constitute more than half of the Soviet labor force (*Zhenshchiny v. SSSR* 1990: 3), they tend to be located in poorly paid sectors of the labor market (Rimashevskaia 1991: 41) and in the lower ranks of the workplace hierarchy.[10] In the public arenas of power (despite quota system representation), they were also virtually invisible in positions of political power. Indeed, women held only about 7 percent of the important secretary positions in the party at even the regional and district level (Strukova 1990: 15). The so-called woman's question was rarely seriously addressed and certainly was never answered within the political system (see Buckley 1989). In the important sphere of reproduction, as decent contraceptives such as birth control pills, diaphragms, and condoms that do not tear were (and are) widely unavailable, abortion is reported as the primary method of family planning.

Despite the persistent occupational segregation and economic stratification along gender lines, the Soviet state did provide benefits to women workers that supported their labor force participation: factories received subsidies from the state to support daycare, and some enterprises provided benefits (e.g. shopping services for certain goods) that often eased the work of consuming and managing a household. Government allowances were granted to the mother of the family. Under Gorbachev, however, state subsidies for such required benefits were cut back in the declining economic situation, and strapped enterprises began to view women as less desirable workers. Despite laws against sexual discrimination, enterprises found ways to dismiss women workers. In the process of privatization, state enterprises have often been offered an opportunity to start up again as if they were new businesses, and, to reduce their own costs, many have closed down sectors that are disproportionately staffed by women or have opened again with a new all-male labor force. Defense industries that have been downsizing in the process of conversion have fired women in disproportionate numbers. And other state enterprises have reduced their staff by firing women for whom they could not find 'appropriate work'.[11] In 1992, economist Judith Shapiro estimated that the percentage of women unemployed due to economic restructuring will eventually be double that of men (1992: 33). According to official statistics, as of January 1993 women constituted 71.9 percent of the unemployed. Substantial numbers of these women are well-educated and experienced engineers and technicians in their late thirties and forties. Unfortunately for them, job advertisements in many of Moscow's newspapers reveal that the positions opening for women in new firms are regularly and heavily targeted at comely younger women, able to 'wear a mini-skirt'.

Despite the need to ameliorate the economic plight of women in the transition, the government has tended to center its attention not on women as independent, politically significant wage earners but as traditional wives, mothers, and supporters of the state. This is reflected in Boris Yel'tsin's comments made on the eve of the national women's holiday in Russia (8 March) in 1991: 'I consider that our women deserve the highest accolades. I should like, personally, on my own behalf, and on behalf of the Supreme Soviet, to thank all of you, dear women, for your great endurance, for your trust and support, and for your work, for the fact that you do not lose your optimism and remain feminine and beautiful.'[12] Within the Russian Supreme Soviet and the new Parliament, little attention has been paid to women in the economy; the more persistent refrain has been about the 'crisis of the Russian family' – the birth rate now stands lower than at any time since World War II, child mortality rates have increased, and politicians have returned to a powerful pronatal ideology. Initial drafts of the new Russian constitution excluded women except for family-based policies. Our own interviews with members of the Supreme Soviet's Joint Committee on Women's Affairs and Protection of the Family, Mother, and Child indicated a central concern with the demographic crisis and a readiness to view increasing crime and alcoholism as proof of a crisis of the Russian family requiring women's (and not men's) attention.[13] Interviews with prominent women deputies in the Supreme Soviet suggest that the refrain that women should return to family care and leave state business to men echoes throughout the Parliament.[14] The implications of such discrimination against women in the labor market and of efforts to return women to home labor are manifold. They reduce not only women's economic resources and labor force participation but also their access to such opportunities as purchasing shares in co-ops undergoing privatization. Discrimination thus supports a tendency toward male monopolization of the privatization process.

Moreover, women's participation in national government has declined precipitously. 'The nomination and election of Deputies to the new parliaments at all levels has proved catastrophic for women – their representation has sharply declined. . . . Preliminary data leave one dumbfounded: One republic parliament has one woman Deputy, another has three, a third has six, and so on.'[15] Thus, prior to the December 1993 elections, only about 5.4 percent of the deputies in the Russian Parliament were women – comparable to the percentages in many Western democracies, but a large drop from the previous Soviet quota system.

Still, perestroika and glasnost did pave the way for a broader-based dialogue about women and women's equality in Soviet and Russian society. The new democratic efforts made possible a women's activism that is directed not by the party or the state but by women themselves. Shut out of the protected quota system, women have become increasingly aware of their truly marginal political status and have responded to it. Their success is uncertain. In December 1993 elections were held for the new parliament. In the Federal Council, women captured only nine of 178 seats (5 percent). Sixty women were elected. to the 440-seat State Duma (13.6 percent). Twenty-one of the women in the Duma were candidates of the political block Women of Russia organized by Alevtina Fedulova, head of the Union of Women of Russia, and Ekaterina Lakhova, President Yel'tsin's adviser on children, family, and women's issues. Over 8 percent of the electorate voted for this block. Fedulova was subsequently named a deputy speaker of the State Duma (Shvedova 1994: 7).

A look at some of the leading movement organizations and activists in Russia illustrates both the emerging interpretive consensus on women's position and the obstacles to building a unified movement. By 1994, more than 300 women's organizations had registered with the Russian Ministry of Justice and many more operate without registration (Ershova *et al.* 1995). Groups focus on women in small business, mothers of soldiers, women in defense conversion, consciousness-raising, and psychological support. There are women's environmental groups, a soup kitchen movement, women's centers, family clubs, communist women's groups, and nationalist and religious groups of women. It is beyond our scope here to give a description and assessment of every women's organization that we have researched; therefore, we focus on a number of organizations that have been highly visible and influential nationally and on several more local organizations. These include the Soviet Women's Committee / Union of Women of Russia; two *zhensovety* (local women's councils); the Center for Gender Studies at the Institute for the Socioeconomic Study of Population of the Russian Academy of Sciences; the GAIA Women's Center; and the

Association of Small Towns. We believe these six groups are illustrative of the range and types of women's activism that are emerging, the problems and tensions that women activists are addressing, and the relations among women's organizations as they seek to develop the base for a national women's movement.

The organization of activism

Soviet Women's Committee/Union of Women of Russia

Any discussion of women's activism in Russia must be situated in an understanding of the historical legacy and contemporary activities of the former Soviet Women's Committee, now the Union of Women of Russia, and of the *zhensovety* (women's councils) associated with it. As we noted earlier, the Soviet Women's Committee is the most long-lived and politically pervasive women's organization; until perestroika, it was concerned almost entirely with advocating peace as a women's issue and propagandizing how communism had solved the woman question. Its titular heads were heroine women like Valentina Grizodubova, a pilot, and Valentina Tereshkova, a cosmonaut, who were supposed to embody the Soviet official myth of the emancipated woman. The Soviet Women's Committee forged links with international women's organizations, attended international forums, and advocated world peace as a women's issue, but it did not focus on women's issues in the Soviet Union. The committee's willingness to embody Soviet propaganda about women's emancipation was evident. Public statements by Tereshkova exemplify that the Soviet Women's Committee shared the party's contradictory position on women, arguing simultaneously for women's equality in labor and for her primary social function as mother:

> I would emphasize that we are given ideal work conditions. . . . When we began working in the service zone, medical science checked our physical condition constantly. Technical personnel are always trying to make our jobs easier. Music is played to lessen the effects of the noise of our looms. We wear headphones to protect our ears. . . . Soviet women do in fact enjoy fully equal rights. Female equality is stressed and guaranteed. Motherhood is regarded in our country as women's greatest social function. The state values motherhood and helps women to raise children.[16]

With perestroika, however, the Soviet Women's Committee did begin to turn its attention toward developing a national agenda. This was due in part to expanded political opportunities and responsibilities and to the recognition of the increasingly difficult position of women in Soviet society.

The organization was awarded seventy-five seats in Gorbachev's Congress of People's Deputies and became the predominant voice in any discussion of women's issues. It should be noted that during perestroika one-third of the seats in the Congress of People's Deputies were reserved for the Communist Party and official organizations. In 1990, this group was detached from the state and formally constituted as a voluntary union of women's councils and non-governmental organizations under the new name of the Union of Women of Russia.

Employing the powerful national and international connections forged during the communist era, the Women's Union conducts its work with support from foundations, international organizations, and individuals, as well as through fundraising and commercial projects. Not surprisingly, this group has also played a major role in educating Western feminists about the impact of the transition from communism on women. Nearly every international forum on women includes a representative from the Union of Women of Russia.

Its major work today, dramatically different from its central focus only eight years ago, is the support of women during the economic crisis. Alevtina Fedulova, president of the union, posits that the economic independence of women is crucial to change what she has come to believe is a patriarchal Russia. The union runs a number of projects designed to assist women in finding employment, retraining, and surviving unemployment. In interviews with us in July 1991, March and December 1992, and June and July 1993, the staff of the Union of Women of Russia reinforced again and again the dramatic shift that has taken place in their priorities as the Soviet Women's Committee and its successor heed the needs of Russian women. Fedulova emphasized that 'our main social basis is working women. No, it is not working women any longer; it is unemployed women. There are major problems; there is a major social crisis'.[17] In focusing on unemployed women, she points out that the union has developed a clear set of activities:

> The first one is assistance to unemployed women.... Once a month we hold a job fair here in our building. We have already had five of them ... over five thousand women came here. The next priority deals with the retraining of women.... The third priority is to give women a sense of social support: personal counselling, legal counselling, psychological counselling and educational counselling. Not only individual women but dozens and hundreds of women come here for help.... The people need us. On that account, we are really accumulating the pain people bring here.[18]

The Union of Women of Russia also engages in more explicitly political activity, particularly at the national level. For example, President Fedulova and her staff have been very active in critiquing draft legislation, conducting public hearings, and submitting concrete proposals to the parliament. In fact, these activities have reinforced their belief that Russia is essentially patriarchal and that women must mobilize as women. As we pointed out earlier, in the December 1993 elections, the Union organized a political block, Women of Russia, that successfully collected the 100,000 signatures necessary to run candidates for election to the parliament. The block was organized and ran on a social welfare platform; it also explicitly denied being a feminist block. According to its pamphlet, 'Why I Vote for the Political Movement Women of Russia', the block stood for ten points:

> 1. Unified democratic Russia with common economic and cultural space, equal rights and opportunities for everyone; 2. state guarantees of education and public health care to all who need them without exceptions; 3. a state-run system of pre-school education of children; availability of day-care centers, and summer camps for children; 4. observance of human rights, observance of the constitution, and independent and strong courts providing fair solution of conflicts; 5. a strong army and state guarantees for decent life of families and servicemen; 6. powerful law enforcement bodies capable of fighting crime and guaranteeing safety to every citizen; 7. search for consent and consolidation in all spheres of life that would lead to civil peace and social stability; 8. development of those productive spheres that relate to basic needs of every family and every person; 9. prohibition of the propaganda of violence and pornography; and 10. cooperation with various countries of the world, resulting in worthy status of Russia in the world community.

Using their organizational infrastructure and contacts with women all over the country, they managed to elect twenty-one women to the State Duma. (Fedulova was one of their candidates, won a seat, and was subsequently named deputy speaker of the Duma.)

Like most of the other women we interviewed, the staff at the Union of Women of Russia emphasized the difficult task of mobilizing women – that is, of empowering women to take the initiative, to see themselves as active agents. Like many other women's groups, the union focuses on building women's confidence; theirs is a 'special (kind of] work to show women that they themselves can do a lot; that they can put their force and their energy and their minds into some concrete undertakings.'[19] But given the Soviet past and the notion that the state should take care of all its citizens, the task of building independence and agency requires an openness to many forms of mobilization and activism. Staff at the Union of Women of Russia recognized the value of the development of new women's organizations (though they seemed to be somewhat skeptical about the viability of many

of them and expressed a strong sense of the need for unity among women).
As Fedulova put it,

> A year ago, an organization would crop up here, another one
> would crop up there, still another one. And people felt free to speak
> about it. Some felt a woman's place was at home, some felt a
> woman's place was only at work. Some felt only women working
> in the same profession should act together. It takes time for women
> to understand that if we're speaking about some high priority
> issues like workplace discrimination, no one organization can
> address this in isolation. It is necessary to come together and
> promote coalitions and general strategy. As for tactics, everyone
> can work on their own. . . . Of course we would like to work in
> closer cooperation with other organizations . . . but we don't want
> to impose anything upon them. We understand [opposition to a
> unitary movement but] maybe it's not very good and we have to
> survive together. It's very sensitive.[20]

Fedulova and her staff recognized the historical legacy of the Soviet
Women's Committee and the suspicion it engendered among some
emerging activist groups. Fedulova also emphasized that the creation of
the Union of Women of Russia was a clear break with the past and the Soviet
Women's Committee.[21]

Zhensovety

The work of the Union of Women of Russia, most notably its recent
success in the parliamentary elections, needs to be viewed, however, in
the context of its national network and its ability to build long-term
coalitions. The *zhensovety*, first created under Khrushchev, were reactivated
during perestroika and began to generate their own agendas. A party
directive placed the *zhensovety* under the leadership of the Soviet Women's
Committee and, as affiliates of an official organization that was able to send
representatives to the newly established Congress of Peoples' Deputies,
they were able to participate in the selection of delegates. Existing *zhensovety*
were reinvigorated and the network of *zhensovety* was expanded (Browning
1992: 99–100).

Thus, the *zhensovety* were at once tied to the Soviet Women's Committee,
whose role was growing in the late 1980s, and were given increased opportunities for activism and mobilization in their own right. Today, in contrast
to the Soviet Women's Committee and its national political agenda, the
zhensovety are highly varied in their politics. Some organizations continue
to have too little social or political impact or voice; others, like the *zhensovet*
of the Central Aerohydrodynamics Institute, led by Ol'ga Besolova, have

been politically active and have taken initiatives independent of the Soviet Women's Committee. Genia Browning reports, for example, that they nominated alternative candidates to the Congress of People's Deputies in opposition to the Moscow *zhensovety*, though unsuccessfully; 'in another example of independence, a workplace *zhensovet* in Dubna defied the town *zhensovet* by hosting the first independent women's forum' (1992: 103). Besolova and other women active in the Central Aerohydrodynamics *zhensovet* have made links with the League of Women Voters in the United States and are involved in developing strategies to educate Russian women about and in political activism. Besolova's belief is that only through educating women at the local level about the basics of political mobilization will women be able to have any effect on national politics. This belief in the centrality of political activity as a way to overcome women's passivity and sense of powerlessness infuses all of their activities, economic and social as well as political.

In contrast, other *zhensovety* have found their political voice in a focus on women, family, and community. The women's committee in Troitsk, a center for scientific work outside Moscow, illustrates this. Some of the women active in this group met through the local computer center for children, which is supported by the Troitsk Institute of Innovation and Thermonuclear Research (TRINITY), the main employer for the town. As a result of the computer center activities, a series of other projects grew out of TRINITY activities, including a 'People-to-People' diplomacy project with families in northern California. Exchanges produced a project that their American partners called the International Women's Trust – Women's Peace Trust. From this, the Troitsk women's committee was established, and organized an international women's conference, began to address problems of families in Troitsk, and sought to 'organize a women's movement in the community.'[22] The Troitsk Women's Committee is now engaged in providing support for invalids, handicapped children, and children in orphanages, relying heavily on American donations. Finally, it has forged a collaborative relationship with a group in Pennsylvania to develop a Junior Achievement program for youngsters in Troitsk.

Unlike Besolova's group, the Troitsk group is clearly a case in which women first came together as mothers and then developed an organization and aims that addressed broader women's issues. At our meeting with the members of the group, we learned that for many of them, their primary concern remained women in the family. As one member put it, 'It wasn't until perestroika that we were able to really look at and discuss problems of women, families, birth control, social violence in the family, marital rape, etc.' They saw one of their biggest tasks as 'convinc[ing] municipal authorities to take domestic violence seriously and to do something about it.' The women of Troitsk were also very concerned about the impact of perestroika and the transition to market economy on women's economic potential. They agreed that 'back to the kitchen' pressure is very strong in Russia today, but they also emphasized that two main factors would keep women in the workforce: (1) financial constraints at home requiring a woman's salary, and (2) the desire of many women, particularly those who have worked for many years, to continue to work as a way to 'fulfill their personality'. They saw the problem of retraining for women as a critical one for their group to address, because they said it was much more difficult for women to change careers than it is for men – the problem being 'moral and psychological' as well as a matter of structural opportunities. They saw women's organization and mobilization as important not only for themselves as women but for the revitalization of their community as well.[23]

Center for Gender Studies

Among the most direct and consistent critics of the legacy and central role of the Soviet Women's Committee has been the Center for Gender Studies at the Institute or the Socio-economic Study of Population of the Russian Academy of Sciences in Moscow. It was founded in April 1990 as the first center for women's studies and research in the country and, as a research center of the academy, is among the most prestigious organizations in Russia. The Center receives funding from the state as well as from international feminists and funding organizations.

Scholars at the Center for Gender Studies emphasized a number of themes as central to their concern with Russian women: the traumatic psychological effects of women's deteriorating economic situation, the difficulties scholars face in presenting feminist interpretations of this situation in public forums, and the need for a truly independent women's movement. These issues are deeply intertwined for the activists at the center. They believe that women are unable to respond actively to their deteriorating situation because of the dramatic shifts in public interpretations of their lives and in part because they have never been able to see themselves as independent actors. As Anastasia Posadskaya, director of the Center, put it, 'Women were constantly told by our propaganda that they are emancipated and have reached all the highest levels of society. . . . Now these women are told that their real place or natural place is in the home, that they will be given a pension from a very early age because the economy does not need their inefficient labor. So at a personal level, this is a terrible frustration; this is confusing.'[24]

Hence, the Center for Gender Studies sees itself as playing both an interpretive and an activist role, in which the bases of women's economic and political powerlessness are described, theorized, and challenged. In part because of its many international contacts and in part because of its very focus, the Center for Gender Studies has been central in the efforts to conceptualize and articulate the distinctive meanings of feminism for Russian women. As Posadskaya states:

> I have thought a lot about what would it mean to be a feminist in this country, about whom we can call feminist and whom we cannot. . . . One thing is that the woman who identifies herself as a feminist understands that women's issues are global and that what is happening here in this country to women and to her personally is an experience which has been shared by millions of women in the whole world. There might be things specific to us Russians, but the secondary position of women, women as a second sex . . . is what feminism recognizes. . . . For our country, I think it is especially important that the ideal of women's emancipation has been used in ways as a facade for non-emancipation, not only for women, but also non-emancipation of men. . . . So for women here it is very important to have their own voice, to speak independently. . . . This accent on independence is very crucial for understanding feminism.[25]

Among its most prominent activities, the Center was responsible for the organization of the first and second Independent Women's Forums in Dubna in March 1991 and November 1992. As the first all-Soviet independent women's meeting, Dubna I, 'Democracy Minus Women is No Democracy', was an important historical event. Two hundred women from forty-eight different women's groups, associations, and parties and twenty-five localities in the Soviet Union came together for three days. Twenty-five guests from Western countries, including Britain, Canada, Germany, Sweden, and the United States, also attended.

Panels and organizational meetings focused on the themes 'Women and Politics', 'Women and the Transition to the Market Economy', 'Feminist Critiques of the Totalitarian Culture', and 'Women and Violence'. Every woman we interviewed praised Dubna I for its conception and highly evaluated her experience of coming together with other women. Dubna I was uniformly seen as an empowering and politically significant event. One of its outcomes was the establishment of a Women's Network 'as a form of cooperation and information between different women's groups and individual women'.[26] Ambitious in its conception, this network has not yet fully realized these goals. Initially it served primarily to provide the planning committee for the organization of Dubna II that ended as a very small group of women, most of whom were at the Center for Gender Studies.

Dubna II, 'From Problems to Strategy', held in November 1992, attracted over 500 participants from Russia and the Independent States and numerous foreign participants. As Posadskaya put it, Dubna II was necessary especially for 'women from remote areas'.[27] There was substantial foreign financial support of the conference. Panels focused on employment and the economy, politics, and a wide range of social dimensions of women's lives.[28] As will be evident in the next section, responses to this Dubna were more mixed, although a formal committee was established to organize a third forum. Posadskaya believes that Russia badly needs a coherent women's movement and that such events and organization are necessary or there will be 'no orientation, no possibility to know what's going on'. Women are afraid of organization, however. 'They don't want it, but now they are starting to see it as a resource, if it is nonhierarchical, and if all centers are equal and decide things equally.'[29]

The Center for Gender Studies and the Union of Women of Russia have been the organizations most visible to Westerners. Apparent differences between them have produced a dichotomizing view of women's activism as either independent or state sponsored. Differences between the two leaders, Fedulova, a former member of the Central Committee of the Communist Party, and Posadskaya, who was never a party member, lend credence to this imagery. So too does the fact that the Center was never tied to the Communist Party. Like all organizations within the Russian Academy of Sciences, however, the Center is state sponsored, and some of its staff have in the past had ties to the Soviet Women's Committee. Given the wide range of women's organizing in Russia, facile polarizations of these two organizations oversimplify tensions in the emerging women's movement.

GAIA

Another organization attests to the problem of dichotomizing the women's movement into a state-sponsored/independent motif. Although GAIA Women's Center is an independent organization, it began in 1990 with funds from a state-sponsored association, and both of its founders are well connected through their academic positions at the USA–Canada Institute of the Russian Academy of Sciences. The GAIA organization initially concentrated its resources and energies on several projects designed to directly help women in their daily lives and to empower women to ease the transition from communism. According to one of its leaders, Nadezhda Shvedova, 'GAIA's task is to create a psychological space for raising women's consciousness. . . . We hope to support women through practical tasks. So the total task is empowerment and raised consciousness.'[30] As Elena Ershova, GAIA's founder, points out, 'In the US, consciousness-raising was a middle- and upper-middle-class phenomenon – they had the time to discuss and ruminate. Our situation is more severe; it is necessary to survive. So it is necessary to raise consciousness through looking at ways of self-support, self-realization, survival.'[31] The activists who founded GAIA share an interpretation of Russia as a deeply patriarchal and authoritarian society. Their goal is to empower women to become autonomous, self-confident, and strong voices in order to advance democracy, build a civil society, and dismantle patriarchal values and practices in Russia. They believe that empowerment can be realized only through women's active participation in grassroots economic, social, and political projects.

Like the Union of Women of Russia, the *zhensovety*, and the Center for Gender Studies, GAIA attempts to cultivate relations with Western feminists and women's organizations. The director of GAIA, Elena Ershova, told us in a 1992 interview that women activists and organizations in Russia needed to develop international contacts for several reasons: (1) to provide material support; (2) to help share experiences of organizing and mobilizing in other countries; and (3) to keep Westerners informed about the status of women and about policies and laws affecting women in Russia so that they might help promote women's rights among Russian policy-makers. The GAIA organization has also tried to encourage international contacts between non-activist Russian women and others in concrete ways. For example, in September 1992 it organized and sponsored an international conference in Moscow on women in the free market economy; more than 400 women participated in the conference, which was designed to help foster business contacts and promote knowledge.

More recently, GAIA has been in the forefront of efforts to develop a political network to lobby the state on behalf of women. Government representatives were invited to attend and participate in the September conference, and indeed, a number of government officials including then Vice President Rutskoi did so. Ershova was an important force in the establishment of an advisory committee on women to the Higher Economic Council of the Supreme Soviet. In December 1992, GAIA took a leadership role in an initiative to create a network among women's organizations in Russia, the Women's League. Finally, although GAIA as an organization did not become involved in the 1993 parliamentary elections, names of some GAIA activists were placed on the candidacy list of the political block Homeland. Many of the signatures of the Homeland block petition, however, were rejected by electoral officials because they came from Russians outside Russia.[32] As a result, block candidates were not allowed to run for office.[33]

Association of Small Towns

The Association of Small Towns stands in sharp contrast to the organizations discussed earlier. This organization results from the vision of a single woman, Tatiana Tsertsvadze, who started it when her physician sister was assigned to a clinic in Venev, a small town about 180 kilometers from Moscow. Venev, originally a wealthy merchant village, is an interesting example of a particularly Soviet phenomenon. Under Soviet rule former prisoners who were not permitted to return to Moscow were assigned to Venev as workers in the nearby mines, and today approximately 50 percent of the town's population is composed of former prisoners, their families, and descendants. When her elderly mother moved to Venev, Tsertsvadze began to visit, to learn the myriad economic and social problems of the region, and to appreciate its historical significance to Russian culture.

Tsertsvadze developed the idea of retraining small-town residents for participation in a market economy through the production of crafts indigenous to the area. Although she began in Venev by contacting town authorities, organizing a public group of town intelligentsia, identifying potential leaders, and seeking workers to join on a project, the program extended to other areas as well.[34] After several years of negotiating and working closely with local authorities and professional women, she initiated a program of economic redevelopment. Some key projects include a small enterprise in which workers produce bath carpets and a shop for handicrafts, especially traditional wood carving. In her estimation, 'This is a very difficult challenge: to see young women who are brought up in an uncultured and inhuman condition, who think being oppressed, being unspiritual is normal; to be just a reproductive source – I can't bear this; I can't agree with this.'[35] But this passivity and fatalism are, she believes, variable throughout the region: 'All towns are so different. Every one has its own face. Some are very ugly. That is a fact. Others are a potentially very strong force.' In some small towns, she points out, there are 'a lot of woodworkers, artisans, and people who want to preserve traditions; there are villages where there is an absence of criminals and an openness to hearing ideas and suggestions, and people with great initiative and ideas.'[36] Tsertsvadze also developed similar programs for redevelopment among similarly sized towns in the general region outside of Moscow. These towns then joined together to form the Association of Small Towns. Although not conceived as a women's project, the Association and its supporters have been almost exclusively women. Problems of alcoholism among men and their seeming lack of interest in economic development have left this important work in the hands of women. Although not directly engaged in national politics, Tsertsvadze none the less understands her work as part of building a Russian women's movement. She attended Dubna I and a business training workshop sponsored by the Center for Gender Studies; she sustains links with members of GAIA and has been working to extend international contacts. Like virtually all the women we interviewed, Tsertsvadze emphasized that this is a period in which women are engaged in a process of self-reflection, self-discovery, and development of a sense of personal agency. Her voice, however, is less explicitly feminist and more religious than others we interviewed. Indeed, her view is that women are more spiritual, more community-minded, more concerned about culture than men. What she shares with the other activists is a sense that if Russian society is to be reformed and rebuilt, women must be central to that process. And she recognizes that women have a secondary position in public life in Russia. In our interviews, Tsertsvadze emphasized the importance of her work as an independent part of a revival of Russian culture and religion, relying entirely on private support. At the same time she is dependent on elected government officials in Venev and other towns to support her work.

Women's activism in contemporary Russia

Two major concerns emerged from our interviews and analysis of the organization of women's activism: the importance of the historical legacy of the Soviet state, and the competition for scarce resources – human, organizational, financial, domestic, and international. Both concerns compose an important part of the context and process of movements building in Russia. The director of GAIA, Elena Ershova, discussing the impact of the Soviet past on the women's movement, said, 'I tell you this so that you will understand the way we are passing now, how information is important to us, and how to think everything over critically again, to re-think our experiences.'[37] Any analysis that neglects or underestimates a legacy that still echoes strongly for contemporary women risks misinterpreting the dynamic process of movement-building in Russia.

The unique historical legacy of the Soviet state, however, cuts two ways. First, there is a distrust of the state and its apparatus that runs deep in virtually all the women activists whom we have interviewed. As we will discuss below, this distrust extends to organizations such as the former Soviet Women's Committee, which served as the state's mouthpiece on women's issues and helped promulgate the myth of sexual equality in the Soviet Union. There is also a recognition that the state has been (and will be until other institutions are created to supplement and/or replace it) chiefly responsible for addressing and solving social issues, including the rights of women. Although every woman activist we met certainly realized that Soviet legislation ensuring women equal rights had little to do with the realities of daily life, not one wished to abrogate or minimize those rights on paper, particularly at this time, as Russia struggles to build a law-based society. Furthermore, given that there have been no private sector institutions to turn to, there has been and continues to be a reliance on the state as problem-solver. This ambivalent attitude toward the state has important consequences for the development of the women's movement in Russia. The acute social upheaval wrought by the transition has also created a range of scarcities extreme even for Russia. These scarcities, combined with the ambivalence about how to use the state as a resource, affect the development of effective and coherent political mobilization.

Legacy of the Soviet state

Elvira Novikova, a scholar and a consultant to the Central Committee during perestroika, speaks eloquently of the legacy of the Soviet state for women's activism. She argues that 'foreign feminists . . . need to listen to us attentively. The central question for me is, who am I? Can I realize my potential? Am I an object of the state? Am I being manipulated by the state? Only in this way can we tell whether the situation of women has been changed.'[38] These concerns about the historical legacy of state manipulation of women's politics are most evident when we examine the position of the Union of Women of Russia. The new generation of feminists and women activists is sometimes quite suspicious of the Union of Women of Russia regardless of its current activities or membership. The degree of suspicion was evident in the development of the Independent Women's Democratic Initiative, NEZHDI (Do not wait), which was launched at a meeting in July 1990 and held its first forum in Dubna on 29–31 May 1991. Its statement on the social and political tasks for women contained a powerful attack on prominent women in the former party and state apparatuses (and so, implicitly, on the Soviet Women's Committee): '"Puppet women" in representative organs of power and "iron ladies" in the director's chair, women elected by no one but appointed by one or other state institution, obedient to the will of the bosses and always ready to carry any directive issued on high – thus has a negative image been created of the woman director, the woman political leader.'[39] A representative of the Soviet Women's Committee was present at the forum but apparently played no role in its development or its activities. In our own interviews with the Soviet Women's Committee in July 1991, we pressed them for an interpretation of the relationship between the Soviet Women's Committee and other groups. The committee members were clearly aware of the attack on them and its implications. According to Fedulova:

> We don't see the Soviet Women's Committee as an umbrella organization, and we don't want centralization. Lenin said, 'Before unity, you should separate.' Many of the new organizations center around charismatic individuals who are opposed to centralization. Many have been set up without the help of the Soviet Women's Committee and many with our help. Some of them would like to unite with the Soviet Women's Committee but still maintain their identity. To those who argue that the Soviet Women's Committee should be disbanded, we say 'We shall work as long as women phone and call.' We think criticism is healthy because, as Andrew Carnegie said, 'You don't kick a dead dog.'[40]

Fedulova emphasized that the task of the Soviet Women's Committee is to change the policy of the state toward women and not to oppose other organizations, clubs, trade unions, or associations should they not wish to work with the Soviet Women's Committee.

After becoming the Union of Women of Russia, this once-powerful committee has faced numerous external challenges to its survival. As a private organization it has had meager state funding, and its tenancy in its own building must now be paid for. One-third of the permanent staff has been fired due to lack of funding, and continued activities such as job training workshops rely very heavily on international support and funding. When we spoke with Fedulova in March 1992, the interview was interrupted briefly when she sought to cash payroll checks at a local state bank, where no money was available. Our sense remains that the Union of Women of Russia is relatively resource-rich (in experience, organizational networks, international contacts, and state connections) but that its history makes it suspect to new organizers and feminist activists.

From our perspective, this is not an organization to be discounted. Indeed, the electoral victory of the Women's Bloc attests to the significance of Fedulova and the Union of Women of Russia. First, because of its prominence, it is the organization to which ordinary women are most likely to turn during the crises generated by the transition. Despite staff cutbacks and fiscal contingencies of enormous impact, this organization has continued to offer workshops for job training; to provide information, referrals, and other support for unemployed women; to serve as a watchdog over political developments; and to sustain important connections with international women's organizations and the United Nations. Second, it is engaged in activities that empower women and appears committed to challenging state actions that would undermine efforts at such empowerment. In this sense, because it is able to take advantage of its historical connections to the state, the Union of Women of Russia is among the most influential organizations articulating women's concerns.

Nevertheless, the lingering suspicions about the role of the Soviet Women's Committee in the old regime prevent it from standing at the forefront of the emerging women's movement. Building trust between them and new reformers will take time. The development of new groups separate from the older organizations, as Ol'ga Besolova stressed, 'is an important process which is underway; each takes itself seriously, so the unification process should not be accelerated.'[41] While both groups of reformers appreciate the need for time and see long-term possibilities for shared work, we are not sanguine that the tensions and suspicions will be overcome in the near future.

On the other hand, everyone recognizes that the state remains a powerful influence in Russian society and that women must bring their own resources to bear in affecting its policies to benefit women. There are certainly organizations and women activists who have been lobbying the government to create and modify policies; the draft law on the family is one example, as are the activities of the Union of Women of Russia and the Center for Gender Studies. Coordinated efforts also took place to establish a consultative body on women's issues to the Higher Economic Council and to develop an informational exchange network of women's organizations, the Women's League. Furthermore, local groups have often discovered they must learn to work with the government in order to achieve their goals and survive. The Association of Small Towns' collaboration with the local council in Venev is a good example of a women's group finding ways to enlist the cooperation of local authorities. Furthermore, the elections of 1993 proved that women were capable of organizing and mobilizing to elect women candidates into office. As Fedulova has asserted, 'If we don't influence politics our interests will be defeated. . . . Now it is men who make politics; they can't take into consideration the aspects of women.'[42]

The historical legacy, then, is a double-edged sword for the building of a women's movement in Russia. Although groups (however reformed) that are identified too closely with the old regime and the state may be considered suspect by newer groups of activists, the historical legacy also compels a certain coherence. Women activists seem to have a clear understanding of the necessity of women's influencing government in the transition. Yet, as the quotation from Novikova suggests, there is a powerful sense among the women activists whom we interviewed that women's mobilization in Russia must have as a primary goal the liberation of women from state control, as an experience distinct from but related to that of their male compatriots. It is a compelling motivator for movement-building, but it is also fraught with insecurity.

Resource scarcity

Problems related to competition for scarce resources (most obviously financial, but also human and organizational) compound these complexities. In former times the Soviet Women's Committee, as the official women's organization in the country, received considerable support from the state. Now the Union of Women of Russia and the other fledgling organizations that are either institutionally based (e.g. the Center for Gender Studies) or free-standing (e.g. the Association of Small Towns) must finance themselves through donations, grants, contracts, or other money-making ventures. Many activists noted in our interviews that, although there is no shortage of ideas or projects, there is the problem of money.[43] And also, increasingly, there is a problem of space. New organizations like GAIA, the Association of Small Towns, and some zhensovety have difficulty in finding any space at all for their activities. Even the Union of Women of Russia, located in Pushkin's residence in central Moscow, now leases the space formerly provided to it by the state. The dire economic circumstances in Russia mean that women's groups are to some extent competing among themselves for resources. This is particularly true, as it is in the West, with regard to support from international foundations and institutions. Dubna II came under harsh criticism from many activists who we spoke to, for instance, because of their perception that conference planners from the Center for Gender Studies were trying to limit interchange (and with it, possible collaboration) between other Russian women's organizations and Western participants.[44]

There is evidence of some competition for human and organizational resources as well. As the unhappiness with Dubna II brought to light, access to foreigners was motivated not simply by a desire to acquire externally generated financial support but also by an interest in acquiring information, expertise, and, to some extent, political visibility both at home and abroad. Furthermore, as organizations develop and seek greater influence, particularly on public policy-making at the national level, grassroots support and affiliation with the local groups become more essential. Thus, some at the Union of Women of Russia have charged that at Dubna II the Center for Gender Studies was attempting to pilfer the Union's extensive network of women's organizations in Russia.

It should not be surprising that competition for scarce resources, for political influence, and for visibility have tended to favor the larger, better-established women's organizations such as the Center for Gender Studies and the Union of Women of Russia, or that some small organizations fear domination by them. To a certain extent, these larger organizations might be seen as victims of their own success, especially given concerns about accumulated and centralized power in any organization. National and local groups have attempted to find bases for collaboration, however.[45] For example, the Center for Gender Studies has assisted smaller organizations and allowed them to have a say in the development of the second Dubna conference. The Troitsk Women's Committee and GAIA have been able to develop contacts in a way that does not portend domination of the smaller organization by the larger group in Moscow. The *zhensovet* at the Central Aerohydrodynamics Institute initiated and led efforts to do political education for women with support from the Union of Women of Russia. These initiatives and recent efforts by a range of organizations to develop an informational exchange network illustrate the possibilities for mutually beneficial cooperation.

Conclusion

Resource competition and varying relations to the state will remain central features of women's organizational politics in Russia. They could generate a mode of interaction among women's groups that entrenches conflicts and distrust among activists, although it is as likely that they are simply outgrowths of the historical legacy and the contextual juncture in which women's politics and mobilization in Russia are located today and that with time can be overcome. We hope that this last will be the case because we see powerful commonalities and ideas emerging from the practices of women activists. Virtually all the activists whom we have interviewed identify women's subordination as existing within a system of patriarchy; all have some conception of Russia as a deeply sexist society; all view their activism as a vehicle for exploring, defining, and understanding the meaning of personality and personal identity. All share the sense that the institutional 'protections' of women under the Soviet state were not 'good' for women; yet all resist the state's efforts to withdraw constitutional guarantees of sexual equality and reduce the (admittedly poor) system of social supports for women and their families. All groups want to transform the state into an arena for advancing women's interests and human rights. Many see their activities not only as benefiting women's interests but also as necessary for the development of a civil society that will be able to advance democracy and ensure that an authoritarian state will not re-emerge. And all believe that in important ways only women can ensure this development of a civil society; indeed, this is where some of the activists seem to embrace essentialist views of women. In the process of organizing, however, activists encounter political forces resentful of their activism, forces that see their activities not only as an unwelcome intrusion into the new politics of men but as a hindrance to the development of economic and governmental reform. Activists constantly face essentialist arguments about women that seek to limit Russian women's autonomy and power. In the process of countering the political essentialism that is so powerful today in Russia, many activists are beginning to share resources more readily and to work together in coordinated ways to combat these negative political and economic effects. Through this process, women may develop a common consciousness and come to articulate and advance a uniquely Russian feminism.

ACKNOWLEDGMENTS

We would like to thank Michigan State University's Office of International Studies and Programs and James Madison College and the International Research and Exchanges Board (IREX) for their generous support of our research. We also appreciate suggestions and reactions to earlier versions of this chapter by Julia Grant, B. Welling Hall, Nadezhda Svhedova, Kenneth Waltzer, and the anonymous reviewers of *Signs*. And we are grateful to Andrew J. Armstrong and Rita Ordiway for their assistance in the preparation of the manuscript. All interviews were conducted by us; they were in either English or Russian. Interviews with Elena Ershova, Anastasia Posadskaya, Nadezhda Shvedova, and Vera Soboleva were conducted in English. We acknowledge with gratitude the translating of Galina Negrustrueva, Ol'ga Zatzephina, and Nadezhda Shvedova, who assisted with translation during Russian language interviews. Interviews and their translations were recorded, with additional translation by Linda Racioppi.

NOTES

1 Ol'ga Besolova, *Zhensovet*, Central Aerohydrodynamics Institute, interview, Moscow, July 1991; and Anastasia Posadskaya, Center for Gender Studies, interview, Moscow, March 1992.

2 Specifically, we interviewed activists in the Soviet Women's Committee/ Union of Women of Russia, Center for Gender Studies at the Institute for the Socio-economic Study of Population of the Russian Academy of Sciences, at the Institute of Philosophy of the Academy Sciences, and the Gender Sciences Workshop at the Foreign Policy Association (headed by Alexander Bessmertnykh). We also interviewed activists from GAIA Women's Center, from Women's Creativity Initiative, the Center for Women's Initiatives, the Association of Small Towns, and the Troitsk Women's Association; the Institute for International Entrepreneurial Development; the Congress of Soviet Women; and Family House, a mother's club associated with the Slavic Association. We met and interviewed women Members of Parliament (both before and after the fall) as well as deputies on several committees related to women; a member of the Higher Economic Committee of the Supreme Soviet; members of local Soviets; the editor and staff of *Sudarushka*, a newspaper for women; as well as a number of successful businesswomen and small businesswomen's group members.

3 See Clements (1991) and Farnsworth (1980) for discussion of Kollontai and other feminists.

4 We would like to acknowledge the influence of Mary Buckley on our own analysis of Soviet history. Her important book *Women and Ideology in the Soviet Union* (1989) has set a standard for subsequent scholarship.

5 See Buckley (1989) for an excellent discussion of the 'solving' of the woman question by Stalin.

6 *Zhensovety* were often established at large workplaces; they were supposed to assist women in harmonizing home and work life in order to make advancement at work more likely.

7 However, the regime had difficulty increasing the birth rate substantially even in the Stalin years, as women refused 'to return to the childbearing practices of the patriarchal peasant family' (Goldman 1991: 266).

8 Clements, however, notes that despite the state's promises to expend more funds on social support services for women and their families, resources were not forthcoming and instead were directed at heavy industry and defense (1991: 276).

9 *Current Digest of the Soviet Press* 43, no. 43 (1991): 22.

10 For example, in the field of education, where almost 75 percent of the teachers are women, women make up less than 40 percent of directors of middle schools, and among those with higher and middle specialist training, women make up only about 7 percent of leading positions (Strukova 1990: 15).

11 *Current Digest of Soviet Press* 44, no. 11 (1992).

12 Foreign Broadcast Information Service-Soviet-91-046 (8 March 1991): 70.
13 Interview with several members of the Joint Committee on Women's Affairs and Protection of the Family, Mother, and Child, Moscow, March 1992.
14 Interviews with Valentina Lenkova, Moscow, December 1992, and with Maria Salliere, Moscow, July 1993.
15 *Current Digest of the Soviet Press* 43, no. 43 (1991): 23.
16 Comments by Valentina Tereshkova quoted in Danmarks Radio video production, *Soviet Women*, 1986.
17 Alevtina Fedulova, interview, Moscow, March 1992.
18 Ibid.
19 Vera Soboleva, interview, Moscow, March 1992.
20 Alevtina Fedulova, interview, Moscow, March 1992.
21 Alevtina Fedulova, interview, Moscow, July 1993.
22 Interview with members of the Troitsk Women's Committee, Troitsk, December 1992.
23 Ibid.
24 Anastasia Posadskaya, interview, Moscow, March 1992.
25 Ibid.
26 Center for Gender Studies, *Occasional Newsletter*, no. 2: 1.
27 Anastasia Posadskaya, interview, Moscow, December 1992.
28 Formal sections included panels addressing 'Women in Business', 'Women Starting Businesses', 'Women's Unemployment', 'Women's Organization in the Workplace', 'The Impact of Military Conversion on Women', 'Rural Women', 'Policy on Women', 'Nationalism and Ethnic Problems', 'Women and Electoral Campaigns', 'Women and Education', 'Women and Violence', 'Women and Health', 'Feminism and New Women's Movements', 'Women and Creativity', 'Women in Religion and Religion for Women', 'Girls Transition from Adolescence to Adulthood', 'Women's International Collaboration', 'Management of Nonprofit Organizations', 'Issues of Institutionalization of the Independent Women's Forum', 'Computers for Women', 'Traditional and Contemporary Families', and 'Women in Politics'. There were also some classes on studying a foreign language, assertiveness training, and 'Listening to Your Body'.
29 Anastasia Posadskaya, interview, Moscow, December 1992.
30 Nadezhda Shvedova, interview, Moscow, July 1991.
31 Elena Ershova, interview, Moscow, July 1991.
32 It should be emphasized that collecting signatures from Russians outside the state of Russia was not an attempt to pad the petition. It was not clear that those Russians, who were eligible to vote, could not sign petitions.
33 Nadezhda Shvedova, interview, Washington, DC, March 1994.
34 The process was not easy: some political resistance and rumors of Central Intelligence Agency connections came from local party officials; townspeople were passive and dependent on Tsertsvadze for the entire project. Only with the election of a new town authority in Venev did she secure much public support.
35 Tatiana Tsertsvadze, interview, Venev, December 1992.
36 Ibid.
37 Elena Ershova, interview, Moscow, July 1991.
38 Elvira Novikova, interview, Moscow, July 1991.
39 The statement was later published as 'Women in Action'.
40 Alevtina Fedulova, interview, Moscow, July 1991.
41 Ol'ga Besolova, interview, Moscow, July 1991.

42 Alevtina Fedulova, interview, Moscow, July 1991.
43 At one research institute we visited, we were asked what research we would like done and were told that it could be done well by them.
44 A second criticism was that the conference organizers were seeking to supplant the leadership role held by the Soviet Women's Committee for so many years. This perception was perhaps fortified by the proceedings at a panel at which one of the participants (who was also a member of the conference planning committee) proposed a hierarchical model for the Russian women's movement, a model which was seen by many present as curiously reminiscent of the structure of the Communist Party of the Soviet Union. Needless to say, the proposal was roundly critiqued by the gathering.
45 Indeed, women activists from the provinces and other areas outside Moscow were equally (and perhaps even more) interested in developing such contacts.

REFERENCES

Atkinson, Dorothy, Dallin, Alexander and Lapidus, Gail (1977) *Women in Russia*. Stanford, CA.: Stanford University Press.
Browning, Genia (1992) 'The Zhensovety Revisited.' In *Perestroika and Soviet Women*, ed. Mary Buckley, pp. 97–117. Cambridge: Cambridge University Press.
Buckley, Mary (1989) *Women and Ideology in the Soviet Union*. Hammondworth: Harvester/Wheatsheaf.
Clements, Barbara Evans (1991) 'Later Developments: Trends in Soviet Women's History, 1930 to the Present.' In *Russia's Women: Accommodation, Resistance, Transformation*, ed. Barbara Evans Clements, Barbara Alpern Engel and Christine D. Worobec, pp. 267–78. Berkeley and Los Angeles: University of California Press.
Ershova, Elena, Racioppi, Linda and See, Katherine O'Sullivan (1995) 'Gender, Social Movements and Multilateralism: A Case Study of Women's Organizing in Russia.' In *Sources of Innovation in Multilateralism*, ed. Michael G. Schechter. Tokyo: United Nations University Press, in press.
Eyerman, Ron and Jamison, Andrew (1991) *Social Movements: A Cognitive Approach*. University Park: Pennsylvania State University Press.
Farnsworth, Beatrice (1980) *Alexandra Kollontai: Socialism, Feminism and the Bolshevik Revolution*. Stanford, CA.: Stanford University Press.
Goldman, Wendy (1991) 'Women, Abortion and the State, 1917–36.' In *Russia's Women: Accommodation, Resistance, Transformation*, ed. Barbara Evans Clements, Barbara Alpern Engel and Christine D. Worobec, pp. 243–66. Berkeley and Los Angeles: University of California Press.
Gorbachev, Mikhail (1987) *Perestroika New Thinking for Our Country and the World*. New York: Harper & Row.
Heldt, Barbara (1992) 'Gynoglasnost: Writing the Feminine.' In *Perestroika and Soviet Women*, ed. Mary Buckley. Cambridge: Cambridge University Press.
Holland, Barbara (1985) *Soviet Sisterhood*. Berkeley and Los Angeles: University of California Press.
Isaak, Jo Anna (1992) 'Reflections of Resistance: Women Artists on Both Sides of the Mir.' *Heresies: A Feminist Publication on Art and Politics* 7 (2, issue 26): 8–37.

Konstantinova, Valentina (1992) 'The Women's Movement in the USSR: A Myth or a Real Challenge?' In *Women in the Face of Change: The Soviet Union, Eastern Europe, and China*, ed. Shirin Rai, Hilary Pilkington and Annie Phizacklea, pp. 200–17. New York: Routledge.

Lapidus, Gail (1978) *Women in Soviet Society*. Berkeley and Los Angeles: University of California Press.

Lipovskaia, Ol'ga (1992) 'New Women's Organizations.' In *Perestroika and Soviet Women*, ed. Mary Buckley, pp. 72–81. Cambridge: Cambridge University Press.

Rimashevskaia, N. M. (1991) *Zhenshchiny v obshchestve: Realii, problemy, prognozy*. Moscow: Nauka.

—— (1992) 'Perestroika and the Status of Women in the Soviet Union.' In *Women in the Face of Change: The Soviet Union, Eastern Europe, and China*, ed. Shirin Rai, Hilary Pilkington and Annie Phizacklea, pp. 11–19. New York: Routledge.

Rossiiskaia Federatsia (1993) 'Doklad Proekt o Vypolnenii v Rossiiskoi Federatsii Konventsii o likvidatsii vsekh form diskriminatsii v otnoshenii zhenshchin.' Pamphlet.

Shapiro, Judith (1992) 'The Industrial Labor Force.' In *Perestroika and Soviet Women*, ed. Mary Buckley, pp. 14–38. Cambridge: Cambridge University Press.

Shvedova, Nadezhda (1994) 'Women in Politics: The Federal Assembly Election Results, 1993 Russia.' Paper presented at the annual meeting of the International Studies Association, Washington DC, 1 April.

Smith, Dorothy E. (1989) 'Sociological Theory: Methods of Writing Patriarchy.' In *Feminism and Sociological Theory*, ed. Ruth Wallace, pp. 34–64. Newbury Park, CA.: Sage.

Stites, Richard (1991) *The Women's Liberation Movement in Russia: Feminism, Nihilism, and Bolshevism, 1860–1930*. Princeton, NJ: Princeton University Press.

Strukova, L. G. 1990. *Trud, Semiia, Byt Sovetskoi Zhenshchiny*. Moscow: Iuridicheskaia Literatura.

Waters, Elizabeth (1991) 'The Female Form in Soviet Political Iconography, 1919–1932.' In *Russia's Women: Accommodation, Resistance, Transformation*, ed. Barbara Evans Clements, Barbara Alpern Engel and Christine D. Worobec, pp. 225–66. Berkeley and Los Angeles: University of California Press.

Zhenshchiny v. SSSR: Statisticheskie Materialy (1990) Moscow: Financy i Statistika.

234

11

ELUDING THE FEMINIST, OVERTHROWING THE MODERN?

Transformations in twentieth-century Iran

Zohreh T. Sullivan

The first chapter in this collection showed the centrality of 'modernity' to both anti-colonial and feminist movements; being modern often entailed accepting 'Western' styles and values, notably a secular or non-religious way of life. However, throughout the entire course of anti-colonial activism, alternate strategies such as pan-Arabism and the revival of Islam had developed. The reinvigoration of Islamic community envisioned the rule of Muslim clerics and the imposition of their teachings throughout society. In this way the Western identity – either capitalist or socialist – that had so shaped and, as many argued, oppressed colonized peoples could be thrown off for a more traditional, authentic one.

Islamic fundamentalism gained ground throughout North Africa and the Middle East, and nowhere more so than in Iran. In 1979 Islam-inspired forces overthrew the brutal and Western-allied government of the Pahlavi dynasty, which had come to power in the 1920s, and replaced it with a religious government. Under the rule of the Ayatollah Khomeini, the restoration of strict gender order and the subordination of women became a touchstone for de-Westernization and thus the basis for the restoration of true independence for Iranians. As Islamic fundamentalism spread in North Africa and the Middle East, feminism became seen as traitorous, and some women activists fled for their lives.

Simultaneously, however, as gender segregation and women's seclusion were restored, opportunities opened up for women. That is, if women were not supposed to have contact with unrelated men, then entire categories of services had to be staffed by women. Thus, women's presence in education, social welfare, and medicine, for example, became stronger. Nor did activism die out, as this chapter suggests. Instead, women found new ways to make their claims and even used old ones, sometimes with dire consequences. This chapter looks at novel forms of resistance and feminism where feminism is outlawed. It proposes that people must see that as oppression changes course, it is always opening up spaces for resistance. Thus students of social movements like feminism should expect neither responses easily identified as 'feminist,' nor consistent slogans and programs over time.

* * *

'Everything is pregnant with its contrary.'
(*Karl Marx*)

The Shaykh Fazl Allah Nuri Expressway cuts through modern Tehran. Five minutes away from the newly named Azadi (Freedom) Square, it intersects with the Jalal al-Ahmad Highway that goes past the Ali Shariati Hospital, the College of Commerce and Administrative Sciences, and the College of Educational Sciences. Shaykh Fazl Allah Nuri was the charismatic conservative cleric who positioned himself against Western modernity and was, in 1909, publicly executed for opposing the first Constitutional Revolution of 1906. 'I speak of being afflicted with "westisis" the way I would speak of being afflicted with cholera,'[1] writes Jalal al-Ahmad in *Westoxification* (*Gharbzadegi*), his famous critique of Pahlavi Iran's mindless mimicry of Western modernity. Any post-revolutionary Islamic government that chooses to name its expressways after Nuri and Al-Ahmad is probably, and self-evidently, being selective about which aspects of modernity to discard. Modernity, with its attendant goals of progress, autonomy, freedom, education, and justice, was quite simply reread as always already a part of the true Islam.

A model of secular modernity, however, had consolidated itself in nineteenth-century Iran through the Constitutional Movement that positioned itself against the practices of the decadent Qajar monarchy by looking to the West for models of nationhood and development. Modernity, however, came with unacknowledged ties to cultural colonization and petroleum politics. While on the macro-level the state bought the package deal, on the micro-level individuals resisted by channeling disturbance into various oppositional patterns of modernity, a countermodernity, as it were, one of whose impulses was shaped into revolutionary Islam.[2] The binary between traditionalism and modernity that sometimes shapes conventional discussions of Iran and the Iranian Revolution is therefore inadequate to a model I prefer, that of the coexistence and tension of each in a dialectical (but not mutually exclusive) relationship with its alterity.

I prefer to see modernity and the issue of women's freedom so integrally linked to it not as agendas but as new ways to package hidden internal agendas. Modernity, antimodernity, and feminism therefore need to be recast in terms of how groups respond to, react against, and use their ideologies. Modernity and feminism become vehicles producing a series of tensions between the ordering impulse of ideological systems and the clumsy challenges of real life. I will suggest not merely the relativity of the modern but the difficulty of reducing these modernities to their Western counterparts.[3] The liberation of women, though not necessary to the larger agendas of modernity, becomes a troubled sign of its possibilities, limits, blind spots, and discontents.

Both modernity and feminism, in Iran and elsewhere, exist in perpetual antithesis with excluded particularities that remain beyond their control, and that return to disrupt their management. The unexpected difficulty of absorbing large programs into experience can be seen in the disparity between how cultural work implements modernity and how it is integrated at the level of personal experience. This chapter will therefore oscillate between public and private narratives: it will rely, in part, on a series of oral narratives I collected, starting in 1990, with Iranian émigrés and exiles that form a book called *Exiled Memories: Identity, Revolution, Iran*. Although the interviews I conducted invited my informants' memories of childhood, revolution, and exile, modernity was a currency that circulated through all their transactions. I will use their voices as a way to reflect on alternative modernities and on the problem of gender in Iran, and as an introduction to groups who narrate competing conceptions of culture and identity that recall projects of modernity during the first Constitutional Revolution of 1905, during the Pahlavi era (1925–1979), and after the Islamic Revolution of 1979. Finally, by using stories of women as dialectical inversions of each other, I argue that although questions of gender and the articulation of gendered roles may come under the dominance of state apparatus, the state does not in the process secure the consent of all its women subjects. In other words, the Islamic State exercises hegemonic control over general politics, education, and culture, but, in the case of women, its hegemony is not tied (to use Ranajit Guha's elegant formulation) to dominance.[4]

Gendering the Iranian past: Shariati, Nuri, and Kasravi

In October 1971, the Shah of Iran and his queen staged the megalomaniacal 2,500-year celebration of Persian monarchy in Persepolis, a ceremony whose quail eggs stuffed with caviar and roast peacock and foie gras were catered by Maxim's of Paris, whose water and wine were flown in from France, whose entertainment was staged by Peter Brook, and whose benediction included a prayer in which the Shah called upon Cyrus, the great Achaemenian king of kings, to 'rest in peace, for we are awake.' At the same time in a small religious center called Hosseineyeh Ershad, Ali Shariati was awakening Iranian dissidents and students to the principles of his countermonarchical manifestos, and calling upon the figure of Fatima, the daughter of the Prophet, as an emblem of revolutionary possibility.

Here we see two ways of recasting symbols from the past (Cyrus and Fatima), the Shah overhauling pre-Islamic Iran to dramatize current 'modernity' and Shariati recovering a woman, Fatima, whose conservative image he empowers with agency and revolutionary wrath against the patriarchal ruler. To the disenchanted masses angered at the petroleum imperialism hidden in the bright packagings of the Shah's 'Great

Civilization,' 'Shariati's fiery and erudite lectures and his reminder of daily life as a source of power and resistance offered alternative models of cultural identity. Imprisoned by the Shah in 1974 and later exiled in France, Shariati is generally recognized (though he died in 1977) as the 'ideologue' for the revolution. Overflowing crowds of dissidents and revolutionaries found new hope in his radical lectures in the early 1970s.

In Paris, Shariati had edited *Iran-e-Azad* (Free Iran), had translated works of Che Guevara and Frantz Fanon, had debated with Fanon about using Islamic unity as a weapon against neocolonialism, and had studied with several famous scholars at the Sorbonne. In his series of influential lectures titled *Return to the Self*, Shariati called for resistance to Western cultural imperialism through a return 'not to the self of a distant past, but a past that is present in the daily life of the people.'[5] This is a self embedded in the social and material practice of everyday life whose power, as Foucault might put it, lies in 'micro' operations and in the reconstitution of the self.

But that newly realized Islamic self was necessarily gender inflected. Woman, Shariati argued, was the easiest path to de-territorialization. 'The West falls upon the soul of the Easterners like termites. . . . they empty out the contents . . . destroy all of the forces of resistance.'[6] Shariati's much celebrated *Fatima Is Fatima* used the figure of the daughter of the prophet Muhammad not only as a model of revolutionary resistance to the monarchy in the 1970s but as a figure who could resolve the current problem of how women could enter modernity and remake themselves as neither Western nor traditional. Its vocabulary and arguments inform almost all subsequent manifestos by women after the revolution.[7] By authenticating a secular concept of womanhood as an alternative to the Pahlavi 'Westoxicated' images of woman, it offered a new and revolutionary model of Islamic womanhood; but it is also a text that once again uses the body of the woman as the site on which to compose national and ethical values. Woman, for Shariati, is at once the greatest hope for and the greatest threat to revolutionary possibility.

Yet it is not Western women he faults but their commodification. In spite of their power to effect social change, women, he claims, allow their desires to be so manipulated that they become vulnerable pawns in capitalist consumption and leisure. Blaming the poverty of modern Iranian culture for providing no alternative other than dead ritual and tradition to women and youth, Shariati addresses the collusion between the oppressor and the oppressed: 'An oppressor cannot perform oppression in the air' (*FF*, p. 108). When, for instance, Chengiz Khan defeated Iran in the fourteenth century, Iran had opened itself to this defeat through internal decomposition, ignorance, and superstition.[8] The same historical decadence, he warns, recurs in current youthful vulnerability to Western ideological exploitation and cultural colonization at whose temple (to lust and sexuality) the first object to be sacrificed is woman (*FF*, p. 90). In language that recalls such social critics as Thorstein Veblen, George Bernard Shaw, and Karl Marx, Shariati reminds his audience of the link between the prostitute and the bourgeois lady, of the cost of unexamined sexuality and commodification. Referring to the marriage of Jackie Kennedy and Aristotle Onassis, he writes, 'The First Lady of America can also be bought for a price. The difference between her and those who stand on the street is one of rate' (FF, p. 97).

Like Frantz Fanon, Shariati rejects the traditional model of woman built around past Islamic cultural traditions; but unlike Fanon, he argues that the traditional image of Islamic woman is an inadequate representation of the revolutionary activism offered within Islam and exemplified by Fatima and her daughter Zainab. More generally and more importantly he affirms Fanon's warning that

> In an underdeveloped country every effort [must be] made to mobilize men and women as quickly as possible; it must guard against the danger of perpetuating the feudal tradition which holds sacred the superiority of the masculine element over the feminine. Women will have exactly the same place as men, not in the clauses of the constitution but in the life of every day: in the factory, at school, and in the parliament.[9]

The 'web' that imprisons and impoverishes modern woman, Shariati writes, is woven out of inherited traditions of conservatism, patriarchy, and ignorance (FF, pp. 109–110). The confinement of women within the home, the gendered splitting of the private and public, and the exclusion of woman from the public sphere are all inadequately premised on the virtues of motherhood and chastity. How, he then asks, can a person 'who is herself incomplete and useless, who is missing a part of her brain and who is excluded from literacy, books, education, discipline, thought, culture, civilization and social manners . . . be worthy of being the nourisher of tomorrow's generation?' (FF, p. 109).

In valorizing the figure of Fatima, not as daughter of Muhammad, wife of Ali, or mother of Hassan, Husain, and Zainab, but as 'herself' (hence the title of the book), Shariati reminds his audience of the denigration to which Islamic culture (not Islam) has subjected the image of women. He contrasts the civility of Qur'anic respect for girls against an Arab poet's advice that fathers of daughters select the grave (over house and husband) as their most suitable son-in-law.

In opposition to the ubiquitous image of the traditional royal family whose patriarch claimed to respect only women who, as 'natural' wives and mothers, were also 'beautiful, feminine, and moderately clever,'[10] Shariati posited another way of seeing. He exposed the scandal of the traditional and unacknowledged traffic in women bartered in a form of unexamined homosocial exchange. The 'fate of woman in our traditional, conservative society' is to grow up in her father's house 'without breathing any free air,' to go 'to her husband's home (her second lord and master) in accordance with an agreement . . . between a buyer and a seller' (*FF*, p. 110). Once she is transferred to her husband's house, 'the marriage licence or ownership papers show both her role and her price. She becomes a respectable servant. A married man means someone who has a servant who works in his house. . . . She is a household laborer and a nurse . . . without any wages; she has no rights' (*FF*, p. 111).

Though he is daring in his critique of the role of women in the traditional Iranian family, the contradictions in Shariati's stance toward women are also significant: on one hand, women are essentially vulnerable to the seductive powers of exploitation and consumerism; but on the other, they have power and agency to construct themselves as warriors, as is evidenced by a series of women scholars and scientists (*FF*, pp. 82–86). So too, Fatima, as the ideal mother, wife, and daughter, can also become the emblem of 'newly created revolutionary values' (*FF*, pp. 129).[11]

Such values are needed, Shariati claimed in *One Followed by an Eternity of Zeros*, to defend the Muslim against neo-imperialism and cultural loss that come to Iran disguised as modernization. The history of Iran is narrated as a 'fall' into colonialism. For Shariati, national authenticity was a necessary antidote to the designs of the multinational markets on individual desire; and cultural authenticity could be found in his philosophically eclectic and religiously armored construction of cultural identity. 'Islam,' Shariati said,

> is the first school of social thought that recognizes the masses as the basis, the fundamental and conscious factor in determining history and society – not the elect as Nietzsche thought, not the aristocracy and nobility as Plato claimed, not great personalities as Carlyle and Emerson believed, not those of pure blood as Alexis Carrel imagined, not the priests or intellectuals, but the masses.[12]

Here we see in Shariati's appeal to the masses and attack on the West an ironic link to Marxism, which is also (ironically) the latest bloom in Western Enlightenment thought. Through the early years of the revolution, Marxist categories and Shariati's language, argument, examples, and tropes became the scaffolding for Islamic feminism and humanism and were appropriated (though unacknowledged) by such groups as the Women's Society of Islamic Revolution, the Iranian women's delegation to the UN Decade for Women's Conference.[13]

Shariati locates the only weapon against global capital in individual agency and the 'self'. This is not an example of strategic essentialism in the service of a naive but necessary fiction of the self; this is a more popular, culturally constructed notion of self as a productive force in the service of nationalism deployed against the de-territorializing imperatives of Western global capital. Eloquent in his defiance of the monarchy *and* the traditional clergy, trained in a contemporary European vocabulary and in Islamic philosophy, Shariati played, according to historian Mohamad Tavakoli, 'a crucial role in constructing an oppositional cultural and political identity based on a system of historical narration organized around Islam.'[14]

That oppositional construction was prefigured by a clergyman of whom Shariati would have disapproved – the late nineteenth-century figure recovered by the Islamic Revolution and celebrated in verse, drama, and modern expressways – Shaykh Fazl Allah Nuri. As leader of the clerical movement against the first Constitutional Movement, his politicization and organization of the clergy, some believe, prepared the way for the 1979 Revolution. Why, he asked, did the Constitutionalists wish to base the Iranian Constitution on equality and freedom? 'The foundation of Islam is obedience and not freedom; and the basis of its commandments is the differentiation of collectivities and the assemblage of the different elements, and not on equality.'[15] Constitutionalism, Shaykh Fazl Allah claimed, was a European invention, 'a fatal disease, a terminal injury,' and he concluded that Western philosophy goes hand in hand with Western tyranny. Shaykh Fazl Allah was not the last to think so.[16] In aiming to halt the movement of Iran into Westernized 'modernity' and plurality, Shaykh Fazl Allah asked for a return to *shari'a* (divine law) as a defense against Western consti- tutional laws (*qanun*) that would turn authority over to the people and Parliament.[17] His stance against modernity and its corollary in women's freedom, articulated in a document titled 'For the Awareness of Muslim Brothers,' warned against the forces that 'spread consumption of alcoholic drinks, promote prostitution, open schools for women, redirect the money that should be spent on religious projects into building of factories, roads, railways and other foreign projects in Iran.'[18]

The historical moment that produced Shaykh Fazl Allah Nuri, modernity, women's education, and the woman's movement also produced its irreducible complexity on an individual level in the life of Nuri's grand- daughter, Zia Ashraf Nasr, whom I interviewed in 1990. Her immediate family mirrored the schism in the country between the clergy who supported and those who opposed the constitution: whereas her grand- father on her father's side was Nuri, her grandfather on her mother's side was Sayyed Tabatabai, one of the leading theologians who backed the Constitutional Movement. In spite of family injunctions against the education of girls, Zia Ashraf persuaded her family to allow her to attend one of the first Muslim girls' schools, Madrassah-'i Namus, that had opened in 1907. A deeply religious woman who sees no contradiction between Islamic philosophy and the freedom of women in the public sphere, she renarrativized the progeny of the Prophet (it is standard knowledge that Muhammad had no male heirs; and Zeinul Abedin, the Prophet's great-grandson, is best known as a perpetually ailing imam) in order to foreground the power of his daughter and granddaughter, Fatima and Zainab. Mrs Nasr faulted the 1979 Revolution as 'un-Islamic':

> This 'Islamic' idea of women you quote to me from Khomeini . . . the disparity between men and women. This should be labeled not 'Islam' but 'Khomeini.' I believe, based on the life of the Prophet and the first leaders of Islam, that Muhammad himself did not discriminate against women. He considered his daughter Fatima superior to men. He made her the beginning. . . . Why? The Prophet had sons from other wives. He had daughters and sons. But he didn't give any of them as much power as he gave this girl. . . . After Fatima, her daughter was privileged – Hazrat Zainab who supervised the caravans, who took care of the family in the desert of Karbala, who brought the family in its imprisonment from Karbala to Medina. There were other men after Imam Hosein's martyrdom – Imam Zeinul Abedin, for instance. But it was a woman, Hazrat Zainab, who supervised the family, who took charge. Even in Yezid's court, it was she who lectured at him, and what a sermon she delivered. She was a woman, yet she was at the head of Islam. Then why should a woman, later on, stay home and the man go out? . . . Now the veil enslaves woman. Now women have been packaged and bundled so one has to guess from the shape. . . . Is it a human being or a black bundle?

Like other girls in the early years of the century, Zia Ashraf Nasr had a gendered education: she was taught to read but not write, in the tradition of limiting women's access to communication though not to learning. She learned to write only after her return to Tehran, after her family's exile in Iraq following the execution of her grandfather, and after the death of the grandmother with whom she lived. By then (1918) she was about fourteen years old and keenly aware of her sharp memory that enabled her to remember a page after glancing at it swiftly. Recalling her early education, she smiled as she told of making it through six grades in six months, and of the many women in her family who broke the family edict against girls attending school: 'Look at the number of strong women in our family who have doctorates in medicine, literature, and other fields. My aunt . . . was the first Iranian woman to go to the American school and learn English . . . to the American Missionary School.' Zia Ashnaf's temperament and life were formed in the crossfire of tradition, change, and modernity, at a time when women began their activities through the formation of organizations, the opening of girls' schools and the publication of women's periodicals.

The movement for women's rights in Iran has a long and well-documented history. Zia Ashraf Nasr experienced its beginnings in her friendship with Iran's leading feminist, Siddiqeh Dowlatabadi, in her involvement with women's societies, and in her struggle for women's enfranchisement. The same Constitutional Revolution that executed her grandfather also generated the start of women's secret societies and a surge in women's resistance to political and social subordination. When, in 1911, it was rumored that some of the Members of Parliament were giving in, again, to Russian demands, women's groups took action. Three hundred women with concealed guns behind their *chadors* (veils) entered the buildings, confronted the leaders of Parliament, tore aside their veils, and threated to kill their husbands, their sons, and themselves if the independence of the Persian people were further eroded.[19]

At the turn of the century, political modernization became identified with nation-building; but the discourse of nationhood, as Afsaneh Najmabadi demonstrates, was consistently gendered. Because the significance of symbolic gendering was never confronted and problematized, it was susceptible to slipping backward into Qur'anic rhetoric of male dominance or forward into the kind of consolidation expressed in the Islamic Republic.[20] Such casual acceptance of gender inequity forged unexpected bonds between secular and religious intellectuals. Ahmad Kasravi, the historian, reformer and jurist, active in the 1930s and 1940s, argued for modernity and women's education, and against the veil. But he also argued against women's right to enter the public sphere in politics, the judiciary, or the civil service.[21]

But women could, Kasravi conceded, participate through their political support of national and necessarily male agendas. Kasravi's importance as a secular modernist lay in his articulation of the need to centralize and integrate the many decentralized groups in the country: the elites, the masses, the clergy, the tribes, the clans, religious sects, and ethnic languages that constituted the 'unintegrated' layers of Iranian society.[22] Gradually as secularism gained power,

> the old tolerant attitude towards cultural heterogeneity was gradually supplanted by an intolerant crusade for national homogeneity: tribal nomadism became associated with rural gangsterism, regional autonomy with administrative anarchy, communal variety with political incompatibility, and linguistic diversity with oriental inefficiency.[23]

Iranian scholars read Ahmad Kasravi, variously, as the most controversial of modern intellectuals, as a theorist of modernity, and as a 'dangerous iconoclast' appropriately murdered for trying to destroy traditional authority.[24] Because of his uncompromising opposition to 'irrationality', he might be called a modernist who rethought Iranian modernism, one who, though a clergyman, celebrated Western science and supported the

Constitutional Revolution in 1906, while he opposed women's liberation and suffrage, Western cultural imperialism, *and* the Shi'a clergy. Arguing for 'puritan rationalism', Kasravi attacked the clergy for superstition. He published over fifty books, a weekly journal, and a daily newspaper all elaborating on his theories of class, society, and 'civilization', laying out his strategies for national integration. A celebrator of urban living, he coined the new Persian word *shahrigari* (urbanization) to contrast it with *biyabangari* (nomadizaton).[25] He also attacked, as reactionary, the most precious art in Persian culture – poetry – because he believed that the habit of recitation and recourse to poetic quotation was a way of avoiding thought. To clarify his position on the fetishizing of poetry and mysticism, he started a book-burning festival at the winter solstice.[26]

Kasravi's dream of unifying Iran was predicated on a paradox: he wished to take its distinctly divided factions and to integrate them into a modern democratic society with one language, one culture, and one central authority. In 1946 a man from an organization called the Devotees of Islam shot Kasravi dead. Kasravi had been brought to court under indictment on charges of slander against Islam. The fable of his failure perhaps illustrates a metaphor (from Kristeva), the banished or the abject returning violently from exclusion to enact its revenge against the center.[27]

Modernizing from above

Such denial of marginal and diverse forces has recurred through the reigns of the Pahlavis and the ayatollahs. As part of his modernizing programs, the Shah set up, in the early 1970s, educational programs for women in villages. Pahlavi father and son, Reza Shah and Mohamad Reza Shah, combined the state policy of crushing opposition with enforced emancipation and modernization. Reza Shah's 1936 decree banning the veil is but a tiny example of how 'modernization from above' was presented as the only way for Iran to enter the modern world.[28] Reza Shah learned from a visit in 1934 to Atatürk's Turkey that the road to modernity necessitated emancipation of civil law from the *shari'a* and thereby the disengaging of secular politics from religion. Political emancipation and equal rights, however, had their dark underside: state repression, a regularized police society, and a consumer-mad 'westoxicated' culture.[29]

The *chador*, forbidden by Reza Shah as part of his enforced program for emancipating women, and associated with the backward and downtrodden during the Pahlavi era, was later used as an emblem of revolutionary protest by women of all castes and classes who marched against the Pahlavi regime. Within the year following the revolution, they were to be surprised by governmental laws that required the *chador* for women who wished to venture outside their homes or enter offices and restaurants. Thus, the *chador* is used by opposing camps for opposite reasons: the veil as a symbol of liberation from the dictatorial state and as an instrument for hegemonizing a revolution by those whose only aim was political power. The following story will suggest yet another take on the *chador*.

One of my interviewees, Pari (a pseudonym), spoke of her efforts, as assistant minister of agriculture, to head the literacy campaign for rural women: 'Neither the government nor I knew what we were doing,' she said. 'The literacy campaign had staffed centers for educating village girls to become "agents of development" who would then return to the villages to effect change.' Six centers were therefore built outside villages in buildings that looked like English boarding-schools, so different from their own environments that Pari found it 'culturally shocking.' The girls were required to learn how to use such Western facilities as tables and chairs, knives and forks, showers, and Western toilets, none of which they had seen before. Also, the girls, who had never slept in beds, were now expected to sleep in bunk beds. Pari tells of how, when they persisted in falling out of their bunk beds in the middle of the night, the administrators found a bizarre solution. They tied the woman on the top to her bed with her *chador*.

The image of the woman bound to her bed with the veil in the larger cause of progressive rights and freedoms, a paradox of modernity, captures the simultaneity of modernity and its underside, of the forces of reason and their bondage, of the necessary reconstruction of identity and the loss of community; it bears witness to modernity as its own gravedigger.[30] 'Everything is pregnant with its contrary.' In its social context, the image recalls the monumental hegemonic vision of Pahlavi Iran, and of the Enlightenment project of modernity that enforced selected citizen rights through repression and violence.

Another event revealed an even darker side of Pari's effort to educate village women. The story of the *chador* tells of the enforcement of knowledge whose dialectic is specific to modernity. This next story suggests a different dialectic endemic to resistance.

Here is her account of her visit as an 'agent of development' going to the village in her official capacity:

> I went to the village and asked for S ——. She didn't come out. The next day I returned and asked for her again, and she didn't come out. Then I found out that the girl had been beaten black and blue by her father, that she couldn't walk for weeks, and that she was ashamed to be seen because I had caused her such humiliation. . . . It was our organization that had made this man so angry. It was us as agents of development who couldn't understand village psychology. . . . The men could not tolerate the fact that someone from outside the village would come and ask to speak to a woman and not to a man. . . . I later found out that when I wasn't present, the women I worked with would, for the smallest thing, ask

permission from their fathers, brothers, and husbands. But then I would reappear and anger the men.

Pari was sent to the village to teach women's rights, which at its most basic level taught women their right *not* to be beaten or abused. But her very presence led to a reactionary violence – the abuse of the women. Pari assumed, as did the state, that social progress would neutralize the need for revolution. Her predicament was that of the modernizing agent taking on the burden of universal modernity, whose enlightened agenda necessarily produced darker consequences than she suspected. Or, as Geoffrey Harpham phrases it 'Enlightenment is always otherwise.'[31]

Pari not only witnessed but inadvertently promoted the collision between the state and its citizens, between modernity and its other, between what Partha Chatterjee might call capital and community, and, on quite another but a connected register, between the premodern, subjugated woman and modernity. Pari's story tells us something too about the problem of modernization that Chatterjee writes of in *The Nation and Its Fragments* – the problem of the suppression of an independent narrative of community, the erasure of respect for the individual that can occur when the importance of individual freedom and individual rights is proclaimed.[32]

Pari tells the story of village women as part of a series of narratives that include herself and the women in her family. But the embedded stories are significant for their differences. Unlike her village counterpart, Pari's own search for autonomy from patriarchal oppression, her own subjection to coercive codes of female behavior and child abuse occurred in an urban setting that privileged her class, and that allowed her to find surrogate communities outside her city and country. But the village women relied on structures of kinship and community within the village. Outside the village a woman faced the multiple unknown threats of the city, whose effect was to alienate the villager from her former community, leaving nothing to fill the void.

Such alienation had also been the unexpected consequence of the White Revolution of 1962–63; the Shah's programs of multiple modernization, coinciding with rapid industrialization and Westernization, resulted in poverty and chaos that followed mass migration from country to city. An Azari woman, Mrs K., whose family owned a village near Tabriz, tells of the effects of the Shah's White Revolution and land reforms on villagers.[33] She recalls that they sold their land and went to the city, where they lived in slums and, if they found jobs, worked as janitors. She described their depression and culture shock: 'Now they [the villagers] come to my brother and complain that they don't know how to live in a city. On arriving in the city, one young man simply walked through a street expecting the cars to stop for him. Instead he was hit by a car and died.'[34] The Iranian displaced by the Shah's reforms could not survive the crash into modernity (any more than could his European counterparts) without the protection of a surrogate organization – perhaps even of the industrial 'Fordist' organizations that had collapsed in the 1970s both in Europe and Iran.

The land reforms, the White Revolution, and associated government projects, however, were premised on Western models of development that opposed a 'backward' agriculture to a modern structure of unified (state) organizations. On the basis of the logic of downward flow from the economy's 'centre of gravity,' from the oil industry to rural sectors, literacy and programmatic learning were to be the first of many steps toward freedom and rights;[35] and the position of villagers, farmers, and women would (it was reasonably assumed) automatically right itself along with the spread of reading, writing, and reason. In fact, the program so angered the men in the village that it exacerbated the injustice it was intended to dispel. Though the 'agents of development' came from above, descending from the skies in state helicopters equipped with institutional power, they failed to take into account the strength of revolutionary power brewing below.

Pari was vaguely aware that the young women in her village would disappear at certain points in the day, but she didn't give this much thought because their usual excuse was prayers. One day in 1978 she went to hold a workshop for women in a village near Shiraz. This time the students who were her village aides disappeared. Frustrated, Pari returned to Tehran and saw soldiers and cannons all over the streets. She asked the taxi driver what was happening. He answered, 'Lady, haven't you been living in Iran?' Didn't she know there was trouble between the government and opposition rebels? She later realized that the women and student aides had disappeared at the same time of day, about 8 p.m., to gather around the radio and hear the BBC news. She should have known that 8 p.m. was not an appropriate time for Muslim prayers, but as a modernized, de-Islamicized Iranian, she didn't. The villagers, who were later to become part of the revolutionary movement, tuned in to radios that suggested an alternative entry into modernity – a new imagining of a society that does what modernity, as they received it, failed to do, one that follows the 'exhaustion' of Pahlavi modernity but sees the possibility of an alternative narrative and activates new patterns of modernity. In the same vein, the message of that new society streamed in on tape cassettes recorded by Khomeini and surreptitiously distributed nationwide, and through underground radio stations and a system of new communication technologies that for the first time linked village life with global centers like London and Paris.

The historian Mohamad Tavakoli told me a slightly different story about 'agents of development' that provides an important example of the appropriation and transformation of state powers, of how individuals used the instruments of Pahlavi modernization in ways other than those the state envisioned, how they took the packet and subverted its agenda. Mohamad's brother, who was part of the Education Corps set up as an arm of state modernization in the early 1970s, found that the opportunity to work in rural Iran yielded unexpected results. Inadvertently, the regime had promoted a hitherto impossible dialogue between the educated urban Iranian and the rural villager. His understanding of the problems of village life politicized his consciousness and spurred the formation of a new revolutionary identity in him and many others. His subsequent involvement with leftist groups was the direct and unintended consequence of the state's programs of development.

Iran's program of literacy and modernization served not only the interests of Big Oil and American foreign policy[36] but also the making of a revolutionary counterculture. The violent protection of US oil investments turned into a narrative that energized the Shah's Iran and mobilized the forces of modernity into a story of progress, development, modernization, and freedom.[37] But what the grand narrative ignored was the presence of another story that challenged its conceptual framework. Partha Chatterjee's narrative of community can perhaps be further complicated through a reading of resistance theory that refuses to allow the colonized (oppressed/subaltern) to be totalized as a stable category, and that investigates histories of insubordination and struggle against institutional and ideological domination.[38]

The state's many ideas of development,[39] all imposed from above, though theoretically plausible, were contradicted by the actual events fueled by the rage of those marginalized by modernization that built up to the Islamic Revolution of 1979. The revolutionaries were multiply determined subjects. The rage of displaced villagers and students drove them into a variety of leftist groups alongside the marginalized *ulema*, or clergy, and the intellectuals who opposed the Shah's US-supported, consumer-driven modernization. The opposition spilt into political spectra that resist easy classification, though for the sake of simplification we can list the conservative Right (the Bazaar) and the conservative Left (Jalal Al-Ahmad in one of his phases), the Islamic Right (Hezb Jumhuri Islami, the Ayatollahs Shariat Madari and Khomeini) and the Islamic Left (Mojaheddin, Ayatollah Taleqani and Ali Shariati), and, finally, a three-way split producing the nationalist Right (the Shah), the nationalist Left (Fadayaan, the National Front), and the nationalist Islamic (Mehdi Bazargan and Ayatollah Taleqani).[40]

But none of these factions was antimodern. The Revolution has been given many labels: against the standard reading of it as a reactionary, traditional, and antimodern revolution, Michel Foucault and Paul Vieille both describe it as a postmodern revolution, and for Anthony Giddens it was a sign of the crisis of modernity.[41] It was not antimodern because Khomeini and his cohorts built on a coalition with secular modernists and leftists, and their early pronouncements invoked, in addition to change and social justice, 'the rights of minorities, the rights of women, and the holding of democratic elections.'[42] Its leading theorists had recognized that the 1950s and 1960s had produced a cultural schizophrenia, and that an 'other' modernity through Islam might be a way to confront 'cultural imperialism' and to address what Shariati called the 'modern calamities' of social and intellectual systems.

Revolution and women's bodies

In Iran's conflicted efforts to construct national, revolutionary, and Islamic modernities the figure of the 'woman' has repeatedly been constituted as the overdetermined sign of an essentialized totality, as a metaphor for a besieged nation, an embattled self, a delicate interiority, the uncontrollable other, the 'unpierced pearl' to be bought and protected, or the sacred interior. As Farzanch Milani observes, women dominate the cultural imaginary by becoming emblems of national identity: 'Forcefully unveiled, they personify the modernization of the nation. Compulsorily veiled, they embody the reinstitution of the Islamic order.'[43]

A dramatic example of the violent repressions unpinning the gendered organization of Iranian cultural practice may be seen in the disruptive power of two women who transgressed the boundaries set by a patriarchal society. In their insistence on equality, independence, and women's emancipation, both women transgressed in ways that are specific to both feminism and modernity. When in the mid-nineteenth century Qurrat al-'Ayn, a woman writer, orator, poet, teacher, and religious rebel, discarded her veil and her submission to Islam and became a celebrated preacher for Babism, she so angered the male elite that she was arrested and executed on orders of the Shah. Before her death in 1852, the sight of her speaking unveiled before large crowds of men left more than a few men deranged. In the most notorious incident, one 'Abdol Khaleq Esfahani is said to have protected his honor by cutting his throat with his own hands.[44]

Sixty years later in the city of Isfahan, another feminist, Siddiqeh Dowlatabadi, daughter of a well-known Muslim religious leader, had her life threatened and was driven into exile. She was the contemporary woman most admired by Zia Ashraf Nasr, who recalled Dowlatabadi's return from Europe as one of the most important events in her life. The year was probably 1927, and Zia Ashraf was attending the *Dar-ol-Moallemat*, a teacher-training institution:

> I was very excited one day to hear that Khanum Dowlatabadi, the progressive leader of women's liberation in Iran, had returned from abroad and was giving a lecture in town. Some of our teachers got ready to go, and I asked to go with them. We went early and waited

for her to arrive in this huge hall with balconies. She entered looking very dignified, very authoritative. She greeted a few people, went behind the desk, and began her lecture. There was silence as she began. But suddenly from the balcony a large pomegranate was thrown at her that landed on the lecture desk, exploded, and all the pomegranate juice splashed on her face and clothes. But Khanum Dowlatabadi was so collected and well composed that she did not pause in her talk: she continued as if nothing had happened. From that day on, I was won over and became devoted to this woman.

This powerful woman who so impressed Mrs Nasr was the aunt to my main informant, Pari. Haji Mirza Hadi, Dowlatabadi's father, had been a Mojtahid (religious jurist) in Isfahan. He married first Khatemeh Begum, who bore him six sons and a daughter, Siddiqeh Dowlatabadi, before the mother fell sick and died. Dowlatabadi arranged for her father to marry his secretary's nine-year-old daughter, after which she took over the care of her father's child wife's two children – one of whom was Pari's mother.

Dowlatabadi raised the two girls and married a doctor, Dr Etezad in 1898. But, so the story goes, she discovered that she was infertile and got divorced. In 1917, she started the first school in Isfahan for women, *Umm Al-Madaris* (Mother of Schools). One of the first graduates of the American College for Women, *Iran Bethel*, her friend, Mehrtaj Rakhshan, became the headmistress of this school. In 1919 Dowlatabadi started a society, *Sherkat Khavateen Isfahan* (Isfahan Women's Cooperative), whose purpose was to change practices she believed harmful to Iran, such as the marriage of girls before the age of fifteen and the import of foreign fabrics. At the same time she started the first major woman's magazine, *Zaban-i Zanan* (Women's Tongue), in Isfahan in 1919. Through this magazine, she argued against the imposition of the veil, for economic and emotional independence of women, for the education of women in ethics, literature, and science, and against the political dependence of Iran on other countries. The aim of this journal, then, was both feminist and nationalist. The biweekly magazine shocked religious groups in Isfahan.

Siddiqeh Dowlatabadi won further national notoriety by criticizing the prime minister (the *vusuq-al-dawlah*), who had signed a treaty giving certain rights to the British. The British retaliated by promising to distribute food to poor Iranians who agreed to gather at the post office in support of the *vusug-aldawlah*. When an emissary from Dowlatabadi arrived at the post office to read out Siddiqeh Dowlatabadi's powerful petition for freedom from British interference and control, the crowd listened intently. After he finished reading, they left without accepting any of the food offered by the British.

The government countered by banning Dowlatabadi's magazine because, by discussing politics, she had transgressed its original purpose and limits. After her life was threatened and her house stoned, she went into hiding. Finally she moved from Isfahan to Tehran, where she started new societies (*anjuman*) for women and published a dictionary of contemporary women. In 1923, she left for Europe and traveled in France, Germany, and Switzerland. She studied at the Sorbonne for a few years and returned to Iran in 1927. She is known as one of the first women in twentieth-century Iran to address crowds publicly without a veil, She gave speeches everywhere, even in the heart of conservative Qum.

While in Europe, she attended the Tenth Congress of the International Alliance for Women's Suffrage in Paris (May 1926). There she met and started a friendship with Margaret Ashby, the president of the International Alliance of Women's Suffrage. Ashby, a New Yorker and mother of two, a housewife and a politician, was also the founder of *Taking Care of Home and Children*. The structure of this magazine influenced the journal Dowlatabadi subsequently edited in Iran, *Name-i-Banovan* (Women's Paper), which was produced under the supervision of the government.

Not only was Dowlatabadi's magazine repeatedly threatened and its publication banned for several months, but she received death threats for her outspoken feminist and political editorials. When in 1936 Reza Shah issued the decree banning the veil, Siddiqeh Dowlatabadi was safe. In 1946 she returned to Europe to attend the Tenth Congress of the Women's International League for Peace and Freedom in Geneva. When she died in 1961 at the age of eighty, Dowlatabadi asked that no veiled woman be allowed to attend her death ceremonies or visit her grave. In 1993, her niece Pari went to visit her grave, whose stone, though defaced by Hezbullahi thugs, still stands. She asked the keeper of the graveyard whose grave this was. He replied, 'I'm not sure. But I think it is the grave of a lewd woman who danced naked in front of cinema theaters.'

A second reading of the Siddiqeh Dowlatabadi story reveals some troubling fault lines. A courageous feminist and activist all her life, she consolidated her feminism along class lines. Her problem could be read as not uncommon to the early history of feminism. Joan Scott, for instance, draws attention to the history of feminism as 'the history of the project of reducing diversities (of class, race, sexuality, ethnicity, politics, religion, and socio-economic status) among females to a common identity of women (usually in opposition to patriarchy, a system of male domination).'[45] Yet Scott also discusses the problem of feminism's repressing differences that could not be eliminated. Such 'repression' of sexuality and class can be seen in a painful and telling incident recorded during my conversations with Pari, about her famous aunt.

Not only was the marriage between her seventy-year-old father and the nine-year-old daughter of his secretary arranged by Siddiqeh Dowlatabadi, the story continues with the following detail: when the girl was in labor before her first menstruation, howling with pain and hanging from the beams in her bedroom, Siddiqeh Dowlatabadi ordered the family to leave her alone. Another relative, unable to bear her cries, went to her aid. When the young wife was fifteen – after giving birth to two daughters, one of whom was Pari's mother – she was widowed. Once again, Siddiqeh Dowlatabadi arranged for her to marry an old man. As Gayle Rubin might say, woman here was the gift, but the exchange partners upon whom this exchange would confer its 'quasi-mystical power of social linkage,' though not necessarily men, operated through a psychic economy where daughter identified with father, and whose power and privilege were male.[46] The locus of the girl's oppression was between power systems (father and daughter) within a sexual system that trafficked in women, more specifically, women of a lower class. Descended from the 'lower-class interloper who had come into the family,' Pari was always aware of her difference from and inferiority to the other Dowlatabadis. And 'difference' perhaps became the category through which Dowlatabadi found more common ground with Margaret Ashby in Paris than with her father's child bride.

Feminist political activism waned during the Pahlavi era, partly because both the Left and the Right were gender blind, partly because various 'societies' were subsumed into the state-sponsored Women's Organization of Iran headed by the Shah's twin sister, Ashraf Pahlavi, Najmabadi describes the shift in attitudes toward women's rights as a movement from activism to tokenism: 'In the first period [the 1930s], women's status was seen as a symbol of modernity of the new nation and the new state. In the second period [the 1970s], it became the symbol of the modernity of the monarch and his progressive benevolence towards women.'[47]

Whereas women had been activists before and during the Islamic Revolution, they found themselves increasingly disenfranchised by the hardened positions taken by the Revolution after its initial 'spring of freedom.' Newly hardened positions ware articulated most publicly by Monireh Gurji, the woman representative responsible for drafting the new Constitution of the Islamic Republic: 'I feel ashamed to talk about "women's rights". Have any of our brothers in this assembly mentioned "men's rights"?'[48] The question elided was well articulated most recently by Mahnaz Afkhami

> [H]ow will Muslim women, particularly those among them who can communicate with others, influence events, and make a difference, be empowered to advance the cause of women's human rights? How can the process be enhanced, facilitated, encouraged? What possibilities exist or can be generated for women activists?[49]

The struggle against the Shah brought out the greatest political participation by women in the history of Iran. Hailed as the 'pillars of Iranian society' by Ayatollah Khomeini, women were soon pilloried into submission, their symbol for revolutionary liberation (the *chador*) turned into a shroud of protective exclusion and bondage. Yet on International Woman's Day – 8 March 1979 – thirty thousand women marched on the streets to protest compulsory veiling and other forms of punishing and disciplining women. The women who marched for women's rights were a heterogenous group who represented social and political organizations as different as the conservative Women's Society of Islamic Revolution and the radical Revolutionary Union of Militant Women, whose parent organization was the Maoist Communist Party of Workers and Peasants.[50]

For the women I interviewed who had participated in this and the next march, the event included moments of unwelcome epiphany.[51] Not only was the march followed by several days of hysterical responses from young Islamic fanatics who roamed the city in search of women they could assault, but it also revealed to them the indifference of leftist organizations to women's issues.

The Women's March of 12 March 1979, for instance, ruptured certainties for Afsaneh Najmabadi by starting the process of breaking up unexamined ideas of unified feminism, recognizing difference, and admitting the multiplicity of class and gender identities. The march had been organized to protest Khomeini's March 7th decree on *hijah* (regulation Islamic dress, not necessarily the *chador*) as a requirement. Najmabadi was about to take her turn (on behalf of a segment of the Socialist Worker's Party) as speaker on a platform. Suddenly something she heard made her so dizzy that she almost fell off the platform: she had heard a woman from another committee say, 'Look at those painted faces in the crowd. I will never go on a march with those women.' Afsaneh's first reaction was that 'of course she was right. A great many women who had come to that rally were exactly the women whom for years we had come to call "the painted dolls of the Pahlavi regime."' But years later as she reflected on her dizzy spell, she wrote:

> Despite nine years of vehement argumentations against crossing class lines, something in my mind had broken down. All I cared about, there and at that moment, was for women of any class, or any ideological affiliation . . . to make a very loud presence felt. . . . For years I thought my dizziness had been caused by the deep anger I had felt. . . . On the body of what we called the Westoxicated painted dolls, we had *fixed* layer upon layer of meaning. . . . This dichotomous mapping of female bodies as representations of revolution and counter-revolution, of moral and immoral, was the common political and cultural language of Islamic and

secular forces at the time, with no room for any 'choreographical' destabilization.[52]

Four months later, on 12 July 1979, when three prostitutes were executed, none of the leftist presses with which Afsaneh Najmabadi was associated thought the event important enough to report. She and other activists like Nayereh Tohidi report their horror at the extent to which the Left had internalized patriachal priorities,[53] at their own inability to counter leftist arguments that head coverings and women's rights were minor issues in the context of the larger political arena of anti-imperial straggles.

Gradually, as evidenced by the writings of Khomeini and Motahari, all differences withered into a single truth: the only acceptable woman in the Islamic state was the Muslim woman who was the 'pillar of the family,' and who abided by all the laws laid down in the *shari'a,* who would accept the misogynist gender coding prescribed for her by the new government's version of Islam. By 1981 (two years after the Revolution), the idea of debating compulsory veiling or women's marches or women's rights seemed a part of the quixotic fantasy that had briefly accompanied a lost revolution.

The role of motherhood, however, was chosen as a charged symbolic site for the Islamic Republic. Motherhood was politicized and valorized, as well as sanctified through association with the clergy's vision of Fatima as ideal mother, wife, and daughter, even as the 'family' and 'family values' were revived as the birthplace for a new and proper Islamic society. Haleh Afshar compares Khomeini's veneration of mothers as 'pillars of the nation,' 'forts of virtue and chastity' who must raise 'brave and enlightened men and weak and united women,' with Hitler's similar claim that women were 'entrusted in the life of the nation with a great task, the care of man, soul, body and mind.'[54] Equality with men is deemed 'degrading' to women because it alienates them from their essential nature. While educated and middle-class women likely to pursue higher education and careers were indignant at definitions of their true 'nature,' the poorest women in the lowest classes were attracted and empowered by Khomeini's decree that husbands were responsible for the care and feeding of their wives. And it was the promise of this protection that kept them ardent supporters of the clergy.

The thrust of the conventional public narrative I have offered above is contradicted and inverted by yet another private account. A story told to me by Mohamad Tavakoli about his sister's rise and resistance to patriarchy, it is also a story about the incommensurability between ideology as it does its cultural work and ideology as it gets absorbed into personal life. Mohamad Tavakoli was born in Chaleh Meidun (below the bazaars in south Tehran) into a family of eight sons and one daughter. All eight brothers and their father saw the little sister as the repository of their honor and therefore, from the age of seven on, the object of their concern, protection, and wrath if, for instance, her *chador* slipped. As was true of other girls in her conservative neighborhood, her movements in public were limited to trips to buy bread or go to school.

When the Revolution started in 1978, she disappeared from her home for three days with no explanation. She was then sixteen years old. When she returned, her angry father and brothers discovered that she had been engaged in making Molotov cocktails during one of the decisive battles between the army and the people. During the family fight that ensued, she wrestled with her father, knocked him to the ground, and kicked him. The father, who ironically had been the most religious member of the family, found that the Revolution had become his daughter's excuse for revolting against him. He left his home and went to his village of origin, promising never to return until his daughter left the house.

Her rejection of paternal power, however, did not preclude subsequent attachments to other centers of male power. In the early 1980s, Mohamad's sister flirted with the possibility of joining various leftist Islamic groups and temporarily even abandoned the *chador*. During the elections for the Assembly of Experts she came into contact with the Party of the Islamic Republic, liked their simplicity and clothing (the men, for instance, wore no ties), and became active in their cause. When she completed this trajectory by marrying a member of the Revolutionary Guard, she continued her education, became principal of a high school, and established an educational collective. Mohamad says that all the brothers are now afraid of her and warn him to be careful of what he writes In letters home. She has recently considered running for Parliament.

The strictures against women therefore contained and nourished their contrary. And in this inversion we see also an inversion of the narrative of bound women in Pari's story about her village work. The collapse of old certainties led to the invention of new spaces for the rethinking of women's issues and the male-engendered narratives of Islamic laws. Ten years after the revolution, women found other ways to avoid confrontation with the regime by critiquing *ijtihad* (legal decisions about the *shari'a*), by reinterpreting gendered readings of the Qur'an, and by demonstrating an active presence in 'every field of artistic creation, professional achievement, educational and industrial institutions, and even in sports.'[55]

Najmabadi draws attention to the new power women have gained through their manipulation of the gendered construction of Islamic political discourse, as a result of which they are configuring new readings of Islam and feminism. Studies of female suicide, of population control, of laws of custody and divorce, of opposition to changes in laws on marriage and polygamy, for instance, appeared in the pages of *Zan-i-Ruz* (Today's Woman).[56]

Seventeen years after the Revolution, evidence suggests that women are beginning not only to have an active presence in politics[57] but also to carve out new possibilities for themselves in social, legal, and political life through public debate in women's magazines, through social and civic activism, and through public office.[58] Small though the number appears, it is significant that nine out of 280 members of the Majlis (Parliament) are women. This number is 4 percent higher than the comparable figure in Turkey, which is assumed to be more 'modern' than Iran. The cabinet includes one woman who serves as adviser on women's issues. After the Beijing conference, the Ministry of Health opened a new position for a female deputy minister. Rafsanjani's daughter, Fayezeh, won the second-highest number of votes in the Majlis during the most recent election.

The counternarrative to these happy statistics is that Rafsanjani's daughter, after being elected to the Majlis, was beaten after a press conference by a group of conservative thought-police who objected to her liberal positions on such issues as appropriate clothing for women who ride bicycles, and her opposition to certain aspects of the status quo: that women are excluded from the judiciary, that they are policed and arrested for improper *hijab*, and that the violation of Islamic gender relations is punishable by flogging. The Persian skill at versified sloganeering (demonstrated all through the marches preceding the Islamic Revolution) took a newly gendered turn during the conservative opposition to the election of Fayezeh Rafsanjani. The slogans began by collapsing two women, Fayezeh and Ayesheh ('A'isha) – the youngest wife of the Prophet, a model of reprehensible womanhood in Shiite Islam. One slogan therefore went as follows: '*Ayesheh ba shotor amad,/Fayezeh ba motor amad*' (Ayesheh came on a camel, Fayezeh came on a motorcycle). Another slogan played on the likeness between her first name and the similar-sounding word meaning "prostitute" – *fahesheh*:

Ayeshe-i-shotor sawar (Ayesheh who rides a camel)
Faheshe-i-motor sawar (Prostitute who rides a motorcycle)

Fayezeh Rafsanjani and the debate about the propriety of women riding bicycles (see *New York Times*, 20 September 1996) is but a small manifestation of a much larger debate about women and power. So too the link between the camel and the bicycle in the second slogan needs to be contextualized in terms of a larger conflict over female activity and transgression that goes back to the seventh-century Battle of the Camel, also known as the first civil war in Islamic society.[59]

The limited space women have carved for themselves has not been freely given. As Haideh Moghissi puts it, 'The Islamic regime has not opened the gates. Women are jumping over the fences.'[60] In particular, four journals are responsible for rearticulating the position of women: *Payam-i-Hajar* (Message of Hagar), *Zari-i-Ruz* (Today's Woman), *Farzaneh* (Wise Woman), and *Zanan* (Women).

While distancing themselves from Western feminism as a limited and Eurocentric category, articles and editorials in three of the four magazines call for a re-examination of male readings of the *shari'a* and the Islamic canon. Their central concerns vary: *Payam-i-Hajar*, for instance, focuses on 'awakening the conscience of the Islamic Republic' to the plight of working women, rural women, state workers, and 'other suffering sisters.' *Zanan*, however, has taken on the radical task of 'decentering the clergy from the domain of interpretation,' questioning legality, justice, and canonical readings of the Qur'an, and advocating 'reading the Qur'an as a woman.'[61] Social critics (Mina Yadigar Azadi and others) challenge readings of specific verses in the Qur'an by refusing to allow claims about ethics to be normative and insisting on the need for historic specificity. By arguing against hegemonic authorities and by admitting into their pages forbidden female voices from the decadent period of monarchy, and from the writings of such Western feminists as Virginia Woolf, Simone de Beauvoir, and Susan Faludi, the new Islamic feminists are, as Najmabadi tells us, collapsing the oppositions between modernity and Islam, secular and Islamic feminism, and feminism and cultural authenticity. In these new alliances we might see a specifically non-Western alternative modernity that rereads and rethinks the failures of the past and present.

Finally, I return to my earlier point about the unexpected consequences of modernity – a package deal whose hidden agendas are surprisingly resisted by those who find ways to put new experiences in the old package. Those new experiences are the contraries with which modernity is always pregnant. Life makes for strange bedfellows. Just as Big Oil, the United States, and the Shah had no intention of producing an Islamic Revolution, so too the Islamic Revolution had no intention of producing its unintended effect: a potential that, though compromised, is realizing itself in a kind of woman's movement specific to and produced by its historical moment – and in a newly politicized public reflected in the approximately 90 percent of people who went to the polls in May 1997, an election that, against conventional predictions, brought in the liberal Ayatollah Khatami. Women are neither 'returning' to a past narrative, nor are they mimicking a Western model of feminism. Instead they struggle to articulate a women's movement in dialectical conflict with each.

NOTES

A shorter and earlier version of this paper was presented at a symposium on Alternative Modernities at Northwestern University in April 1996. For their generous conversations, comments, and criticisms on either the early or the late version of this essay. I want to thank: Lila Abu-Lughod, Susan Bazargan, Jim Hurt, Afsaneh Najmabadi, Robert Parker, Richard Powers, Mohamad Tavakoli, Joe Valente, and Paul Vieille.

1 Jalal Al-Ahmad, *Plagued by the West*, trans. Paul Sprachman (Delmar, NY: Coward, McCann, and Geoghegan, 1981), p. 3. Al-Ahmad was one of many intellectuals and social critics who theorized the importance of political Islam in terms made familiar by Marxist socialism. Other representative figures in this group were Mehdi Bazargan and Abol Hassan Banisadr. His influential term *Gharbzadegi* has been translated alternatively as 'westernitis' or 'westoxification'.

2 See Parvin Paidar's *Women and the Political Process in Twentieth-Century Iran* (Cambridge: Cambridge University Press, 1995) for a provocative linkage of two Iranian revolutions (1906 and 1979) with modernity, a movement that in Iran was 'broadly defined . . . as a socio-political process which promised the establishment of economic prosperity, social and technological progress, social justice, political freedom and national independence' (p. 24).

3 Keya Ganguly insists on the *agrammaticality* of different cultural modernities to discuss the 'messiness and incommensurable aspects of distinguishing, perhaps in the dark, the ruptures and syntheses produced in the encounter between a putatively universal grammar of subjectivity and its multiple, historically specific variations.' 'Carnal Knowledge: Visuality and the Modern in *Charulata*,' *Camera Obscura* 37 (1996): 157–86.

4 See Ranajit Guha, 'Dominance without Hegemony and its Historiography,' *Subaltern Studies* VI, ed. Guha (Delhi: Oxford University Press, 1980), pp. 210–309. Guha focuses on ninteenth-century colonial society in India, where he sees the state exerting domination without hegemony – the necessary consent of all classes.

5 Shariati, *Bazgasht bih Khvish*, p. 316, quoted in Mohamad Tavakoli, 'The Constitutional Revolution of 1905–1906 and the Islamic Revolution of 1978–1979' (Ph.D. diss., University of Chicago, 1988), p. 124. This is not essentialist authenticity, and not a fixed definition of the self based on a fantasmatic past. That was the model of self used by the clergy and accounts for Shariati's excommunication by the religious Right.

6 Ali Shariati, *Fatima Is Fatima*, trans. Laleh Bakhtiar (Tehran: The Shariati Foundation, n.d.), p. 105. Hereafter cited parenthetically as *FF*.

7 Some of the documents by women compiled in Azar Tabari and Nahid Yeganeh's *In the Shadow of Islam: The Women's Movement in Iran* (London: Zed Press, 1982) include lengthy examples lifted from Shariati's book almost as if the authors had internalized his argument and metaphors.

8 Shariati's argument is reminiscent of Fanon's chapter 'On National Culture,' in *The Wretched of the Earth*, trans. Constance Farrington (New York: Grove, 1963), in which he examines the problems of constructing a new identity forged out of a dead past and a bourgeois travesty of an imagined European present.

9 Fanon, *The Wretched of the Earth*, p. 202.

10 Oriana Fallaci, *Interviews with History* (Boston, MA: Houghton Mifflin, 1976), p. 272.

11 See William R. Darrow, 'Woman's Place and the Place of Women in the Iranian Revolution,' in *Women, Religion and Social Change*, ed. Yvonne Yazbeck Haddad and Ellison Banks Findly (Albany: State University of New York Press, 1985), pp. 307–20, for a valuable reading of the ambivalent discourse of

women's rights in the Islamic Constitution and its sources in earlier writings by Shariati and Motahari.

12 Ali Shariati, *On the Sociology of Islam*, trans. Hamid Algar (Berkeley, CA: Misan Press, 1979), p. 49.

13 See, for example, Tabari and Yeganeh, *In the Shadow of Islam*, pp. 173, 176, 189, 190.

14 See Mohamad Tavakoli, 'Modernist Refashioning of Iran' (unpublished Ms.)

15 Quoted in Said Amir Arjomand, *Authority and Political Culture in Shi'ism* (Albany: State University of New York Press, 1988), p. 357.

16 Derek Walcott refers to 'Progress as history's dirty joke' and its excuse for extermination, genocide, war, and slavery; Levinas – using Hegel, Husserl, Heidegger, and Sartre as evidence – has also attacked Western ontology as a philosophy based, he claims, on 'a horror of the other.' Emmanuel Levinas, 'The Trace of the Other,' in *Deconstruction in Context*, ed. Mark C. Taylor (University of Chicago Press, 1986), pp. 346–47. Levinas proposes ethics in place of ontology, substituting respect for the other (justice) in place of desire (freedom).

17 The irony here is that while Nuri claimed that he did not wish to build Iran out of the *ash* (stew) of the British, he was glad to sell out land and monopolies to the Russians. For a reading of this entangled relationship, see Michael M. J. Fischer, *Iran: From Religious Dispute to Revolution* (Cambridge, MA: Harvard University Press, 1980), pp. 5–51. See also Vanessa Martin's *Islam and Modernism: The Iranian Revolution of 1906* (Syracuse, NY: Syracuse University Press, 1989). Although Nuri's stance later became the basis for what is now referred to as traditionalist ideology, he does not fit into the category of the 'premodern' traditional because he takes modernity as a counter and articulates a position against it.

18 Quoted in Paidar, *Women and the Political Process*, p. 65.

19 See Eliz Sanasarian, *The Women's Rights Movement in Iran* (New York: Praeger, 1982), pp. 20–21. See also Haideh Moghissi, *Populism and Feminism in Iran: Women's Struggle in a Male-Defined Revolutionary Movement* (New York: St Martin's Press, 1994); and Paidar, *Women and the Political Process*.

20 See Afsaneh Najmabadi's forthcoming *Daughters of Quchan: Re-membering the Forgotten Gender of the Iranian Constitutional Revolution* (Syracuse, NY: Syracuse University Press) and her unpublished Ms. 'Female Suns and Male Lions: The Gendered Tropes of Iranian Modernity.'

21 See Moghissi, *Populism and Feminism in Iran*, pp. 82 ff. She quotes from Ahmad Kasravi, *Khaharan va Dokhtaran-e Ma* (Our sisters and daughters), 2nd edn (Bethesda, MD: Iranbooks, 1992), pp. 13–31.

22 Ervand Abrahamian, 'Kasravi: The Integrative Nationalist of Iran,' *Middle East Studies*, October 1973, 271–95. This illuminating essay narrates the history of Iran as a story of linguistic, religious, and tribal factions and communal struggles. Abrahamian suggests what is at stake in political modernization by recalling differences in the use of the term 'national integration,' which for Clifford Geertz means the 'aggregation of communal groups into nations' and for Leonard Binder suggests the closing of gaps 'between elites and masses through the building of new national values and state institutions' (p. 272).

23 Ibid., p. 273.

24 Ibid.

25 Ibid., p. 280. See also Fischer, *Iran*, for its discussions of theological disputes.

26 For all these details, I am indebted mostly to Abrahamian, 'Kasravi,' and Roy Mottahedeh, *The Mantle of the Prophet* (New York: Pantheon, 1985), pp. 98–105.

Abrahamian sees the book burning and Kasravi's desire to cleanse Persian of mystical poetry and foreign words as a typically extreme strategy whose effect was to alienate communists and intellectuals who would otherwise have supported Kasravi. He therefore sees the failure to compromise as the cause of Kasravi's downfall. For an account of a typical debate between Khomeini and Kasravi in the 1940s, see Fischer, *Iran*, pp. 130–33.

27 Julia Kristeva, *Powers of Horror: An Essay on Abjection*, trans. Leon Rodiez (New York: Columbia University Press, 1982).

28 See Nikki Keddie, *Roots of Revolution* (New Haven: Yale University Press, 1981), pp. 93 ff.; and Kumari Jayawardena, *Feminism and Nationalism in the Third World* (London: Zed Books, 1986), pp. 57–72.

29 See Geoffrey Galt Harpham, 'So . . . What *Is* Enlightenment? An Inquisition into Modernity' *Critical Inquiry*, (spring 1994): 551–56, for a sharp reading of the Inquisition as embodiment of the paradox, self-division, darkness, and 'dialectic' of the Enlightenment.

30 This familiar image from Marx has been used to advantage most recently in David Lyon, *Postmodernity* (Minneapolis: University of Minnesota Press, 1994), p. 21. Terry Eagleton uses the image to describe capitalism, which 'gives birth to its own gravedigger, nurturing the acolyte who will one day stab the high priest in the back,' in *Criticism and Ideology* (London: New Left Books, 1976), p. 133.

31 Harpham, 'So . . . What *Is* Englightenment?', p. 333.

32 Partha Chatterjee, *The Nation and Its Fragments* (Princeton, NJ: Princeton University Press, 1993), p. 234.

33 In 1963, explaining his program in the language of popular revolution, the Shah embarked on 'the Revolution of the Shah and the People' that included reforms such as voting rights for women, the formation of a literacy corps, and land reforms. See also Afsaneh Najmabadi, *Land Reform and Social Change in Iran* (Salt Lake City: University of Utah Press, 1987), for a valuable study of the effects of the land reforms of 1962–72 on the economy of rural societies, and of the problems in translating into other cultures the European model for agrarian development.

34 We must recognize that this is the narrative of a landowner and not of a peasant. The White Revolution was also seen as liberation by many peasants, some of whom organized street demonstrations during the 1960s in support of its aims.

35 See Haleh Afshar, 'An Assessment of Agricultural Development Policies in Iran,' in *Iran: A Revolution in Turmoil* (Albany: State University of New York Press, 1985), pp. 58–79. She points to misconceived national planning and to statistics that demonstrate, over a forty-five year span, a lack of linkage between central and rural economies: 'The oil industry was a highly developed, capital-intensive producer of unprocessed oil, mainly for consumption of the West. Oil formed an enclave of development with no backward and little forward linkage to the indigenous sector' (p. 59).

36 After the CIA *coup* of 1953 Iran's political and economic enmeshment turned from Britain and the Soviet Union to the United States, whose paranoia about the Soviet threat from the 1950s to the 1970s translated into massive military and economic assistance. Before the 1953 *coup*, the country had been indirectly controlled by Britain and the Soviet Union. The Shah is reported to have complained that ambassadors from the two countries handed him a list of candidates each time there was an election to the Majlis: see Mehran Kamrava, *Revolution in Iran: The Roots of Turmoil* (New York: Routledge, 1990), p. 30.

37 See Chatterjee, *The Nation and Its Fragments*, p. 235.

38 See Benita Parry, 'Resistance Theory / Theorizing Resistance or Two Cheers for Nativism,' in *Colonial Discourse/Postcolonial Theory*, ed. Francis Barker, Peter Hulme, and Margaret Iversen (Manchester: Manchester University Press, 1994), pp. 172–96; Lila Abu-Lughod, 'The Romance of Resistance: Tracing Transformations of Power through Bedouin Women,' *American Ethnologist* 17 (1990): 41–55.

39 See Anthony Giddens, *Central Problems in Social Theory: Action, Structure and Contradiction in Social Analysis* (Berkeley and Los Angeles: University of California Press, 1979), pp. 226 ff. Discussing the uneven development of different sectors of social systems, Giddens writes of two models of unfolding development in Marx: one a progressive model moving toward empowering workers, neighborhoods, unions, and the proletariat; and the other, a 'second theory of revolution,' that 'anticipates a conception of uneven development,' that 'involves the idea that the conditions intiating revolutionary trans- formation are to be found in the conjunction of the retarded and the advanced: the sort of explosive situation Marx saw to exist in Germany in the late 1840s, and in Russia some thirty years later' (pp. 226–27).

   See also Marshall Berman's persuasive and relevant argument about the 'tragedy of development' in *All That Is Solid Melts into Air* (New York: Penguin, 1982): 'In so-called underdeveloped countries, systematic plans for rapid development have generally meant systematic repression of the masses,' a repression that he says takes two forms. 'The first form has involved squeezing every last drop of labor power out of the masses – Faust's "human sacrifices bled, / tortured screams would pierce the night" – in order to build up the forces of production, and at the same time drastically restricting mass consumption so as to create a surplus for reinvestment in the economy. The second form entails seemingly gratuitous acts of destruction – Faust's destruction of Philemon and Baucis and their bells and trees – not to create any material utility but to make the symbolic point that the new society must burn all its bridges so there can be no turning back' (pp. 75–76).

40 Although I am indebted to conversations with Mohamad Tavakoli for my understanding of differences, he warns me to resist such facile simplifications because each of the figures I name belongs just as easily in other categories.

41 See Ali Mirsepassi-Ashtiani, 'The Crisis of Secular Politics and the Rise of Political Islam in Iran,' *Social Text* (spring 1994): 51–84, for an important reading of the revolution as a 'historical turning point in the crisis of modern secular politics.' Foucault's comment appeared, according to Ashtiani, in an interview in a Persian paper, *Akhtar* 4 (spring 1987): 43. Paul Vieille's comments were made in Champaign-Urbana, both in conversations and public talks.

42 See Cheryl Benard and Zalmay Khalilzad, '*The Government of God*' (New York: Columbia University Press, 1984), p. 39. When Karim Sanjabi, the leader of the National Front, visited Khomeini in France, he emerged from their meeting with a shared understanding of Islam and democracy as foundations. This convinced secularists that the theologians would step aside once the Revolution had been won. Later, however, Khomeini refused to include the word 'democracy'. It was, he said, 'a Western import and Islam sufficed.' See Keddie, *Roots of Revolution*, p. 252.

43 Farzaneh Milani, *Veils and Words: The Emerging Voices of Iranian Women Writers* (Syracuse: Syracuse University Press, 1992), p. 4.

44 Ibid., p. 86.

45 Introduction to *Feminism and History*, ed. Joan Wallach Scott (Oxford: Oxford University Press, 1996), p. 4.

46 See Gayle Rubin, 'The Traffic in Women: Notes on the "Political Economy" of Sex,' in Scott, *Feminism and History*, pp. 105–51.

47 Afsaneh Najmabadi, 'Hazards of Modernity and Morality: Women, State and Ideology in Contemporary Iran,' in *Women, Islam and the State*, ed. Deniz Kandiyoti (Philadelphia: Temple University Press, 1991), p. 63.

48 Nahid Yeganeh, 'Women's Struggles in the Islamic Republic of Iran,' in Tabari and Yeganeh, *In the Shadow of Islam*, p. 55. Gurji was the chosen woman representative in the Assembly of Experts. She continued in this speech to say that Islam does not separate women's from men's rights. 'We have only the rights of human beings.'

49 Introduction to *Faith and Freedom: Women's Human Rights in the Muslim World*, ed. Mahnaz Afkhami (Syracuse: Syracuse University Press, 1995), p. 5.

50 My source is the section entitled 'Women's Organizations in Iran,' in Tabari and Yeganeh, *In the Shadow of Islam*. This useful book includes documents on the question of women spanning the period from Khomeini to the Tudeh Party. It also lists positions taken by thirteen major and ten smaller women's organizations on the Revolution.

51 See Afsaneh Najmabadi, 'Without a Place to Rest the Sole of My Foot,' *Emergences* (fall 1992): 84–102, for an account of her participation in the march, her questioning of the mapping of female bodies as representations of revolution and counter-revolution, and her disillusionment with leftist organizations for their refusal to take public positions on the terror against women when three prostitutes were executed on 12 July 1979.

52 Ibid., pp. 91–92.

53 Ibid., p. 92.

54 See Haleh Afshar, 'Khomeini's Teachings and Their Implications for Iranian Women,' in Tabari and Yeganeh, *In the Shadow of Islam*, pp. 75–90. She quotes from C. Kirkpatrick's *Women in Nazi Germany* (London: Jarrolds, 1939), p. 100.

55 Afsaneh Najmabadi, 'Feminisms in an Islamic Republic,' in *Gender, Islam, and Social Change*, ed. Yvonne Haddad and John Esposito (New York: Oxford University Press, 1998), pp. 59–84.

56 See Paidar, *Women and the Political Process*, pp. 265–363, on the 'Discourse of Islamization,' for a valuable survey of the Islamic Republic's policies on women.

57 For this information, I am grateful to Nayereh Tohidi, who has recently visited Iran and written on the changing social positions of women (see n. 58).

58 See Moghissi, *Populism and Feminism in Iran*. See also Valentine Moghadam, ed., *Identity Politics and Women: Cultural Reassertions and Feminisms in an International Perspective* (Boulder, CO: Westview Press, 1994); and Nayereh Tohidi, 'Modernity, Islamization, and Women in Iran,' in *Gender and National Identity: Women and Politics in Muslim Societies*, ed. Valentine Moghadam (London: Zed Books, 1994).

59 See D. A. Spellberg, *Politics, Gender, and the Islamic Past: The Legacy of 'A'isha bint Abi Bakr* (New York: Columbia University Press, 1994), pp. 132 ff., for an insightful reading of conflicting interpretations of 'A'isha's role in the Battle of the Cammel in Sunni and Shi'a sources. This event is read as the cause of the split in the Prophet's household after his death. Most of his wives opposed 'A'isha's involvement in politics on the grounds (according to Shi'a sources) that women belonged in their tents rather than on battlefields. 'Retrospectively

cast in the historical record as the defeated political activist, 'A'isha is scripted to defend an untenable legacy as a woman already defined by the errors of female transgression' (p. 137).

60 Moghissi, *Populism and Feminism in Iran*, p. 183.
61 For the details on magazines, I am entirely indebted to Najmabadi's 'Feminisms in an Islamic Republic.'

12

HUMAN RIGHTS ARE WOMEN'S RIGHT

Amnesty International and the family

Saba Bahar

Women's movements have had formal international ties since 1902 when the International Woman Suffrage Alliance was organized. In the late twentieth century, globalization of the economy, technology, information, and politics made connections among women more widespread. In particular, international meetings became important to women's movements from the mid-1970s. These meetings were the occasion for publishing statistics on women in individual nations and evaluating women's situation globally. They provided publicity for the incredible poverty of most women, their victimization physically and politically, and the need to remedy these harsh conditions. Global organizations like Amnesty International and Human Rights Watch came to see that their work had focused too strictly on male political prisoners, the treatment of combatants, and other issues relating only to men. Feminism was reaching beyond national governments and constituencies to a global audience.

A major achievement of the last two decades of the twentieth century was the formulation of projects on human rights as they pertained to women. Human rights are defined in a variety of ways, from the right to food and shelter to a life free from violence and abuse. Women's failure to enjoy equal human rights emerged from these international conferences – for example, in Nairobi, Houston, and Beijing – as a common bond for women in countries of the North and South alike. Since World War II the number of people killed globally in wars of liberation, civil wars, ethnic war, and interstate war has passed the fifty million mark. It has been estimated that these wars and the accompanying rape have disproportionately impacted women. Domestic violence and rape in the course of everyday life constituted another common thread and one that seemed a progressively greater threat. This chapter charts the emergence of human rights as a feminist theme in the 1980s and 1990s and its intersection with other activist agendas. Human rights activism, its advocates maintain, has the potential for reinvigorating political life at the local level because it encompasses basic needs. In this respect it replaces or complements the older concept of equal rights around which women and people of color had organized earlier in the century. It reclaims politics for people, and this is what feminism needs.

* * *

During the past twenty years, the campaigns and interventions of feminist movements all over the world have forced the human rights movement to undergo a radical change by redefining the concept 'human rights.' Although committed to the notion of 'universal human rights,' feminist activists and scholars have nevertheless argued that human rights are not static and fixed but are determined by historical moments and struggles. As Charlotte Bunch, a key figure in the movement, states, the 'dynamism and ongoing relevance [of human rights] stem from the fact that more people are claiming them and, in the process, expanding the meaning of "rights" to incorporate their own hopes and needs' (Bunch 1995: 13).

Until recently the international human rights movement was defined in terms of the interests of those who first promoted it: Western-educated, propertied men. It therefore focused primarily on the state's infringement of public civil rights, including the right to free expression, to political association, and to a fair trial. It ignored or refused to intervene, however, when violations occurred within the private sphere of the home and when not directly caused by the state. Many human rights violations against women, including domestic violence, female genital mutilation, sexual slavery, forced pregnancies, and sterilization, are committed within the family and by private individuals or organizations. Because they occur in private, such violations have been uncontested by human rights activists. This view of human rights reinforces the artificial distinction between the public and the private spheres and fails to take into consideration how the inaction or discrimination of the state causes violent action in the home (Bunch 1995; Roth 1995).

The women's human rights movement has called into question this artificial distinction. Informed by their demands for urgent action and by feminist critiques of the state, such as those articulated by Catharine MacKinnon (1989) and Carole Pateman (1988), the movement calls attention to the state's role in maintaining and reproducing a gender hierarchy. By upholding a legislative and juridical system based almost entirely on male experiences, by attributing and enlarging the scope of male power within the family, and by failing to intervene against the status quo of women's social subordination, the state adopts and perpetuates male power (Romany 1995). Because of the state's complicity, violence in the family can ultimately be traced back to the state and its assumptions regarding gender roles and hierarchies within the family. As a result, the liberal distinction between private/family and public/state falls.

Feminist scholars and activists have questioned the state's responsibility for domestic violence.[1] In several countries, including Peru and Egypt, husbands have the legal right to beat and even kill their wives if they suspect them of committing adultery (Amnesty International 1995a; Merrus 1995; Roth 1995).[2] Here, the state is explicitly upholding male power within the family and thereby sanctioning a double standard. Elsewhere, the state is complicit in a less direct manner: although domestic violence is penalized, the judiciary fails to prosecute such cases systematically and/or applies lesser sentences (Beasley and Thomas 1994). In such cases, the state is discriminating against its female citizens. Brazilian 'honor' killings exemplify this form of discrimination. Brazilian women's rights activists investigated and documented the extent to which Brazilian courts and prosecutors accepted the 'honor' defense (that the man's honor was damaged because of the woman's behavior) to accusations of domestic violence. In doing so, these activists brought the state's responsibility for private human rights violations to international attention: the US-based Human Rights Watch, a non-governmental human rights organization, extended the study as one of the first in its Women's Rights Project (Beasley and Thomas 1994; Roth 1995).

That the law reflects male experience serves to keep women in violent relationships. In France, for example, family law stipulates that the partner who leaves the relationship abandons his/her rights to shared housing. Such a law restrains women who are trying to leave violent relationships: they often have no place to go, especially given the paucity of shelters and if they want to keep their children (Delphy 1995). By automatically vesting the right to housing in the 'abandoned' partners, the law ignores women who leave violent relationships with few resources of their own.[3] More important, a woman who leaves a violent relationship cannot be considered to be 'abandoning' her partner in the same sense as a man who leaves in order to avoid financial, parental, and social responsibilities. By failing to distinguish between these two forms of abandonment, the French state upholds social norms that discriminate against women.

Feminist human rights activists are thus doing more than merely expanding the notion of human rights. They are questioning the political and social foundations on which the notion of 'rights' rests; they are undermining the distinction between public and private, and challenging the social contract that is the basis for such distinctions. This re-evaluation argues that implicit to a public social contract is a hidden and forgotten sexual contract, which naturalizes family relations in terms of a gendered hierarchy.[4] It explores how the social contract has been founded with assumptions about gendered subjects as well as gender relations within the family. To incorporate the demands and vindications of this movement, therefore, involves more than merely focusing on woman's human rights; it demands a reconsideration of the definition of 'human rights,' of social contract theory, of theories of the family, and of the relationship between the state and the gendered citizen. Ultimately, such a reconsideration will have an impact not only on the lives of women but also on a global agenda for improved social, economic, and political standards of living.

Feminist scholars and activists have vindicated women's human rights, promulgated a new theory of social contract, and in doing so, have transformed the internationally contested terrain of 'human rights.' In response, several organizations have incorporated the feminist mandate. In 1989, Amnesty International, probably one of the most globally renowned non-governmental human rights groups, finally began to focus on the issue of violence against women. By organizing formal working groups responsible for documenting violations and in consultation with women's organizations from several countries, Amnesty International recognized that an overwhelming number of political activists, community organizers, and trade unionists are women. It concluded that women suffer more violations of human rights than any other group in the world, both in times of war and through traditional practices excused by culture (see Amnesty International 1991).[5] This documentation also forced the human rights organization to rethink the terms of its mandate, namely 'action to oppose arbitrary detention on political grounds' (Amnesty International 1995a: 11). To address the specific violence that women experience, the organization had to reconsider not only the private/public division but also its own emphasis on state-related violence against women. It did so by examining the manner in which government discrimination against women directly contributes to human rights violations against women (Sidhu and Chatterjee 1995). The result of this documentation and of this theoretical reorientation appear in its 1995 report *Human rights are women's right* (1995a) and in the fifteen-point platform for action that appears in the appendix to this report.

Comparing the demands that follow Amnesty International's first report on human rights violations against women, *Women in the front line* (1991) with its more recent *Human rights are women's right* (1995a) reveals some of the changes in Amnesty International's position on these violations. The 1991 report focuses primarily on women activists who have been persecuted by the state, and extensively covers the forms of abuses that women specifically suffer, including rape, sexual humiliation, and inadequate medical attention. The 1995 report, in comparison, emphasizes that government-sponsored discrimination against women contributes *directly* to human rights violations in the private sphere. The 1991 report concludes with twelve steps to protect women's human rights; in the 1995 report, this has been extended to fifteen steps. In fact, four steps are new, because one step was dropped from the 1991 platform. These steps call for the recognition that women's human rights are universal and indivisible (point 1); the eradication of discrimination, which denies women human rights (point 3); and the promotion of women's rights as human rights through official programs of education and training (point 14). A fourth new step, 'Armed political groups should safeguard women's human rights' (point 15) recognizes the manner in which armed political groups may also function like the state. The 1991 report rejected this last point, claiming that it is 'governments which have jurisdiction to determine criminal responsibility and to bring to justice those responsible for violent attacks on government authorities, security forces, and civilians' (Amnesty International 1991: 3). A final difference between the two platforms is the suppression of point 9 of the 1991 platform, 'Prevent human rights violations against women who are members of ethnic minorities' (Amnesty International 1991: 52–54; Amnesty International 1995a: 118–30).[6]

In addition to these new steps, the more recent report modifies a number of points. Instead of simply demanding a stop to 'disappearances' and extrajudicial executions, point 6 demands that the victims be compensated. Although this demand is included in the bullets under the main heading of the 1991 report, it has less importance than if it were integral to the heading itself. In addition to asking governments to support the work of relevant intergovernmental organizations, point 13 of the 1995 report (as opposed to point 12 of the 1991) asks for support for the work of non-governmental organizations, referring in the explanatory paragraphs to the activities of women activists.

Thus, both the additions and the modifications to the 1995 report suggest a greater focus on government discriminatory action and thereby a more complicated theorization of the relationship between the private and public spheres. They testify to Amnesty International's ongoing commitment to concrete action opposing women's human rights violations. This theorization and this commitment are all the more difficult given the variety of cultural and regional concepts of the family and of gender roles within it. Indeed, Amnesty International's opposition to certain forms of gender discrimination almost inevitably leads to charges of cultural imperialism and/or of Western bias. Clearly, part of the difficulty Amnesty International faces is negotiating a position that acknowledges the opposing claims of universal human rights and cultural practices.

Without underestimating the difficulties of this task, I nevertheless argue that Amnesty International's conflicting commitments both to its original mandate on state-based violence and to the recognition of violence in the private sphere, and specifically the family, results in a somewhat ambivalent, hence problematic and unsatisfactory, stance. Amnesty International's commitment to contesting violence only in the public sphere results in upholding assumptions about the family, about gender relations within the family, and about the gendered subject. After examining these empirical and theoretical gaps, I turn to another problematic area in this report, namely the manner in which a 'naturalized' family contract becomes the model for a social contract. By relying on this model, the report transfers assumptions about gendered subjects and gender hierarchies within the family to the state, thereby reproducing the image of a weak, dependent female child demanding protection and help from powerful and paternal state figures.

By analyzing Amnesty International's report on violence against women, I am not interested in condemning the human rights organization, especially one that has demonstrated an effective and genuine commitment to combating human rights violations all over the world. On the contrary, what interests me here are the limits that a traditional approach to human rights violations, emphasizing exclusively the public sphere, can set to contesting violations more generally. As long as the relation between the public and the private sphere, the state and the family is not re-theorized, many human rights violations against women will remain undocumented, regardless of avowed commitments.

Family violence as state violence

In preparation for the Fourth World Conference on Women in September 1995, Amnesty International launched a six-month campaign entitled 'Human Rights Are Women's Right,' which addressed the problems of violence against women. The press release for this campaign states that it focuses on three areas where governments fail to protect women's human rights: 'during wars and conflicts, when repressed because of their activism, and stemming from discrimination against women' (Amnesty International 1995b). Amnesty International explains that its new focus is informed by the activities of different feminist grassroots organizations that contest the distinction between private and public spheres, in particular between domestic and government violence. Nevertheless, the new focus still reiterates the organizations founding mandate for action, namely:

> To oppose a set of grave violations of the rights to freedom of expression and freedom from discrimination, and of the right to physical and mental integrity. In particular, Amnesty International opposes arbitrary detention on political grounds, believing that no one should be imprisoned as a prisoner of conscience and that no political prisoner should be imprisoned without a prompt and fair trial. Amnesty International also takes action to oppose torture, the death penalty, extrajudicial executions and other forms of arbitrary killing, and 'disappearances.'
>
> (Amnesty International 1995a: 11)

The mandate continues to emphasize freedom of expression freedom from discrimination and the right to a fair trial, which have come to be known as 'first generation rights,' that is, public and civil rights.[7] Only certain human rights victims are protected by Amnesty International (prisoners of conscience and political prisoners). Only specific human rights violations are enumerated in this paragraph: imprisonment, torture, death penalties, and extrajudicial executions are all crimes of the state. Finally, the report focuses on the public sphere in addressing the specific violation of women's human rights. Amnesty International opposes violence committed against women by governments and armed political groups, including the use of rape as an instrument of torture, forced gynaecological examinations for women in custody, and government persecution on the grounds of sexual orientation. Amnesty International therefore merely expands the concept of 'human rights' to include women by mentioning abuses and punishments that concern women only in these same arenas.

This mandate does not, however, radically redefine 'human rights.' By upholding specifically civil rights, it maintains the private/public split and sees human rights as rights to be protected and guaranteed almost exclusively in the public sphere. It ignores violations in the family and by private individuals, even when the state sanctions them. As such, it maintains a conventional and liberal conception of the state and of the social contract and fails to explore the extent to which the state adopts the standpoint of male power.

Because of this failure, a number of violations against women's human rights remain undocumented and ignored in the report. Although the report mentions abuses committed against women in the private sphere (including domestic violence, genital mutilation, and forced prostitution), these abuses are not its focus. Female genital mutilation (FGM) is discussed only in an appendix to the document.[8] There, the report discusses a number of different international and national efforts to stop the practice.

The existence of government policy regarding the practice suggests that FGM cannot be regarded as merely a 'private, family affair,' but one where the state can intervene. Burkina Faso, Egypt, Sudan, Sweden, and the United Kingdom have either legislation or ministerial regulations against it *per se*. In Canada, Côte d'Ivoire, France, Guinea Bissau, Kenya, and the Netherlands, FGM falls under existing legislation or application of case law. A number of countries where FGM is traditionally practiced have signed treaties and charters recognizing the right to physical and mental integrity and prohibiting gender discrimination. They have made official statements condemning it. Despite these laws and treaties, few governments have prosecuted or punished practitioners (Sullivan and Toubia 1993). This situation recalls the Brazilian 'honor' killings discussed above: the state is more lenient when it comes to prosecuting crimes committed against women in the name of 'tradition' and the family.

The Amnesty International report mentions the United Nations High Commission on Refugees' position on forced genital mutilation. The commission recognizes, as a claim for refugee status, the risks of forced genital mutilation and/or of facing persecution for opposing the practice when these risks are combined with an absence of state protection. Despite this recommendation and national legislation against the practice, few countries grant asylum to women on these grounds alone. In France for example, the petition for asylum from a woman from Mali was denied. Whereas the board's decision recognized FGM as a means of persecution, it argued that the Mali government was not responsible for it. It indicated that although there is no legislation against FGM in Mali, the authorities nevertheless support campaigns against it (Leiss and Boesjes 1994). The decision thus equates mere support for campaigns with government action. Amnesty International's decision to relegate FGM to an appendix reproduces this decision. It fails to address adequately violations of human rights in the private sphere, even when such violence can be prevented or punished by state action.

Although Amnesty International campaigns against the systematic rape of the women of Bosnia-Herzegovina, it overlooks another form of violence against women common to certain wars: an increase in domestic violence. In contrast to this report, Belgrade feminists Lepa Mladjenovic and Vera Litricin have documented the increase of domestic violence in the Serbian capital since the beginning of the war. They argue that the percentage of guns among violent men has doubled, and identify 'the Post-TV News Violence Syndrome' whereby men are more violent against their wives after exposure to nationalistic propaganda (Mladjenovic and Litricin 1993).

Nor does the 1995 Amnesty International report take a position against practices in which the privacy of the family merges with racist and sexist immigration laws in many Western countries. These laws directly contribute to keeping many immigrant women of color in violent marriages. One such law is the UK's 'primary purpose' law, which stipulates that in marriages between a British resident/national and a non-British resident, the married couple must live together for one year in the United Kingdom before an independent residency status will be accorded to the non-resident. As a result of this law, women who have found themselves in violent relations before the year is over are in extremely difficult positions: they must choose either to endure the violence at the risk of their lives or risk deportation (Bhabha and Shutter 1994).[9]

The report's silence on this issue is all the more telling given its claim that 'women who come from minority or marginalized groups are in double jeopardy. Discriminated against as women, they are also victims of prejudice' (Amnesty International 1995a: 85–86). In this context, it mentions the rape of Dalit and Adivasi women in India by police officers and of a French citizen of Tunisian descent by both Italian and French border police. The failure to discuss the nefarious 'primary purpose' law in relation to these other instances seems to be justified by an arbitrary distinction between 'public' violence (committed by public officers in public places) and private violence (committed by individuals in their own domestic space). That the latter is directly engendered by the state's discriminatory actions and laws remains unexamined and/or is excused as a private, family matter.

Although the report considers as part of its mandate the manner in which 'judicial systems discriminate against women by sentencing them more harshly than men convicted of the same offences' (Amnesty International 1995a: 85–86), it fails to address the manner in which judicial systems sentence women to forced sterilization as punishments for crimes they might have committed. Recently, for instance, a United States judge allowed a woman who pleaded guilty to using cocaine to choose between two sentences: sterilization or three months in jail and a $750 fine (Associated Press 1995a).[10] It is unlikely that a man guilty of a similar crime would face a similar choice. The question that needs to be asked here is whether such an oversight is merely an empirical one or whether it reflects a more general failure of Amnesty International to theorize reproductive rights as human rights. Given the report's strange silence with respect to these violations, I would argue the second position.

The report mentions forced gynecological exams in custody; such a violation, however, is not strictly speaking a reproductive rights issue. Rather, it is either a health or a sexual harassment issue. It is, moreover, important to recall that the report only contests such violations when committed in custody, that is, by public officials as part of their public function. Violations committed by doctors and health officers in the private section go undocumented.

The only mention of women's reproductive rights to appear in the 1995 report regards pregnant women in custody. It urges that special action be taken to protect their special health needs. It mentions the risks of injury to the fetus, of miscarriage, and of giving birth in harsh prison conditions as forms of human rights violations (Amnesty International 1995a: 87, 123). It also condemns forced pregnancies that result from rape (e.g. Amnesty International 1995a: 22). Amnesty International, however, ignores the relationship between the human right to reproductive rights and state population policies, focusing only on the health rights of pregnant women in custody and not the reproductive right of women more generally to choose when and if they want to be pregnant.

Feminist theorists and activists have, in contrast, repeatedly argued that reproductive rights are legislated in national laws and therefore cannot be considered merely as 'private rights.' Where reproductive rights are concerned, public policy intersects directly with private choice. For instance, the legal age of marriage is directly related to women's reproductive health and rights. When this age is low or when the law is not enforced, as in Nigeria and Zaire, adolescent girls face the often mortal consequences of adolescent pregnancy (Cook 1995). Moreover, reproductive choice is also directly imposed by the state, as in the case of restrictive abortion laws or in forced, government-imposed sterilization.[11] Indeed, a number of different countries, from the United States to India to Brazil, have forced reproductive choices on women by sterilizing them without their informed consent (Hartmann 1987; Heise 1995; Mirsky and Radlert 1994). At other times, the state remains complicit with male household heads by giving them control over women's bodies. In India and Kenya, for example, spousal permission is often a condition for the dispensation of contraceptives. Such policies not only deny reproductive choice to women but also place them at risk of violence at having raised an issue often conflated with 'infidelity' or of abandonment (when the male spouse decides that he has a mouthful too many to feed) (Cook 1995, Heise 1995).

Finally, in countries where a somewhat progressive reproductive policy does exist, governments discriminate against women citizens by failing to prosecute attempts to deny women legal abortion. France and the United States, where abortion is legal, have been reluctant to prosecute groups that have attempted to block women's access to clinics through both non-violent and violent means (Cook 1995; Heise 1995). The French government even wanted to grant amnesty to anti-abortion protesters convicted of interfering with clinics, even though this bid was later dropped (Associated Press 1995b). Moreover, a French court recently acquitted anti-abortion activists on the grounds that the fetus is 'a future human being,' despite the fact that such a definition is in direct contradiction with the country's abortion legislation (Reuters 1995). This case is being appealed.

These examples suggest that despite the silence, women's reproductive rights fall within Amnesty International's mandate.[12] Moreover, when violations are examined in relation to a country's natalist politics, the complicity between state power and family power is revealed. Indeed, is it possible to consider the French state's laxness *vis-à-vis* anti-abortion activists without examining its recent policies on family benefits? French feminists have argued that the new law paying parents when they abandon active employment for child-rearing (*'allocation parentale d' éducation'*) is not so much a recognition of the value of women's work in the household as it is a pronatalist policy, encouraging couples to have more children and women to return to the family sphere to do so (Delphy 1995; Jenson and Sineau 1995).[13]

That this policy is pronatalist and not aimed at improving women's situation is revealed in the way in which the policy was crafted. The benefits were originally intended to encourage couples to have a third child, but under the Balladur government they were extended to the second. The birth of each additional child justifies the payment of a new fixed sum. The benefits are very low, and the fixed sum for each additional child is very limited. Furthermore, as first designed, only employed parents could benefit from the *allocation parentale d'éducation*; this stipulation was subsequently dropped following parliamentary opposition. The law nevertheless stipulates that until the child's third birthday, waged employment can be exercised for no longer than a year.[14] It makes no provisions to guarantee the resumption of employment (Jenson and Sineau 1995).

Given existing gendered wage disparities, the effect of the policy is to move employed women out of the workplace and into the home. This is so even though the policy does not distinguish between men and women. Because the couple itself must decide which spouse will give up a job to bring up the child, the very low sum of the benefit ultimately encourages women, who tend to earn lower wages, to abandon employment for the fixed sum. In doing so, women are not rewarded for their new 'career choice'; their male partners are (Delphy 1995; Jenson and Sineau 1995). Once again, the very low sum paid is at stake: the social security benefits are not sufficient without another full-time wage-earner.

By adopting such a policy, then, the French state is not simply encouraging the birth of more children; it is also reinforcing both gender discrimination in the workforce and implicit assumptions about the gendered division of labor within the family. As Delphy writes, 'It is not the recognition of the value of this work, but rather a subsidy to the patriarchal structure of the family' (Delphy 1995: 26; my translation) The state, at least in this instance, has chosen the patriarchal family as the unit through which it implements its own natalist policies.

The Amnesty International report addresses the state complicity with male power in the private sphere most convincingly when discussing the specific vulnerability of women refugees, asylum-seekers, and displaced women. It documents how government officials, from border guards to refugee camp supervisors, abuse their public office to sexually exploit women and girl refugees, and demand sex in exchange for refugee status. Governments turn blind eyes to violations of women's human rights when they do not punish male officials for breaching legislated codes of conduct. While not directly complicit in upholding male power, the state nevertheless fails to act against it.

The report also mentions the particular cruelty of asylum procedures in European countries. It takes a position against the 'safe country policy,' which claims that certain countries are 'safe' and that refugees from these countries do not have any justified basis for making an asylum claim. The designation of the 'safe' country is often a political decision, having little to do with political conditions in the country itself. India, for instance, is considered a 'safe' country, which is why no Sikh or Kashmiri activist has ever been able to lodge a successful asylum claim in a European country (see Fekete and Webber 1994).[15] Although this policy does not affect women uniquely, it nevertheless makes access to safe refuge for women more difficult. Indeed, although women and children are the majority of the world refugee population, they are nevertheless the minority of those who succeed in obtaining asylum in European and North American countries.

This disparity is due to the difficulties of the escape journey, where women are more vulnerable, to policies such as the 'safe country' policy, and to the asylum process itself. The report insists that the latter may entail specific difficulties for women:

> Often those hearing asylum applications fail to categorise violations women's rights as persecution. The asylum process itself, which requires applicants to tell strangers in uniform what has happened to them – often repeatedly – works against women victims of rape and sexual abuse. Many are too ashamed or traumatized to tell their stories, especially to men.
>
> (Amnesty International 1995a: 27)

Here the report highlights how the asylum process fails to take into account the specificity of women's experiences. It is deaf to violations of women's rights as persecution, and it is insensitive to the difficulty of recounting a traumatic event, given the social and cultural taboos surrounding rape.

Finally, point 11 of Amnesty International's fifteen-point platform specifically recommends that 'procedures for the determination of refugee status . . . should provide interviewers trained to be sensitive to the issues of gender and culture, as well as to recognize the specific protection needs of women refugees and asylum seekers' (Amnesty International 1995a: 126). This move asks that women refugees be given individual treatment and not be regarded as part of their families. Unlike discriminatory immigration legislation such as Britain's primary purpose law, it makes women legally and often financially independent of their male relatives and protects them from possibly violent marriages and relationships. And yet, the report does not go as far as Canada's Immigration and Refugee Board, which since March 1993 has recognized gender-specific refugee claims. Under these guidelines an Ecuadorian woman systematically abused by her husband and a Chinese woman threatened by forced sterilization both qualified for asylum (Kelly 1994).

I have been arguing that despite its implicit acknowledgment of the demands of the women's human rights movement, Amnesty International nevertheless continues to uphold the public/private distinction that this very acknowledgment questions. Because of this failure to question the public/private distinction, even such a progressive human rights organization does not adequately explore the manner in which the state is often either directly complicit or willfully blind to violence in the private domain; it does not explore how the patriarchal state depends on the patriarchal family to consolidate its own authority. This theoretical weakness, in turn, results in a number of crucial empirical oversights. The shortcomings that I have been addressing here are, then, less importantly about limitations in the position of Amnesty International itself, and more importantly about problems concerning the relation between the public/ state and the private/family. This relation needs to be systematically re-interrogated, re-conceptualized and re-theorized in order to produce and engage a more effective platform for the global human rights movement.

Amnesty International's models for political action

Even if Amnesty International does not specifically address the issue of private violence, it does specify that government action should be taken to prevent it. At least five of the fifteen steps proclaim what governments *should not* do and suggest what they *should* do, thereby articulating a proscriptive and prescriptive model for political action (Amnesty International 1995a: 118–37). I would now like to examine this model, its reification of the patriarchal family and of gendered relations within the family. I argue that despite its commitments to recognizing women's human rights, Amnesty International continues to reproduce an image of passive, dependent women who need paternal families and states to protect them. This image ultimately relies on assumptions of a patriarchal family where female child-rearers depend on strong male figures for protection.

Amnesty International's prescription for action is in many ways informed by the paternalistic politics of the Rousseauian social contract in insisting on the necessity of government action to protect women against private and public violence. Rousseau situates the original model of political relations in the family (Rousseau [1762] 1992: 29–31). Though not an explicit contract, Rousseau's vision of family ties is constructed via an exchange: in return for love (the love they receive from their children), fathers will provide them with the care and attention necessary for their preservation. Rousseau also assumes that the head of the family unit is the father and that exchanges are contracted with him and not the mother. The original exchange thus depends on dual presuppositions of natural family ties (fathers are *naturally* heads of the household) and of a necessarily unequal relation between fathers and children (children are *necessarily* dependent on fathers for their self-preservation). Rousseau establishes an analogy between these natural and necessary family ties and the social order. He suggests that heads of state are like fathers, and that citizens are like children, the main difference between the family and the social contract being that the state does not receive love in exchange for its protection, but power.

As figured in Amnesty International's report and in the proposed platform for action, government is a paternal power whose specific duty is to help its necessarily dependent female citizens with the care and attention needed for their survival. Such a contract thus implies that the female citizen/resident/refugee, in her gender-specific relation to the state, is like a child: *necessarily* and *naturally* weak, dependent, and requiring particular attention and protection. Focusing on violence against women, Amnesty International's paternal politics implies that women are either lesser men, in so far as they require special attention and help to become full citizens, or that they are lesser citizens, without complete access to rights and responsibilities.[16]

Amnesty International's 1995 campaign points then to a political paradox: how to guarantee women's rights without reproducing a paternalistic and patriarchal relationship similar to that which has engendered the violations of these very rights.[17] Such a position, however, fails to recognize the extent to which women can and have defined their own political agenda and have entered into negotiation with the state, not as weak, dependent, and lesser individuals but rather as autonomous, self-determined political actors. Instead this formulation reproduces the image of passive women who must be protected by fathers and governments from everyday violence.

At times, the Amnesty International report contests such an image. At the end of the introduction to *Human rights are women's right*, Amnesty International proclaims that the future actions of the global human rights movement must depend on the demands of women themselves:

> Women's voices can be heard over the world: demanding justice, protesting against discrimination, claiming rights, mourning dead husbands and comforting raped daughters. The job of the human rights movement is to make governments listen and ensure that they take action to protect and promote women's human rights.
> (Amnesty International 1995a: 14)

The paragraph establishes a distinction between the voices of women and the ears of governments and human rights movements. Here, women themselves engage in action, by recounting, demanding, protesting, claiming, mourning, and comforting. More important, the actions occur both in the public sphere of the state and in the private sphere of the family. Women's voices are both solacing, in keeping with a more traditional maternal role, and denunciatory, breaking away from such a role. These voices should set the agenda for political action, suggests the report.

The Amnesty International report documents the contributions of individual women activists, including labor, political, human rights, and community activists. It also recognizes the accomplishments of 'grassroots campaigning, usually by independent women's rights organizations' (Amnesty International 1995a: 8). This acknowledgment is an important step toward the recognition of the political action of women as independent agents.

Indeed, diverse women's groups have forced the issue of violence against women on to the agenda of international, intergovernmental conferences. In 1979, when the UN Convention on the Elimination of All Forms of

Discrimination against Women was adopted, it contained no clause dealing specifically with violence against women. Systematic lobbying by grass-roots feminist activists forced attention to the extent of the problem, not only by documenting the violence against women (that is, both the harm done to the individual woman and the adverse consequences for society as a whole) but also by providing refuge to and assistance for women threatened by domestic violence. Violence against women thus became one of the key issues in improving the condition of women as outlined in the *Nairobi forward-looking strategies* (United Nations 1994). It forced Amnesty International itself to recognize that women were underrepresented in their research and to resolve in the 1989 meeting of the International Council, to improve and increase 'its efforts to protect women's human rights' at every level of its work (Friedman 1995). Setting violence against women on the agenda of human rights violation is thus the result of the collective action of women; it is the result of the demands made by women on governments to fulfill their part of the contract. The history of such movements questions the Rousseauian model of a social contract founded on a naturalized and necessary patriarchal family contract. It suggests instead that women participate *independently* in order to make their own demands on the state.

But with the exception of point 13, Amnesty International's fifteen-point platform for action does not specifically address the agency and the actions of these grassroots organizations in deciding how violence against women and gender discrimination should be prevented and eliminated. Point 13 requests that governments 'support the work of relevant intergovernmental and non-governmental organizations' (Amnesty International 1995a: 127), introducing an extra-governmental instance that will counsel and monitor the intentions and behavior of the state in the matter. In the paragraphs that comment and explain this point, however, 'women activists and non-governmental organizations which work for the promotion and protection of women's human rights' are mentioned only once (Amnesty International 1995a: 127).[18]

The conflicts that arose in the preparation for the Fourth World Conference on Women in Beijing exemplify the importance of this demand. Some governments and international agencies attempted to refuse the participation of women's groups. In France, feminists and grassroots organizations were not consulted in the preparation for the conference until after the official government agenda was determined (Delphy 1995). More-over, women's non-governmental organizations faced obstacles to effective participation. These obstacles included denial of accreditation, exclusion from the drafting process, and delays in producing the Conference Platform (Center for Women's Global Leadership 1995). Some non-governmental organizations concerned with women's issues in China-Tibet and Iran were even barred from the conference because of political considerations and regardless of their commitment to women's rights (Kabel 1995; News Service 1995). Feminist activists and organizations protested against these obstacles. Amnesty International, in direct compliance with point 13 of its fifteen-point platform, took up the campaign. By complying with the demands of feminist and grassroots activists, the non-governmental organization began to rewrite the narrative of the passive female victim awaiting the intervention of the paternal state or human rights organizations, which underlies much of Amnesty International's 1995 report.

If point 13 and its application in the context of the Fourth World Conference articulate a new model for political action, one which does not assume a mutalized patriarchal family contract and hence a dependent female subject, then moments of the Amnesty International report revert to the image of the passive woman. An example is to be found in the following description of the devastation of our *fin-de-siécle*:

> As the 20th century draws to a close, women who have taken no part in conflicts are being murdered, raped and mutilated. Others have to endure the loneliness and vulnerability of separation and bereavement. Hardship and deprivation face women who have to support a family alone, in an economy itself distorted by the violence. Millions of women have lost their homes, their possessions, their friends and their roots as they search for safety.
>
> (Amnesty International 1995a: 29–30)

Here women are portrayed as quietly succumbing, silent victims. By suggesting that 'women . . . have taken no part in conflicts,' the passage reiterates an image of military society where only the male soldiers contribute to the defensive or offensive strategy of the country. It neglects to portray the manner in which a militarized society is dependent on the labor of women, mothers, workers, and ideologues even as the violence that such a society encourages has direct repercussions on their lives. Although the verb 'to search' implies a form of resistance and active engagement in history, 'to endure' and 'to support' suggest fatalistic resignation to the conditions of war.

By evoking the construction of a passive victim of history in this passage, I do not seek to contest the harsh reality, the absence of any real choice for women (and men) during war and the repeated failures such women must confront. I am, rather, questioning how such sweeping descriptions efface the women who resist and organize against such devastation, even if in very minimal and limited ways. Women have fled; they have contacted and constructed family networks; they have created new lives for themselves and for their families when they have reached zones of safety.

The absence of female agency in such representations points to underlying assumptions about family structures and gender roles within these structures. These descriptions must be read in conjunction with other passages implying that the 'natural' condition of the world is one where 'weaker' women are protected by 'stronger' men and governments and where patriarchal families act in the best interests of women. In discussing the war in Afghanistan, for example, the report describes Afghanistan as a

> country ravaged by a conflict in which civilians, far from being protected by their non-combatant status, have been deliberately targeted and where women, far from being protected by their gender, have been attacked because of it. Continued fighting over control of territory results in the killing of countless civilians caught in cross-fire, including women and children. As territory changes hands after a long battle, an entire local population may become the target of retaliatory punishment, mainly torture and killings, by the new warlord if he decides that they had cooperated with the previous warlord. A warlord's fighters are usually rewarded by the property they loot or confiscate from the conquered population. This again usually involves massacre of the male members of the families and raping of the women.
>
> (Amnesty International 1995a: 34)

The passage suggests that the 'unnatural' condition in which Afghanistan finds itself lies in the disappearance of an ideal family and state order which 'protects' women. The absence of a strong government and of male family or clan leaders who can contain these conflicting factions results in the massacre and torture of civilians. The report thus overlooks the fact that often it is precisely such a government and such families which are responsible for the worst discrimination and the exclusion of women from public and political life. The rhetoric of this passage reproduces this exclusion by drawing a distinction between civilians more generally and women more specifically, almost as if women were not part of the civilian population. It also states that males are massacred, whereas women are raped, ignoring the fact that rape, in such a context, is often followed by murder or suicide.

Implicit in such descriptions is the conception of women as dependent caregivers first and political actors second. Men, as fathers and husbands, protect these weaker beings. The Amnesty International report mentions that women 'suffer especially. . . . They make most of the world's refugees and displaced people. They are left to *rear families* by themselves' (Amnesty International 1995a: 18; my emphasis). Whereas this statement may be simply asserting an empirical fact concerning the overwhelming percentage of poor displaced and refugee women, it implies that female-headed, single-parent families are 'unnatural' and prevail only during times of conflict and war, as a symptom of a deeper social malady. This implication does not take into account the reality of many such families all over the world, even where military strife is not the order of the day. It points to the endurance of the myth of the patriarchal family, thereby preventing the recognition of female-headed households.

Elsewhere, the report states, 'The nation state has all but collapsed in some parts of the world, splintering into patchworks of territory controlled by competing warlords. Caught in the cross-fire, women from the poorest and most vulnerable sections of society have nowhere to turn. When the rule of law breaks down, there is no authority to protect the weak from the strong' (Amnesty International 1995a: 31–32). Here too, the 'nation state' and the 'law' are figured as intervening to protect the naturally weaker women from the stronger elements of society. Such generalizations fail to recall that the nation state has often been directly responsible for maintaining women as the poorer and more vulnerable members of society in their 'naturally' weaker role. It overlooks the fact that poor women often perceive the nation state and the law as their enemies (Heise 1995). Finally, it ignores the fact that the poor – and especially poor women – have organized collectively to protect themselves from the strong authority of the law. After all, the mothers and grandmothers of the Plaza de Mayo in Argentina, standing up 'in the midst of one of the most brutal dictatorships . . . protested the disappearance of their children' (Bunch 1995: 17), not only introduced the concept of disappearance as a violation of a human right but also helped bring down the dictatorship.

Conclusion

In examining Amnesty International's report and recommendations on the violations of women's human rights, I have tried to argue that the human rights organization continues to retain many presuppositions about the division between the public and private spheres, about the gendered female subject, and about gender relations within the family. I have also indicated where the organization attempts to break away from such assumptions, and to articulate alternative modes of thinking about the relationship between the state and the family, of state responsibility for violence in the private sphere, and of female agency in political action. In the first section of this chapter, although I criticize the 1995 report's silence on domestic abuse, I also point to its more radical position on asylum and refugee laws. In the second section, I argue that Amnesty International relies on an implicit model of a female gendered subject who is passive and dependent on paternal instances. I also indicate areas where the report is directly inspired by and subject to the demands of the women's movement all over the world. Thus, despite replicating implicit assumptions about the state, the family, and gender roles, Amnesty International has a more-than-verbal commitment to feminist critiques of state responsibility and of the family.

I suggest that these opposing positions result from Amnesty International's commitment to its original founding mandate for action directed against governments committing human rights violations in the public sphere versus a realignment of this mandate in response to the feminist transformation of the concept of human rights.

A question that I would like to raise in these final concluding remarks is: Given this central contradiction, maintaining both a traditional androcentric conception of human rights and recognizing the need to redefine these rights in the light of violations against women, how can we envisage the continuing role of non-governmental human rights organizations such as Amnesty International in the movement for women's human rights? I would argue, first, that despite the theoretical and empirical limitations articulated above, it is important not to minimize the concrete actions taken. Forcing the international community to recognize rape – even if only in conflict situations – as torture and a crime is in itself a significant step in a world that continues to ignore this form of systematic violence against women. Likewise, intervening in the illegal arrests, tortures, and extra-judicial executions of political and social activists cannot be minimized.

Second and perhaps more important, an independent women's movement with its own mandate and commitments must and will continue to grow. The mothers of Plaza de Mayo certainly did not wait for the approbation of organizations like Amnesty International to protest the disappearance of their children. They thereby introduced a new concept to human rights definitions. Lepa Mladjenovic contests violence against women in the former Yugoslavia away from the 'real' theater of the war. African women's grassroots groups organize against the practice of female genital mutilation. Feminist activists in India protest against the introduction of reproductive technology, such as Norplant and the anti-fertility vaccine, which are often not only harmful for women's health but also part of a classist, racist, and sexist population policy.

Feminist activists from around the world who want to affirm their solidarity with local struggles should take their cues from these grassroots movements, allowing them to define the agenda for the movement in a manner relevant to their local, cultural, and national contexts. In doing so, they should also exert pressure on Amnesty International and other international human rights organizations to recognize the demands of these groups and to continue to rethink the limitations that its founding charter imposes on the women's human rights movement. This political agenda should, finally, also inform the work of continuing scholarship on the concept of 'human rights,' on the division between the public and the private, on the relationship between the family and the state with specific reference to violence against women. What is at stake here is more than Amnesty International's mandate, more than feminist scholarship on the family, more than the success of different grassroots movements for women's rights. It is the articulation of new forms of knowledge and of politics for a more just and equitable society.

ACKNOWLEDGMENTS

I thank Janice Stewart, the anonymous readers of the manuscript, and the editors of this special issue of *Hypatia* for helping me work through and improve on earlier drafts of this chapter. Ellen Feder and Eva Feder Kirray were particularly helpful with their incisive comments and their endless patience.

NOTES

1 For a more complete account of how domestic violence falls within the domain of state responsibility and for a historical and theoretical consideration of how it came to be considered as an international human rights issue by one human rights organization, Human Rights Watch, see Beasley and Thomas (1994); Roth (1995).

2 Throughout this chapter, I compare the experiences of women in a number of countries. I realize that generalizations tend to ignore differences among women and fail to distinguish between political regimes. It is problematic to compare countries subject to the draconian policies of the World Bank and the International Monetary Fund with those who impose them. Even within one country women do not experience state and family oppression in the same way. Despite this, I nevertheless want to call attention to the manner in which violence against women and the state's complicity in it often cuts across lines of nationality, culture, race, and class.

3 The opposite case can also be made, namely that traditionally, it is often men who have abandoned women and children and that by attributing the common household to the abandoned partner the law is in fact taking into account women's experience. Although this may have been the case historically, the reality in today's France has changed and it is this change that needs to be considered.

4 For a critical discussion of the relationship between the 'public' social contract and the 'private' sexual contract which determines it, see Pateman (1988). Examining the works of contract theorists Hobbes, Locke, and Rousseau, Pateman argues that the construction of modern social theory (the 'social contract') depends on a forgotten but earlier private subordination (the 'sexual contract'). Although I do not agree with all the conclusions Pateman derives from this argument, I would insist in the context of this chapter that much of the distinction between public and private sphere lies in overlooking the implicitly gendered social contract.

5 Brief histories of Amnesty International's work on women are to be found in Friedman (1995); Sidhu and Chatterjee (1995).

6 I will not speculate on the reasons for this suppression.

7 The three 'generations' of rights referred to here include civil and political rights (first generation); economic, social, and cultural rights (second generation); and governing collective or group rights (third generation). Because it implies

progress and hierarchy, this metaphor is controversial. Moreover, Charlesworth has argued that although they seem to take into account women's rights 'progressively' by undermining the public/private division, the theorization of all three 'generations' of rights is contingent on a male life (see Charlesworth 1995).

8 This decision may also be due to Amnesty International's unease in taking a position against traditional cultural practices and of laying itself open to accusations of 'cultural imperialism.' It is important to recall, however, that African women themselves are organizing against female genital mutilation, often with only limited cooperation from their governments. For further information on grassroots actions against the practice, see Dorkenoo (1994).

9 See Nair (1994) and Narayan (1995) for discussions on similar laws in France and the United States respectively.

10 The conviction was later voided because there was no written record that the woman had waived her right to an attorney when she pleaded no contest. The constitutional basis for this sentence, however, was not questioned.

11 Interestingly enough, however, although *Human rights are women's right* does not mention human rights violations resulting from reproductive control, the 1995 Amnesty International report on violence against women in China does. Chapter 6 of the report is entitled 'Human Rights Violations Resulting from Enforced Birth Control' (Amnesty International 1995c). *Human rights are women's right*, on the other hand, includes the testimony of a Chinese woman, staring that the Chinese Public Security Bureau had threatened that 'if any of us were found pregnant, we would be sent to the hospital and forced to have an abortion' (Amnesty International 1995a: 92). It does not, however, analyze this testimony in the light of reproductive rights.

12 Another area where women's reproductive rights and human rights are being continually undermined is in the recent developments in high-technology biomedical reproductive techniques, including in vitro fertilization, surrogacy, and sex predetermination. India's population control programs have called female feticide after amniocentesis the 'most ideal and rational solution to the population explosion' (Raymond 1993: 22). The efforts of the Forum against Prenatal Sex Determination and Preselection Techniques, a coalition of Indian women's groups and health activists, helped prohibt such a 'method.' Legislation on surrogacy (as it is known in wealthy Western 'consumer' countries) and baby-farming (as it is known in poor Third World 'producer' ones) will have direct consequences on the manner in which women exercise economic, moral, and personal control over their bodies as 'reproductive sites.' As research and developments in artificial reproduction continue, women's human rights activists will have to continue to monitor and to act against the possible misogyny in this area. See Raymond (1993) for an overview of developments and for an indictment of their intrinsic misogyny.

13 For a more extensive discussion of the *allocation parentale d'éducation* and of Mitterrand's family politics pertaining to women, see Jenson and Sineau (1995: chap. 8).

14 This condition also forbids paid professional training.

15 An equally exclusionary policy is the 'third country' policy which allows European governments to deny entrance to refugees who have transited via 'safe third countries.' Such policies are part of a systematic attempt to build a European fortress which denies entrance to those of non-white European origins (see Fekete and Webber 1994).

16 The argument might be made that Amnesty International adopts a similar

position when discussing men. To such an argument, I would respond as follows. First, until the human rights organization tackled the question of women's human rights, it concentrated on individual prisoners of conscience and political prisoners, where paternalism does not arise as an issue. As I have tried to argue in this chapter, dealing with violations of women's human rights implies a reconsideration of the very concept of 'human rights,' of the liberal division between the public and the private and of action to oppose violations. Of course – and this is the second point – such a reconsideration will necessarily have an impact on the human rights of men (i.e. the gendered male subject), and it is very likely that the analysis I am developing with respect to women might also be made with respect to men.

17 Carole Paterman articulates a similar paradox when discussing women's participation in the welfare state. She argues that women have been historically excluded from the public sphere of work precisely because it has been defined in terms of male standards and experiences. Women, according to Pateman, have as a result only two alternatives: accept masculine standards at the risk of failing to comply with them and risking further exclusion, or accept fewer – or at the least a different order of – citizenship rights. See Pateman (1989). Whereas I agree with her analysis of women's historical exclusion, I would also insist on other alternatives for women's political participation.

18 As mentioned, this demand has been added to the original twelve points of the 1991 report and platform for action.

REFERENCES

Amnesty International (1991) *Women in the front line.* ACT 77/01/91. New York: Amnesty International Publications.

—— (1995a) *Human rights are women's right.* ACT 77/01/95. London: Amnesty International Publications.

—— (1995b) 'Women: "Invisible victims of human rights violations."' 8 March, news release.

—— (1995c) *Women in China: imprisoned and abused for dissent.* ASA 17/29/95. New York: Amnesty International Publications.

Associated Press (1995a) 'Judge will vacate sterilization order for pregnant cocaine user.' *ClariNet e.News,* 13 February, clari.women.reproduction.

—— (1995b) 'France issues abortion ruling'. *ClariNet e.News,* 21 July, clari.women.reproduction.

Beasley, Michele E. and Thomas, Dorothy Q. (1994) 'Domestic violence as a human rights issue.' In *The public nature of private violence: the discovery of domestic abuse,* ed. Martha Albertson Fineman and Roxanne Mykitiuk. London: Routledge.

Bhabha, Jacqueline and Shutter, Sue (1994) *Women's movement: women under immigration, nationality and refugee law.* London: Trentham Books.

Bunch, Charlotte (1995) 'Transforming human rights from a feminist perspective.' In *Women's rights, human rights: international feminist perspectives.* See Peters and Wolper 1995.

Center for Women's Global Leadership (1995) Press statement. 30 March.

Charlesworth, Hilary (1995) 'What are "women's international human rights"?'

In *Human rights of women: national and international perspectives*, ed. Rebecca Cook. Philadelphia: University of Pennsylvania Press.

Cook, Rebecca J. (1995) 'International human rights and women's reproductive health.' In *Women's rights, human rights: international feminist perspectives*. See Peters and Wolper 1995.

Delphy, Christine (1995) 'Egalité, équivalence et équité: la position de l'Etat français au regard du droit international.' *Nouvelles questions féministes* 16(1): 5–58.

Dorkenoo, Efua (1994) *Female genital mutilation: good practice and prevention*. London: Minority Report.

Fekete, Liz and Webber, Francis (1994) *Inside racist Europe*. London: The Institute of Race Relations.

Freedman, Elisabeth (1995) 'Women's human rights: the emergence of a movement.' In *Women's rights, human rights: international feminist perspectives*. See Peters and Wolper 1995.

Hartmann, Betsy (1987) *Reproductive rights and wrongs: the global politics of population control and contraceptive choice*. New York: Harper and Row.

Heise, Lori (1995) 'Freedom close to home: the impact of violence against women on reproductive rights.' In *Women's rights, human rights: international feminist perspectives*. See Peters and Wolper 1995.

Jenson, Jane and Sineau, Mariette (1995) *Mitterrand et les Françaises: un rendez-vous manqué*. Paris: Presses de la fondation nationale des sciences politiques.

Kabel, Marcus (Reuters) (1995) 'U.N. bans 11 groups from world women's conference.' *ClariNet e.News*, 21 July, clari.women.reproduction.

Kelly, Nancy (1994) 'Making the asylum process work for women refugees.' *Covert Action* 4: 38–44.

Leiss, Anne and Boesjes, Ruby (1994) *Female asylum seekers: a comparative study concerning policy and jurisprudence in the Netherlands, Germany, France, the United Kingdom, Also dealing summarily with Belgium and Canada*. Amsterdam: Dutch Refugee Council.

MacKinnon, Catherine A. (1989) *Toward a feminist theory of the state*. Cambridge, MA: Harvard University Press.

Merius, Julie (1995) 'State discriminatory family law and customary abuses.' In *Women's rights, human rights: international feminist perspectives*. See Peters and Wolper 1995.

Mirsty, Judith and Radlett, Marty (eds) (1994) *Private decision, public debate: women, reproduction and population*. London: Panos.

Mladjenovic, Lepa and Litricin, Vera (1993) 'Belgrade feminists 1992: separation, guilt and identity crisis.' Transcribed by Tanya Renne. *Feminist Review* 45: 113–19.

Nair, Sumi (1994) *Lettre à Charles Pasqua de la part de ceux qui ne sont pas bien nés*. Paris: Edition de Seuil.

Narayan, Uma (1995) '"Male-order" brides: immigrant women, domestic violence, and immigration law.' *Hypatia* 10(1): 104–9.

News Service (1995) *UN world conference on women: genuine NGOs should not be blocked by political self-interest*. New York: Amnesty International.

Pateman, Carole (1988) *The sexual contract*. Stanford, CA: Stanford University Press.

—— (1989) 'The patriarchal welfare state.' In *The disorder of women: democracy, feminism, and political theory*. Stanford, CA: Stanford University Press.

Peters, Julia and Wolper, Andrea (1995) *Women's rights, human rights: international feminist perspectives*. New York: Routledge.

Raymond, Janice G. (1993) *Women as wombs*. San Francisco, CA: Harper.

Reuters (1995) 'Dispute over French anti-abortion case.' *ClariNet e.News*, 5 July, clari.women.reproduction.

Romany, Celina (1995) State responsibility goes private: a feminist critique of the public/private distinction in international human rights law. In *Women's rights, human rights: International feminist perspectives*. See Peters and Wolper 1995.

Roth, Kenneth (1995) 'Domestic violence as an international human rights issue.' In *Human rights of women: national and international perspectives*, ed. Rebecca J. Cook. Philadelphia: University of Pennsylvania Press.

Rousseau, Jean-Jacques [1762] (1992) *Du Contrat social*. Edition établie par Pierre Burgelin. Paris: GF-Flammarion.

Sidhu, Gretchen and Chatterjee, Patralekha (1995) 'Human rights: amnesty takes a limited stand.' *Women's Feature Service*. New Delhi, India, 12 May.

Sullivan, Donna and Toubia, Nahid (1993) *Female genital mutilation and human rights*. Unpublished report prepared for the World Conference on Human Rights, Vienna, June.

United Nations (1994) *Background information: conference to set women's agenda into the next century*. DPI/1424.Rev 1. UN.

13

THE NGO-IZATION OF FEMINISM

Institutionalization and institution building within the German women's movements[1]

Sabine Lang

Globalization has changed the nature of women's activism, giving rise, for example, to NGOs or non-governmental organizations such as foundations or private action groups, especially in the past two decades. Like the activism of individual women in Iran, the NGO gives a new form to efforts on behalf of women. However, instead of fighting the state, as in the case of Muslim feminists, the organizations that provide feminists with jobs to promote social welfare or employment are often allied with state commissions and bureaucracies to attain their ends. NGOs come in all shapes and sizes, from massive, longstanding US foundations like Ford and Rockefeller to the local groups of African activists working to combat AIDS or child abuse. NGOs blanket the globe, with the wealthiest ones able to set research agendas, to decide on areas in which women should develop economically, and to determine criteria for receiving social welfare assistance. Some help women devise political strategies for obtaining benefits from local and national governments, while others help them get elected to office. Has the NGO replaced community-based feminism? As NGOs (in their many different forms) have gained ground, some analysts see the development of a class of 'femocrats' who decide, often unilaterally, what is best for women. Although their decisions may be salutary, they have another consequence. As this chapter on the decline of feminist activism in the newly reunified Germany shows, the heavy presence of NGOs does not necessarily build feminist energy at either the grassroots or national level. While it may empower women or improve their lives, it can also silence them and bring real disadvantages. The reality of a visible women's 'movement' is replaced by the professionalization of feminism, resting in the policy decisions of a few individuals. Although the case is German, the phenomenon is worldwide.

* * *

The creation of a more 'women-friendly' civil society was one of the myths associated with the peaceful revolution of 1989 in East Germany. Many East German women therefore watched the rising public demand for unification with suspicion: 'Do we want to reunite with the men in Bonn and replace the dictatorship of the politburo with that of the chancellor's office?' was a rhetorical question frequently asked by the newly founded women's movement in the GDR.[2] Apprehension about the gendered structure of the West German state and skepticism about distributions of power and social influence were widespread among East German feminists. And indeed, while West German women hoped that with unification some of the progressive women's policies of the GDR state would find their way into new legislation, the outcome of the unification treaty and subsequent German policy decisions have disappointed such hopes.

Why didn't the overhaul of the East German political system and its social and economic foundations bring about considerable improvement in the status of women? And why didn't this in turn result in large-scale mobilization? Have women indeed become a silent majority? Why was neither of the women's movements in East or West Germany visible in public discourse? And why did they seem to be disillusioned with each other as much as with their impact in the transformation period?

I argue that beyond economic insecurity and life-management priorities, beyond the different histories and ideologies of the two women's movements, lies a topical taboo: an area that is hardly ever discussed. This area concerns the forces of feminist organization building and institutionalization that have replaced movement activism and have decisively altered, if not abolished, women's movements in their traditional forms. The primary mobilizing forces for women's issues in Germany – the 'new' women's movement of the West, created in the 1970s, and the women's movement of the East, with its organization, UFV (Unabhängiger Frauenverband [Independent Women's Union]), formed in 1989 – have been separately engaged in similar processes of organization building and institutionalization. As a result, both put less emphasis on traditional movement goals such as the politicization and mobilization of a feminist public. In effect, both German women's movements have metamorphosed from overarching movements into small-scale professionalized organizations. They no longer focus on mobilizing feminists for the rebuilding of a democratic public sphere but have turned into women's non-governmental organizations (NGOs) with strong ties to the state. This change has had ambivalent consequences.

The effects of this radical reorientation are visible in structure, ideology, program, and strategy. The transition from movement to NGO brought with it a structural emphasis on professionalized but decentralized small-scale organizations and a turn from anti-hierarchical to more hierarchical structures. Ideologically, there is a tendency to translate the 'traditionally' complex feminist agenda of emancipation and equality into specific single issues and a form of politics with a predominantly state-oriented focus. While feminist movement building was once about the establishment of new democratic counterculture, feminist organizations today are about issue-specific intervention and pragmatic strategies that have a strong employment focus.

German unification: the (re)production of gendered society

Whether East Germans took to the streets or left the country in 1989, the impulse for democratic reform was not voiced in gender-specific terms.[3] Mobilization occurred as a response to the lack of civil society under state socialism, where organized political resistance or dissidence had been sanctioned by the state. Yet the revolutionary establishment of a functioning democratic public sphere occurred within the context of an accelerating influx of West German political culture and its institutions as well as the breakdown of the East German economy.

With unification, East Germans entered a liberal democracy and a market economy with its promise of individual and pluralist participation, on the one hand, and its structural, economic, and corporatist restraints on the other. Within this seemingly wider civic space lurked the discovery that the freedoms acquired were, in Isaiah Berlin's distinction, negative freedoms, that is, *freedoms from*, rather than substantial positive and creative freedoms, *freedoms to*.[4] Freedom from repression, which permitted public speaking, or even the 'afforded possibilities of concerted action and social self-organization,'[5] did not necessarily translate into the creation of new opportunity structures, new itineraries for participation, or new jobs. Nor did it entail the freedom to decide which features of the socialist system's women's policies would be worth transporting into the newly unified German society. Instead, in the former GDR, women lost their jobs disproportionately. While in 1989 there were 4.3 million women in the GDR with jobs, by November 1994 only 59 percent of those were still employed, as compared to 70 percent of the men.[6] Women were specifically pushed out of high-income and comparatively high-status positions in areas such as public management or the universities.[7] Without much overt public discouragement, the rates of women applying for traditional male jobs in, for example, the building sector or certain technical sciences decreased rapidly. Women were by and large the first to lose jobs and the first to adopt more family-centered roles as an immediately available option. The primary, visible actors in the civil public sphere of the former East Germany turned out to be men, thus mirroring Western political public and its predominantly male actors.

But women in the former West Germany also feel the costs of this transformation, primarily in the experience of having to share those public resources that, until 1989, had been allocated for women's centers and special programs by federal and state agencies. To take one example out of many: The West Berlin Parliament established a program in 1990, the C1 Program, which enabled West Berlin universities to hire sixty-four women assistant professors and qualify them for full professorships as part of state affirmative action policy. Now that the united city has three universities in West Berlin and four more universities in East Berlin (not including the professional training colleges and private colleges), the same resources have to be divided among a much larger number of institutions, which leads to increasing competition and provokes fear among West German feminists that their advances – achieved under prosperous economic conditions and a stable social welfare system – are in danger.

Yet beyond what one might subsume under the topic of distributive struggles, West German feminists were wary of the transformation because their 'feminisms' were criticized by East German women as ideologically rigid, essentialist, and ahistorical. As compared to other Eastern European societies, where feminism has been a 'no-word' for some time, East German women claimed an independent version of feminism for themselves. In this sense, the divisions between East and West German women were more than rhetorical digressions or definitional quarrels. They represented power struggles over agendas and strategies in the public sphere. West German feminists insisted on the need for East and West German women to adopt a common voice, underestimating the problem of hegemony within this commonality. Ultimately, they were disappointed with the reluctance of Eastern women to adopt the language and the terminology of Western feminisms.

There were, of course, other reasons for the lack of a public presence for a women's agenda during unification. The Eastern civic public needed women's voices at exactly a time when individual life management and the demands of the new market economy had priority for most. Developments in the university system put enormous strain on women intellectuals in the arts and sciences, who were about to be marginalized by being forced either into limited contracts or, if they wanted to qualify for the academic market, into doing research in mainstream areas that by definition excluded feminist approaches and topics. An audible civic voice for women would also have required media and other communication resources, but a strong feminist journalistic tradition was missing in Germany.[8]

Yet while such structural, economic, and psychological constraints do account for the lack of broad and massive mobilization among women, they do not sufficiently explain the two movements' overarching invisibility or the paralysis of their public voice. There seems to have been a set of impediments that added to the quietude of the movements and their

293

activists and which ultimately fostered overall civic silence during the transformation period.

Feminist movements and the politics of organization

Both West and East German feminist movements lacked the means to counteract discriminatory policies invoked and regenerated during unification. One of the central obstacles to mobilization was a rising trend in the East and West German movements alike toward a new politics of organization. That politics at first took on different shapes in the East and the West, yet ultimately it seems as though sisterhood has converged in what I call the establishment of NGOs instead of political movements.

Feminists and civil society after state socialism

While the GDR had carved out semi-private niches for women's groups within the Church and academia, most political organizing around women's issues was channeled through the official state women's organization, the Demokratische Frauenbund Deutschlands (DFD). Representation of women in Parliament was granted through a prescribed number of seats for the DFD, which defined its agenda strictly according to party doctrine.[9] Analyzing these East German niches as bastions for women within a Gramscian understanding of civil society[10] underestimates the regime's effective strategy of appeasement in these small and highly state-infiltrated spaces and the official repression against critical public discourse. Even within the broadest possible definition put forward earlier – treating civil society as a space for concerted action and social self-organization – East German society allowed neither for the evolution of such a sphere nor for a political public to sustain it.

In 1989, however, there was a surprisingly quick turnaround. When, on 3 December, approximately a thousand women gathered in an old theater in East Berlin to found the UFV, the focus of its interventionist politics was the reform of state socialism. There was at first little discussion about how to broaden the organization. Participants were well aware that the majority of Eastern women might perceive their customary style and political rhetoric as alienating and that most women in the GDR did not identify with feminism in its Western form.[11] Besides, the acceleration of political change demanded concentration on interventionist strategies and a feminist agenda within the existing state. The 'immediate demands' (Sofortforderungen) presented by the UFV on this founding day did not include reflections on its feminist framework or its ideological substance, nor an invitation for GDR women to join debates and open a new feminist public forum. Instead, the eleven articles of the 'immediate demands' document were pointedly geared toward government and SED party institutions, demanding among other things the establishment of an affirmative action fund administered by the GDR ministers' cabinet – but with 'guaranteed access for the independent women's movement.'[12] This reality focus was appropriate at the time, taking into account the political power structure a few weeks after the breaking down of the wall. An equally strong institutional focus occurred in the demand that the UFV be represented in the first alternative central policy-making institution, the Central Roundtable in East Berlin, where negotiations among the protagonists of the old system, the Church, and the civil movements took place. The UFV was at first not admitted and acquired a seat at this central policy-formation institution only after intense negotiations. Even though the political space had been widened substantially, the terms of trade between representatives of the old regime and actors from the civil rights movements had remained gender-exclusive.[13]

The UFV served (with others) as a catalyst for establishing civil society. Yet what it initially set out to achieve was political participation and representation *within* the existing and then reformed socialist political system through a feminist expansion or redefinition of its institutions. Its political agenda was thus largely directed toward state policies, and their implementation. Central for policy implementation became the Women's Equality Offices, which, under pressure from the UFV, were established in every community with a population over 10,000.[14] Their efforts were primarily directed at the acquisition of state resources for women's centers, shelters, and job-creation programs. UFV politics shared this orientation toward state reform, and this in turn had repercussions for its own organizational structure.[15]

When the UFV held its fifth congress, called 'Against Individualization,' in 1993, it had no more than 300 members in all of the new states. After two years of separatism, West German women were allowed to participate.[16] By December 1994, the UFV orchestrated a symbolic funeral for its old claim 'Without women you cannot make a state' and coined the more realistic phrase, 'Yes, without women there can be a state!'[17] The state of affairs was summarized by this disillusioned statement: 'The women's movement [of the] East has ended up where it never wanted to be: in a societal and political niche without influence. In this it caught up with the West German movement in no time.'[18] Thus, the primary focus of the UFV – to foster women's participation within established institutions such as parties, unions, foundations, and corporatist representative bodies – had failed. Ironically, it had been a similar experience, namely that existing social institutions and options for political participation were male-centered, that had turned the West German feminist movement into a quest for autonomy and a separatist women's culture in the 1970s.

West German corporatism and the women's movement

West German society rests on an institutional political system that features corporatism, consensus, and cooperative federalism[19] and thus is, in comparison to less corporate social structures, more resistant to challenges from the political margins. By corporatism I refer to a 'web of institutional linkages between state and society,'[20] which, in contrast to pluralist lobbying as a political strategy, is confined to a limited number of institutions. These institutions have a history as corporatist partners of the state and have developed hierarchical structures, specific representational bodies, and functionally differentiated agendas. Through these special links centralized and powerful interest groups such as the German unions and economic chambers are incorporated on a regular basis in the process of policy formulation. State decision making and its implementation relies on consensual agenda formulation with these corporatist actors.[21]

The politics of the West German feminist movement have been developing in opposition to this patriarchal web of centralized and powerful interest groups and parapublic institutions.[22] It is within this corporatist political paradigm that the ideological focus of women's mobilization in West Germany, during the 1970s and into the 1980s, namely the insistence on 'autonomy,' becomes meaningful. Women articulated their refusal to be subsumed and co-opted by structures that allowed for neither easy access to nor the active incorporation of a feminist agenda. Instead, the gender-specific distribution of power was at first challenged not in the institutional realm of society and state but within the structures of family and personal gender relations. Feminist culture thus served as a source of identity production in and against existing repressive social structures, prevalent cultural codes, and patriarchal symbols.

A first wave of institutionalization of women's claims happened – instigated by the Green Party – when specific women's equality issues were taken up by the Social Democrats and other established political parties. The most visible result of the equality debates in the labor force are the Women's Equality Offices which have since become compulsory for many public institutions and executive bodies, again from the local to the federal level. Yet while institutional feminism and femocracy blossomed in the early 1990s, resulting in the establishment of women's ministries or, at least, the establishment of state secretaries in all German states, and women's offices and affirmative action plans in most of the large institutions, the visibility of women's movement politics in East and West Germany declined.

The public silence that accompanied the legislative process of reshaping the abortion law after unification is a striking example of an issue in which the feminist movements were almost invisible. After a progressive parliamentary initiative sponsored by Social Democrats, Liberals, Democratic Socialists, and even a few Conservatives succeeded, an abortion law was approved that guaranteed a general right to abortion during the first twelve weeks of pregnancy. The German constitutional court overruled this law in May 1993 and required a stronger pro-life focus from the legislature. The court ruling stated that abortion in the first twelve weeks would not have to be punished but would none the less have to be considered unlawful. This established a moral bind for women, counselors, and doctors by claiming that abortion as such would be against the moral code of society and law. The constitutional court's judges also required that counseling have a strong pro-life orientation and that health insurance could not be required to pay for an abortion.[23]

The ruling turned out to be a paradigmatic text for the backlash against women in the transformation period – and yet there was very little protest by feminist activists. A week before the official decision, the basic outlines of the verdict had already been leaked by the media. But it was mostly Social Democratic women's ministries of the state legislatures and members of the Green and Social Democratic women's caucuses who called for protests and demonstrations on the day of the ruling. Nearly a thousand women protested in Berlin; 300 protested in Cologne, and 400 in Hamburg and Munich. Compared to the big pro-choice rallies of the mid-1970s, this was a clear and traumatic defeat for feminist mobilization. The movements were almost invisible – feminist civil society had turned a central political and symbolic issue over to medical associations, the churches, pro-life organizations, Parliament, and, ultimately, the courts.[24] 'We were infuriated, but we did not know where to go to protest' was a phrase frequently heard in Berlin in the month following the court's ruling.

But in terms of feminist politics there was more at stake here than the defeat of feminist positions on abortion. The institutionally absorbed policy formulation in the abortion issue reflects not just on the individual political abstention of women, but also on a lack of organization and mobilization of movement structures. While there are decentralized networks of women's projects and centers, organized decision-making processes for interventionist strategies do not seem to exist within the movement.

Beyond the organizational problems that both German feminist movements face in setting up specific agendas and developing policy strategies, there are also conflicts bound up with membership and ideology. In terms of membership, many women, but especially young German women, do not want to be labeled 'feminists' or be identified with the claims made by their mothers. In effect, the women's movement appears to be aging without young successors. The age cohort in Berlin feminist centers and projects is at present between thirty and fifty. Ideological rifts are bound up with the realization that the feminist principle of anti-hierarchical and decentralized organizational structures has not been effective in mobilizing resources for such crucial issues as abortion, the constitutional debate, or the National Women's Strike Day in March 1994. The West German women's movement has also put a strong emphasis on autonomy, creating a separatist culture of feminist projects, health and educational centers, shelters, etc. This quest for and insistence on autonomy is, as I will point out below, a fragile construct and is undermined by the effects of an increasing financial dependence on the state.

Thus, the apparent political apathy among East and West German women toward such crucial issues as abortion cannot be attributed simply to economic individualism and distance from established politics, but must be seen in relation to the general lack of feminist mobilization strategies. The lack of mobilization is in turn the result of specific forms of institutionalization in the women's movements. We have arrived at the present phase of the West German feminist movement, a phase in which the two women's movements move from their asymmetric histories and converge in similar processes. We witness at present the 'NGO-ization' of the feminist movements. NGO-ization occurs, I will argue, in response to developments within German social and political institutions and tends to reduce feminist NGOs to marginalized forces within corporatist civil society. Before I go into greater detail about the specific form that NGO-ization takes, I will take a quick and, for the purpose of this argument, selective look at the relationship between the German state and feminist organizations.

The German state and feminist organization

The internal dynamics that changed feminist movement politics into organizational politics were the result of several factors, among the most important of which were the selective regulation practices of German state agencies. Ironically, the *institutionalization of the feminist movement* is the unwanted and also unintended consequence of a core demand of the West German feminist movement during its successful fight against unpaid labor and the campaign to convince state institutions to support socially important women's work (such as in shelters, women's centers, and feminist job training institutions). The Berlin Senate financed some 250 women's projects in 1994. The approximately 120 initiatives that received funds directly from the State Ministry for Women were subsidized with approximately US$20 million in 1994.[25] Others are state or federally funded through intermediate institutions such as the Federal Agency for Employment or by state-specific labor market programs.

Since unification, in East Berlin alone, some ninety women's projects with about 1,500 jobs were financed with federal and/or Berlin state funds. Considering rent, salaries, maintenance, or jobs through federal work creation and retraining programs (ABM and FuU), the women's infrastructure and the feminist job market are at this point thoroughly dependent on state financing. What I describe for East and West Berlin is equally relevant for all five new states of the ex-GDR. Women's shelters, centers, developmental training programs, etc., have been almost exclusively financed by the Federal Ministry for Women and Youth and the Federal Agency for Employment, and a considerable amount of Federal funds were distributed through the oldest institutional and politically centerist-conservative organization of women in Germany, the German Women's Council (Deutscher Frauenrat).

What must be interpreted, on the one hand, as a strong state focus on supporting women's issues and anti-discrimination policies must, on the other hand, also be analyzed in relation to questions of power allocation, dependency, and regulatory force. The most active parts of the autonomous women's movement are at this point highly dependent on those structures and institutions that feminism has identified as thresholds against gender equality and which, feminists claim, should be targets of subversion and change. This dependency goes beyond a functional relationship based on finances. It includes state decisions about which initiative does or does not get financed.[26]

This specific German observation might be generalized to a certain degree: Western governments have suddenly over the course of the past few years discovered NGOs as central organizations of civil society. At the World Social Summit, which took place in March 1995 in Copenhagen, there were about 120 references in the official declaration either to NGOs directly or to the important role of civil society in counteracting social injustice, creating jobs, etc.[27] NGOs are more and more called upon to replace state activities in the social sector and function as repair networks for economic and political disintegration processes. But is it not more accurate to describe NGOs as SGOs, that is, semi-governmental organizations, in that they are thoroughly dependent on the distributive influence of state agencies and that their politics and their policies will have to correspond with the specific agenda setting of respective state politics? To put the problem differently, if NGOs don't want only to engage in social repair work, but actually want to change structural features of a certain political agenda, how successful can they be when they are dependent on exactly the structures that need to be transformed? In so far as public funding excludes public discourse about this funding and thus excludes the public from the details of the state–society relationship, public funding also tends to preclude public voice.

The consequence should by no means be to renounce public funding. But the present weakness of the movement lies in its inability to articulate and expose these dependences. Instead, each project and initiative tends to adopt the premise of secrecy and to deal with those dependences rather defensively. The structural mechanisms of such dependences might prove especially problematic in times of fiscal crisis, when cutbacks in the social sector cause distribution fights among these 'benefit recipients.'[28] Some of the effects are already visible. Segmentation and competition within the movement inhibit the focus on a common agenda; internal lobbying takes the place of joint public pressure and public lobbying. This means, in effect, too little presence in the public discourses of civil society; instead, energy is put into private lobbying strategies to secure jobs and finances.

I am aware that the point I'm raising might easily be misunderstood in that it ignores other gatekeepers of the public sphere, like the selectivity of the media, in deciding on public topics. Nor do I intend that my argument put into question the legitimacy and necessity of state funding for feminist initiatives. Quite the contrary: I would argue that these financial involvements have to be exposed more by feminists and turned into a collective and public bargaining power for feminist claims so as to prevent them from becoming strongly individualist dependencies. Additionally, I want to point to the dangers that are built into a feminist strategy that focuses primarily, or even solely, on the stabilization of initiatives and centers and as such loses the impetus to develop larger feminist publics, stronger voices, and more interventionist means. If we put this dependency in the larger context of the decline of welfare states in Western Europe,[29] then the question is where future resources will be accumulated for critical state gender politics and for social mobilization against the divisions that discriminate anew against women (social security reforms, etc.).

The feminist movements as NGOs

German feminist project advocate Renate Rieger has recently published a collection of essays on the state of the feminist movement, ironically entitled *The Laming of the Shrew*.[30] The authors included in this collection all share a sense of disillusionment and crisis. To explain this common perception, Rieger identifies four major shifts within project culture. One is that women now look to feminist projects more for jobs than for feminist political ideas. Many women dropped out of the UFV and went – as state-financed workers – into women's projects. The dependence on state-financed work creation programs (ABM) has resulted in a high rate of fluctuation because these programs only run for up to two years per person. This in turn prevents continuity within the project agenda. Second, cutbacks in social policies are anticipated and produce high levels of insecurity. Third, as women look for traditional recognition for their work and tend to become more conscious about pay, projects become less attractive. Fourth, project women are disillusioned because work conditions have not substantially differed from non-feminist work contexts.[31] In sum, the utopia of feminist havens in heartless societies has vanished.

These shifts, which, on the one hand, are structural and, on the other hand, are ideological and 'personal,' have encouraged a stronger focus on organization building and professionalization. This entails a conviction that voluntary work and engagement should be replaced by paid-labor. It implies a commitment to effectiveness and the re-employment of hierarchical structures.[32] It means negotiating money and contracts with local, regional, and federal bureaucracies, and carving up projects so that they fulfill the logic and meet the standards of funders such as the European Community. It gives a new weight to public relations and the search for funding for such jobs in women's projects. In short, project organization is oriented toward internal project consolidation, lobbying power, and public relations rather than public mobilization. Professionalization refers to the projects' attitude toward their work, which shifts from the creation of feminist spaces for 'alternative' modes of life and work to 'job' attitudes and to an identification with being a part of the formal tertiary sector.

NGO-ization may well be more effective in issue-oriented politics, cooperation with the media, and state institutions. But the question to be kept in mind is the degree to which this effectiveness will be paid for by dependency and the translation or relocation of political agendas. Dependence on femocratic structures within the state, that is, on women's offices and ministries on the local, state, and federal level, work so long as these institutions have strong positions and bargaining power within state decision-making processes. What may also be lost in this development is the possibility of forming broader networks and institutions that may indeed have the power to mobilize along central feminist issues and challenge the gendered structure of civil society within the established organizations and parties. Feminist NGOs are in danger of adapting to the vertical structure of current political life, even if their ideological focus remains a participatory and horizontally oriented political structure in which gender-conscious policies have become part of every level of decision making.

As women's movements professionalize and as their dependence on the state increases, unification has resulted in decreasing participation by women in the institutions of the political system. There is a noticeable downward trend: engagement in feminist issues is becoming less popular in the 1990s. In the 1994 elections to the German Parliament, all parties except the Liberals (FDP) and the Party of Democratic Socialism (PDS) put forward considerably fewer women candidates than in 1990. The number of female direct candidates[33] for parliamentary seats went down in the Conservative Party (CDU) from 15.2 percent to 13.4 percent, the Social Democratic Party (SPD) from 31.2 percent to to 23.2 percent, and the Green Party from 34.6 percent to 28.3 percent.[34] Even in the Green Party there is an increasing reluctance among women to specialize in women's issues,[35] because this concentration is said to reduce the chances of achieving higher office and visibility in all parties. This development is mirrored by a decline in young women's interest in politics. During the first elections in united Germany in 1990, only 60.4 percent of young West German women between twenty-one and twenty-five voted, as compared to 82 percent of women between forty-five and fifty and 84.2 percent of women aged fifty to sixty.[36]

And in the first elections to the European Parliament in the united Germany, less than half of young women between eighteen and twenty-four even went to vote.[37] Whereas political interest among young men aged twenty to thirty increased, it decreased in the same age cohort of young women.[38] Generally, German women express considerably less interest in politics than German men: In 1992, in a representative study, 66 percent of the women claimed to have very little or no interest in politics, as opposed to only 41 percent of the men.[39]

In the light of these developments, the feminist turn from collective mobilization to NGOs becomes understandable and at the same time even more problematic. Where there is a decreasing constituency and demand for mobilization, institutions must learn and change. But, as Mary Douglas has pointed out, institutions are 'cognitive communities' that do not simply respond to societal trends but have a stake in generating social and self-knowledge themselves.[40] Feminist institution building would have to refocus on engendering civil society and specifically its corporatist German version, not by reproducing its secretive structures and hierarchical bonds with the state, but by generating more public voice and knowledge and by working hard at alternative institution building.

NOTES

1 I would like to thank Margit Mayer, Birgit Sauer, Roscha Schmidt, and Brigitte Young for their stimulating discussions and references on the topic.
2 Ina Merkel, 'Manifest für eine autonome Frauenbewegung,' *Tageszeitung*, 5 December 1989.
3 While gender-specific issues did come up occasionally within the GDR literary semi-public (see, for example, Irmtraud Morgner, *Leben und Abenteuer der. Trobadora Beatriz nach Zeugnissen ihrer Spiel frau Laura* (Darmstadt: Leucterhand Verlag, 1976) and were the focus of a few semi-clandestine academic women's groups, the dominant political, academic, and media discourses did not give voice to feminist standpoints and debates.
4 Isaiah Berlin, 'Two Concepts of Freedom,' *Deutsche Zeitschrift für Philosophie* 41, no. 4 (1992): 741–55.
5 Christopher G.A. Bryant, 'Social Self-organisation, Civility and Sociology: A Comment on Kumar's "Civil Society,"' *British Journal of Sociology* 44, 3 (1993): 399.
6 Bundesanstalt für Arbeit, Abt. Statistik, Eckwerte des Arbeitsmarktes Bundesrepublik Deutschland, 1995.
7 Brigitte Young, 'Asychronitäten der deutsch-deutschen Frauenbewegung.'
8 The same holds true for women's presence in the media professions in general. While in 1970 women made up 29 percent of German journalists, they accounted for only 31 percent in 1994. This figure also indicates how massive numbers of women from the former East German media sector – where they held about 50 percent of the posts – were forced into unemployment during the transformation. At present only three out of ten journalists at daily newspapers in Germany are women. In the political sections of the media women journalists

still hold only 25 percent of the jobs (IG Medien/Forschungsgruppe Journalismus, *Frauen in Journalismus* (Dortmund: I.G. Medien Verlag, 1995).

9 Myra Marx Ferree, 'Institutionalizing Gender Equality: Feminist Politics and Equality Offices,' *German Politics and Society* 24/25 (1991): 58.

10 Anna Schwarz, 'Gramscis Zivilgesellschaft und die Analyse der Umbruchprozesse in der DDR, *Das Argument* 193 (1992): 418.

11 Irene Dölling, 'Between Hope and Hoplessness: Women in the GDR after the "Turning Point,"' *Feminist Review* 39 (1991): 3.

12 *Tageszeitung-taz*, Berlin (daily newspaper), 3 December 1989.

13 Birgit Sauer, 'Der "Runde Tisch" und die Raumaufteilung der Demokratie. Eine politische Institution des Übergangs?' in Birgitta Nedelmann (ed.), *Politische Institutionen im Wandel. Sonderheft der Kölner Zeitschrift für Soziologie und Sozialpsychologie* (Opladen: Westdeutscher Verlag, 1995), pp. 108–25.

14 The purpose of these offices as part of the executive branch is mainly to implement and coordinate women's policies. In doing so the Women's Equality Offices are supposed to evaluate legislation, to cooperate with women's groups and organizations, and to regularly inform central government agencies on women's concerns.

15 Anne Hampele, 'Frauenbewegung in den Ländern der ehemaligen DDR,' *Forschungsjournal Neue Soziale Bewegungen* 1 (1992): 34–41.

16 *Tageszeitung-taz*, Berlin (daily newspaper), 7 June 1993.

17 Ulrike Helwerth, 'Ohne Frauen ist ein Staat zu machen,' *Freitag* 51 (16 December 1994): 14.

18 Ibid.; translation by author.

19 Simon Bulmer (ed.), *The Changing Agenda of West German Public Policy* (Aldershot: Dartmouth, 1989).

20 Peter Katzenstein, *Policy and Politics in West Germany: The Growth of a Semi-Sovereign State* (Philadelphia, PA: Temple University Press, 1987).

21 Roland Czada, 'Korporatismus,' in Dieter Nohlen (ed.), *Wörterbuch Staat und Politik* (Munich: Piper, 1991), p. 322.

22 Brigitte Young, *German Unification, the State, and Gender* (New Haven, CT: Yale University Press, 1996).

23 This turns the right to abortion into a socially stratified right, since abortions in Germany are very expensive. In addition, in almost all other European countries health insurance is required to pay for abortions.

24 In June 1995 a revised version of the abortion law was voted on in Parliament and accepted.

25 Fiscal plan Senatsverwaltung für Arbeit und Frauen, 18 02, 1994.

26 Do state agencies think public relations jobs necessary in feminist projects? Or are they the first to be cut in times of recession? How much public opposition by their 'benefit recipients' (*Zuwendungsempfänger* is the official term for German state funding of projects) do state agencies tolerate?

27 *Tageszeitung-taz*, Berlin (daily newspaper), 10 March 1995.

28 Brigitte Young, 'Asynchronitäten der deutsch-deutschen Frauenbewegung.'

29 Ibid.

30 Renate Rieger (ed.), *Der Widerspenstigen Lähmung? Frauenprojekte zwischen Autonomie und Anpassung* (Frankfurt: Campus Verlag, 1993).

31 Ibid., p. 16.

32 Ibid.

33 Direct candidates campaign to gain a mandate in a specific voting district (*Direktmandat*). Other candidates are put up through party lists.

34 *Frankfurter Allgemeine Zeitung*, Frankfurt (daily newspaper), 8 October 1994.

35 *Freitag*, Berlin (weekly magazine), 30 September 1994.
36 *Tagesspiegel*, Berlin (daily newspaper), 9 January 1994.
37 *Frankfurter Rundschau*, Frankfurt (daily newspaper), 14 October 1994.
38 *Tagesspiegel*, Berlin (daily newspaper), 9 January 1994.
39 Institut für Demoskopie Allensbach (ed.), *Frauen in Deutschland. Lebensver-hältnisse, Lebensstile und Zukunftserwartungen. Die Schering-Frauenstudie '93* (Köln, 1993).
40 Mary Douglas, *How Institutions Think* (Syracuse: Syracuse University Press, 1986), p. 127.

14

SOME REFLECTIONS ON UNITED STATES WOMEN OF COLOR AND THE UNITED NATIONS FOURTH WORLD CONFERENCE ON WOMEN AND NGO FORUM IN BEIJING, CHINA

Mallika Dutt

Like gender and sexuality, race has been at the forefront of what has come to be known as 'identity politics' – that is, political activism based on advancing the interests of particular groups such as women or gays and lesbians. International meetings not only allowed common themes like human rights to reshape the feminist agenda, they also fostered reconsideration of any number of issues, including those of personal identity. Global migration and travel, one scholar has shown, could upset one's notion of color-based identity. At international meetings whiteness had no positive value, while women of color who migrated to the United States from countries where their color had no racist consequences could suddenly find themselves in the midst of US color-codings of human value. Simultaneously a woman of color from the US could find – as did the author of this description of the conference of women at Beijing in 1995 – that her grievances were only legitimate on the basis of her position in the United States. In comparison to women globally she was among the extremely privileged, not a sister but an advantaged stranger from the North. Moreover, women of color from outside the US had created a more vibrant and effective activism than had most Western feminists. If feminism has called into question men's identity based on their assumed superiority, it has also called much else into question. This constant questioning has made feminisms historically feared. It has also made feminism a major force in critical political thinking, activism for global change, and the quest for human justice.

* * *

Over a year has passed since 40,000 women gathered at the United Nations Fourth World Conference on Women in Beijing. A watershed event in the history of global women's movements, Beijing had an important impact on women's movements in the United States. Seven thousand US women participated in the conference, and many of them were women of color. This chapter reflects on the role and participation of women of color in the women's conference and explores the possible implications of the impact of Beijing on political trends in the United States. Conversations with nine women of color organizers and activists (Alice Cardona, Idélisse Malavé, Lori Pourier, Catherine Powell, Beth Richie, Loretta Ross, Peggy Saika, Rinku Sen, and Ingrid Washinawatok) are interwoven into my own analysis of and involvement in the largest United Nations gathering in history. Of the nine women, three are African American, two are Latina, two are Native American, and two are Asian American. Seven of them attended the Beijing conference; the two who did not go were involved in several pre-Beijing activities.

Four main themes emerged from my conversations and observations. The first was the vibrancy and power of the global women's movement and the corresponding lack of unity and strength in US counterparts. The second had to do with the globalization of the world economy and its impact on the United States. The third concerned the tension experienced around the category 'women of color,' and the fourth led from the profound transformation in consciousness post-Beijing to the struggle to implement that transformation into day-to-day organizing.

Discovering the power of global women's movements

For most women from the United States, Beijing was an eye-opening, humbling, and transformative experience. US women were startled by the sophisticated analysis and well-organized and powerful voices of women from other parts of the world, particularly those of women from the South. Saddled with years of imperialist history along with its corresponding baggage of US superiority, racism, xenophobia, and insularity, women in the United States seldom connect issues of local organizing to international arenas. Even long-time activists and organizers perceive women in other parts of the world as more oppressed, less organized, less vocal, and certainly not as 'feminist' as their US counterparts. Images like female genital mutilation, dowry deaths, and public stoning of women form the dominant perception about the lives of women overseas. The discovery that these 'victims' were in fact a far more powerful voice for change in the 1990s than the women's movement in the United States has provided an important starting point in changing the nature of the dialogue between women in the United States and women in other parts of the world.

For women of color, the discovery and connection with strong voices from the South was particularly important. Almost all the women I spoke with described the sense of global solidarity, pride, and affirmation that they experienced in Beijing. This sense of affirmation had greater resonance, because of the sense of siege that pervades the political environment in the United States, with the attacks on women and communities of color, particularly immigrant women, African American women on welfare, and lesbians. Feelings of frustration and impotence that defined women's political activism in the United States were shattered by the atmosphere of collective power that was palpable in Beijing. As Cathy Powell, an attorney with the NAACP Legal Defense Fund, so eloquently stated,

> 'Although I was depressed about the US women's movement, I felt very proud to be part of a global environment which has been a source of great inspiration in my work. I met amazing women in amazing struggles and feel very affirmed by the loose and diverse broader global women's movement.'

The global solidarity and breadth of issues that were discussed in Beijing brought into stark relief the constraints of single-issue and single-identity organizing in the United States. For Peggy Saika, an environmental justice activist and executive director of the Asian Pacific Environmental Network, the overarching lesson of Beijing was the interconnectedness of issues and people. Indeed, although activists in the United States see connections when they come together across identity or issue lines, the opportunities to do so are few. In Beijing, Saika felt the connections every day, with 40,000 women from around the world discussing everything from peace to education.

The fragmentation of the US women's movement was visually represented in the dialogues that took place in the regional tents. At the NGO Forum, women from different regions gathered in their geographic tents to share ideas, network, and develop strategies. Idélisse Malavé, a litigator for Puerto Rican civil rights, now vice-president of the Ms Foundation, said the Latin American tent was like a festival where an organizing committee held thematic workshops, meetings, and strategy discussions. Women tried to build a common ideological base through dialogue, a process Malavé found very powerful. In contrast, the North American tent was empty and sterile, used only sporadically as an *ad hoc* meeting place, while both US women of color and white women from North America and Europe gathered in more active areas.

Understanding the place of the United States in the global arena

Women of color left Beijing with a heightened awareness of the interaction of local and global forces on women in the United States, particularly economic forces. The adverse impact on women of the globalization of the world economy was a central theme at the NGO Forum. Women from the United States discovered that their stories of social service cutbacks, loss of jobs, corporate downsizing, attacks on women on welfare, and an increase in women's poverty were echoed by women from the South who described the impact of structural adjustment programs in their countries. Women from the South, however, had a far more sophisticated analysis of the role of international organizations like the World Bank and the International Monetary Fund (both dominated by the US government), as well as the role of international capital markets and transnational corporations in the economic marginalization and exploitation of women.

Beijing helped Loretta Ross, organizer in the National Black Women's Health Project and executive director of the Center for Human Rights Education, understand that the globalization of the economy had to be an integral part of her organizing in the United States. For her, Beijing meant questioning the 'American dream' which assumes the ability to acquire and consume material goods if one works hard enough, an assumption called into question by the world economy, which makes working-class people and people of color dispensable. This meant that the economic assumptions that had guided US social change movements needed to be re-evaluated. It became clear to Ross that if US women did not build global movements like an international human rights movement and a global labor movement, they would become part of the global free-fall.

Lori Pourier, who staffs the Indigenous Women's Network, said:

'Beijing opened my eyes to the role of international decision makers. My experience of racism was limited to living as an indigenous woman in the border town of Pine Ridge, South Dakota. I had been too focused on the trust responsibilities of the US government and was not looking at the global picture.'

Meeting indigenous women from other parts of the world who were grappling not only with the impact of dictatorships but also with the impact of institutions like the World Bank, the International Monetary Fund, the World Trade Organization, and transnational corporations, helped Pourier to understand the role of the United States in these organizations as well as the role of global forces within the United States.

Ingrid Washinawatok, a citizen of the Menominee Nation and co-chair of the Indigenous Women's Network, said that Beijing allowed the indigenous women who attended to 'step out of their views of their own oppression to go, hear, share, and feel the oppression of other women. This was important because if you stay too localized and only within your own people, it atrophies you, makes you resentful, and leads to inaction.'

Searching for identity and location in Beijing

For many women of color who sought to create bonds with women from their continents of origin, Beijing was often painful. The difficulties encountered by women of color in connecting with these women were interwoven with the history of their migration to the United States. For African American women, the legacy of slavery meant that few know their specific countries of origin, and claiming common ground with African women was more difficult for them than the geographic and cultural connections through which Asian American and Latinas have a ready frame of reference. For indigenous women, whose presence in and claim to the United States precedes all other ethnic and racial communities, ideas of self-determination and sovereignty resonate most closely with indigenous women from other parts of the world. However, despite these differences in location, in Beijing, all women of color had to overcome the suspicion and hostility that came from being perceived as 'Americans' by women from the South.

Negatively held perceptions of Americans as interfering, arrogant, ignorant, insensitive, and imperialist were ascribed to women of color as well as to white women from the United States. These attitudes forced women of color constantly to confront the role of the United States as an aggressor and violator of human rights even as they perceived themselves as oppositional forces within the country. Thus, as Rinku Sen, co-director of the Center for Third World Organizing, stated, women of color had continually to make decisions about how they identified themselves in relation to women from the South. Although some expected to make immediate connections with women from their home countries, others were more careful in how they identified themselves – as women from the South living in the North, as women of color from the United States, as immigrant women, or as women from their particular ethnic or racial background. According to Sen, women of color sought self-definitions to avoid rejection by their Southern counterparts.

As many women from both the United States and the South have pointed out, US women have usually been involved with women in other countries in the context of academic research, development aid, or involvement in other women's movements. Thus, hundreds of dissertations have been written about women's lives in the Third World by women from the United States, but rarely do women from the South come to 'study' US women or write dissertations on government abuse of women on welfare or the attacks by the religious Right on abortion providers in this country. Similarly, women from other parts of the world have not presumed to define the agenda of US women's movements in the same way that some women from this country have insisted that women's movements in other countries prioritize female genital mutilation, dowry deaths, or religious persecution. This simplistic understanding of women's lives ignores the depth and breadth of women's organizing in other parts of the world. The anger felt by women from other parts of the world at this often racist and culturally biased perception of their work has been exacerbated by the fact that most US women's movements have seldom addressed the role played by their own government in the violations of women's human rights the world over whether through the training of military personnel for dictatorships, the location of military bases, the programs of the World Bank or the International Monetary Fund, or the actions of US corporations overseas.

On being 'women of color' and organizing for Beijing

Women of color today appear to be far more focused on organizing within their own ethnic communities than across color lines. This was particularly apparent among the women I interviewed for this chapter. The primary self-identification through which women described their experiences around Beijing was as African American or Asian American, Latina, or indigenous women even when their political work was located in a broader context and they had gone to the conference as part of a multi-ethnic team. The term 'women of color' was most easily embraced by African American women, but even they described their experiences primarily through the context of their own racial/ethnic identity. Indigenous women seemed to be the best-organized constituency of women from the United States, and articulated their concerns and issues differently from other women of color.

Alice Cardona was dissatisfied with the term 'women of color.' She said the term came from African American women's attempt to be more inclusive but that it failed to reflect the social context of different communities. Cardona's group, the National Latina Caucus, went to Beijing as Latinas, an identity they used primarily to disassociate from white women who were perceived as imperialist or insensitive. For Cardona, the issue of identity is 'a question of community consciousness and not of color.'

An interesting phenomenon in Beijing was the contrast between the power of Asian women's movements in the regions compared with the relative marginalization of Asian American women in the United States. Person after person commented on the strength, diversity, and leadership of women's movements in India, the Philippines, Japan, and other parts of Asia. According to Loretta Ross, Asian women were the best organized force in Beijing; she wondered what impact this would have on Asian American women in the United States. Although the visibility of Asian women was affirming for Peggy Saika, it also reinforced the fragility of Asian American women and their inability to be front and center in the US political scene.

Efforts to bring together different communities of women of color for pre-conference organizing were limited to local and regional initiatives, with the exception of the US indigenous women. Indigenous women in the United States met systematically for nine months and produced an eighty-page document that reflected the feedback, input, and writing of women from around the country. In Beijing, this document became the North American contribution to a global indigenous women's statement of their concerns. Although African American, Latina, and Asian American women also drafted their own statements in Beijing, the statement by indigenous women was the most comprehensive.

Although they were the best organized as a group, indigenous women did not fully identify as 'women of color.' As Ingrid Washinawatok described it, for indigenous women, solidarity with other women of color in the United States is complicated by the reality that women of color are just as much interlopers on Native people's lands as are white people. Communities of color and immigrant communities are often disrespectful of indigenous peoples; share the same value systems as white people in terms of acquisition of wealth, resources, and power; and can be as insensitive to the needs of indigenous peoples. Thus, the concerns of other women of color conflict with or differ from indigenous women's struggles around self-determination, land, sovereignty, and survival. In Beijing, therefore, the primary focus of US indigenous women was to meet indigenous peoples from around the world and to build an international network. This network will act across common issues of nuclear waste, land rights, and sovereignty issues and to monitor actions at the United Nations which affect indigenous peoples. Alliances with other women of color were useful in certain contexts, but indigenous women did not feel that they always fit into the general agenda of women of color.

Transforming consciousness into action

All the women I spoke with described a profound shift in their consciousness post-Beijing. Almost all shared the same vision for future social change organizing, but few have been able to make these ideas concrete. According to Rinku Sen, women have developed a new language describing themselves and their work, but this has not yet changed day-to-day organizing. It has also been difficult for women who were in Beijing to share their experiences adequately with women who did not attend the conference.

311

Despite the challenges, the common themes articulated by those who went to Beijing provides a shared basis for action. Many women urged increasing the focus on community organizing and base building. Their first priority was organizing within their own ethnic communities. Alice Cardona articulated the need to refocus on one's own community and then connect with other women of color to coalesce around clear goals. Similarly, Peggy Saika described her efforts to build an Asian American and Pacific Islander women's movement that shifted the focus from service-oriented organizations to base-building and advocacy groups. All these women described plans for national post-Beijing meetings of their particular identity groups. They also felt more opportunities to meet across issue and identity lines were crucial, and they called for better international networking and global connections.

Opportunities lost and found

Beijing provided women of color with singular opportunities to catapult themselves into leadership within organizations in the United States – opportunities that have not been realized. On the other hand, the energy and excitement of those who went continues to provide hope that new directions will emerge in the organizing of women of color.

Women of color were unable to utilize the pre-Beijing process to build a national movement or network when such a network was critical. Hundreds of meetings and conferences took place prior to Beijing (including ten regional meetings convened by the Women's Bureau of the Department of Labor); yet few attempted to share agendas, goals, ideas, and strategies to develop concerted plans of action. The energy that took women to Beijing did not get transformed into a powerful voice for the human rights of women of color.

Moreover, women of color did not understand the importance of the Beijing Platform for Action as a tool to influence public policy in the United States. The Platform for Action was negotiated by approximately 181 governments, including our own, to reflect the commitments of UN member countries to half the world's population. Although women globally were involved in regional and UN efforts to lobby their governments and establish themselves as players in their own public policy processes, few US women of color even realized that the Beijing conference comprised an official governmental conference as well as an NGO forum. Because of their lack of preparation, it was difficult for women of color in Beijing to represent their interests adequately or affect the process. Again, the one exception was the indigenous women's caucus. However, their efforts at influencing the Platform for Action would have benefited from a strong and powerful lobby by women of color who had agreed to shared goals.

Despite these missed opportunities, the excitement and energy that Beijing has generated provides the possibility of forging stronger directions, coalitions, agendas, and movements of women of color to address the present political climate. However, some important shifts in consciousness are necessary before such a possibility is realized.

Although women of color must focus on their own ethnic communities in order to build strong bases for political action, it is also critical that they begin to provide much-needed national leadership that crosses ethnic and identity lines. US women's movements today are suffering from an acute crisis in leadership, vision, and direction. Women of color who are local leaders must develop and share their critical lessons, strategies, and analyses with a wider constituency of people. If women of color continue only to define themselves in the context of their communities, they perpetuate the problem of white women being perceived as national leaders while women of color are seen only as speaking for their own particular ethnicity or concern. It is important that leadership be assumed out of a sense of accountability and responsibility, but it is also important that marginalized communities understand their power as well as their victimization.

Women from other parts of the world demonstrated the potential to speak as leaders while articulating a complex analysis of their exploitation and oppression. US women of color returned from Beijing with pride and affirmation, which should provide the basis for moving from margin to center in a way that redefines both. Our ability to build a true democracy that values and protects the human rights of all its constituents hangs in the balance.

ACKNOWLEDGMENTS

I would like to thank Alice Cardona, Idélisse Malavé, Lori Pourier, Catherine Powell, Beth Richie, Loretta Ross, Peggy Saika, Rinku Sen, and Ingrid Washinawatok for their generosity with their time, thoughts, and analysis. I would also like to thank Charlotte Bunch and Claudia Hinojosa for their feedback.

INDEX

Hitler, Adolf 255
Ho Chi Minh 49
Hockney, David 166
Homosexual Law Reform Society (UK) 166, 172
Hong Mi Young 134
House Un-American Activities Committee (HUAC) 143
Human Rights Commission of the United Nations 133
Human Rights Watch 265, 268; Women's Rights Project 268

Idris, Hawa 23, 30
Independent Women's Democratic Initiative (Russia) 226
Independent Women's Union (UFV, Germany) 291, 294–5, 300
Indigenous Women's Network 308
Indochinese Communist Party 48–9, 50
Inkatha Freedom Party (IFP, SA) 69, 71–2
Institute of Women's Research (Korea) 125
International Federation of Women Lawyers 112
International Monetary Fund 5, 308, 310
International Woman Suffrage Alliance 252, 265
International Women's Trust – Women's Peace Trust 219
International Women's Year Action Group (Japan) 187, 193
Islam 13; Egypt 20, 22–3, 25, 29–32, 34, 36–8; Iran 235, 237, 239–45

James, Michael 173–6
Japan Socialist Party 191, 193, 196
Jeannette Rankin Brigade (USA) 160
Johnson, Lyndon 158
Jones, Juno 174–5, 177
Jun Yeonny 129, 131

Kabira, Wanjiku 106, 113
Kanogo, Tabitha 115
Kasravi, Ahmad 244–5
Kazim, Safinaz 31, 33, 34–7
Kennedy, Jacqueline 240
Kennedy, J.F. 144, 152
Kenya African National Union (KANU) 104–9, 113
Kenya Finance Trust 112

Kenyatta, Jomo 104
Kerouac, Jack 145
Khamis, Muhammad 'Atiya 26
Khasiani, Shanyisa 109
Khatami, Ayatollah 258
Khomeini, Ayatollah Ruhollah 35, 235, 248–9, 254–5
Kim Eun Shil 126
Kim Jae Kyu 124
Kim Young Sam, President 133
King, Martin Luther, Jr. 149
Kollontai, Aleksandra 210
Korean CIA 122, 124
Korean Council for Women Drafted under Japanese Rule 131–2
Korean Sexual Violence Relief Center 129, 133
Korean War (1950–53) 129
Korean Women Workers Association (KWWA) 127–8
Korean Women's Association for Democracy and Sisterhood 128
Korean Women's Associations United (KWAU) 125, 132–5
Kwon Young Ja 134

Lakhova, Ekaterina 214
Langley, Esme 167
Le So Sun 123
Le Tan Danh 55
League of University and Institutes' Young Women 25
League of Women Voters: Kenya 113; USA 147, 154, 219
Lee Sun Shim 132
Lenin, V.I. 208, 226
Liberal Democratic Party (Japan) 191, 193, 196
Liberal Party (FPD, Germany) 296, 301
Likimani, M. 114
Lille, Patricia De 72
Lopata, Helen 146
Lufty, Huda 36

Maathai, Wangari 113, 116
MacArthur, General Douglas 182, 184
MacKinnon, Catherine 267
Maendeleo Ya Wanawake (MYWO, Kenya) 108–9, 111, 113
Makeba, Miriam 68
Makhluf, Shaikh Hasanayn 28
Malavé, Idélise 306–7
Mandela, Winnie 68

Pan-Arab Feminist Conference 24
Party for Democratic Socialism
(Germany) 296, 301
Party of the Islamic Republic 256
Pateman, Carole 267
Paulista Association of Solidarity in
Unemployment 94
Peterson, Esther 152
Plato 170
Posadskaya, Anastasia 220–2
Posner, Blanche 143
post-industrial society 5
Pourier, Lori 306–8
Powell, Catherine 306–7
Power, Lisa 175
Progressive Party (South Africa) 72

Qutb, Sayyid 31

race 7–8, 144, 148–52, 157–9, 305–13
Rafsanjani, Fayezeh 257
Rakhshan, Mehrtaj 251
rape 7–8, 54, 84, 125, 129–33, 265–6,
272–4, 279, 281–2
Rape Crisis Center (Tokyo) 186
Rashid, Fatma Ni'mat 24
Rawalt, Marguerite 152
Research Center for Women's Study
(Korea) 130
revisionism ix–x
Revolutionary Union of Militant
Women (Iran) 254
Rhie, Maria Chol Soon 123
Richie, Beth 306
Rieger, Renate 300
Robinson, Rubye Doris Smith 150
Rogers, Nick 173
Roh Tae Woo, General 125
Roosevelt, Eleanor 152
Ross, Loretta 306, 308, 310
Rousseau, J.-J. 278
Rubin, Gayle 253
Rubin, Lillian 147
Ruddick, Sara 156
Russell, Ken 174
Russian Revolution (1917) 45, 205,
208–10

Sabri, Sayyid 28
Sadat, Anwar 31, 32, 34, 35
Sadat, Jihan 32, 34
Sa'id, Amina 30, 31, 33
Saika, Peggy 306–7

Saitô Chiyo 185
Saniyya Teachers School 18
Scott, Joan 252
Seichô no Ie (Japan) 194
Sen, Rinku 306, 308–9, 311
sexuality 7–8, 130–2, 146, 158, 160,
166–79, 189–90, 193, 255, 257
Shafiq, Duriyya 24, 27, 28
Shapiro, Judith 213
Sha'rawi, Huda 19, 21, 23, 24, 25
Shariati, Ali 238–42
Shaw, George Bernard 240
Shim Mi Ja 131
Shinjuku Women's Liberation Center
(Japan) 186
Shufuren (Japan) 184
Shvedova, Nadezhda 222
Sidki, Isma'il 20
Sidqi, Ni'mat 33
Simon, Paul 166
Skocpol, Theda 59
Smith, Howard 154, 171
Smith, Margaret Chase 154
Social Democratic Party (SPD,
Germany) 296, 301
Socialist Workers' party (Iran) 254
Sôhyô (Japan Council of Trade Unions)
191
Southern Christian Leadership
Conference (SCLC, USA) 149
Soviet Women's Committee/Union of
Women of Russia 214–20, 222–3,
225–9
SPD Women's Caucus (FRG) 297
Stalin, Josef 205, 208–10
Stamp, Patricia 102
Stewart, Rod 166
Student Nonviolent Coordinating
Committee (SNCC, USA) 150, 157,
159
Students for a Democratic Society
(SDS, USA) 157–8
Suzman, Helen 72

Tabatabai, Sayyed 242
Tanaka Sumiko 188
Tatakua Onnatachi (Japan) 186
Tavakoli, Mohamad 242, 248, 255
Tereshkova, Valentina 215
Tocqueville, Alexis de 59
Tohidi, Nayereh 255
Trieu Au 48
Trung sisters 48

318